PENGUIN HANDBOOKS

COOKING FOR SPECIAL DIETS

Bee Nilson was born in New Zealand where she received her professional training. After graduating as Bachelor of Home Science of the University of Otago, she came to England and settled in London where she has been teaching and writing about cookery and nutrition ever since. She is a State Registered Dietitian, a member of the British Dietetic Association, the New Zealand Dietetic Association, and the Nutrition Society. She also holds the Diploma in Education of London University.

During the war she was at the Ministry of Food and compiled the *A.B.C. of Cookery* and other Stationery Office publications. Her other books include the Penguin Handbook *The Penguin Cookery Book* (now in its twelfth printing), *The Book of Meat Cookery*, *Pears Family Cookbook*, and *Deep Freeze Cooking*.

COOKING FOR SPECIAL DIETS

BEE NILSON

Second Edition

Penguin Books

Penguin Books Ltd, Harmondsworth, Middlesex, England
Penguin Books Inc., 7110 Ambassador Road, Baltimore, Maryland 21207, U.S.A.
Penguin Books Australia Ltd, Ringwood, Victoria, Australia
Penguin Books Canada Ltd, 41 Steelcase Road West, Markham, Ontario, Canada
Penguin Books (N.Z.) Ltd, 182-190 Wairau Road, Auckland 10, New Zealand

First published 1964
Reprinted 1968
Second Edition 1971
Reprinted 1973, 1974

Made and printed in Great Britain
by Cox & Wyman Ltd, London, Reading and Fakenham
Set in Monotype Garamond

Contents

RECIPES

Preface

WHEN a patient at home is advised to have something other than a normal diet, it is often difficult for the home cook to translate the doctor's instructions into acceptable and varied meals. This is a book to help cope with such a situation.

To help in understanding the need for a special diet each chapter carries a brief description of the diseases being discussed and indicates why special diets are frequently advised as part of the treatment.

What follows aims at expanding and interpreting the dietary advice the doctor gives. This is done by discussing changes needed in usual eating habits, in cooking methods, and by giving a quick reference list of foods usually allowed, which includes suggestions for recipes, cross-referenced to the recipe section at the end of the book.

Then follows a meal-pattern based on the good normal diet, on average eating habits in Great Britain, and on the needs of the diet, with fourteen suggested menus for dinner meals and the same for meals suitable for high tea, supper, or lunch. The meal-pattern, together with the list of foods allowed, will help the cook to compile meals of familiar foods, while the menus are designed to suggest something a little different for an occasional change.

Even people on diets often want to have celebrations, eat out, or take picnic and sandwich meals. Suggestions have been included for these wherever appropriate. For celebration meals the menus have been chosen using dishes which appear on most restaurant and hotel menus, but recipes are given for home use.

The many labour-saving devices which are a help in diet cookery have been mentioned, but allowance is also made for those who have to cook with basic equipment only.

Many special foods are manufactured for use in diets, and while it is not essential to use any of these, they have been included as another means of introducing variety, as has reference to many packet and convenience foods in common use.

It must be emphasized that the book is intended only as a help in carrying out the doctor's advice on dietary treatment and the suggestions contained herein should not be followed without medical approval.

*

I would like to thank all who have helped me in the production of this book but especially Mrs E. Scott and Miss A. M. Brown of the British Dietetic Association for advice and criticism, and the Dietetic Diploma students of the Northern Polytechnic who, during the course of their training, have cooked and eaten many of the menus and recipes.

In addition I would like to thank the Controller of Her Majesty's Stationery Office for permission to use the Medical Research Council Special Report Series No. 297, *The Composition of Foods*, for purposes of calculating the nutritive value of recipes and compiling food exchange lists. Also the many food manufacturers who have so generously supplied me with information about their products.

And finally I wish to acknowledge the writings of many experts on nutrition whose work I have consulted during my years of teaching nutrition and in compiling this book.

London
1963 BEE NILSON

Preface to Second Edition

In this new edition diets no longer considered important have been eliminated, all have been extensively revised, while the 'Overweight' and 'Diabetes' chapters have been enlarged.

I am most grateful for the help given me in this revision by Miss Anne Lace, State Registered Dietitian.

London
1971 BEE NILSON

CHAPTER I

Introduction

Why Special Diets are Prescribed

Sometimes diets are prescribed because part of the body (e.g. the digestive system) is not functioning normally and a modified diet will give it a chance to rest and recover.

Sometimes the general health is poor because the body is being over-generously supplied with food (obesity) or given insufficient food (underweight and nutritional anaemia). Then a change in diet can help to correct the condition.

Sometimes the body's ability to deal with waste products (e.g. salt) is impaired and dietary restriction (low-salt diet) will help the treatment.

The Usual Procedure

The doctor decides whether a special diet should be given and he is the person who should be consulted before any changes are made to his prescription.

If a dietitian is available the doctor sends the patient and the person who is to do the cooking to her to have the management of the diet explained in terms of menus and cooking, and she advises and guides the patient in consultation with the doctor.

Unfortunately there are not nearly enough dietitians for those who need help, and so the more common procedure is for the doctor to give the patient a sheet of instructions outlining the diet, and the patient and the home cook do the best they can to put it into practice.

Fitting the Diet into the Family Meals

It is well recognized today that a diet is unlikely to be followed at home if it entails a great deal of special cooking, and consequently the complicated diets of a few years ago have been largely discarded in favour of simpler ones which do not disrupt the family cooking unduly.

Throughout the book suggestions have been made for fitting a diet in with the family meals wherever possible. In some cases, of course, a certain amount of special cooking is unavoidable, but for the sake of the peace of mind of the patient and all in the family this should be done with as little fuss as possible.

The over-anxious housewife who continually discusses the difficulties of the diet she is coping with is quite liable by her bad psychology to do so much emotional damage to the patient that it counteracts much of the good effect the diet might have.

SPECIAL KITCHEN EQUIPMENT

Purées and sieving. Sieving is a most time-consuming job, but is frequently needed for vegetables and for making many puddings. The simplest way of making a purée is to use an electric blender or liquidizer, either a separate machine or an attachment on a mixing machine. This will make food sufficiently fine for most diets. Actual sieving is usually needed only for patients on a low-residue diet. Sieving attachments on an electric mixing machine are the easiest to use.

The most efficient hand-operated ones are Moulinex, which are fairly readily available in a wide variety of sizes. They are much cheaper than electric machines.

For potatoes and other root vegetables a ricer is useful.

Mincing. Mincing, especially of meat, is needed for many dishes. Best is a mincing attachment on an electric mixer or a small separate electric mincing machine, which is surprisingly cheap for what it does. There are many efficient hand-operated ones and, if the mincer is reassembled after washing and drying and put back on the work bench, it is always ready and therefore seems much less troublesome than if it has to be extracted from cupboard or drawer and assembled each time it is wanted.

Making fruit and vegetable juices. Where lots of fluids are needed a juice extractor is a great help. These are sold as separate electric machines or as an attachment for a mixing machine. They make juices from any fruits or vegetables in a matter of seconds. For fruit juices only, a fruit press is very good.

For measuring fluids a graduated measure is essential, preferably marked in fluid ounces as well as pints.

For cooking milk mixtures without burning and for keeping food hot a double boiler or porringer is easier to use than the improvised basin over a pan of boiling water.

A pressure cooker is a great time-saver with foods requiring long boiling and also makes food soft quickly for subsequent sieving. But take care not to overcook vegetables in it or you will lose a lot of vitamin C, which all sick people need in generous amounts.

For serving and cooking, individual-sized heat-resistant dishes and tumblers are a good investment, being useful for many other occasions too.

For keeping food fresh and safe a refrigerator is a great boon. It also saves trips to the shops and enables food to be prepared in advance and stored safely.

A *freezer* can greatly reduce the labour of diet preparation, especially when the foods required are not suitable for the rest of the family. Several portions of the diet food may be cooked and the surplus frozen for future use. It is particularly useful for things like salt-free and gluten-free bread, cakes, and puddings and for special sauces and soups.

Saucepans and stewpans of good quality make cooking easier whatever the kind of stove you use. This is even more so in the case of diet cooking, as so much milk is used, and thick purées which stick badly in thin pans, especially when they are used on a naked flame.

Oven casseroles. Some are designed for use on the hotplate or gas burner as well as in the oven and they are great time-savers. If they are pretty enough to serve the food in they are more useful still and they do keep the food hot.

Aids to hot and cold food service for the patient in bed. There are various devices on the market for keeping plated food hot and these are useful when hot food has to be transported some distance in cold weather, when there is likely to be delay in service, or when the patient is a slow eater.

The best of these, if you can manage to find one, is the nursery plate with hot-water compartment underneath.

Aluminium plate-covers are quite inexpensive and can be heated in the oven. One of these plus a really hot plate will keep food hot for most occasions. Be sure to remove the cover for the patient if it should be very hot and don't have the plate hot enough to burn his fingers.

Stainless-steel serving dishes with lids retain heat a long time, and individual dishes of this type or of heavy earthenware are a good investment.

If you should possess a portable electric warming plate and have facilities for using it in the bedroom, this is a wonderful help.

Vacuum flasks and containers of various types and sizes are available and are equally useful for keeping hot foods hot and cold ones cold, and especially for leaving at the bedside with hot or cold drinks for the patient to take as desired.

The Basis of Special Diets

Special diets are all modifications of a good normal diet.

It is generally accepted that a special diet should be as like a normal diet as possible, that is, have as few modifications as possible and still achieve its purpose.

There are several reasons for this policy: it causes less change in the eating habits of the patient, is easier to manage at home, and is therefore more likely to be followed than a more bizarre diet. In addition, the general nutritional state of the patient is more likely to be good if the normal diet is followed with only slight modification.

The patient's likes and dislikes should naturally be considered, and these, together with the modifications made necessary by the disease, determine how the diet will be compiled.

THE GOOD NORMAL DIET

The good normal diet has five main constituents:

1. *Protein.* This substance is the basis of all life and the main constituent of body cells. Protein is continually being removed from cells and replaced by fresh supplies. During growth more cells are made and more protein needed. In illness there is a destruction of body protein of varying degrees of severity and this must be replaced from the food. In fact, the only place from which protein is obtained for growth, repair, and maintenance of the body cells is the food eaten.

The chief sources of protein in the average diet in Great Britain are bread and cereals, milk and cheese, meats, game, poultry, fish, and eggs. Pulses and nuts are important protein sources for the vegetarian and vegan.

Some food proteins are better quality than others, but the best of all is a good mixture such as is found in a well-varied diet.

2. *Fats.* These include oil and solid fats. They are burnt by the body as a fuel to give energy, they act as an insulating layer against cold and injury to organs, and they form a fundamental part of all cell structure. How much and what kind of fat is best for humans is still a subject of scientific research and much difference of opinion amongst medical authorities.

The chief sources of fat are butter, margarine, dripping, cooking fat, fatty meat, oils, and cream.

3. *Carbohydrates.* These also are burnt as fuel to give energy. If an excess is eaten it is converted to fat and stored as a reserve fuel. When these reserves become too large the person is overweight or obese.

The carbohydrates used for fuel by the body are starches and sugars of all kinds, found in nearly all foods, but especially in bread, flour, rice, barley, oats, sugar, treacle, honey, sweet fruits, potatoes, cakes, biscuits, confectionery and jams.

The best foods are those containing other essential substances (e.g. vitamins) as well as carbohydrates. These are bread and cereals, and potatoes. Sugars consist only of carbohydrates and nutritionally are some of the poorest foods available.

4. *Minerals.* These form part of the body's structure (e.g. bone) and also regulate and control normal functions of the body. They include such things as calcium, which is needed for good bones and teeth: iron, for good red blood; iodine, to prevent goitre; fluorine, for strong teeth; and a host of others. They are found in a wide variety of foods and a good basic diet should provide plenty. The most important sources are: *calcium*: bread, flour, milk, and cheese; *iron*: liver, heart, kidney, corned beef, beef, bread; *iodine*: drinking-water (if not from an iodine-deficient area), fish, iodized salt; *fluorine*: drinking-water (unless it is from a fluorine-deficient area). In some districts fluorine is added to deficient drinking-water and has been responsible for improvements in children's teeth in these areas.

5. *Vitamins.* These substances are essential to life and are present in food in very small amounts and in some cases in a very limited range of foods so that unless care is exercised in choosing a diet they may be missed out.

Their general job is to control body functions, which they do in a variety of ways. Chief among the vitamins are:

Vitamin A and carotene, needed for normal growth and for healthy eyes. Vitamin A is found in butter, margarine, oily fish, and cod- and halibut-liver oils, while carotene is found in green and red vegetables.

Vitamin B complex, needed for the processes by which energy is obtained from carbohydrates, fats and proteins, and found in cereals, bread, meat, vegetables, milk and cheese, eggs, yeast and yeast extracts, and meat extracts.

Vitamin C, needed for normal health of many parts of the body, including blood vessels, teeth and gums, bones and cartilage, and for wound healing. It is found only in fruits and vegetables, especially fresh ones.

Vitamin D, needed for strong bones and teeth and the prevention of rickets. It can be obtained from sunshine, but most people have to rely on getting it from margarine, butter, oily fish, and cod and halibut liver oils.

Foods to Include Daily

To know about these five main constituents or nutrients in a good diet is one thing; to plan diets using a good mixture of them is a little more difficult.

To help people plan good diets many basic menu-planning guides have been devised. Here is one of them.

Include the following (daily, unless otherwise stated).

Milk. 1 pint (2c.). This includes milk used in cooking as well as for beverages.

Or, instead of 1 pint (2 c.) of milk have *one* of the following: ½ pint milk (1 c.) plus 1 oz. (1 inch cube) cheese, 2 oz. cheese, ¼ pint (½ c.) full-cream evaporated milk, 2 oz. (4 heaped Tbs.) dried full-cream milk-powder, 1 pint (2 c.) yogurt, 4 oz. cottage cheese (1 c.).

Skimmed milk (milk with cream removed) is not an adequate exchange for whole milk as it lacks the vitamins found in cream, but it is a useful supplement to other milks and for low-fat and low-calorie diets; all varieties of cheese are similar nutritionally except a true cream cheese which is more like butter in composition.

Eggs. One daily. Either as an egg dish or used in cakes and puddings. Nutritionally of very high value and important in most special diets.

Fats. 1½ oz. (3 Tbs.) butter or margarine. 1 teaspoon cod-liver oil or equivalent for children and teenagers. Other fats and oils for cooking in moderation.

Meat, game, poultry, fish. At least one good helping a day. Children 1 oz. or more, adults 3–4 oz. 2 oz. of cheese or 2 eggs are a substitute for a 4-oz. portion of meat. Include either liver, heart, or kidney, *and* either herring, kipper, sardine, or tinned salmon at least once a week. These are rich sources of many important vitamins.

Vegetables and fruits. Serve two portions daily from this list:

4 oz. freshly cooked cabbage

5–6 oz. freshly cooked potato (1–2 medium)
1–2 oz. raw vegetables, such as watercress, cabbage, brussels sprouts. (Lettuce will not do: the equivalent amount would be 4–8 oz. i.e. one to two large lettuces.)
1 orange
1 grapefruit
1 dose blackcurrant syrup or purée or rose-hip syrup
4 oz. (2 medium) tomato
$\frac{1}{8}$ pint (5 Tbs.) orange or grapefruit juice (fresh or canned)
$\frac{1}{4}$ pint ($\frac{1}{2}$ c.) tomato juice (fresh or canned)
Include other vegetables and fruit to give variety to the diet.

Bread and flour. The need for these varies with the age and activity of the person and the type of meal eaten. Those leading a sedentary life and having two or three cooked meals a day do not need more than 2 or 3 oz. (2–3 slices) of bread. Children, teenagers, active adults, and those having sandwich lunches will need more. Bread should not be substituted for any of the foods already listed. Cereals and cakes and flour confectionery are extras to add variety to the diet but should not be eaten instead of other foods.

Sugar preserves and sweets. Nutritionally, these are extras to give variety and their proper place is at the end of, rather than between, meals.

Condiments. These are important for making food palatable and giving pleasure. With some people they are liable to cause digestive troubles if used in large amounts. Iodized salt is advised in all areas where the drinking-water is lacking in iodine.

Meal-Patterns

The number of meals eaten daily, and the kind, is a matter of tradition and habit. Some people eat once or twice a day only, others six or seven times. It is generally agreed that more frequent, smaller meals are better than one or two very large ones and that whatever other meal is skipped it should not be breakfast. Missing this meal means going for a very long time without food, which tends to produce fatigue during the morning.

Below is the daily meal-pattern found to be the most widespread in Great Britain. This has been used as the basic meal-pattern for special diets.

For sick people it is also better to have several meals a day as their appetite is frequently small and they won't eat enough unless they eat often.

For Adults and Older Children:

On waking (*optional*). Tea or fruit juice.

Breakfast. Fruit juice or stewed or fresh fruit; cereal with milk or a cooked dish (egg, bacon, meat, fish), or cheese, bread or toast and preserves, beverage.

Mid-morning. Beverage.

Midday. Soup or hors d'œuvre or fruit juice (optional), meat or fish or eggs or cheese, vegetables, sweet or cheese, raw fruit or celery.

Afternoon. Beverage, sandwiches, and cake (optional).

Evening. Soup (optional), meat or fish or egg or cheese with vegetable or salad or made into sandwiches. Bread and butter, cooked or fresh fruit or cold pudding or fruit and cheese.

Bedtime. Milk drink (optional).

For Small Children (1–5 Years)

On waking. Fruit juice.

Breakfast (8–8.30 a.m.). Porridge or cereal, crisp toast or rusk, butter or margarine, marmalade, jam, or honey, milk to drink; in addition, one of the following: egg, bacon or ham (1–2 tablespoons), steamed, grilled, or creamed fish (1–2 tablespoons), herrings, sardines or herring roes (1–2 tablespoons).

Mid-morning. Milky drink.

Midday. Meat, liver, fish, or rabbit (1–3 tablespoons), potato cooked in various ways (1 medium), green vegetables (1–2 tablespoons), milk pudding plus stewed fruit, or steamed or baked sponge or pastry, water to drink, piece of raw apple or carrot.

Tea (4.45–5.0 p.m.). Brown bread or toast with butter or margarine, and jam, honey, or yeast extract, home-made cake or biscuits, raw fruit or salad, milk to drink. In addition one of the following: egg dish, cheese (¾–1 oz., 1 inch cube), cold meat or ham (1–2 tablespoons), fish (1–2 tablespoons), pudding of junket or milk and fruit (1–2 tablespoons).

Bedtime. Milk.

Sweets. After dinner but not between meals.

Quantity of Basic Daily Foods for Children and Adolescents

Milk. 1–1½ pints (2–3 c.)

Eggs. 1.

Meat, fish offal, chicken, or cheese. **1 oz. for young children,** increasing to 3 oz for older ones.

Green vegetables or salads. 1–2 oz for young children, increasing to 4–6 oz. for older ones.

Potatoes and root vegetables. 1 oz. for young children, increasing to ¼–½ lb. for older ones.

Butter or margarine. ⅛–¾ oz. (1 Tbs.) for young children, increasing to 2–3 oz. (4–6 Tbs.) for older ones.

Bread. 2 oz. (2 slices) for young children, increasing to ½–¾ lb. (8–12 slices) for older ones.

Cod-liver oil. A dose for all ages.

Good Cooking is Important

Poor-quality cooking not only makes food unpalatable but can also reduce its nutritive value and make it difficult to digest. Sick people frequently have digestive difficulties. For the sake of the patient, special care should be given to the following:

Cheese should be lightly cooked only. A high temperature tends to make it tough and stringy and very indigestible.

Meat should be of good quality and cooked thoroughly, but do not overcook. Underdone meat is always a possible source of food poisoning and should not be given to sick people.

Fish should be cooked thoroughly and gently and preferably not fried, as the fat makes it indigestible. Grilling or baking are better methods.

Eggs lightly cooked are more digestible than raw and safer from the risk of food poisoning. Hard-boiled eggs are best chopped or mashed to make them easier to digest.

Vegetables should be carefully cooked and served at once. The water-soluble vitamin C is important to all sick people and is easily lost by careless cooking. Boil vegetables in very little water, cook them quickly and drain and serve at once. Don't serve reheated vegetables as this causes them to lose vitamin C. Don't prepare salads far in advance.

Cereals and flour mixtures should be cooked thoroughly. Uncooked starch is very difficult to digest; therefore all sauces, cereal puddings, and so on should be cooked adequately.

Fats and frying. Many special diets recommend omitting fried food because it tends to be indigestible. This is particularly the case when food is fried in fat which is not hot enough or in fat which has been allowed to become overheated. In the former case the food is greasy and very indigestible and in the latter the overheated fat acts as an irritant to the stomach.

Fruits. Raw fruits should be prepared just before service and likewise fruit juices. Open canned juices just before using and store remains, covered, in a refrigerator.

Preserved Foods

In most homes preserved foods form only a small part of any diet and the differences in composition between fresh and preserved are therefore comparatively unimportant. It is when preserved foods are extensively used that these differences should be taken into account.

Canned Foods

If canned meats form the bulk of the meat eaten, it should be remembered that the process of canning destroys most, if not all, of the vitamin B_1. As most people get about one-fifth of their daily intake from meats, some compensation for this loss is needed, for example, eating more vegetables, using whole-wheat flour and wheat germ.

If canned vegetables replace fresh ones there is likely to be a reduction in the intake of vitamin B_1 and C. About one-fifth of the total B_1 usually comes from vegetables so if both canned meat and canned vegetables are used other sources of B_1 will be most important.

Over fifty per cent of most people's vitamin C comes from vegetables, thirty-three per cent of this being from potatoes, so if fresh potatoes are available the solution is to step up their consumption. Failing this, fresh fruit and fruit juices should be taken instead. Canned fruits retain vitamin C better than canned vegetables, especially if they are eaten without being heated up. Canned orange, grapefruit, and tomato juice, and canned blackcurrants, are all good sources of vitamin C.

Vitamin C is especially important to all sick people and therefore the best sources available should always be used.

With other canned foods such as milk and fish, any changes in nutritive value are comparatively unimportant.

Frozen Foods

If these are stored at the correct temperature they lose very little nutritive value and compare favourably with fresh.

Dried Foods

Ordinary dried fruits and vegetables lose practically all their vitamin C and are not adequate substitutes for the fresh.

Modern dehydrated vegetables which are properly gas-packed in sealed tins retain vitamin C but lose it rapidly after the tins are opened. Instant and flaked potatoes usually contain less vitamin C than fresh potatoes and, if used to replace the fresh, more vitamin-rich fruits and fruit juices should be given to compensate.

AFD, or accelerated freeze-dried, foods if properly packed compare favourably with fresh foods.

Good Presentation is Important

Attractively served food encourages the patient to eat the diet as well as giving pleasure.

Simple decorations are best and the use of coloured china and individual portions and dishes a great help. Avoid hectic colours and synthetic flavours.

Hot food should be really hot and cold food well chilled, as lukewarm food of either kind is unappetizing. Salads should be crisp and appetizing.

Make sure the food is easy to handle without making a mess of the patient and the bedclothes.

If possible, serve vegetables in separate dishes for the patient to help himself to what he wants. The tray should be big enough to hold the dishes comfortably but light in weight. Utensils should be lightweight. Small knives and forks are easier to manage. Use individual condiment sets, milk jugs, and other small containers.

Clean Handling of Food is Important

IT IS INDEED VERY IMPORTANT. People who are weakened by illness (and the very young and the very old) are more susceptible to food poisoning than the average person and the results are more serious.

Contamination from the hands of people preparing food is the chief cause of trouble. It is advisable not to handle food unless absolutely necessary (use forks or tongs instead) and certainly not to handle food which is to be served without further cooking.

If you are careful about the following points you will do a lot to avoid trouble:

Hands. Scrub thoroughly before handling any of the patient's food and always after visiting the toilet or using your handkerchief or having a cigarette.

Meat. Cook it carefully and thoroughly and serve as soon as cooked. DO NOT cook in advance and warm up. If the recipe uses cooked meat be sure that it is fresh and not a stale left-over. NEVER handle cooked cold meat, use fork or tongs instead, and never leave it exposed to dust and flies or in a warm place. Don't store minced meat but use it up at once.

Jellies and cold sweets made in advance should be kept in a cold place and used up the next day. Cold sweets made without gelatine can be put in the deep freeze.

Milk. Leave in bottles until required. Store in a cold place and protect from flies.

Eggs. Store in a cold place. Separated yolks and whites or whole eggs broken out of their shells should be covered and stored in a cold place and then cooked thoroughly when used. It is better to use eggs lightly cooked rather than raw when they may be infected even in the shell. When raw eggs are used in cold jellies or in other sweets, chill the mixture quickly and use up as soon as set. If there should be any infection in the egg, storing in the warm will cause a rapid multiplication of the dangerous organisms and this is a cause of food poisoning.

Storage without a refrigerator. Put all foods in the coldest possible place, on marble or slate or stone if possible, and cover with metal gauze covers or muslin or, for short periods, polythene covers. Milk and jellies and moulds can be put in a dish of cold water with damp muslin over the top dipping into the water.

Washing up. Be very careful and thorough. It is safer to rinse afterwards in very hot water and drain without wiping.

NOTE. The reference numbers given in the following pages, in food lists, meal patterns, and menus, refer to recipe numbers. The recipe section begins on page 225.

CHAPTER 2

General Diets

THIS chapter is a guide to what you should do when the doctor recommends for the patient one of the following general diets: 1. A liquid or fluid diet. 2. A semi-solid or soft diet. 3. A light diet.

These are the most commonly prescribed of all diets. Frequently the patient is started on liquids for a day or so and then progresses through the other general diets to recovery and the good normal diet.

THE LIQUID OR FLUID DIET

The fluid diet is used when the patient is very weak and ill and has no appetite, for diseases of the throat and oesophagus (gullet) which make swallowing difficult and painful, for fractured jaws when chewing is impossible, or when the intestine is diseased or inflamed and the patient cannot digest solid foods.

How the Normal Diet is Modified

The very sick may only be able to have boiled water, glucose drinks, and diluted fruit juices. These make a very inadequate diet and the patient is restricted to them for the shortest possible time. Thereafter, a fluid diet which is as much like the normal diet as possible is given. It is very important to see that all the foods present in the good normal diet are included in one form or another, especially if the liquid diet is likely to continue for any length of time.

The chief modification needed is in consistency. The fluid diet includes any foods which are liquid at normal body temperature, such as all the foods we normally call liquids, plus those which melt at body temperature, such as jellies and ice creams. Some very soft foods such as junkets and custards are usually allowed as well.

Sometimes digestion is impaired and it is advisable to leave out any foods liable to cause discomfort, such as very fatty or highly seasoned foods or those containing anything likely to scratch a sore gullet or intestine or make it sting, e.g. strong vinegar; or very acid fruit juices given neat, e.g. lemon or orange.

The number of meals a day also needs altering, especially when the patient's appetite is poor. Small frequent feeds (every 2 hours) are often needed to make sure that the day's total is sufficient.

When it is impossible for the fluid diet to provide all the patient's needs the doctor will supplement it by pills or medicine containing the missing nutrients (particularly vitamins and minerals). It is most important to see that these are taken as prescribed.

Fitting in with Family Meals

In many cases items from the normal family menu will be found suitable, so that special preparation for the diet can be reduced at normal family meal times, and the quickly prepared fluids used for between-meal feeds for the patient.

If an electric blender is available, many of the normal family dishes can be converted to liquid form, e.g. stews, casseroles and soups, and milk puddings; in fact practically any food can be turned into a liquid by adding stock or milk to bring the mixture to drinking consistency. This not only has the advantage of cutting down the amount of special cooking needed, but also gives the patient familiar flavours, which often makes the fluids more acceptable than special brews of unfamiliar types of foods.

Useful Special Foods (For names and addresses of manufacturers, see Appendix.)

While an adequate fluid diet can be provided without the aid of special foods, it is sometimes difficult to get the patient to take enough normal foods. It is then that the concentrated special foods are very useful. Some of these provide all the nutrients needed in a normal diet, while others are designed to increase the intake of certain nutrients such as protein and vitamins.

All the products need to be used with skill and imagination or the patient will quickly tire of the flavours. Most of the manufacturers will supply information on the use of their products in fluid diets.

CAUTION. These are all concentrated products and if used too enthusiastically can cause discomfort and indigestion. If this happens they should be discontinued or used in much smaller amounts. A little and often is better than big doses.

Complan (Glaxo) is made from dried milk with vitamins and minerals added. It can be made up with just water, or with milk, or added to any other fluid. It has a slightly sweet taste and care is needed in adding it to savoury foods.

Prosol (Trufood) is a good source of protein and calcium and also supplies vitamins of the B complex. It can be added to any liquid, sweet, or savoury.

Casilan (Glaxo) is a very concentrated source of protein and calcium. It can be added to any liquid, sweet or savoury, but use it carefully or the patient may find it too concentrated.

Full-cream dried milk (infant milks) provides all the nutrients of fresh milk in a concentrated form and can be used to enrich fresh milk in the proportion of 2 oz. (4 heaped Tbs.) full cream dried to 1 pt (2 c.) of liquid milk. Be sure the powder is in good condition, as if it is stale it gives a rancid taste to the liquid. It will be found to be a very acceptable supplement to most people, as it does not introduce a strange flavour.

Instant dried skimmed milk (available from most Grocers and Chemists) (cream removed before drying) is concentrated milk, especially useful when a less fatty fluid is required (2 oz. (4 heaped Tbs.) powder to 1 pt (2 c.) is the usual proportion). It also has the advantage of being the cheapest protein supplement available and of having a flavour acceptable to most people. It lacks the fat-soluble vitamins A and D found in full-cream milk and should therefore not be used to replace whole milk and cream but as an addition to them. Fluids for a low-fat diet are discussed in Chapter 4.

Evaporated or unsweetened condensed milk can be added to any fluid, sweet or savoury.

Yogurt has no more nutritive value than other forms of milk but gives variety, especially for people who prefer less sweet fluids.

Yeast extracts are useful supplements to savoury fluids, providing additional B vitamins.

Fluids rich in vitamin C include blackcurrant syrup and purées; rose-hip syrup and mixtures such as rose-hip and orange; guava juice; apple juice fortified with vitamin C. They can be used alone as fruit drinks or added to milk.

Glucose is used for sweetening and increasing the calorie value of foods. It has the advantage of being less sweet than ordinary sugar so more can be used. It is also absorbed and used by the body more quickly than other sugars. It is better to use it to sweeten milk and fruit-juice drinks, rather than just in the form of glucose and water. Glucose alone is not so well used by the body as glucose plus vitamins supplied by milk, eggs, and other ingredients used in fluid feeds. Powdered glucose must be mixed with warm liquid to make it dissolve.

Suitable Foods

Beverages. Tea, coffee, cocoa, chocolate, fruit cordials, carbonated beverages, milk beverages, yeast and meat extracts, malted milks and other proprietary milk beverages, milk shakes. See also recipes Nos. 1–39.

It should be remembered that many fruit cordials and carbonated beverages are thirst-quenchers rather than foods and should not form too large a part of the diet.

Cereals. Cornflour, arrowroot (see No. 21), and potato flour are used to thicken milk and fruit juices. Strained oatmeal gruel, strained infant cereals made into a thin gruel with milk (No. 22).

Cheese. Grated mild cheese or mild processed cheese can be melted gently in liquids. Cottage cheese sieved and diluted or made liquid in an electric blender (Nos. 53 and 57).

Condiments. Moderate amounts only.

Eggs. As Egg nogs (Nos. 14–18); in soft cooked and thin custards (see Nos. 138–9, 397, and 442); in soups, egg broth (No. 58), and in any other liquid. Eggs are important for providing iron likely to be lacking in a fluid diet.

Fats, oil and cream. Any may be added as desired. Cream, melted butter, and margarine add vitamins A and D and calories.

Fish. Sieved or put through an electric blender for soups.

Fruit. Fresh, canned, or frozen strained juices and purées added to any liquid. If the throat is sore very acid juice, e.g. orange, lemon, blackcurrant, should be avoided unless mixed with some other fluid.

Meat, game, and poultry. Any may be used to make soups and stocks (see pages 237–46). If an electric blender is available, meat stews and other moist mixtures can be converted to liquids. Lightly cooked tender meats such as liver and chicken can be sieved and added to liquids.

Milk is the basis of all fluid diets. All kinds are allowed. Use dried and evaporated milks for a concentrated source (see Nos. 1–10) and to give variety. Also yogurt – plain and flavoured.

Puddings. All jellies provided they contain no whole fruit, skin, or pips (see Nos. 399, 407, 409, 420, 461–76), junkets (No. 480), custards (Nos. 397, 440–1), ice cream (Nos. 445–9, 454–5), water ices (Nos. 457–9), sherbets (Nos. 458 and 460). Canned strained foods make good fluid feeds if diluted with milk.

Soups and stocks. Any allowed so long as they are strained or blended finely in an electric blender. Packet and canned soups, strained or blended, may be used if they have a mild flavour. Dried milk, yeast extracts, cream, eggs, and permitted cereals can be added to increase the nutritive value and give variety.

Soups will form the basis of the diet for people who prefer

savoury to sweet liquids, and their adequate fortification with other ingredients is important as their basis, stock, has a lower nutritive value than milk. Cream soups made with a milk basis, plus vegetable purées are among the best to use. Nourishing soups are Nos. 53, 56, 57, 58, 75, 77, 78.

Sugars. Any may be used for sweetening liquids. Glucose is less sweet than ordinary sugar and more can be used. Black treacle, honey, and brown sugar all help to give variety.

Vegetables. Fresh, frozen, or canned for making stocks and soups and as purées added to milk and other liquid. Canned vegetable juices, and vegetable juices made with an electric juice extractor (Nos. 27–32) are all good. Strained canned vegetables can be thinned with milk or stock to make beverages.

Meal-Pattern

Type 1 is based on eight two-hourly feeds with additional ones if needed. Each feed equals approximately 8–10 fluid ounces (1 cup).

8 a.m. Strained and enriched cereal (No. 22).
10 a.m. Egg nog (Nos. 14–18).
12 noon Cream vegetable soup (No. 77).
2 p.m. Pudding from the list or fruit juice with glucose.
4 p.m. Milk drink of malted milk or coffee or chocolate.
6 p.m. Milk drink with sieved or blended meat or fish or melted cheese (Nos. 42, 53, 54, 64).
8 p.m. Pudding from the list or fruit juice with glucose.
10 p.m. Fortified milk drink (Nos. 2–13, 17 and 18).
Additional fruit or milk drink as desired.

Include daily 2 pints (4 c.) of milk, one of which may be fortified (No. 1 e), and 3 oz. (6 level Tbs.) or more of sugar or glucose. If savoury drinks are preferred substitute 2 Tbs. of double cream for each 1 oz. (2 level Tbs.) of sugar or glucose omitted from the day's diet.

Type 2 is for the more normal appetite.

On waking. Tea with plenty of milk and sugar or fruit juice with glucose.

Breakfast. 4–6 fl. oz. ($\frac{1}{2}$–$\frac{3}{4}$ c.) strained cereal or gruel with milk and sugar (No. 22), 8–10 fl. oz. (1 c.) egg nog (Nos. 14 and 16–18).

Mid-morning. 8–10 fl. oz. (1 c.) milk drink.

Midday. 4 fl. oz. ($\frac{1}{2}$ c.) fruit juice with glucose, 8 fl. oz. (1 c.) thick soup or meat stew made liquid in the electric blender, 2–3 oz. (50–100 g.) pudding from the list, 6 fl. oz. ($\frac{3}{4}$ c.) beverage.

Tea. 2–3 oz. (50–100 g.) ice cream or pudding from the list, 8 fl. oz. (1 c.) milk drink.

Evening. 4–6 fl. oz. ($\frac{1}{2}$–$\frac{3}{4}$ c.) fruit juices with glucose, 6–8 fl. oz. ($\frac{3}{4}$–1 c.) cream or milk soup or meat or fish dish made liquid in the electric blender, 2–3 oz. (50–100 g.) pudding from the list.

Bedtime. 8–10 fl. oz. ($\frac{3}{4}$–1 c.) milk drink.

Additional beverages between meals if desired. (Either milk, or fruit juices sweetened with glucose.)

THE SEMI-SOLID OR SOFT DIET

The soft diet is usually used for patients who have been on fluids and are progressing towards more solid foods. They are not on it for long but soon change to the light diet and then the good normal diet.

It may also be prescribed when there are chewing and swallowing difficulties not sufficiently severe to need a completely fluid diet.

How the Normal Diet is Modified

By preparing food in such a way that it can be broken up in the mouth without difficulty and easily swallowed. This is the modification needed for those whose only trouble is difficulty in chewing and swallowing.

Highly seasoned and indigestible foods are excluded but the basis is the same as the good normal diet (page 15). Any of the foods recommended for fluid diets are also suitable here.

Fitting in with Family Meals

Special cooking should not be necessary unless the family insists on a diet of fried foods and highly seasoned and indigestible ones.

Items from the ordinary good family diet (see pages 15–20) can be chopped, mashed, and pulverized to a suitable consistency. Alternatively, cook something suitable for the patient and add a solid supplement for the rest of the family, for example toast with soup, biscuits with soft puddings, raw salad or fresh fruit to end the meal.

Useful Special Foods

Because patients usually have a small appetite it is necessary to supplement the diet with the special foods listed on pages 26–8 for the fluid diet. These can be given most conveniently as between-meals drinks but can be used in addition to the more solid foods.

Many convenience foods can help to save time when preparing the diet; for example, strained baby foods which are already in a soft condition and can be used alone or as a basis for recipes requiring purées; many canned and packet soups already in purée form or which are easily strained or pulped before use; canned fruits and vegetables easily and quickly pulped; many frozen puddings are soft foods when thawed; and many other convenience foods can be used for making other dishes quickly.

CAUTION. Be sure the patient gets either some fresh fruit every day or blackcurrant or rose-hip syrup as a source of vitamin C.

Suitable Foods

Beverages. Milk drinks, coffee, tea, soft drinks, fruit and vegetable juices (see Nos. 1–39). Very cold drinks are soothing when the throat is sore.

Biscuits. Any plain or sweet ones which do not contain nuts or dried fruits can be dunked in a beverage or softened slowly in the mouth.

Breads and scones. Any day-old breads and scones made with white flour. Soft rolls.

Cakes. Plain sponges (Nos. 568–9, 573, and 575), and madeira cake (No. 560), angel cake (Nos. 548–9). Any light cake which does not contain spices or dried fruit. Fairy cakes. Madeleines (No. 561).

Cereals. Cooked infant cereals or groats, cornflakes, puffed rice or rice crispies, white flour, spaghetti, macaroni, noodles, and other pasta, white rice, semolina, cornflour, arrowroot, potato starch.

Cheese. Any of the milder kinds grated or melted gently in a sauce or soup. Cottage cheeses are very useful in this diet (see Nos. 35, 160–1, and 168).

Condiments and garnishes. Moderate amounts of salt, chopped parsley, chopped or sieved egg.

Eggs. Any way except fried. Hard-boiled eggs should be mashed or chopped finely.

Fats, oil, and cream. All allowed but use in moderation and do not fry.

Fish. Any white fish, fresh or frozen, grilled, baked, steamed, or boiled. (No skin or bones.) Canned salmon, herrings, sardines, and tuna fish (bones out).

Fruits. Cooked or canned apples, peaches, apricots, and pears with skins and seeds removed, any other cooked or ripe fruits if pulverized in an electric blender, ripe raw banana or ripe avocado pear. Any fruit juices. Baked apples (pulp sieved), blackcurrant or rose-hip syrup. See also Nos. 396–405, 407–11, 413, 416, 420, 429.

If the throat is sore avoid acid fruits and juices, e.g. lemon or orange.

Meat. It may be necessary to serve meat minced or pulverized, but ask the doctor about it. Minced cooked meat can be reheated in gravy or sauce but it must be freshly cooked, not left-overs. Otherwise use tender roast or grilled or boiled or stewed veal, lamb, or beef, or any minced meat, tender chicken or turkey (no skin), sweetbreads, brains, grilled liver (not ox), tender ham (no fat or gristle).

Milk. Any kind is allowed, including enriched milk (see page 227). Yogurt plain or flavoured. Very cold milk is soothing when the throat is sore.

Preserves. Any without skins or pips.

Puddings. Any of the following without whole fruit, nuts, or dried fruit. Custard, cornflour pudding, instant whips, desserts, rice pudding, sago or tapioca, bread puddings, ices, jellies and gelatine puddings, steamed and baked light sponges (No. 498), fruit fools and whips with puréed fruit, soufflés, junkets, or any other smooth light puddings.

Sauces and gravy. Any allowed as long as it is not highly seasoned or contains whole pieces of vegetable or fruit.

Soups and stocks. Any stocks. Soups should be sieved or mixed in the electric blender. Packet and tinned soups may be used provided they are sieved or blended. Evaporated milk, yogurt, or dried milk can be added to enrich them.

Sugars and sugar confectionery. Any allowed, including honey and syrup. Soft sweets such as jujubes, marshmallows, and chocolates.

Vegetables. Any fresh, canned, or frozen except strong-flavoured ones such as onions. They can be cooked and sieved or mashed or finely chopped. Potatoes can be served in any way except fried and roast. Cauliflower may be served without sieving if the flower part only is used. Skinned or sieved or pulverized tomatoes served any way except fried, any vegetable juices, tender lettuce finely chopped, chopped parsley, asparagus tips, sieved, fresh, or frozen young green peas.

Meal-Pattern

Choose from the list of suitable foods on pages 32–4.

On waking. Tea or fruit juice.

Breakfast. Sieved fruit or fruit juices. Cereal from the list, milk, cream, and sugar. Egg. Bread or roll with butter or margarine. Hot beverage with milk or cream and sugar.

Mid-morning. Milk drink or other beverage, biscuit.

Midday. Soup (if desired) or fruit juice. Meat or fish or poultry.

Potato or pasta or boiled rice. Vegetables. Pudding. Milky coffee or tea.

Tea. Tea or coffee with thin bread and butter, cake or biscuit.

Evening. Soup (if desired). Egg, cheese, meat, or fish dish. Vegetables if desired. Bread and butter, or fruit, or pudding from the list. Milky coffee or tea.

Bedtime. Milk drink. Biscuit.

NOTE. Midday and evening meals are interchangeable.

Lunch, High Tea, or Supper Menus

1

Tomato juice
Cheese pudding (No. 166) *or* Soufflé (No. 183)
Compôte of apples
Small piece of sponge cake

2

Hot Marmite drink
Poached egg mornay (No. 188)
Thin bread and butter
Strawberry fool (No. 396)

3

Cream of pea soup (No. 77) (young green peas)
Ham custard (No. 192)
Thin bread and butter
Stuffed oranges (No. 432)

4

Egg and yogurt mould (No. 194) with chopped lettuce
Tomato concassé (No. 359)
Bridge rolls and butter
Chocolate blancmange with cream and sieved raspberries

5

Salmon loaf (No. 232), with Tomato sauce (No. 108)
Bread and butter
Lemon water ice (No. 457)
Sponge fingers

6

Creamed soft roes (No. 237) in border of Duchess potatoes (No. 349 e)
Strawberry whip (No. 409), *or* Mousse (No. 399-402)
Sponge cake

7

Bacon omelette (No. 172)
Tomato sauce (No. 108)
Bread and butter
Apple trifle (No. 506)

8

Chicken jelly (No. 281)
Asparagus tips with mayonnaise
Bread and butter
Individual orange baked custards (No. 440)

9

Steamed fish and rice mould (No. 229)
Anchovy sauce (No. 91)
Garnish of chopped tender lettuce heart
Banana and blackcurrant sundae (No. 450)

10

Dairy soup (No. 57)
Minced ham and chopped tomato sandwiches
Raw banana

11

Cream of tomato soup (No. 77)
Cottage cheese on bridge rolls
Compôte of fresh or canned peaches

12

Eggs mimosa (No. 195)
Toast fingers
Raspberry summer pudding (No. 437)
Cream

13

Tomato juice
Ham mousse (No. 279)
Chopped lettuce
Madeleines (No. 561)

14

Liver terrapin (No. 308)
Crisp toast
Peach melba (No. 451)
Sponge cake

Dinner Menus

1

Canned or fresh orange juice
Tender roast veal (minced if necessary), with gravy
Purée of potatoes (No. 349 h)
Sieved spinach
Crème au caramel (No. 441)

2

Cream of spinach soup (No. 77)
Grilled white fish (No. 203)
Parsley butter (No. 99)
Creamed potatoes (No. 349)
Grilled tomatoes
Egg jelly (No. 463)

3

Cream of green pea soup (No. 77) (young, fresh, or frozen peas)
Creamed chicken in macaroni ring (No. 322)
Tomato concassé (No. 359)
Chocolate mousse (Nos. 438-9)

4

Cream of tomato soup (No. 77)
Poached white fish (No. 205) with egg sauce (No. 83)
Purée of potatoes (No. 349 h) with chopped parsley or watercress
Steamed canary pudding (No. 498)
Orange sauce (No. 145)

5

Mushroom soup (No. 66)
Creamed sweetbreads (No. 310)
Purée of potatoes and carrots (No. 354)
Swedish apple cake (No. 416)

6

Pineapple juice
Creamed veal (No. 322) in border of Duchess potatoes (No. 349 e)
Purée of young green peas
Trifle (No. 508)

7

Cream of celery soup (No. 77)
Minced liver in tomato sauce (No. 302)
A few cooked and chopped brussels sprouts
Baked trifle (No. 507)

8

Vegetable juices, hot or cold
Tripe soubise (No. 316)
Potato purée (No. 349 h)
Purée of green peas
Coffee Spanish cream (No. 462)

9

Consommé
Tender boiled lamb
Parsley sauce (No. 80)
Purée of potatoes (No. 349 h)
Mashed young carrots
Fruit mousse (Nos. 399–404)

10

Cream of asparagus soup (No. 77)
Baked cheese custard (No. 163)
Fresh tomato purée
Grapefruit jelly (No. 466)
Sponge cake (No. 568 or 569)

11

Tomato juice
Tender roast chicken
Bread sauce
Purée of potatoes (No. 349 h)
Parsley to garnish
Vanilla ice (No. 454) and Melba sauce (No. 146)

12

Cream of pea soup (young green peas) (No. 77)
Beef mould (No. 260)
Tomato sauce (No. 108)
Creamed potatoes (No. 349)
Gooseberry fool (No. 396)

13

Tomato yogurt (No. 24)
Roast breast of turkey
Bread sauce
Duchess potatoes (No. 349 e)
Mashed young carrots
Apple snow (No. 413)

14

Tomato jelly with chopped lettuce (No. 362)
Liver pilaf (No. 305) (liver chopped or minced)
Floating island (No. 442)

THE LIGHT DIET

The light diet is used when the patient is not seriously ill but is not well enough to take a normal diet and needs simple, easily digested foods.

NOTE. Light does *not* mean soft and sloppy, with sieved vegetables.

How the Normal Diet is Modified

By concentrating on simple cooking methods, and leaving out highly seasoned foods, strongly flavoured vegetables, tough meats, rich fatty and fried foods, and rich cakes and pastry.

People who are ill enough to need a light diet often suffer damage and wastage of body tissues and therefore need plenty of protein and vitamins in their food and frequently a high-calorie diet as well. They may not have regained their normal appetite, and small meals of concentrated foods are therefore indicated. Food supplements such as dried milks are useful here.

Fitting in with Family Meals

This kind of diet is quite suitable for the rest of the family and no special cooking should be required for the patient unless the diet has to go on for a long time in which case it becomes boring for the family used to richer food.

Useful Special Foods

These are only required if the patient has a very small appetite and are probably best used in drinks given between meals. For details of the supplements and liquids see pages 26–8 and Nos. 1–11.

Foods Usually Allowed

Beverages. Any kind.
Biscuits. Any kind.

Bread and scones. All except very new bread and hot scones.

Cakes. Plain cakes of all kinds.

Cereals. Any kind.

Cheese. All kinds so long as they do not give the patient indigestion.

Condiments. Salt and pepper. Avoid pickles and heavy spices as these may cause discomfort.

Eggs. Cooked any way but fried.

Fats, oils, and cream. Any kind in moderation.

Fish. White fish cooked any way except fried. Canned salmon and tuna fish.

Fruit. Any kind as long as very tough skins are removed.

Meat. All kinds, simply cooked and tender cuts.

Milk. All kinds allowed, as much as possible being included. The concentrated milks, evaporated and dried, are useful for increasing the protein and calorie content of the diet. Yogurt helps to give variety.

Preserves. Any kind.

Puddings. All allowed except rich pastry and suet puddings.

Sauces and gravies. All except the very highly seasoned and rich ones.

Soups and stocks. Any may be used. Cream soups are most nourishing for this diet.

Sugars and sugar confectionery. All kinds.

Vegetables. All kinds except fried, and very strongly flavoured ones, if they cause indigestion. Salad vegetables such as lettuce, endives, tomatoes, watercress, chicory, beetroot, tender raw brussels sprouts, shredded or grated raw carrot, and cucumber if it does not cause discomfort.

Meal-Pattern

Breakfast. Fruit juices, porridge or cereal with milk, cream and sugar. Fish, egg, or bacon. Bread or toast with preserves, and butter. Weak tea, or milky coffee.

Mid-morning. Enriched milk drink, Nos. 1–11.

Midday. Soup if desired or fruit juice (not many can manage three courses). Fish or meat or cheese or egg dish. Vegetable. Pudding or cheese and biscuits.

Tea. Bread and butter, preserves or other spreads, plain cake, weak tea.

Evening. Soup and a main dish of fish or meat or cheese or egg. Alternatively, a main dish with sweet or cake.

Bedtime. Enriched milk drink (Nos. 1–13, 18).

NOTE. Midday and evening meals are interchangeable.

Include these daily:

1½ pints (3 c.) milk, some of it enriched.
1 egg.
2 portions of meat or fish or poultry or offal or cheese.
2 portions of fresh vegetable.
1 portion of fruit or fruit juice.
1–2 oz (2–4 level Tbs.) butter.
Bread, and other foods according to appetite.

Lunch, High Tea, or Supper Menus

1

Scalloped scallops (No. 236)
Mashed potatoes (No. 349)
Fresh lemon jelly (No. 467)

2

Asparagus soup (No. 77)
Creamed soft roes on toast (No. 237)
Tomato garnish

3

Salmon au gratin (No. 230)
Green salad
Bread and butter
Apple snow (No. 413)
Sweet biscuit

4

Minced liver in tomato sauce (No. 302)
Toast
Fruit fool (No. 396)

5

Cream of chicken soup (No. 54)
Ham custard (No. 192)
Bread and butter
Fresh orange

6

Egg broth (No. 58)
Chicken in jelly (No. 281)
Rémoulade sauce (No. 116)
Sliced tomato
Bread and butter

7

Dairy soup (No. 57)
Veal mould (No. 325)
Tomato salad (No. 393)
Roll and butter

8

Tripe and egg pie (No. 314)
Baked tomatoes
Toast
Coffee Spanish cream (No. 462)

9

Cream of celery soup (No. 77)
Liver terrapin (No. 308)
Fresh fruit

10

Cream of tomato soup (No. 77)
Poached eggs mornay (No. 188)
Toast
Fresh fruit

11

Scalloped eggs and ham (No. 196)
Toast
Fruit whip or mousse (Nos. 399 or 409)

12

Brain soup (No. 51)
Toast
Eggs Crécy (No. 189)

13

Tomato and Marmite soup (No. 74)
Cheese custard (No. 163)
Toast or bread and butter
Fresh fruit

14

Fish shape (No. 223)
Anchovy sauce (No. 91)
Green salad
Crème au caramel (No. 441)

Dinner Menus

1

Plaice or sole mornay (No. 242)
Boiled potatoes
Lettuce salad
Vanilla ice (No. 454) with blackcurrant syrup

2

Grilled white fish (No. 203)
Parsley butter (No. 99)
Creamed potatoes (No. 349)
Grilled tomatoes
Fresh orange jelly (No. 467) and cream

3

Poached fillets of sole or plaice (No. 205)
Egg and lemon sauce (No. 100)
Creamed potatoes (No. 349)
Green peas
Strawberry mousse (Nos. 399–401)

4

Fish Florentine (No. 218)
Creamed potatoes (No. 349)
Refrigerated peach flan (No. 490)

5

Veal blanquette (No. 320)
Boiled macaroni or noodles
Spinach
Norwegian trifle (No. 479)

6

Creamed sweetbreads (No. 310)
Mashed potatoes (No. 349)
Carrot purée
Egg jelly (No. 463)

7

Tripe au gratin (No. 315)
Mashed potatoes
Brussels sprouts
Vanilla mousse (No. 454) with sauce Melba (No. 146)

8

Steamed chicken and rice (No. 277)
Lettuce salad
Blackcurrant jelly (No. 465) with green grapes

9

Steamed lamb chop (No. 297)
Tomato sauce (No. 108)
Cauliflower sprigs Polonaise (No. 335)
Creamed potatoes (No. 349)
Chocolate mousse (No. 438 or 439)

10

Lamb stew (No. 298)
Spinach
Boiled potatoes
Baked trifle (No. 507)

11

Boiled chicken with noodles (No. 269)
Green beans
Fruit purée ice (No. 460)

12

Beef mould (No. 260)
Mushroom sauce (No. 105)
Brussels sprouts
Floating island (No. 442)

13

Fillets of plaice or sole with mushrooms (No. 244)
Creamed potatoes (No. 349)
Tomatoes concassé (No. 359)
Frozen fruit mousse (No. 455)

14

Sole or plaice with cream and grapes (No. 235)
Duchess potatoes (No. 349 e)
Fruit juice custard (No. 397)
Langues de chat (No. 542)

CHAPTER 3

Diseases of the Digestive System

THE digestive system consists of:

1. The alimentary canal, which has the following parts: mouth and throat or pharynx; oesophagus or gullet; stomach; small intestine consisting of duodenum, ileum and jejunum; the large intestine or colon or lower bowel; the rectum and anus.
2. The salivary glands.
3. The liver and gall bladder.
4. The pancreas.

Food has to be broken up physically (chewing and churning) into small pieces and mixed with digestive fluids secreted by the salivary glands, the walls of the stomach and small intestine, the liver and gall bladder, and the pancreas. These fluids add water to moisten the food, and enzymes and other substances which change its chemical composition and turn it into a suitable form to pass through the walls of the small intestine (absorption) into the blood. The residue passes along the colon, water being re-absorbed from the now liquid residue, and is finally passed out of the body (faeces or stools) via the rectum and anus.

The Mouth, Throat, and Gullet

There can be many causes of difficulty in chewing and swallowing. Among these are laziness in chewing, defective and missing teeth, sore throat (a variety of causes), fractured jaw, carcinoma or cancer of the parts, bulbar palsy (defective muscles in the walls of the gullet which makes swallowing difficult).

Diets usually prescribed are either the fluid diet (see page 25), or the soft or semi-solid diet (see page 31), both designed to present the food in a form which the defective system can handle. As this type of diet may have to continue for some time, it is most important that it should be based on a good normal diet (page 15), otherwise nutritional deficiencies will be liable to arise.

The Stomach

The stomach acts as a reservoir for the food and releases

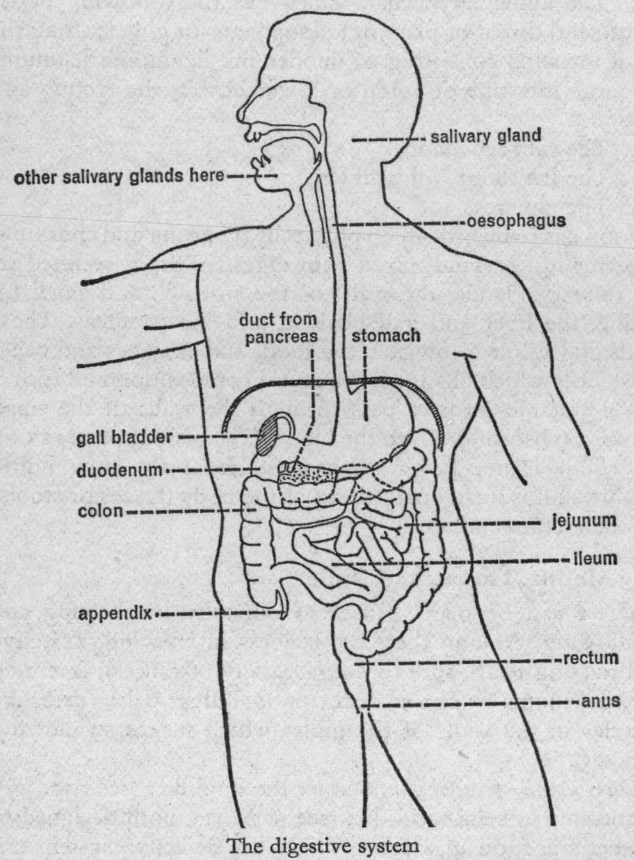

The digestive system

small amounts at regular intervals into the duodenum. While in the stomach the food is churned by muscular contractions, mixed with digestive fluid (including hydrochloric acid), and reduced to a semi-fluid soft mass (chyme). Many defects can occur in this part of the system. They include:

1. *Dyspepsia* or *indigestion* are terms used to cover a collection of symptoms such as heartburn, nausea, distention, belching, and flatulence.

The diet will vary with the cause of the trouble and will be prescribed by the doctor. Frequently the recommendations include the following:

Eating a well-cooked varied normal diet (see page 15).
Not overeating (i.e. smaller meals).
Taking fluids between meals only.
Eating more slowly and chewing thoroughly.
Avoiding very fatty and fried foods.

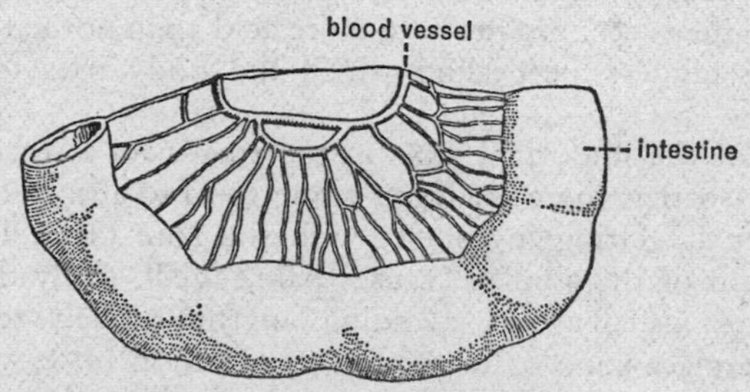

A loop of the intestine showing blood vessels into which digested foods pass

Avoiding flatulence-producing vegetables like onions, radishes, cabbage, pulses, nuts, and anything found to cause discomfort in the individual.
Not eating full meals when very tired or physically or emotionally under strain.

When a special diet is prescribed it is usually a low-fibre diet (page 50).

2. *Gastritis* is inflammation of the lining of the stomach and has many causes. The diet is usually designed to rest the stomach and in the acute stages may consist of water only. It then progresses to the fluid diet (see page 25), and finally to the low-fibre diet (see page 50), or to the light diet (see page 38), and then to the normal one.

For chronic gastritis the low-fibre diet is usually prescribed with only small portions of food at a time.

3. *Peptic ulcers* include both gastric or stomach ulcers and duodenal ulcers.

The cause of ulcers is not known and therefore the treatment is not really known either, though time and custom have shown certain procedures to be beneficial in the majority of cases. The ulcer is a sore in the lining of the stomach or duodenum, the lining having been partially destroyed. The pain felt by the patient is due to hydrochloric acid produced in the stomach coming into contact with the sore place. Ulcer patients seem to produce more acid than normal people and this hinders the healing which the body tries to carry out.

One of the important aims in the treatment is to eat frequently so that there is always some food to absorb the acid and stop it getting in contact with the sore place. Because distention of the stomach causes pain, small, easily digested meals are usually best, avoiding anything likely to make the sore place sting or to scratch (e.g. lemon juice, vinegar, pickles and spices, coarse and scratchy fruits and vegetables and cereals; very hot foods, strong alcohol, strong tea and coffee).

In the early stages of treatment the diet may be chiefly milk, which will be given in various forms at hourly or two-hourly intervals; from there the patient progresses to the low-fibre diet (see page 50).

Some patients, however, are allowed to eat anything they fancy which they find does not cause pain. Others are recommended to have the low-fibre diet, others simply a light diet (see page 38).

The Liver and Gall Bladder

The liver secretes bile which is a fluid important in fat digestion. The gall bladder stores the bile and releases it into the duodenum as required. The diseases affecting these parts are dealt with in Chapter 4, pages 82–94.

The Pancreas

The pancreas secretes digestive enzymes to deal with fats, carbohydrates, and proteins. Diseases of the pancreas which reduce these secretions are called mal-absorption diseases and are dealt with in the following section.

The pancreas also secretes insulin, a hormone needed for the proper use of carbohydrates (starches and sugars). Failure in insulin supplies leads to diabetes, discussed in Chapter 5, pages 95–114.

The Small Intestine

The upper part is the duodenum which receives bile from the gall bladder and the digestive fluids from the pancreas. It also secretes other digestive juices in its own wall. The lower parts, jejunum and ileum, are where the major portion of digested food is absorbed through the walls of the intestine into the blood. Apart from duodenal ulcers, the main diseases of the small intestine are those known as mal-absorption disorders, that is, diseases which prevent the food being completely digested and absorbed into the blood. This in turn leads to something very like a condition of starvation and malnourishment, and the whole body will eventually feel the effects. Chief amongst these conditions are:

1. *Coeliac Condition.* This is most frequently diagnosed in young children between the ages of six months and six years but it also occurs in older children, adolescents, and adults of any age-group. In the coeliac condition the intestine is hyper-sensitive to proteins found in gluten, a normal

constituent of some cereals, with the result that the sufferer is unable to absorb food properly and many distressing symptoms result. The child suffers from malnutrition and fails to grow normally; the adult, too, is malnourished, and both adults and children have unpleasant fatty stools due to the inability of the intestine to deal with fat in the normal way.

In the early stages of treatment the amount of fat in the diet will be restricted, but once the patient has responded to the gluten-free diet normal amounts of fat can usually be taken. The chief sources of gluten are wheat, rye, barley, oats, in that order. Some people with the coeliac condition are advised to avoid all four cereals, others are allowed to have barley and oats but not wheat or rye.

Diet is the only treatment known for this disease. For the gluten-free diet, see pages 60–74.

2. *Steatorrhoea.* This disease is characterized by faulty absorption of fat. It may be due to a failure in the secretion of bile, to a failure on the part of the pancreas which normally secretes fat-digesting enzymes, or to a defect of absorption similar to that which occurs in the coeliac condition. If the last is the trouble the patient will be put on a gluten-free diet (see page 60); if the trouble is failure in the fat-digesting mechanism the diet will be a low-fat one (see page 84).

3. *Tropical sprue.* This is another disease where there is poor fat absorption and a low-fat diet with a good protein intake is usually prescribed (page 84).

The Large Intestine or Colon

After digestion and absorption, the undigested residue (faeces) passes slowly along the large intestine, and the water which was secreted in digestive fluids is largely re-absorbed. Among the diseases of the large intestine are:

1. *Spastic constipation*, due to a spasm in the muscular wall of the intestine. This obstructs the normal passage of the faeces. The usual dietary treatment is a low-fibre diet, the diet gradually returning to normal as the patient improves.

2. *Atonic constipation.* This condition is often known as the 'lazy colon'. It is due to poor condition of the muscular walls of the intestine whose contractions (peristalsis) are responsible for moving the faeces along the colon to the rectum for final elimination.

There are many causes of this kind of constipation, but frequently it is due to a faulty diet too low in fibre and the usual dietary treatment is a high-fibre diet (see page 75).

3. *Diarrhoea.* Among the many causes are disturbed emotional states, food poisoning, dysentery, typhoid fever, ulcerative colitis, over-active peristalsis, and inflammation of the lining of the intestine. Because the patient with diarrhoea passes liquid stools there is a great loss of fluid from the body and a high fluid intake is part of the diet.

As the intestine is inflamed, digestion and absorption are poor and therefore the food should be very easy to digest and should not contain coarse fibre or anything which will leave an indigestible residue that may scratch the sore intestine. The diet usually prescribed is the low-fibre diet (see page 50).

MILK DIET FOR ULCERS

The milk diet is based on hourly or two-hourly feeds which consist mainly of flavoured milk taken 5 fl. oz. ($\frac{1}{2}$ c.) at a time. These feeds are given from 7 a.m. or earlier if awake, to 10 p.m., or bedtime. The patient should have a Thermos of milk drink by the bed to have if awake during the night.

Flavourings usually allowed in the milk are weak tea, Ovaltine, Horlicks, Bengers, cocoa, Marmite, blackcurrant purée, Milo, Bournvita, drinking chocolate.

Other foods usually allowed are some milk puddings in small portions as alternatives to or in addition to some of the milk feeds, e.g. junkets, milk jellies, egg custards, blancmange, milk pudding (cornflour, ground-rice, semolina, sago); strained oatmeal porridge or groats made with milk for breakfast; creamed soups as alternatives to the milk, important for introducing a little butter into the diet (see No. 77); plain biscuit or rusks two at a time occasionally if there is no vomiting or pain. These may be spread with butter.

The juice of two oranges diluted with water is allowed throughout the day and may be taken in small amounts between milk feeds whenever the patient is thirsty.

Daily amount of food usually allowed (CHECK THIS WITH THE DOCTOR). Milk 4 pints (8 c.), 2 eggs, 1–2 teaspoons butter, juice of 2 oranges, 2 portions of cream of vegetable soup. If vitamins are prescribed by the doctor, make sure the patient takes them regularly as directed.

Transition to the low-fibre diet is usually gradual, with breakfast, midday, and 6-p.m. milk feeds being replaced by the sort of meals advised in the low-fibre diet until finally the patient is fully on to the new diet.

THE LOW-FIBRE DIET
(or LOW-ROUGHAGE, LOW-RESIDUE, BLAND, OR GASTRIC DIET)

This diet is often prescribed for conditions such as gastritis, peptic ulcer, spastic constipation and diarrhoea (see pages 46–9).

How the Normal Diet is Modified

1. By avoiding all coarse fibres which may act as an irritant to an inflamed intestine. Coarse fibres are found in such foods as:

Fruits (especially raw, and in the peel, pips, and pith).

Whole-grain cereals (brown breads, whole-grain or brown crispbreads, such as Ryvita, and wholemeal biscuits such as digestive biscuits or oatcakes).

Nuts.

Pulses (dried peas, beans, lentils, processed peas).

Stringy vegetables (especially stalks and overmature vegetables, celery, skins of peas, broad beans, and potatoes).

Gristly and stringy meat (can be softened by long, slow cooking).

Stringy fish such as lobster and crab.

CAUTION. Vegetables and fruit in *some form* must be included in this diet, as in all others, because they are the only sources of vitamin C, which has important healing properties. The amount and kind which can be tolerated varies with the patient. Some can only have them sieved or in the form of juices, others can have small amounts of the tender soft parts of many cooked vegetables and some raw and canned fruits (see list, pages 53–5).

2. Certain foods may cause discomfort and are best avoided, for example, strongly flavoured vegetables such as onions, turnips, radishes, green and red peppers; strongly smoked and pickled meat and fish such as kippers or heavily smoked bacon; strong coffee and tea; alcohol; and large quantities of salt, pepper and other seasonings.

3. By avoiding fried foods (grill or bake instead).

4. By avoiding extremes of temperature, that is, very hot or very cold food. (Ice cream should be eaten very slowly.)

5. By avoiding any other foods known to cause discomfort in the individual.

Fitting in with Family Meals

Special cooking can largely be avoided if the patient's diet is made the basis of the family meals. Vegetables and fruit can be left whole for the family and some whole-grain cereals provided as extras, e.g. coarse breakfast cereals and whole-wheat bread as an alternative to the white the patient must have.

It won't hurt the family to forgo highly seasoned and fried foods for a while, but if this is not acceptable extra seasonings and spices can be added to the family's portion.

As explained on page 46 for peptic ulcers, regular meals at frequent intervals are an important part of the treatment. For a suitable meal pattern, see page 55.

Advice to Relatives

The diseases which need a low-fibre diet are frequently

those made worse by worry and stress. The family can help by not making a lot of fuss over the diet and by encouraging the patient to enjoy the food. To avoid hurry, bickering, and argument at the table is also a help, and do not try to force the patient to eat when he or she is very tired or upset. Give him a warm milk drink instead, and after a rest period a light meal should be taken. Also, be very sure all food is freshly cooked, and handled and stored in a clean manner (see page 23).

Cooking Methods are Important

OUT: frying, because it makes food indigestible and smoking-hot fat contains a substance (acrolein) which irritates the lining of the intestine. No-so-hot fat makes food greasy and indigestible.

IN: grilling or baking instead, and much better for the rest of the family too.

Also IN: poaching, boiling, baking, and stewing (sieve or strain the gravy and don't use lots of onions, seasonings and herbs).

Careful cooking of vegetables is important to preserve the maximum amount of vitamin C. Purée vegetables while they are hot, reheat quickly, and serve at once.

Useful Special Foods

Strained infant foods in small tins and vitamin C-rich syrup, such as blackcurrant and rose-hip syrup.

Foods Usually Allowed

CAUTION. Check this list with your doctor or dietitian. Make sure you use all the foods allowed so as to provide variety and prevent boredom. Try to find acceptable ways of cooking each permitted food.

Beverages. Freshly made weak tea and coffee, cocoa and drinking chocolate, Complan, Ovaltine, Horlicks, Bengers, Allenbury's Diet, Bournvita, Milo, and other patent milk foods.

When flatulence is present beverages may be confined to between meals only.

Milk drinks, fruit and vegetable juices (see Nos. 1–18, 20–24, 26–38).

Biscuits. Any except those made with wholemeal flour (e.g. digestive), oatmeal or rolled oats, or containing coconut, other nuts, dried fruit, or spices.

Breads. Day-old white or brown bread or rolls (but not coarse wholemeal), Melba toast, rusks, plain scones, crisp toast buttered cold.

Cakes. Plain sponges, Madeira cake, and any plain soft cakes which are not highly spiced or with dried fruits. Avoid rich pastries and doughnuts and doughy buns.

Cereals, starches, and pasta. Breakfast cereals: Rice Krispies, Cornflakes, Puffed Rice, infant cereal, fine oatmeal porridge or groats, wheat germ. Others: white flour, cornflour, arrowroot, potato flour, semolina, sago, tapioca, custard powder. Pasta: macaroni, spaghetti, noodles, and any others.

Cheese. All mild ones including cottage and cream cheese. Melt hard cheeses in a sauce or use in cooking, but not baked or grilled to form a hard crust.

Condiments and garnishes. Moderate amounts of salt, very small amounts cinnamon, all-spice, mace, paprika pepper; finely chopped parsley, chopped hard-boiled whole egg, or the sieved yolk.

Eggs. Any way except fried or curried or other highly seasoned methods.

Fats, oils, and cream. Butter, margarine, oils, cream, peanut butter, home-made mayonnaise, and salad cream (using less vinegar, or lemon instead).

Fish. Any kind of white fish, fresh or frozen. Cooked any way except fried, soused, or other highly seasoned methods. Also allowed are soft roes, herrings with all skin and bone removed, tinned or fresh salmon, pilchards or sardines (bones and skin mashed or removed), oysters.

Fruit. Baked apple (pulp only), soft cooked or canned apple, sweet cherries, peaches, apricots, pears (no skin or pips), other cooked fruits if sieved, raw ripe bananas, fruit juices (better at the end of a meal). Some orange or grapefruit or tomato juice should be given daily, or rose-hip syrup or black-currant syrup. Orange or grapefruit sections with all skin and pith removed are sometimes allowed, also very ripe melon, ripe raw avocado pear, pears (no peel or pips), peaches (no skin).

Meat, game, and poultry. Tender roast or boiled meats; chicken; rabbit; turkey and offal any way but fried, and other meats if minced. Grilled lamb cutlets, tender steak, and broiler chicken, steamed lamb cutlets, lightly grilled mild bacon, luncheon meat, boiled ham or tongue.

Milk. All kinds allowed. Milk forms the most important part of the diet, especially for between-meal drinks. Yogurt also allowed.

Preserves. Any sieved jams, all jellies, honey, golden syrup, sieved or jelly marmalade, lemon curd.

Puddings. All milk puddings, ice cream (no whole fruit). Jellies (no whole fruit), custards, sherbets, light steamed or baked sponge puddings, queen of puddings, meringues, trifle (no whole fruit), fruit (see above), fruit mousse, creams, fruit fools. See recipe index.

Sauces and gravies. Those made with milk or vegetable or fish stock and lightly seasoned with salt. Tomato purée, red-currant or other jelly with meat. Home-made salad cream and mayonnaise (see Fats, above).

Soups and stocks. Home-made vegetable ones only, and all should be sieved. Vegetable and fish stocks, Marmite. Avoid those made with strongly flavoured vegetables. Cream soups are the best (see No. 77).

Sugars and sugar confectionery. All sugars allowed. Plain or milk chocolate, boiled sweets after meals, including barley sugar.

Vegetables. Potatoes in any way except fried, roasted or sautéed. Cooked and sieved or mashed carrots, young green peas (fresh or frozen), beetroot, spinach, spring cabbage, asparagus tips, tomatoes, whole marrow, flower of cauliflower, raw ripe tomatoes (skin and seed removed), inner tender leaves of lettuce finely chopped.

Meal-Pattern

Using foods from the list, page 52.

On waking. Very weak tea.

Breakfast. Cereal with milk and sugar *or* egg or white fish or kedgeree or soft roes or crisply grilled bacon or cold boiled bacon or ham. Bread or crisp toast, butter or margarine, and preserves. Very weak tea with milk, or a little strained and diluted fruit juice (4 Tbs.).

Mid-morning. 5 fl. oz. (½ c.) milk drink. Plain biscuit or plain cake or sandwich.

Midday. Meat or fish or poultry, vegetable, potatoes. Sweet. Fruit juice as at breakfast.

Tea. Weak tea, permitted cake, sandwiches or bread and butter or crisp toast.

Evening. Meat or fish or egg or cheese dish with vegetables if desired. Alternatively, serve a milky soup and sandwiches. Crisp toast or rusks or bread and preserves or permitted cake or pudding. Milk flavoured as desired. Fruit juices as at breakfast.

Bedtime. Milk drink.

Include these foods daily:

CAUTION. Check this list with your doctor or dietitian.

2 pints (4 c.) liquid milk or its equivalent in dried or evaporated milk (see page 17).
3 oz. meat, poultry, or fish (average portion).
2 eggs or 1 egg and 1 oz. cheese.
1 oz. (2 level Tbs.) butter or margarine.
¼ pt (½ c.) fruit or tomato juice.
3–4 oz. potatoes (1 medium).
3–4 oz. vegetables (average portion).
Bread and cakes and cereals as required.

Eating Out

Choose from these items:

Soups. Cream soups, fruit juices, tomato juice, or vegetable juices.

Eggs. Plain omelette. Boiled, scrambled, poached.

Fish. Grilled (remove bones and skin from herrings and other small fish), roes on toast, sardines on toast (mash the bones), fried fish in batter (but leave the batter).

Meats. Tender roast and grilled. Boiled lamb (not caper sauce) or lean ham, cold roast beef or lamb, roast, grilled, or boiled chicken or turkey, cold chicken.

Vegetables. Potatoes, mashed, boiled, baked, or roast (leave the skins). Mashed carrots, spinach purée, cauliflower (leave the stalks), and marrow.

Puddings. Milk pudding, custards, jellies (no whole fruit), plain steamed or baked sponge, ice cream or water ices (no whole fruit), or plain biscuits and mild cheese.

Fruits. Ripe banana or fruit juices.

Breads. Usually those in a restaurant are fairly new so ask for thin unbuttered toast instead or Melba toast or rusk or water biscuit or cream-crackers or bread sticks (*grissini*).

For other items, see permitted food list, page 52.

Sandwich Meals

Breads. Day-old white or brown (not coarse wholemeal), rusks, plain scones, day-old soft rolls, finger rolls, French bread, Viennese bread, milk twists, cottage loaves, cream-crackers, water biscuits, breakfast biscuits.

Fillings, Savoury. Canned pilchards, sardines, tuna fish well mashed, chopped hard-boiled egg with home-made salad cream or mayonnaise, home-made liver pâté (No. 303 or 304). Cheese from list, cottage cheese with permitted flavourings, sliced tender cold meat, minced meat with permitted sauces and flavourings, Marmite. *Sweet.* Sieved jams, jellies, and honey.

Other sweet foods. Cooked stewed fruit from the list or cold sweets, in containers. Biscuit or cake from the list. Plain ice cream if available. Plain chocolate and boiled sweets.

Beverages. Milk drinks or permitted soups, in Thermos flasks. Cold milk.

Extras. Plain biscuits and permitted cheese, hard-boiled eggs.

Fruit. Ripe banana, fruit juices in small polythene bottles, rose-hip syrup, ripe pears, peaches, grapes, and orange segments if allowed.

A suitable meal would consist of:
2 substantial sandwiches with meat, egg, cheese, or fish filling.
1 sweet sandwich or cake or ice cream or chocolate.
Permitted fruit or fruit juice.
Beverage.

Lunch, High Tea, or Supper Menus

1

Cream of asparagus soup (No. 77)
Chicken sandwiches
Piece of Genoese sponge (No. 568)

2

Creamed soft roes (No. 237)
Tomatoes concassée (No. 359)
Meringue glacé (No. 452)

3

Dairy soup (No. 57)
Ham sandwiches
Fresh orange jelly and cream (No. 467)

4

Cauliflower with salmon sauce (No. 231)
Crisp toast
Madeleines (No. 561)

5

Brain soup (No. 51)
Bread and butter
Strawberry mousse (No. 400 or 402)

6

Baked fish in Béchamel sauce (No. 202)
Mashed potatoes
Apricot whip (No. 409) or mousse (Nos. 399–402)

7

Vichyssoise (No. 78)
Lean tender lamb sandwiches with tender chopped lettuce

8

Mimosa eggs (No. 195) on toast
Coffee cream (No. 461)
Fresh orange juice

9

Tender roast beef sandwiches with tomato concassée (No. 359)
Coffee junket (No. 480)
Whipped cream

10

Soufflé omelette (No. 180) with tomato sauce (No. 108)
Bread and butter
Ice cream with fruit sauce (Nos. 143–6)

11

Cream of spinach soup (No. 77)
Cream cheese sandwiches
Canned peaches

12

Grilled herring fish cake (No. 224) with Dutch sauce (No. 84)
Blackcurrant jelly (No. 465)
Sponge cake (No. 568 or 569)

13

Cream of chicken soup (No. 54)
Egg sandwiches
Arrowroot cookies (No. 537)

14

Scalloped egg and ham (No. 196)
Crisp toast
Coffee Spanish cream (No. 462)

Dinner Menus

1

Pot-roasted broiler (No. 274)
Boiled potatoes
Chopped tender lettuce heart salad *or* spinach purée
Egg jelly (No. 463)
Red fruit purée or sauce (No. 146)

2

Salmon loaf (No. 232)
Egg sauce (No. 83)
Mashed potatoes
Young green peas (sieved)
Banana mould (No. 420)

3

Fillets of fish with lemon sauce (No. 103)
Creamed potatoes with chopped parsley (No. 349)
Raspberry fool (No. 396)

4

Steamed lamb cutlets (No. 297)
Tomato sauce (No. 108)
Potato purée (No. 349 h)
Crème au caramel (No. 441)
Orange juice

5

Stewed kidney (No. 285)
Boiled potatoes
Carrot purée
Caramel rice cream (No. 492)
Blackcurrant syrup and grapefruit juice mixed

6

Grilled beef patties (tender meat) (No. 262)
Tomato purée
Mashed potatoes
Floating island (No. 442)
Piece of sponge cake (No. 568 or 569)

7

Braised sweetbreads (No. 311) (with the vegetables sieved)
Creamed potatoes (No. 349)
Spinach purée
Apple trifle (No. 506)

8

Steamed stuffed fillets of sole *or* plaice (No. 245)
Grilled potato and cheese balls (No. 351)
Chopped tender lettuce heart salad
Fruit juice custard (No. 397)
Sweet biscuit

9

Beef mould (No. 260)
Cauliflower sprigs
Parsley sauce (No. 80)
Golden jelly (No. 469) with cream

10

Rice and fish mould (No. 229) with cheese sauce (No. 81)
Young green peas
Chocolate mousse (No. 438 or 439)

11

Creamed chicken in noodle *or* macaroni ring (No. 322)
Sieved spinach
Orange mousse (No. 399)

12

Scalloped brains (No. 278)
Creamed potatoes (No. 349)
Mashed carrots
Frozen fruit mousse (No. 455)

13

Lamb stew (No. 298) (gravy sieved)
Young peas (sieved)
Creamed potatoes (No. 349)
Jelly (No. 465) with cream or custard sauce (No. 139)

14

Minced liver in tomato sauce (No. 302)
Creamed potatoes (No. 349)
Steamed canary pudding (No. 498), with orange sauce (No. 145) *or* Melba sauce (No. 146)

Celebration Meals

1

Grilled fresh salmon with parsley butter, and lemon (a small portion)
Roast turkey
Potato purée
Spinach purée
Peach Melba (No. 451)

2

Ripe avocado pear with lemon juice
Tender grilled fillet steak
Potato purée
Young green peas
Charlotte russe (No. 509)

THE GLUTEN-FREE DIET FOR THE COELIAC CONDITION

How the Normal Diet is Modified

This diet should be as normal as possible in all respects, especially for a child, to ensure general good nutrition and growth and to avoid as far as possible making the child conscious of being different from others.

The only modification needed to a normal diet is the elimination of anything made with wheat-flour, oats, barley, or rye. Gluten-free flours are used for making bread and all baked goods and for thickening purposes. Most baking has to be done at home to ensure the right ingredients are used, and no packet, tinned, or other commercial products can be used unless the article is known to contain no wheat-flour, oats, barley, or rye (see list below).

Foods to Avoid

All foods made with flour such as bread, scones, cakes, biscuits, crispbreads, pastry and all puddings made with flour, bread or cake-crumbs; semolina; pasta such as macaroni, spaghetti, ravioli, noodles; pancakes; Yorkshire pudding; wheat breakfast cereals such as shredded wheat, Weetabix, and wheat flakes; cornflour, custard powder, blancmange and packet puddings. All foods made with rye flour such as rye bread and crispbreads. Some people need to avoid things made with barley and oats as well.

Sausages, meat pies; sausage rolls; canned meats, game and poultry; canned fish in sauce; meat and fish pastes; fried foods coated with batter or crumbs.

Packet and bottled sauces; packet and canned soups; stock cubes; meat cubes.

Cheese spreads and processed cheese; packet suet; baked beans and other vegetables in sauce; strained and junior vegetables; canned or packet vegetables with added ingredients; bottled mayonnaise and salad dressings.

Pie fillings; strained and junior fruit; peanut butter; mincemeat and lemon curd; compound peppers; mustard; packet condiments; pickles.

Confectionery and sweets; cocoa and chocolate drinks; proprietary drinks; ice cream; baking powder.

Fitting in with Family Meals

Except for the special bread most of the foods allowed in the coeliac diet are suitable for general family meals. As far as possible avoid special cooking for the coeliac member of the family, especially a child, so that they can be normal and eat the same foods as the rest.

List 1. Special Foods Used in the Diet

Foods in this list are all prescribable under the National Health Service for patients on a gluten-free diet and may be obtained from the chemist:

Gluten-free Flours: Energen wheat-starch; Rite-Diet gluten-free flour (Welfare Foods); Tritamyl gluten-free flour (Procea).
Gluten-free bread: Rite-Diet gluten-free bread (Welfare Foods).
Gluten-free biscuits, Farley gluten-free biscuits; Liga gluten-free biscuits; Rite-Diet gluten-free biscuits (Welfare Foods).

List 2. Foods Usually Allowed

Beverages. Tea or coffee (fresh or soluble), cocoa (Fry or

Bournville), fruit juices and squashes, Milo, Nesquick, Bournvita, Cadbury drinking chocolate, Bovril, Virol, Marmite, vegetable juices and tomato juice.

Biscuits. Only those made without wheat-flour, rye, oats, or barley. Special biscuits, see List 1. For gluten-free recipes, see Nos. 535, 536, 539, 543.

Breads. Only those made with gluten-free flour. See List 1. For recipes, see Nos. 512–14.

Cakes. Only those made without wheat-flour, rye, oats or barley. For gluten-free recipes, see Nos. 549–52, 562–4, 566–7, 568 Variation, 571–2. Also Rite-Diet gluten-free rich fruit cake (Welfare Foods).

Cereals, Flours, Starches and Pas a. Those given in List 1 and also cornflour (Boots or Brown and Polson), arrowroot, potato flour or fecule, rice (including ground rice and rice flour), cornflakes, rice Krispies, Puffa Puffa rice, Frosties, Ricicles, and Aprotein Dietetic pasta (Carlo Erba).

Cheese. All kinds except cheese spreads and processed cheese. Gluten-free cheese spreads are Armour, Fine Fare, Kraft and Swiss Knight.

Condiments. Salt and pure pepper (not compound), herbs, spices, vinegar, French mustard (Noels), ready-mixed mustard (Sainsbury), curry powder (Heinz and Noels), pickles (beetroot, gherkins, onions, red cabbage, walnuts, capers, olives).

Eggs served any way provided gluten-free ingredients are used.

Fats, oils and cream. Any allowed including fresh and canned cream. Suet should be fresh grated, not packet.

Fish. All kinds, but not fried in batter or coated in crumbs unless gluten-free flour and crumbs are used. Canned fish in oil.

Fruit. Any kind, raw, frozen, canned or dried.

Meat, game and poultry. Any fresh meat, bacon, ham, offal, game and poultry. Canned lambs' tongues, ox tongue, ham, corned beef, luncheon meat (Plumrose), pork luncheon meat

(Plumrose), chopped pork (Plumrose, Harris), Frankfurter sausages, salami.

Milk. All kinds allowed, fresh, canned or dried.

Nuts. Any kind, plain or salted. Peanut butter (Gales, Mapleton, Sun-Pat).

Preserves. Jams, marmalade, jelly, mincemeat (Robertson), lemon curd (Gales, Robertson).

Puddings. Only those made with gluten-free flour, bread or cereal. Canned creamed rice, sago and tapioca, blancmanges (Birds, Brown and Polsons), instant whips (Birds), ice cream (Lyons Maid, all except those containing cake, Wall's vanilla brickette and vanilla tubs, Cornish ice cream and super choc bar); St Ivel's Readimix.

Other suitable puddings will be found in the recipe section, see index. With some recipes, only the 'variation' is gluten-free. Suitable recipes include ice cream Nos. 445–9, 454 and 455, water ices Nos. 456–60, banana and chocolate creams, fruit purée dessert, fruit soufflé, steamed sponge (No. 505), lemon snow, caramel oranges, jellies, fruit juice custard, chocolate mousse, Norwegian trifle, refrigerated flan, fruit whip, lemon meringue rice, rice soufflé, fruit fools, custards, pineapple and orange mould, stuffed oranges, stuffed apple, orange and grapefruit cup, fruit mousses, gooseberry and banana compôte, grapefruit and prune salad, grapes and tangerines, fruit meringue, coffee Spanish cream, junket, coffee cream, caramel rice cream, fruit whip, Yorkshire pudding, floating island, baked trifle, apple snow, egg jelly.

Sauces and Gravy. Thin gravy No. 94, or sauces and gravy thickened with gluten-free flour or cereal or with eggs. Home-made mayonnaise No. 115, salad dressings Nos. 109 and 112, French dressing No. 113. Other sauce recipes can have gluten-free flour substituted for the wheat-flour, or use cornflour. For proportions, see page 66. Gluten-free gravy browning (Bisto, Heinz), Salad Cream (C.W.S., Crosse and Blackwell, Heinz), Tomato Ketchup (C.W.S., Chef, H.P., Heinz).

Soups and Stocks. Any home-made stock, stock cubes (Lemco, Maggi), canned consommé, and real turtle soup. Other soups, read the labels, see below. Home-made soups thickened with gluten-free flours and using other ingredients in the list of foods allowed. See also Nos. 42–4, 46–7, 52–3, 55–9, 62–4, 66–7, 69–71, 74, 75, 78.

Sugar and sugar confectionery. Sugar, glucose, honey, syrup, treacle. Boiled sweets, chocolate (Marks and Spencer's plain chocolate bars; Nestlés all chocolate bars; Rowntree's Aero and After Eight; Suchard, all chocolates).

Vegetables. Any kind, fresh, frozen or canned, without a sauce unless this is made with gluten-free ingredients (read the label).

Proprietary Foods – Checking Labels

Packet, canned and other proprietary foods are liable to have the ingredients changed from time to time and it is always wise to read the labels before using any of them. Beware of any which contain 'starch' (including wheat-starch and edible starch), 'flour', 'cereal', or 'hydrolysed protein'. With some it will also be necessary to watch out for the inclusion of oats and barley products.

The Coeliac Society, P.O. Box No. 181, London NW2 2QY, maintains an up-to-date list of proprietary foods which, at the time of compiling the list, are guaranteed gluten-free by the manufacturers. This list can be purchased from the Society.

Meal-Pattern for a Young Child

On waking. Fruit juice.

Breakfast. Permitted cereal. Egg or fish or bacon. Gluten-free bread, toast, or rusks. Butter or margarine. Marmalade. Milk drink.

Mid-morning. Milk drink.

Midday. Meat or alternative, potatoes and vegetables. Milk pudding. Piece of raw fruit.

Tea. Milk drink. Gluten-free bread made into sandwiches, or egg or cheese dish. Milk pudding and fruit if desired. Piece of raw fruit.

Bedtime. Milk drink.

Daily Allowance of Basic Food

In the average diet, wheat-flour and bread are an important source of protein and, with the exception of Rite-Diet, gluten-free flours are a poor source of protein; therefore more protein from other sources should be included in this diet (e.g. more milk, eggs, meat, fish, and cheese) than the normal child might have. See normal diet, page 15.

Dried skimmed milk used to enrich ordinary milk is a cheap way of increasing the protein, while if a child dislikes ordinary cheese, cottage cheese is a good alternative to it. Undiluted evaporated milk instead of cream can also be used. For ways of using these products, see page 227 and Recipe Index.

Changes Needed in Cooking Methods

The only change, but a big one, is the substitution of gluten-free flour and cereals (see Lists 1 and 2), for ordinary wheat-flour, in all cooking.

Because gluten-free flour lacks protein it tends to make rather dry and crumbly cakes and biscuits, and the bread sometimes has a more cake-like texture than when made with ordinary flour. If some gluten-free source of protein is added, the results are better. Eggs, dried milk powder or Casilan or Soya flour are the best to add. Rite-Diet gluten-free flour already has protein added to it. Other gluten-free flours can have dried skimmed milk added in the proportions of 2 oz. (4 heaped Tbs.) dried skimmed milk to 6 oz. (1½ level c.) gluten-free flour or wheat starch; or 1 oz (2½ level Tbs.) Casilan to 7 oz. (1½ c.) flour or starch; in either case count the mixture as equivalent to 8 oz. gluten-free flour.

Bread can be made with yeast, see recipe No. 512, or with baking powder, No. 514.

Good results can be obtained by mixing gluten-free flours or wheat starch with other gluten-free products such as cornflour, rice flour or potato flour. These often give better results than when the gluten-free flour or wheat starch is used by itself.

Cakes and biscuits with generous amounts of egg and/or fat are usually the most successful, see page 62, 'Cakes'.

For thickening sauces, gravies and soups, use gluten-free flours from Lists 1 and 2. Use about half the amount of gluten-free flour, wheat-starch, cornflour or potato flour as you would of ordinary flour. Sauces made with potato flour are cooked as soon as the mixture thickens.

Gluten-free baking powders are made by Glenville and Sainsbury, and Glenville also make a gluten-free golden raising powder. Gluten-free baking powders can be made at home using either of the following recipes:

Gluten-free Baking Powder (1)

3 oz. cornflour
3½ oz. bicarbonate of soda
2 oz. cream of tartar
2 oz. tartaric acid (get from chemist)

Mix all ingredients together and pass through a very fine sieve two or three times. Store in an airtight tin and in a dry place and label it.

Gluten-free Baking Powder (2)

4 oz. cream of tartar
2 oz. bicarbonate of soda
4 oz. ground rice or rice flour

NOTE. Mix as before. The reason for including some tartaric acid is that the baking powder begins to work before the mixture goes in the oven and gives a lighter result with small cakes and scones. Most commercial baking powders contain tartaric acid or something which has the same effect.

As these two home-made baking powders contain quite a lot of cornflour or rice flour to keep them dry, more needs to be used than with a commercial baking powder. The recipes given in the book are for use with home-made baking powder;

when substituting a commercial powder, use half the quantities given in the recipes.

Midday Dinner Menus for a Young Child

1

Rice and fish mould (No. 229)
Parsley sauce (No. 80) (gluten-free thickening)
Green peas
Banana and chocolate cream (No. 419)

2

Beef mould (No. 260) (gluten-free crumbs)
Brown sauce (No. 96)
Brussels sprouts
Junket (No. 480)
Piece of raw apple

3

Grilled beef patties (No. 262)
Baked tomatoes
Mashed potatoes
Orange baked custard (No. 443) (use whole milk)

4

Lamb stew (No. 298)
Cabbage
Rice soufflé (No. 496) with rose-hip syrup
Piece of raw apple

5

Tripe au gratin (No. 315) (gluten-free flour and crumbs)
Mashed potatoes
Carrots
Milk and fruit juice jelly (No. 472)
Gluten-free rusk or biscuit

6

Mincemeat loaf (No. 258) (gluten-free crumbs)
Baked jacket potatoes (No. 348)
Brussels sprouts
Trifle (No. 508) made with gluten-free sponge (No. 572)

7

Grilled fish cakes (No. 224 or 225)
Egg sauce (No. 83) (gluten-free thickening)
Grilled tomatoes
Lemon meringue rice (No. 494)
Piece of raw fruit

8

Stuffed tomatoes (No. 364)
Creamed potatoes (No. 349)
Steamed sponge pudding (No. 505)
Jam sauce (No. 141)
Piece of raw fruit

9

Creamed soft roes (No. 237) in potato nest
Green peas
Fresh orange-juice jelly (No. 467)
Gluten-free rusk or biscuit

10

Steamed lamb chop (No. 297)
Tomato sauce (No. 108) (gluten-free thickening)
Mashed potato
Chopped leeks
Poor knight's fritters (No. 520) (using gluten-free bread)
Piece of raw fruit

11

Fish au gratin (No. 220) (gluten-free crumbs and sauce)
Baked tomato
Green peas
Baked Yorkshire pudding (No. 158 or 159) with honey or syrup sauce (No. 148)
Piece of raw apple

12

Creamed veal in potato nest (No. 322) (gluten-free sauce)
Chopped spinach
Chopped carrots
Egg jelly (No. 463)
Jam sauce (No. 143)
Gluten-free rusk

13

Minced veal in tomato sauce (No. 108) (gluten-free thickening)
Mashed potatoes
Chopped green beans
Home-made ice cream (No. 454) or from List 2, page 63
Stewed fruit with rusk (gluten-free)

14

Grilled lamb patties (No. 290)
Mashed potatoes
Chopped carrots with parsley sauce (No. 80) (gluten-free thickening)
Chocolate junket (No. 480) with fresh orange pulp
Rusk (gluten-free)

NOTE. Instead of raw fruit or rusk at the end of a meal try a piece of raw carrot or celery for a change.

Tea Menus for a Young Child

1

Scrambled egg romaine (No. 193)
Gluten-free toast and butter
Ripe pear
Milk drink

2

Home-made blackcurrant juice jelly with grapes (No. 465)
Cheese sandwiches
Piece of celery
Milk drink

3

Cheese spread sandwiches, List 2, page 62
Gluten-free sponge cake (No. 566)
Piece of apple
Milk drink

4

Cottage cheese and lettuce sandwiches
Fresh fruit jelly (No. 464)
Milk drink

5

Egg in a nest (No. 191) on gluten-free toast
Bread and honey
Piece of orange
Milk drink

6

Golden omelette (No. 178) (gluten-free bread)
Fruit salad and cream
Gluten-free biscuit
Milk drink

7

Grilled cheese and potato balls (No. 351)
Grilled tomatoes
Gluten-free crisp toast or rusk and honey
Milk drink

8

Herring spread sandwiches (No. 533) *or* sardine sandwiches
Junket (No. 480) and raw apple and orange salad
Milk drink

9

Cod's roe pie (No. 211)
Toast and honey
Piece of apple
Milk drink

10

Smoked fish kedgeree (No. 227)
Toast and honey
Raw orange
Milk drink

11

Canned salmon au gratin (No. 230)
Crisp toast, preserves
Piece of raw apple
Milk drink

12

Liver terrapin (using gluten-free flour) (No. 308) with fingers of toast
Fresh fruit jelly (No. 464)
Milk drink

13

Herring roe spread (No. 531) on fingers of gluten-free bread *or* toast
Fairy cake (No. 550)
Orange
Milk drink

14

Neapolitan sandwiches (No. 530) using gluten-free bread
Gluten-free cake (No. 567)
Raw apple
Milk drink

Suggestions for a Birthday Party for a Child

Try to choose items which all the children will like and which at the same time are suitable for the gluten-free diet.

Sandwiches. As the bread will be unfamiliar to most of the guests it is wiser to give open sandwiches only and to toast the bread or use it made into rusks, but keep the latter small and easy to handle.

Toppings for these sandwiches could include: any of the savoury items in List 2, page 61, cottage cheese and celery or chopped chives, herring roe spread (No. 531), herring spread (No. 533), egg filling (Nos. 527 and 528), flaked fish with salad dressing from List 2, canned salmon and sardines, chopped apple and celery, meat fillings (No. 527) with gluten-free sauces.

Other savoury items. A dish of small pieces of cheese. Potato crisps. Small pieces of celery heart stuffed with cheese. Dates stuffed with cottage cheese.

Sweet items. The birthday cake could be an iced Butter sponge (No. 566). Other popular sweet items include: jellies, all kinds including those made with evaporated milk and fruit and cream. Trifle (No. 508) made with angel cake (No. 549) or gluten-free sponge (No. 572). Home-made ice cream (No. 445 or 454 or from List 2), water ices (Nos. 456–60), iced lollies, caramel oranges (No. 430), Norwegian trifle (No. 479), refrigerated flan (Nos. 488 and 489), individual creme au caramel (No. 441), stuffed oranges (No. 432), meringues (No. 562 or 563), almond fingers (No. 536), chocolate crisps (No. 539), doughnuts (No. 526), Pavlova cake and fresh fruit (No. 564).

Christmas Cooking

Stuffings for the meat can be made with stale or dried gluten-free breadcrumbs or crushed cornflakes. Christmas cake (see No. 551), Christmas pudding (see No. 501, variation), Chocolate Log – use sponge roll recipe (No. 567) using cocoa from those in List 2, page 61.

Lunch, High Tea, or Supper Menus for the Older Child or Adult

1

Liver pâté (No. 303 or 304)
Celery and sprout salad (No. 372)
Home-made dressing (No. 112 or 115)
Gluten-free toast with butter
Sponge cakes (No. 566)

2

Fillets of fish with lemon sauce (No. 222) (gluten-free thickening)
Tomato garnish
Gooseberry and banana compôte (No. 423)
Gluten-free biscuit

3

Cream of pea soup (No. 77) (gluten-free thickening)
Ham mousse (No. 279)
Chicory salad (No. 374)
Gluten-free toast

4

Baked rice with cheese (No. 162)
Baked tomatoes
Fruit salad
Almond fingers (No. 535)

5

Creamed soft roes on toast (No. 237) (gluten-free thickening)
Waldorf salad (No. 394)
Chocolate Swiss roll (No. 567)

6

Soufflé omelette (No. 180)
Pineapple and lettuce salad (No. 389)
Gluten-free toast
Iced fairy cakes (No. 550)

7

Chicken in jelly (No. 281)
Gluten-free toast
Grapefruit and beetroot salad (No. 382)
Cornflour meringues (No. 562)

8

Tomato juice cocktail (No. 71)
Fricassée of eggs (No. 199) (gluten-free thickening)
Mashed potatoes
Grapefruit and prune salad (No. 424)
Sponge drop kisses (No. 571)

9

Ham custard (No. 192)
Gluten-free toast fingers
Endive salad
Jellied apples (No. 412)
Gluten-free biscuits

10

Tomato bouillon (No. 70)
Chicken and mushroom salad (No. 373)
Gluten-free toast
Sweet loaf (No. 514) with butter and jam

11

Liver pilaf (No. 305)
Lettuce salad
Ice cream (No. 454) and fruit salad

12

Cream of carrot soup (No. 77) (gluten-free thickening)
Tangerine and cottage cheese salad (No. 378)
Gluten-free toast
Chocolate blancmange and cream

13

Fish kedgeree (No. 227)
Tomato and cucumber salad
Banana and chocolate cream (No. 419)

14

Tomato soup (No. 74)
Cheese omelette (No. 173)
Toast (gluten-free)
Fresh fruit, gluten-free cake

Dinner Menus for the Older Child or Adult

1

Grapefruit
Sole mornay (No. 242) (gluten-free flour for the sauce)
Mashed potatoes
Baked or grilled tomatoes
Ice cream (No. 445 or 454)
Fruit
Gluten-free biscuit

2

Cream of spinach soup (No. 77) using gluten-free flour
Sole meunière with orange (No. 238)
Mashed potatoes
Apple snow (No. 413)

3

Fruit soup (No. 59)
Oven-fried fish (No. 204) with lemon wedges
Duchess potatoes (No. 349 e)
Baked stuffed tomatoes (No. 364)
Caramel rice cream (No. 492)

4

Broth (No. 46)
Liver provençale (No. 306) (gluten-free thickening)
Creamed potatoes
Peas or green beans
Norwegian trifle (No. 479)

5

Fruit cocktail (No. 395)
Veal ragoût with green peas (No. 327) (gluten-free thickening)
Boiled potatoes
Coffee Spanish cream (No. 462)

6

Cauliflower and anchovy salad (No. 371)
Liver shashlik (No. 307)
Boiled rice or boiled potatoes
Refrigerated peach flan (No. 490)

7

Jellied consommé with mushrooms (No. 60)
Dish of boiled lambs' tongues (No. 318) (gluten-free thickening)
Creamed potatoes
Spinach
Grapes and tangerines (No. 427)
Gluten-free biscuit or sponge

8

Cucumber soup (No. 56)
Fried chicken and almonds (No. 271)
Boiled rice with lettuce salad
Pineapple orange mould (No. 436)

9

Tomato bouillon (No. 70)
Roast shoulder of lamb with rice stuffing (No. 294)
Carrots and sprouts
Crème au caramel (No. 441)

10

Julienne soup (No. 46)
Baked lamb chops with tomato and cheese (No. 286)
Baked jacket potatoes (No. 348)
Lemon cream (No. 481)

11

Vichyssoise (No. 78)
Steamed chicken and rice (No. 277)
Lettuce salad
Caramel oranges (No. 430)
Gluten-free cake or biscuit

12

Grapefruit
American meat loaf (No. 258)
Tomato sauce (No. 106)
Baked jacket potatoes (No. 348)
Brussels sprouts
Chocolate mousse (No. 438)

13

Brain soup (No. 51) (gluten-free thickening)
Pressed chicken (No. 275)
Celery and sprout salad (No. 372)
Roll and butter
Orange mousse (No. 399)
Chocolate crisps (No. 539)

14

Consommé
Sole or plaice aux crevettes (No. 239)
Creamed potatoes
Lettuce salad and French dressing
Fruit fool (No. 396)
Gluten-free biscuits

Sandwich Meals

Breads. Gluten-free bread cut thin with lots of filling.

Sandwich fillings, Savoury. Cheese, meat minced and mixed with gluten-free sauces, fish mashed with salad and salad dressing (No. 109 or 112), eggs, sliced tender cold meat. These can be taken in separate small containers to spread on rusks or biscuits. *Sweet.* Sweet gluten-free loaf (No. 514), chocolate from List 2. Gluten-free cakes (see page 62).

Extras. Hard-boiled eggs. Nuts.

Fruit. Any allowed; as an alternative take celery.

Beverages. Home-made soups in flask. Milk. Any beverages from List 2.

A suitable meal would consist of:

Two substantial sandwiches with a meat, fish, egg, or cheese filling. One sweet bread sandwich or permitted cake. Ripe banana or other raw fruit. Beverage.

Eating Out

Choose from these foods:

Soups. Consommé and clear soups (no noodles or spaghetti or toast).

Fruit juices or tomato juice or vegetable juices.

Hors d'œuvre. Melon, grapefruit, sardine, smoked salmon, fish dressed with oil and vinegar, vegetables dressed with oil and vinegar, potato crisps, fruit cocktail.

Eggs. Omelettes. Boiled, fried, scrambled, or poached (leave the toast).

Fish. Grilled, boiled, or poached with melted butter sauce or lemon. Fried in batter (leave the batter). Cold fish with lemon or oil-and-vinegar dressing.

Meat. Roast or grilled, any kind (no stuffing or thickened gravy or sauces). Cold roast or boiled meat or poultry.

Vegetables. Any kind. Sauces should be thickened with cornflour.

Pudding. Stewed fruit, rice pudding, plain and fruit jellies, fruit salad and cream, water ices, fresh fruit *or* have cheese, (not processed) with raw fruit (e.g. apple, pear, or grapes).

For other items see food List 2.

Celebration Meals

Instead of bread, have a good portion of potato. Avoid thickened sauces and go for 'straight' cooking.

1

Clear turtle soup
Rump steak
Potato chips
Leaf spinach or green peas
Pears à la Condé (No. 495) *or*
Cheese with grapes or pears

2

Smoked trout with lemon wedges
Mixed grill (leave the sausage or anything in batter)
Chipped potatoes
Green peas
Crème au caramel (No. 441) *or*
Fresh fruit salad with meringues and cream *or*
Cheese with fresh fruit

THE HIGH-FIBRE DIET

This diet is prescribed for Atonic constipation, see page 49.

How the Normal Diet is Modified

The normal diet is modified mainly by increasing the amounts of raw and cooked fruits, nuts, and vegetables, and by substituting wholemeal bread for white bread and either oatmeal, rolled-oat porridge, or whole-wheat breakfast cereals and All-Bran for the refined cereals like cornflakes or rice cereals. The whole-grain cereals contain a considerable amount of fibre which is not digested and adds bulk to the faeces. This in turn stimulates the muscular contractions of the intestine (peristalsis) and so relieves the condition.

Plenty of fluid (3 pints (6 c.) or more daily) is usually prescribed to help keep the faeces soft. A hot drink in the early morning on an empty stomach stimulates peristalsis by passing rapidly through the empty intestine to the colon.

The amount of fat or oil taken is frequently increased as that stimulates the flow of bile and bile in turn stimulates peristalsis.

Fitting in with Family Meals

No special cooking is required for this patient. If the rest of the family cannot have a high-fibre diet the simplest way of giving extra fibre to the constipated person is by providing wholemeal bread and breakfast cereals for them and liberal amounts of raw fruit, dried fruit, and nuts to eat at the end of the meal in place of the usual pudding and/or for between-meals snacks.

Useful Special Foods

Real wholemeal flour is known as 100-per-cent or whole-wheat flour. Unfortunately bread made from this is usually more expensive than 'brown' bread which contains less fibre than wholemeal but more than white bread. Many millers make whole-wheat flours and some of them also provide recipes for using it in all types of cooking. Health Food Stores also sell it and some bakers and grocers.

Many of the crispbreads are made from whole grains, e.g. Ryvita, Brown Rye King.

All-Bran is well known as a breakfast cereal but it can also be used in cooking and recipes are available from the manufacturers, Kellogg, who also make Bran Flakes. Washed bran can be used in cooking too, and is usually sold through Health Food Stores.

Suitable Foods

Beverages. Any kind. Liberal amounts of water (3 pints (6 c.) daily at least).

Biscuits. Wheaten and oat biscuits of all kinds, oat cakes. See also recipes for Nutties (No. 544), Bran biscuits (No. 538).

Breads and scones. Any made with 100-per-cent whole-wheat flour. Also dark rye bread and pumpernickel, whole-grain crispbread. See also recipes for brown baking powder bread (No. 519), and brown honey scones (No. 524).

Cakes. Made with 100-per-cent whole-wheat flour or oatmeal or rolled oats, and with dried fruit and nuts. See recipe for whole-wheat fruit cake (No. 555), treacle parkin (No. 574), whole-wheat gingerbread (No. 556), treacle gingerbread (No. 558), Kolac (No. 559), fruit squares (No. 484).

Cereals and pasta. Whole-grain ones such as 100-per-cent whole-wheat flour, rolled oats, oatmeal, washed bran, brown rice, Weetabix, Shredded Wheat, wheat flakes, All-Bran, wheatgerm.

Cheese. All kinds.

Condiments. All kinds.

Eggs. All kinds.

Fats, oils, and cream. All kinds.

Fish. All kinds in moderate amounts.

Fruit. All kinds in generous amounts with as much as possible eaten raw. Dried fruits should be included.

Meat, game, and poultry. All kinds in moderate amounts.

Milk. All kinds.

Nuts. All kinds – used in cooking too.

Preserves. Whole fruit ones of all kinds. Chunky marmalade, jam with pips and seeds.

Puddings. These can be mainly of fruit, fresh, raw and dried being the best. In recipes using breadcrumbs, wholemeal can be substituted for fresh ones and whole flour for white flour in most others. Many using fruit will be found in the recipe section, see index.

Sauces and gravies. Any kind.

Soups and stocks. Any kind.

Sugar and sugar confectionery. All kinds. Black treacle often has a laxative effect. Sweets containing nuts are useful and sweets made with dried fruits. See No. 422.

Vegetables. All kinds with as much as possible eaten raw. Pulses have a very high fibre content.

Meal-Pattern

On waking. Glass of hot water, or lemon juice with hot water or tea.

Breakfast. Permitted cereal with fruit, milk, and/or cream. Egg or bacon or fish or meat. Wholemeal bread, toast, or oat cakes. Butter and preserves. Beverage.

Mid-morning. Beverages only.

Midday. Vegetable soup. Meat and fish, plenty of vegetables (some raw), potatoes. Pudding with fruit or nuts. If cheese is taken instead, serve with wheaten biscuits or oat cakes, and raw fruit or salad vegetables.

Tea. Sandwiches made from wholemeal bread, and filling containing vegetables, nuts, and dried fruits. Permitted cakes. Tea.

Evening. Meat or fish. Vegetable or salad. Wholemeal bread, scones, or oat cake. Fruit. Tea or coffee.

Bedtime. Hot water or other hot fluid.

Lunch, High Tea, or Supper Menus

1

Herring salad (No. 383)
Oatcakes and butter
Fresh fruit

2

Fish salad (No. 381)
Wholemeal bread and butter
Baked stuffed apple (No. 414)

3

Eggs lyonnaise (No. 198)
Wholemeal toast
Prunes in cider (No. 435)

4

Spanish omelette (No. 181)
Crispbread and butter
Pear salad

5

Eggs à la crécy (No. 189)
Wholemeal rolls and butter
Fresh fruit in jelly
Cream

6

Celery au gratin with grilled bacon rolls (No. 330)
Wholemeal bread and butter
Currant patties (No. 483)

7

Lamb cutlets with aspic (No. 289)
Mixed salad
Wholemeal bread and butter
Cheese and fruit

8

Corned beef salad (No. 375)
Whole wheat crispbread and butter
Stuffed oranges (No. 432)

9

Broad beans and bacon (No. 334)
Wholemeal bread and butter
Oatcakes and cheese
Fresh fruit

10

Fried herrings with oatmeal
Lemon and parsley garnish
Oatcakes and butter
Brown honey scones with butter (No. 524)
Fresh fruit

11

Beef and vegetable soup (No. 42)
Dutch salad bowl (No. 380)
Wholemeal bread and butter
Bran biscuits (No. 538)
Butter and honey

12

Potted meat (No. 264)
Salad
Dried fruit compôte (No. 421)
Nutties (No. 544)

13

Scrambled eggs romaine (No. 193)
Wholemeal rolls and butter
Fresh fruit and nuts

14

Chicory with cheese and bacon (No. 340)
Brown rye bread and butter
Summer pudding (No. 437) with cream

Dinner Menus

1

Vegetable broth (not sieved) (Nos. 44–7)
Bacon hot-pot (No. 247)
Green salad
Raw apple

2

Grapefruit
Beef casserole with tomatoes (No. 250)
Boiled potatoes
Green beans
Fruit squares (No. 484)

3

Minestrone (No. 65)
Veal mould (No. 325)
Tomato and sweet pepper salad (No. 392)
Wholemeal bread and butter
Carrot plum pudding (No. 501)
Lemon sauce (No. 144)

4

Fish cocktail (No. 207)
Roast pork and red cabbage (No. 342)
Baked jacket potatoes (No. 348)
Grapefruit and date salad (No. 425)

5

Prawn cocktail (No. 209)
Fillets mignon with mushroom sauce (No. 105) and watercress
Sauté potatoes
Honey, apple, and nut salad (No. 428)

6

Tomato juice cocktail (No. 71)
Braised beef with prunes and wine (No. 249)
Green beans
Celery and cheese
Raw fruit

7

Beef and vegetable soup (No. 42)
Fish Florentine (No. 218)
Mashed potatoes
Grape and tangerine salad (No. 427)

8

Cod à la boulangère (No. 206)
Nut salad with peas (No. 386)
Fruit flan and cream

9

Onion soup (No. 67)
Haricot mutton (No. 291)
Boiled potatoes
Mashed swedes and turnip
Apple crumble (No. 410)

10

Lentil soup (No. 62)
Liver provençale (No. 306)
Boiled potatoes
Lettuce salad
Orange baked custard (No. 443)

11

Grapefruit and orange cocktail (No. 395)
Goulash (No. 252)
Cabbage
Kolac (No. 559)

12

Mushroom soup (No. 66)
Steak and onions
Fried potatoes
Green salad
Refrigerated flan (No. 488) using whole-wheat cereal

13

Broth Julienne (No. 46)
Lamb ragoût with butter beans (No. 293)
Brussels sprouts
Celery and cheese
Raw fruit

14

Pickled herring or smoked salmon
Whole-wheat bread and butter
Chicken with almonds (No. 271)
Boiled rice
Chicory Polonaise (No. 336)
Fresh fruit salad with cider (No. 406)

Sandwich Meals

Breads. Coarse wholemeal bread, whole rye and wheat crispbread, pumpernickel, dark rye bread, oat cakes.

Sandwich fillings. Any with salad vegetables and/or nuts (see pages 421–3).

Sweet course. Nutties (No. 544), treacle parkin (No. 574), fruit squares (No. 484), Kolac (No. 559), whole-wheat fruit cake (No. 555), whole-wheat gingerbread (No. 556), oat biscuits (No. 545), dried fruits.

Extras. Nuts, celery, strips of raw carrot, radishes.

Fruit. Any fresh fruit.

Beverages. Any.

A suitable meal would consist of:

Two substantial sandwiches with thick filling of meat, fish, egg, or cheese with salad vegetables.
One of the permitted cakes or dried fruits or nuts.
Fresh fruit.
Beverages.

CHAPTER 4

Diseases of the Liver, Gall Bladder and Bile Duct

THESE include hepatitis, sometimes called catarrhal jaundice, cirrhosis, obstructive jaundice, chronic cholecystitis, and gall stones.

The Organs Involved

In the body they are compactly grouped together but they have been spread out here to show the parts clearly.

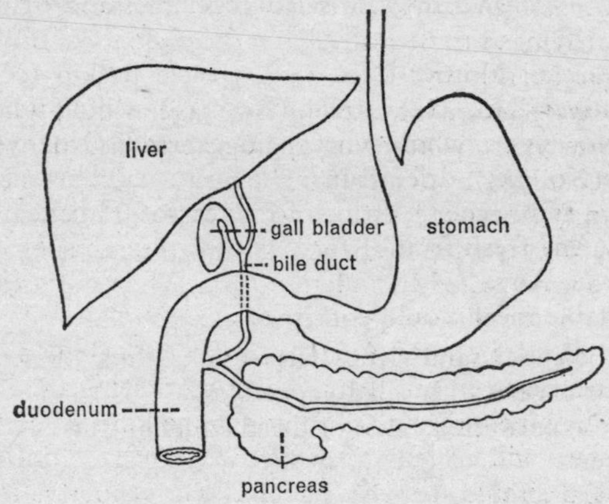

The liver, gall bladder, and bile ducts

The liver is one of the most important organs in the body. After digestion has been completed, most food constituents are transported from the intestine to the liver via the portal vein. Many undergo chemical change in the liver and some are stored there. In addition, the liver manufactures bile, which is passed to the gall bladder for storage and eventually to the small intestine where it performs a vital function in fat digestion. Anything wrong with the liver will affect the nourishment and well-being of the whole body.

Hepatitis, also called infective or infectious hepatitis or catarrhal jaundice, is inflammation of the liver believed to be caused by a virus. The damaged liver fails to produce bile properly and this leads to an inability to digest fat, to loss of appetite, and a tendency for certain foods to cause discomfort and indigestion. The diet usually prescribed is a low-fat diet. A very low-fat diet is unpalatable to most people and it is more usual today to prescribe a moderate fat restriction such as that given on page 84. The amount of fat the patient can tolerate varies considerably.

A good protein intake is recommended and plenty of carbohydrate to supply the calories which would come from fat in a normal diet. In acute and early stages of the disease amounts of protein may need to be restricted if the patient cannot tolerate the larger quantities.

Obstructive jaundice is caused by blockage in the bile passages which prevents bile reaching the intestine and hence brings about an inability to digest fat. The diet usually prescribed is a low-fat diet (see page 84).

Cholecystitis is a disturbance in the function of the gall bladder accompanied by inflammation. When fat is eaten and passes into the intestine, it causes contraction of the gall bladder. As it is important to try and rest the gall bladder, fat is usually restricted in this diet. The low-fat diet (page 84) is the one usually given, though the amount and kind of fat a patient can tolerate will usually vary considerably. A good protein intake is desirable, though patients with cholecystitis often cannot tolerate high-protein foods, such as drinks fortified with dried milks.

Gall stones are due to a change in composition of the bile when cholesterol crystallizes out, or is precipitated, to form calculi or stones. Many people who suffer from gall stones are obese and have to be put on a reducing diet (see page 115); others usually have some fat restriction in their diet (see page 84).

Cirrhosis is degeneration of liver tissue which has many causes including malnutrition. Dietary treatment recommended will vary with the cause and the condition of the patient.

THE LOW-FAT DIET

How the Normal Diet is Modified

By avoiding all fatty foods such as fried foods, pastry, most cakes, and fatty meats. Skimmed milk is frequently substituted for full-cream milk, and cheese restricted to cottage or curd varieties.

A very-low-fat diet is so unpalatable to most people that it is avoided if possible and a moderate restriction (see below) used instead.

In the normal diet fat is an important source of calories and in order to maintain a good intake in the low-fat diet, extra sugar is given in the form of glucose, which is less sickly than ordinary sugar.

A good protein intake is achieved by giving plenty of lean meat, chicken, white fish, egg whites, and skimmed milk. Where a high-protein intake is desirable these foods are supplemented by the use of fortified milk, see No. 1(e).

Any food or flavouring which causes discomfort in the individual patient should be omitted from the diet.

The patient will probably often need coaxing to take food, but diet is an important part of the treatment and any effort needed to make it attractive and acceptable is well worth while. If money saved by not having to buy fats and full-cream milk can be spent on the more expensive fish such as halibut, turbot, and sole, and on luxury fruit and vegetables, this helps to make the restrictions seem less irksome.

Foods with a Very High Fat Content

Butter, margarine, lard, cooking fat, suet, dripping, oils, cream, cream cheese, mayonnaise, salad cream, fried foods, fat bacon and ham, fat lamb and pork, nuts (except chestnuts), cheese, chocolate, cakes, pastry, and puddings made with fat, pies and made-up meat and savoury dishes, sauces made with fat, cream or oil.

Foods with a Low Fat Content

All vegetables if cooked without fat, all fruit except avocado pear and olives, sugar, honey, jam, syrup, black tea and coffee, fruit drinks, Bovril and Marmite. White fish (see list, page 88), skimmed milk, plain bread and flour, macaroni and other pasta, rice, semolina, custard powder, breakfast cereals, cornflour.

Manufactured and Packet Foods with a Low Fat Content

To find out whether these foods contain fat, read the list of ingredients on the label. Apart from 'fat', words to look out for are 'milk', 'full-cream milk', 'oil', 'glycerol esters', 'glycerides' and 'cream'. On the other hand 'skim milk solids' or 'milk solids non-fat' are fat-free.

Some bakers' cakes are low-fat, for example, meringues without a cream filling, swiss rolls with jam filling, small sponge cakes or trifle sponges. Commercial Angel cake usually has a high fat content; for home-made without fat, see recipes Nos. 148–9.

Fitting in with Family Meals

This is not difficult if the rest of the family does not insist on a diet largely made up of fried and other fatty foods. Menus and recipes for the low-fat diet are quite suitable for general family cooking; the additional fat needed by other members of the family can be taken in the form of butter or margarine on bread and cooked vegetables, as cream on puddings, or in the fats used in cakes, biscuits, and pastry.

Cooking Methods are Important

OUT: frying and braising.

IN: boiling and steaming, grilling and roasting or baking without fat or oil, stewing with no preliminary frying, and all thickening made by the blending method. Trim off fat before cooking. Serve fatless gravy or sauces (see page 89). Fish cakes and rissoles can be baked or grilled. Grilled meat is nicer if served with something moist like tomato purée or vegetables moistened with a fatless sauce. When boiling meat, it is better to cook vegetables separately, otherwise they are liable to absorb fat from the stock.

OUT: sauces and gravies made by the roux method or containing eggs or cream.

IN: the blending method for all thickening.

Useful Special Foods

Liquid skimmed milk is ordinary milk with the cream removed. It is used to replace whole milk where fat is severely restricted, and in addition to the allowance of ordinary milk in the moderately fat-restricted diet. Skimmed milk can be used in beverages and in general cooking and is cheaper than whole milk. If your dairy does not supply skimmed milk, dried skimmed milk is a good substitute, or you can ask your doctor if it is all right to use whole milk with the cream poured or siphoned off. Homogenized milk is full-cream milk and the cream cannot be separated in this way.

Instant dried skimmed milk may be used in place of liquid skimmed milk or added to it to increase the protein content in the proportion of 2 oz. (4 heaped Tbs.) of powder to 1 pt (2 c.) of liquid skimmed milk. It may also be added to any whole milk allowed in the diet to give enriched or fortified milk, see No. 1 (e).

Skimmed milk cottage cheese is usually the only cheese allowed in the low-fat diet. It can be purchased at some dairies and delicatessens though it frequently has cream added and is thus not fat-free. Skimmed milk cottage cheese can be made at home, see No. 161.

Machine-skimmed sweetened condensed milk may be used in place of liquid milk for puddings and sweet beverages.

Yogurt. Eden Vale fat-free, and all varieties of Ski yogurt are suitable.

Glucose. When a high-carbohydrate or high-calorie diet is

recommended, glucose can be used in place of sugar. As it is less sweet than sugar more can be used. Glucose is sold as a powder, which dissolves readily when mixed with warm water, and can be sprinkled dry on food. It is also sold as 'liquid' glucose which is a viscous fluid like syrup and can be used in the same way.

Foods Usually Allowed

CAUTION. This list should be checked with your doctor or dietitian and not added to without permission.

Beverages. Tea with lemon or skimmed milk, black coffee, or white coffee made with skimmed milk, soft drinks, Bovril and Marmite, vegetable and fruit juices, fat-free stocks, vegetable stocks. See also Nos. 19, 20, 23, 25, 26, 28–32, 36.

Biscuits. Plain, such as water biscuits.

Breads. Day-old bread, Melba toast (No. 522), home-made rusks (No. 523), crisp toast.

Cakes. Angel cakes (Nos. 548 and 549), meringues (Nos. 562 and 563), and any other fatless and eggless cakes. See Nos. 546, 557 and 564.

It is advisable to make cakes at home to ensure that they contain no fat. If whole eggs are allowed, the true sponge made with eggs, sugar and flour may be used (see Nos. 569, 571 and 573). As most of the cakes are rather sweet, the patient may prefer to eat them as a dessert with a sharp stewed fruit. Those made with treacle, honey, or syrup have a pleasant moist texture if kept in a tin for several days before cutting. Avoid spices and dried fruit if they give the patient indigestion.

Cereals, starches, and pasta. All are allowed, although the fibre in coarse cereals like oatmeal and All-Bran may cause discomfort. Rice, spaghetti, semolina, and macaroni are all permitted if served without fat.

Cheese. Cottage cheese made from skimmed milk.

Condiments. All allowed so long as they do not cause discomfort. It is advisable to be moderate with seasoning.

Eggs. Egg whites are allowed, but there should not be too many used raw. The doctor may allow some whole eggs provided they are cooked without fat; ask him. They may be boiled, poached, used in custards with skimmed milk, and in any way without fat.

Fats, oil, and cream. None at all are allowed in a very-low-fat diet. Be sure to consult the doctor, who may allow 1 oz (2 level Tbs.) of butter or margarine or 4 Tbs. single cream daily.

Fish. Fresh or smoked white fish, for example, cod, haddock, halibut, whiting, sole, plaice, turbot, hake. Do not fry or cook in any way using fat, oil, or cream. Instead boil, steam, bake, grill, or souse. See Nos. 202, 203, 205, 239, 240.

Fruit. All kinds are allowed except avocado pear and olives. If the fibre in fruit causes discomfort, serve it sieved or as juices. The doctor will advise on this.

Meat. Very lean beef, ham, veal, turkey or chicken, sweetbreads, tripe, liver, kidney. It may be boiled, baked, or grilled, with no added fat. If the fat restriction is not very severe the doctor may allow 1 oz. (1 rasher) grilled lean bacon per day. See also Nos. 256, 262, 264, 266, 270, 272, 277, 281, 283, 285, 298, 300, 303, 317.

Milk. Fresh skimmed milk, dried skimmed milk, machine-skimmed sweetened condensed milk, fortified milks (see No. 1). In some diets a certain amount of whol milk is allowed. Ask the doctor about this. Fat-free yogurt is allowed.

Preserves. All are allowed except lemon curd, mincemeat, and peanut butter.

Puddings. All cereal puddings made with skimmed milk and without added fat or cream, custard powder custard, and egg-white custard made with skimmed milk, see snow custard (No. 444), skimmed milk junket. Any gelatine pudding provided it contains no whole milk, evaporated milk, cream, or other fat. Water ices and sherbets (Nos. 456–60). If whole eggs are allowed make ordinary egg custard with skimmed milk, and fruit fools using custard made with skimmed milk. Summer pudding (No. 437), bread pudding (No. 511), pineapple and orange mould (No. 436), apple snow (No. 413), Ohio pudding (No. 503), trifle (No. 508), and any plain jelly and fruit pudding (see recipe index).

Sauces and gravies. These should all be home-made without fat, oil, or cream, and mild seasoning is advisable. Only lemon juice, vinegar, or a fatless dressing is allowed with salad. See Nos. 110 and 120–9, sweet sauces (Nos. 130–2, 140–9).

Soups and stocks. Home-made fat-free vegetable soups (see Nos. 43–9, 55, 59, 64, 71, 72, 76), vegetable stocks, canned vegetable juices, clear meat soup with all fat removed, canned consommé, liquid from boiled and canned vegetables, tomato juice, Marmite or Bovril.

Sugars. All allowed, including syrup, honey, and treacle.

Vegetables. Any vegetable cooked without fat, oil, or cream. If the fibre causes discomfort serve vegetables sieved. Avoid strongly flavoured ones if they cause indigestion. Use raw tender salad vegetables, according to the doctor's advice. Use cooking liquid to make a fatless sauce. See No. 122.

Meal-Pattern

Based on the list of foods allowed. Check these with the doctor or dietitian.

On waking. Tea or glass of fortified fruit juice.

Breakfast. Cereal or porridge with skimmed milk and any of the sugars, stewed fruit. Fruit juice may be added to the cereal. 1–2 slices of bread, toast, or rusks, a scraping of butter or margarine if allowed, preserves, tea or coffee, plus grilled lean bacon, egg, or fish, if allowed.

Mid-morning. Fortified beverage, tea, or coffee, plain biscuit.

Midday. Soup, tomato juice, or fruit juice. 3 oz. meat or fish, vegetables, potatoes. Pudding or fresh fruit; egg may be added to the pudding if allowed. If permitted, biscuits and cheese to follow. Tea or coffee.

Tea. 2 slices bread or toast, or a sandwich with meat, chicken, or egg filling. Preserves or Marmite. Salad (optional). Cake, or plain biscuits as allowed. Tea.

Evening. 3 oz. meat or fish, vegetables or salad. 2 slices bread or toast, preserves, a scraping of butter if allowed, *or* pudding. Tea or coffee.

Bedtime. Fortified milk or fruit juice, plain biscuit.

NOTE. Items in the midday and evening meals are interchangeable to suit the needs and habits of the patient.

Lunch, High Tea, or Supper Menus

1

Sole aux crevettes (No. 239)
Mashed potato (No. 349 a)
Fruit salad
Angel cake (No. 548 or 549)

2

Fish salad (No. 381)
Bread or roll
Fruit Whip (No. 408)
Sweet rusk (No. 523)

3

Rice and fish mould (No. 229)
Tomato salad
Low-fat dressing (No. 110)
Rusks or toast (No. 522 or 523)
Honey

4

Minced liver in tomato sauce (No. 302)
Crisp toast
Lemon-filled sponge (Nos. 569 and 576)
Raw fruit

5

Potted meat (No. 264)
Chicory salad (No. 374)
Low-fat dressing (No. 110)
Bread or roll
Junket (No. 480)
Fruit salad

6

Chicken in jelly (No. 281)
Brussels sprouts and celery salad (No. 372)
Low-fat dressing (No. 110)
Crisp toast
Snow custard (No. 444) with caramel sauce (No. 132)

7

Grilled beef patties (No. 262) with tomatoes and mushrooms
Toast
Stewed apples
Raisin cookies (No. 546)

8

Stewed sweetbreads (No. 313)
Mashed potatoes (No. 349 a)
Fruit purée and meringue (No. 563)

9

Steamed chicken and rice (No. 277)
Raw fruit
Gingerbread (No. 557)

10

Cottage cheese salad (No. 377)
Roll or roast
Summer pudding (No. 437)
Custard sauce (No. 140)

11

Lean cold boiled ham
Tomato jelly (No. 362)
Crisp toast
Trifle (No. 508)

12

Lamb cutlets in aspic (No. 288 or 289)
Orange salad (No. 387) (omit oil)
Melba toast
Bread with Marmite and cottage cheese

13

Grilled kidney, tomato, and mushroom
Mashed potatoes (No. 349 a)
Raspberry meringue (No. 398)

14

'Creamed' fish (No. 214) in border of mashed potatoes (No. 349 a)
Beetroot dressed with lemon juice
Fruit jelly (Nos. 464–7)
Sponge cake (No. 569)

Dinner Menus

1

Jellied consommé with mushroom (No. 60)
Poached turbot *or* other white fish (No. 205)
Caper sauce (No. 129)
Boiled potatoes, green peas
Fruit salad
Meringue (No. 563)

2

Prawn cocktail (No. 209)
Lamb stew (No. 298)
Tender French or runner beans
Additional potato if desired
Sweetened cottage cheese (No. 168) *or*
Plain cottage cheese with celery sticks
Water biscuits

3

Liver pâté (No. 303)
Very lean boiled ham
Spinach purée
Boiled potatoes
Caramel rice pudding (No. 493)
Garnished fresh orange slices

4

Tomato soup (No. 70)
Very lean roast beef
Baked jacket potatoes
Carrots in parsley sauce (No. 125)
Apple snow (No. 413)

5

Orange juice
Casserole of veal (No. 321) served in a border of mashed potatoes (No. 349 a)
Green vegetables
Low-fat milk jelly (No. 473) with raspberries

6

Fruit cocktail (No. 395)
Grilled liver and mushrooms (No. 301)
Sweet pepper and tomato sauce (No. 107)
Mashed potatoes (No. 349 a)
Fruit soufflé (No. 407)

7

Asparagus soup (No. 76)
Cold roast or boiled lean lamb
Potato salad (No. 390) with fatless dressing (No. 110)
Lettuce salad with lemon juice dressing
Ohio pudding (No. 503)
Custard sauce (No. 140)

8

Celery soup (No. 76)
Fish casserole (No. 213)
Mashed potatoes (No. 349 a)
Blackcurrant jelly with green grapes (No. 465)

9

Consommé
Lamb shashlik (No. 295)
Boiled rice
Lemon water ice (No. 457) *or*
Stewed fruit and angel cake (No. 548 or 549)

10

Tomato juice frappé (No. 72)
Chicken casserole with rice (No. 270)
Green peas *or* beans
Baked banana and prunes (No. 418)

11

Green pea soup (No. 76)
Marinaded steak (No. 266)
Boiled potatoes
Leaf spinach or purée
Pineapple sherbet (No. 456)

12

Carrot soup (No. 76 or 47)
Stewed kidney (No. 285)
Boiled macaroni
Lettuce salad with lemon juice dressing
Snow custard (No. 444)
Stewed fruit

13

Grapefruit juice
Chicken paprika (No. 272)
Baked potato
Green vegetable
Apple mousse (No. 404)

14

Fat-free broth (Nos. 43–9)
Veal mould (No. 325)
Orange salad (No. 387) (omit oil)
Pears in red wine sauce (No. 434)

Celebration Menus

1	2
Grapefruit cocktail (No. 395)	Consommé
Grilled turbot with lemon	Grilled entrecôte steak
Boiled potatoes	Boiled new potatoes
Peas	Grilled tomatoes
Water ice or sherbet (Nos. 456–9)	Fresh fruit salad
	Meringue (no cream) (No. 563)

Eating Out

This is difficult because so much fat is used in hotel and restaurant cooking, but choose from the following:

First course. Consommé or other clear soup, fruit juice, tomato juice, vegetable juices, grapefruit, melon.

Fish. Grilled (lemon juice instead of sauce), fried in batter (leave the batter), boiled or poached white fish (lemon juice instead of sauce).

Meat. Very lean roast, grilled, or boiled (no gravies or sauces).

Vegetables. Any plain boiled without fats or sauces. Salad vegetables dressed with lemon juice or vinegar.

Puddings. Canned or stewed fruits, fresh fruit, fruit salad with unfilled meringues instead of cream, plain jellies, fruit jellies, water ices and sherbets.

The Sandwich Meal

Bread. Day-old brown or white bread. Home-made rusks (No. 523), French bread, water biscuits.

Sandwich fillings. As the amount of butter or margarine allowed in the diet will be very small, the bread may have to be used unspread. This means that fillings must be moist, generous in quantity, and tasty, if the sandwiches are to be palatable. The open type of sandwich is best because a greater amount of filling can be used. They are improved if the bread is first toasted.

Alternatively some filling can be carried separately in a small plastic box with a wooden spatula and eaten with home-made scones or rusks, French bread, Melba toast, or water biscuits.

Savoury fillings. 1. Minced cooked lean meat, liver, or kidney moistened with a little fatless gravy or sauce. Bottled sauce if allowed.

2. Canned or cooked asparagus moistened with a little fatless salad dressing.

3. Cooked, flaked white fish moistened with a little fatless salad dressing and mixed with shredded lettuce or chopped tomatoes.

4. Chopped apple mixed with shredded lettuce and fatless salad dressing.

5. Cooked, mashed sweetbreads moistened with a little fatless sauce or salad dressing.

6. Slices of any of the permitted cooked meats with chutney.

7. Vegetable or meat extract.

8. Any salad vegetable allowed, with salt and pepper or a little fatless salad dressing.

9. Cottage or curd cheese mixed with a little fatless salad dressing and chopped herbs or pickles.

Sweet fillings. Cottage or curd cheese mixed with blackcurrant purée or jelly or sieved marmalade. Chopped dates mixed with lemon juice or grated apple, chopped crystallized ginger mixed with honey or syrup.

Sweet course. Cakes or biscuits from the list, page 87, dried fruit, boiled sweets, puddings from the list.

Fruit. Fresh fruit or fruit salad in a carton.

Beverages. Any made with skimmed milk. Soups (see list). Bovril, Marmite, vegetable and fruit juices.

A suitable meal would consist of:

2 slices of bread.

$\frac{1}{4}$–$\frac{1}{2}$ oz. ($\frac{1}{2}$–1 level Tbs.) butter, if allowed.

3 oz. lean meat or chicken or other meat or fish allowed or skimmed milk cottage cheese.

A small piece of permitted cake or biscuit.

Coffee or tea.

Fresh fruit or salad.

CHAPTER 5

Diabetes

DIABETES is a disease in which the body is unable to use carbohydrates (starches and sugars) for energy production in the normal way because of an inadequate supply of insulin from the pancreas.

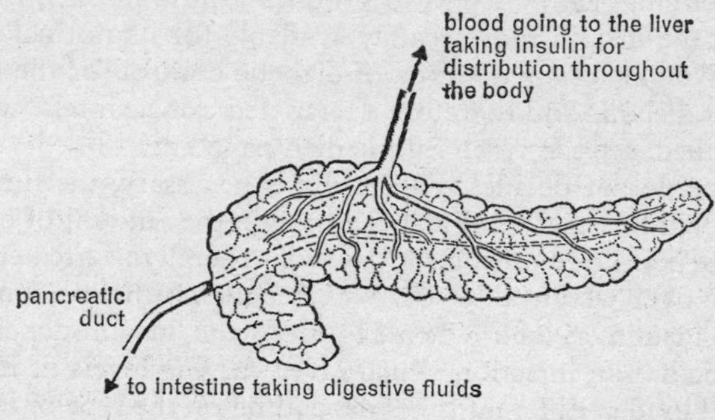

The pancreas

Insulin is made in special cells called the Islets of Langerhans and passes from there into the blood which carries it to the muscles and other tissues.

During digestion carbohydrates are broken down into the simple sugars, chief of which is glucose. This is absorbed into the blood and transported to the tissues, where it is burnt, with the aid of insulin, to give energy. When insufficient insulin is available glucose is not used up, but accumulates in the blood and is finally disposed of through the kidneys. A large amount of water is needed to do this and this causes the passing of large amounts of urine. This and the resulting thirst are common symptoms of diabetes.

The urine of a normal person is free from sugar, so that

testing for sugar is one of the routine checks in diagnosis and treatment of diabetes.

How the Normal Diet is Modified

This involves a control of the quantity of carbohydrate in the diet, the amount prescribed being a reflection of the individual's tolerance for foods containing carbohydrate.

Diabetics who are over-weight are generally able to control their diabetes by dietary restrictions alone, or by dietary restrictions and tablets which may have the effect of stimulating a rather sluggish pancreas to produce a little insulin; or else makes the insulin more readily available for its normal function. Weight loss is the crux of diabetic control for the over-weight diabetic and therefore a restricted calorie intake will be prescribed, see the 1,000 calorie diet, page 121.

If the doctor decides that insulin is necessary, the times of meals will be strictly regulated although the amount of carbohydrate permitted during the day will generally be greater than for the over-weight diabetic. Whereas the normal person produces insulin as and when required, the insulin-dependent diabetic has an injection which gives varying levels of insulin in the blood at different times depending on the type of insulin chosen. The aim of treatment is to keep the level of sugar in the blood within the normal range and since it is carbohydrate which balances insulin, the need for carbohydrate will depend on the duration and peak of action of the insulin. The amount of carbohydrate must be sufficient to cover the period of time when the insulin is having its greatest impact on lowering the blood sugar level.

Exercise too has an insulin-like effect by drawing sugar from the blood for energy purposes.

Diabetics on insulin should always carry some form of carbohydrate in case of emergency such as unexpected strenuous activity or a delayed meal. Glucose or sugar to be taken with a little water is the easiest form of concentrated carbohydrate to carry for emergency use. It is also advisable for diabetics always to carry on them a card indicating that they are diabetic and giving their home address and telephone number and that of their doctor, together with details of their insulin dose.

The use of concentrated sources of carbohydrate such as sugar should be restricted to emergencies; foods such as bread give a more sustained release of carbohydrate, regulated to balance the action of the injected insulin.

The doctor will prescribe the number and timing of meals and the amount of carbohydrate to have at each meal. This is an individual prescription which should be carefully followed.

In the early stages of treatment, where strict control is important, careful weighing or measuring may be advised initially to help the diabetic to recognize quantities. Patients who are used to their diet can usually judge quantities by sight.

Fitting in with Family Meals

It will be seen from the typical meal-patterns (pages 108–9 that the diabetic diet is based on normal family meals, but the patient has to learn to eat only specified quantities of the foods containing carbohydrate.

Some alternative to the usual high-carbohydrate pudding is needed. Raw fruit or stewed fruit sweetened with saccharin or other sugar substitute is the simplest alternative.

Small portions of pudding with a low-carbohydrate content can sometimes be included. To enable a wide range of recipes to be used, carbohydrate and calorie values have been estimated for most of those in this book.

Cooking Methods are Important

As sugar, flour, and bread are the three most common sources of carbohydrate in a normal diet, and as they are used liberally in normal cooking, some modification of recipes and methods will enable the diabetic to eat the food without having to consider its carbohydrate content. The following suggestions will be found useful.

Gravies and sauces. Instead of custard powder, make a real egg custard (No. 139), sweetening with sugar substitute. Savoury sauces may be thickened with whole egg or egg yolk just before serving.

Build up a collection of sauce recipes which do not require thickening (see Nos. 98, 99, 102, 106 and 107, 113, 115–17, 119). Serve gravies unthickened (see No. 94); boil rapidly to reduce the volume, and concentrate the flavour. Apple and mint sauce can be sweetened with sugar substitutes. Use home-made salad dressings without sugar or flour or other starchy thickening, see Nos. 113 and 115 (omit sugar).

Frying. If done in batter the patient will have to leave the batter. Crushed starch-reduced rolls may be used for coating in place of breadcrumbs. Grilling is always to be preferred to frying and better for the rest of the family too.

Stewing fruit. Stew slowly in the oven, without sweetening. Very little sugar will then be needed for sweetening for the family and liquid sugar substitute can be added to the patient's portion.

Jellies. Ordinary packet jellies are all unsuitable because of the high sugar content, but fresh fruit juices, unsweetened or with sugar substitute, can be used (see Nos. 464, 466–8, 470, 478). They will, however, need to be counted as exchanges for carbohydrates. Some very expensive diabetic jelly is available.

Meat stews or braises. Vegetables from free list (see page 105), or small amounts from exchange list (see page 104), for flavouring only. Use only enough liquid to prevent burning, so that the unthickened gravy is not watery. For white stews, such as veal, lamb, or chicken, egg yolk may be used at the last minute for thickening and binding, or use tomato purée. If an electric blender is available, blend the gravy with any suitable vegetables and the vegetable purée formed will thicken the gravy.

Boiled meats. Serve some of the unthickened liquid as gravy. Cook meat in a small pan with just enough water to cover with a bouquet garni for flavouring.

Roasts. Serve thin gravy (No. 94). No stuffings are allowed, but the herbs used in stuffing may be rubbed into the meat, or put inside (e.g. with poultry), as can chopped bacon and chopped mushrooms.

Curries. Make with the minimum of liquid and no thickening. Suitable accompaniments would be cauliflower, green beans, raw diced cucumber, raw sweet peppers, wedges of lemon, tomatoes, and coconut.

Cheese dishes. Instead of cheese sauce, sprinkle grated cheese on cooked vegetables or fish and melt and brown lightly under the grill, e.g. vegetable au gratin (No. 330).

Useful Special Foods. (*For addresses of manufacturers, see Appendix*)

The desirable goal for a diabetic is to eat normal foods, controlling portions and choice of foods to needs. This makes special foods (which are usually very expensive) unnecessary as regular items of the diet. They do, however, give variety, especially for older and less adaptable patients who are not prepared to forgo familiar and favourite foods or to make much change in their eating habits.

Saccharin is the oldest and most widely used sugar substitute. It has no carbohydrate or calorie value. To make a liquid for sweetening purposes dissolve 50 tables in ¼ pt (½ c.) warm water and use 1 teaspoon to sweeten an average portion of pudding. For the average palate 1 tablet of saccharin (0·2 grains) will replace ½ oz. (1 level Tbs.) sugar.

Sorbitol (Howard's of Ilford Ltd) is a carbohydrate. It appears not to need insulin for its breakdown in the body and therefore many doctors allow it as a sugar substitute for non-obese diabetics. It is sold in powder form and can be used for making cakes in similar proportions to ordinary sugar. While it reduces the carbohydrate value per cake it does not reduce the calorie value and considerably increases the cost.

CAUTION. Never use foods containing Sorbitol without the doctor's permission; and do not use them in amounts greater than those prescribed. Sorbitol has a laxative effect and more than 1–2 oz. daily is liable to cause diarrhoea. The obese diabetic must not have any at all unless the Sorbitol is counted for calorie value.

Sweetex (Boots) is a sugar substitute sold in three forms:

Sweetex tablets, containing soluble saccharin (1 tablet = 1 teaspoon of sugar);

Sweetex powder, containing 98 per cent Sorbitol with some saccharin and with about four times the sweetening power of sugar itself, whereas Sorbitol alone is only two-thirds as sweet as sugar. Since less Sweetex powder has to be used, the calorie value is correspondingly less;

Sweetex liquid, containing saccharin and glycerine, and with a value of 1 calorie per 10 drops. The sweetening power is about 15 times that of sugar (4 drops = 1 teaspoon of sugar).

Saxin (Burroughs Wellcome & Co.) is sold in tablets or in solution. It has no carbohydrate or calorie value and can be used freely (1 tablet = 1 teaspoon of sugar; 2–3 drops of liquid = 1 teaspoon of sugar).

Hermesetas (Hermes Sweeteners). Available as tablets or liquid. 1 tablet equals approximately 2 lumps of sugar in sweetness, or 4 tablets equal 1 oz. (2 level Tbs.) of sugar. 1 teaspoon of the liquid equals one pound (2 level c.) of sugar. Hermesetas can be added to food during cooking and does not produce the bitterness characteristic of many other sweeteners. When using tablets for cooking, dissolve them in a little liquid before adding them to the other ingredients. To make a syrup for stewing fruit, dissolve 10–16 tablets in 1 pint (2 c.) of water, the amount depending on the tartness of the fruit.

Biscoids (Andomis product) contain saccharin. 1 tablet equals 1 teaspoon of sugar in sweetness.

Energen Non-sugar Sweetener (Energen Foods) contains saccharin. 1 tablet equals 1 teaspoon of sugar in sweetness.

The Carbohydrate Content of Proprietary Foods.

There are many ‘low-sugar’, ‘low-carbohydrate’, ‘low-calorie’, and ‘starch-reduced’ products on the market, the majority of them more expensive than normal foods. They do not always contain less carbohydrate than normal foods, though many do.

The carbohydrate and calorific values per portion or per ounce should be on the packet and can be compared with normal food; for example:

1 slice (1 oz. approx.) of normal white bread contains 15 grams of carbohydrate and gives 70 calories.

1 oz. (1 level c.) cornflakes contains 25 grams of carbohydratc and gives 104 calories

Diabetic fruit squashes contain much less carbohydrate than normal ones and the unsweetened canned fruit, or canned fruit with sorbitol, has less carbohydrate than ordinary canned fruits. Fruits with sorbitol, however, have about the same calorific value as ordinary fruit canned with sugar syrup.

Diabetic marmalades and jams contain less carbohydrate than those sweetened with sugar although, when made with sorbitol, the calorific value is the same as with sugar preserves.

6 starch-reduced rolls have about the same carbohydrate content as 1 slice of bread, but more calories.

1 starch-reduced crispbread has less carbohydrate and a lower calorific value than a slice of bread.

Weight-watchers need to remember that several starch-reduced rolls will take a lot of butter and jam on them and these add to both the carbohydrate and calorific values.

Diabetic chocolate has much less carbohydrate than ordinary chocolate but the calorific value is about the same.

The British Diabetic Association, in conjunction with the British Dietetic Association, publish a list of the carbohydrate values of proprietary foods. These may be purchased from the British Diabetic Association, 3/6 Alfred Place, London, WC1.

Foods Usually Allowed

Beverages. Tea and coffee, ground and soluble, with milk from allowance and permitted sugar substitute. Diabetic fruit squashes, fruit juices (see exchange list, page 107), cocoa, Horlicks, Ovaltine (see exchange list, page 107), lemon juice with non-sugar sweetening, soda water, Vichy water, Oxo, Bovril, Marmite, clear soups allowed freely. Whisky, brandy, gin, rum, and dry red and white wines and very dry sherry, only in exchange amounts (see page 108) or in amounts allowed by your doctor.

Biscuits. Only as exchanges for bread (see page 103).

Breads. Only in weighed amounts as prescribed by the doctor.

Cakes. Best excluded or very small portions as exchanges for bread. See carbohydrate values in recipes.

Cereals, starches, and pasta. Only as bread exchanges (see page 103).

Cheese. Average portion (1–2 oz.), usually allowed twice daily as a meat substitute.

Condiments and herbs. Any allowed.

Eggs. Allowed for breakfast, in cooking, or as a meat substitute for the midday or evening meal.

Fats, oils, and cream. Butter and margarine in amounts prescribed, others allowed for cooking in moderation.

Fish. As an alternative to meat in the three main meals, cooked without flour batters or bread or flour coating and without thickened sauces unless the thickening is counted as a carbohydrate exchange.

Fruit. Average helpings of grapefruit, lemon juice, rhubarb, gooseberries (all sweetened with saccharin). Other fruits only as in the exchange list (page 105).

Meat, game, and poultry. Average portions allowed at the three main meals. Cooked without added flour, bread, cereals, pasta, or vegetables from list (see page 104), unless these are counted in the day's allowance of carbohydrate, as must be sausages (unless known to be made of meat only), meat pies, and other made-up dishes unless the ingredients are known (see recipes). Canned corned beef and other canned meats allowed only if the label says there is no added flour, cereal, or rusk.

Milk. From the day's allowance as prescribed or as in the exchange list (page 104).

Nuts. Only as in exchange list (page 107).

Preserves. Only as in exchange list (page 107).

Puddings. Either fruit from the list or a small portion of pudding as an exchange for bread (see carbohydrate values in the recipes).

Sauces and gravies. Only unthickened ones allowed unless they are taken as exchanges for bread (see carbohydrate values in the recipes). Worcester sauce is allowed, thin gravy (see No. 94).

Soups and stocks. Clear soups, meat or yeast extract. Others only as carbohydrate exchanges (see carbohydrate in recipes).

Sugars and sugar confectionery are excluded unless as very occasional exchanges for bread (see list, page 107).

Vegetables. Average helping of some allowed (see list, page 105). Others in exchange amounts only (see list, page 104).

Carbohydrate Exchanges

Each food in the following exchange lists contains about 10 grams of carbohydrate.

Bread, and Foods often eaten in place of Bread

Bread, white or brown	$\frac{1}{2}$ slice thick cut sliced large loaf, or $\frac{2}{3}$ slice thin cut sliced large loaf, or 1 slice small sliced loaf
Bread, Cambridge formula	2 slices cut approx. $\frac{1}{2}$ in. thick
Nimble	$1\frac{1}{2}$ slices sliced loaf
Biscuits, plain, semi-sweet (e.g. Marie, Nice or small tea Matzos)	2 biscuits
Starch reduced rolls	3 rolls
Starch reduced crispbread	4 biscuits
Ryvita	$1\frac{1}{2}$ biscuits
All-Bran	3 level tablespoons
Cornflakes or other unsweetened breakfast cereal	3 heaped tablespoons
Porridge made with oats	4 level tablespoons

Macaroni, spaghetti, noodles, boiled	2 heaped tablespoons
Rice, boiled	1 heaped tablespoon
Potatoes, boiled	1 the size of an egg
mashed	1 heaped tablespoon
Baked beans	2 level tablespoons
Canned processed peas	2 heaped tablespoons

Milk

Fresh or sterilized	$\frac{1}{3}$ pint or 14 tablespoons
Sweetened condensed	$1\frac{1}{2}$ tablespoons
Evaporated unsweetened	6 tablespoons
Instant dried skimmed milk, or non-fat milk	$1\frac{1}{2}$ tablespoons or $\frac{1}{3}$ pint reconstituted
Yogurt, plain or natural	1 carton (approx. $\frac{1}{4}$ pint or $\frac{1}{2}$ c.)
Plain ice cream	1 small cornet or 1 small brickette

Meat

Sausages	2 sausages
Chipolatas	4 chipolatas

The following recipes contain negligible amounts of carbohydrate:

Goulash No. 252; Grilled Beef Patty No. 262; Potted Meat No. 264; Pot-Roasted Broiler No. 274; Pressed Chicken No. 275; Grilled Lamb Chops with Herbs No. 287; Lamb Cutlets in Aspic No. 288; Grilled Lamb Patties No. 290; Lamb Shashlik No. 295; Grilled Liver with Mushrooms No. 301; Liver Shashlik No. 307; Veal Mould No. 325; Veal Parmesan No. 326.

Vegetables

Beans, fresh or canned, broad, butter, haricot and baked beans	2 level tablespoons
Beetroot	1 small

Carrots, boiled	2 large
mashed	4 heaped tablespoons
Corn, fresh	½ large cob
canned	2 level tablespoons
Lentils, boiled	2 level tablespoons
Onions, fried	2½ heaped tablespoons
Parsnips, boiled and mashed	2 heaped tablespoons
Peas, fresh or frozen, boiled	4 heaped tablespoons
canned processed	2 heaped tablespoons
Potatoes, boiled	1 the size of an egg
chips	4 large chips
mashed	1 heaped tablespoon
roast	1 small

Free List (Vegetables)

An average helping of the following will provide negligible amounts of carbohydrate:

Aubergine, artichoke (globe and Jerusalem), asparagus, broccoli, Brussels sprouts, cabbage, cauliflower, celery, chicory, cucumber, egg plant, endive, French beans, kohl rabi, lettuce, marrow, mushrooms, mustard and cress, okra, pumpkin, radishes, runner beans, sauerkraut, sea kale beet, Swiss chard, sweet peppers, spring greens, spinach, tomatoes, turnips, watercress.

Fresh Fruit or Fruit Frozen without Sugar

Stewed and baked fruits should be cooked without sugar; most non-sugar sweeteners need to be added after cooking, see page 99.

Apples	1 medium
Apricots	3 large
Avocado pear	1 medium
Banana, ripe	1 small
Cherries, raw	20
stewed	3 tablespoons
Damsons	10
Figs	1 large
Gooseberries, dessert	12

Grapes	10
Greengages	4
Melon	1 large slice
Nectarines	2
Oranges	1 large
Peaches	1 medium
Pears	1 medium
Pineapple	2 heaped tablespoons, diced
Plums	3 large
Raspberries	6 heaped tablespoons
Strawberries	15 large
Tangerines	2

Dried Fruit

Apricots	6 halves, cooked without sugar
Currants	1 level tablespoon
Dates	4
Figs	1 large, cooked without sugar
Peaches	2 halves, cooked without sugar
Prunes	4 medium, cooked without sugar
Raisins	1 level tablespoon
Sultanas	1 level tablespoon

Canned Fruit

Alfonal and Dietade canned fruits in water may be used in place of fresh fruit, with non-sugar sweeteners added. The following exchange figures include fruit plus liquid: one 7 oz. (198 g.) can of fruit salad, pineapple (except crush), pears, peaches, cherries and apricots can be used as a 10-gram carbohydrate exchange.

A third of a can of Dietade pineapple crush equals 10 grams of carbohydrate.

Free List (*Fresh Fruit or Fruit Frozen without Sugar*)

An average helping of any of the following will give negligible amounts of carbohydrate, provided they are cooked and served without sugar: blackberries, currants (red, white or black), green gooseberries, grapefruit, lemon juice, loganberries, olives, paw-paw and rhubarb.

Nuts

The only nuts likely to be eaten in quantities large enough to need counting for carbohydrate are:

Chestnuts	1 oz. shelled
Peanuts	4 oz. shelled

With all the rest, approximately ½ lb. shelled contains 10 grams of carbohydrate. With most nuts 1 lb. yields ½ lb. when shelled.

Soups

The following have negligible carbohydrate in an average portion:

Consommé, Crosse and Blackwell Julienne, Jellied Consommé with mushrooms, No. 60.

Recipes giving approximately 10 grams of carbohydrate per portion are:

Onion Broth No. 45, Brain Soup No. 51, Cheese Soup No. 53, Cream of Chicken Soup No. 54, Dairy Soup No. 57, Egg Broth No. 58, and Mushroom Soup No. 66.

Sugars and Preserves

Sugar or glucose for an emergency	2 heaped teaspoons or 3 small lumps
Lemon curd	3 level teaspoons
Jam, honey, marmalade, syrup, treacle	1 level teaspoon

Average helpings of diabetic jams and marmalades allowed freely except to those on a reducing diet.

Drinks

Bengers, Bournvita, Horlicks, Ovaltine	2 heaped teaspoons
Cocoa powder	5 heaped teaspoons
Orange juice, fresh or canned, unsweetened	8 tablespoons
Pineapple juice, canned, unsweetened	6 tablespoons

Average portions of unsweetened tomato or grapefruit juice contain negligible amounts of carbohydrate.

Ale, strong	$\frac{1}{3}$ pint (190 millilitres)
Beer, draught bitter	$\frac{3}{4}$ pint (426 millilitres)
bottled	1 pint (568 millilitres)
Cider, bottled dry	$\frac{3}{4}$ pint (426 millilitres)
sweet	$\frac{1}{2}$ pint (284 millilitres)
Stout, bottled	$\frac{1}{2}$ pint (284 millilitres)

The following contain negligible amounts of carbohydrate when used in normal quantities:

Soda water, sugar-free tonic waters, dry sherry, Burgundy, Beaujolais, Chianti, Medoc, spirits, and Champagne. Dry white wines have negligible carbohydrate but Graves and Sauternes need to be counted.

A 6 fl. oz. (170 ml.) wine glass full of Sauternes will contain approximately 10 grams of carbohydrate; with Graves 1$\frac{1}{2}$ such glasses full would contain approximately 10 grams of carbohydrate. Thus one standard restaurant-type glass of wine, half-full should be counted as 5 grams for Sauternes and 3 grams for the Graves.

Meal-Patterns

The meal-pattern will be prescribed by the doctor according to the type and amount of insulin being given and the needs of the patient.

As an example of a diabetic meal-pattern a typical 150-gram carbohydrate diet is given below, showing the distribution of carbohydrate throughout the day and how this is translated into meals by using the exchange lists.

Following this are some suggested menus of suitable carbohydrate values for the diet, showing how calculated recipes such as those in this book can be used to give variety.

150-gram Carbohydrate Diet

Breakfast	40 g.
Mid-morning	10 g.
Midday	30 g.
Tea	10 g.
Evening	40 g.
Bedtime	20 g.
Total	150 g.

A Typical Day's Meals Using Exchange Lists

Breakfast		
4 level tablespoons porridge made with oats	10 g.	
7 tablespoons milk or ½ cup	5 g.	
1 egg, poached or boiled	—	
1½ slices bread thin cut large loaf	25 g.	
Butter and diabetic marmalade	—	
Tea with milk to colour	—	40 g.
Mid-morning		
Bovril, or tea with milk to colour	—	
2 Marie biscuits or other semi-sweet biscuits	10 g.	10 g.
Midday		
Roast lamb	—	
2 small roast potatoes	20 g.	
Green vegetable	—	
1 medium baked apple (non-sugar sweetener)	10 g.	30 g.
Tea		
Tea with milk to colour	—	
⅔ slice bread thin cut large loaf	10 g.	
Butter and diabetic jam	—	10 g.
Evening		
Cold ham	—	
2 boiled potatoes each the size of an egg made into salad with French dressing	20 g.	
Tomato and lettuce	—	
1 small ripe banana	10 g.	
2 semi-sweet biscuits	10 g.	40 g.
Bedtime		
⅓ pint (⅔ c.) milk	10 g.	
2 heaped teaspoons Horlicks or Ovaltine	10 g.	20 g.
	Total	150 g.

Menus

Most of the recipes in this book have been calculated for carbohydrate content per portion. The portions recommended are fairly generous in most cases and you may find that many of them come within your own carbohydrate allowance if you eat a smaller portion.

The menus which follow use recipes and the exchange lists to make meals of 30- and 40-gram carbohydrate content.

30-gram Carbohydrate Menus

1

Goulash (No. 252) (3 g.)
4 heaped Tbs. boiled noodles (20 g.)
Spinach or cabbage
1 medium orange (7 g.)

2

Grilled fish (No. 203)
Parsley Butter (No. 99)
2 heaped Tbs. mashed potato (20 g.)
1 grilled tomato
Apple Snow (No. 413) made with sugar substitute (10 g.)

3

Pot-roasted Broiler (No. 274)
2 small roast potatoes (20 g.)
Brussels sprouts
Port Wine Jelly (No. 471) (10 g.)

4

Sole or Plaice Meunière à l'Orange (No. 238) (5 g.)
2 egg-sized boiled potatoes (20 g.)
2 heaped Tbs. boiled green peas (5 g.)
Stewed blackberries sweetened with sugar substitute or use other fruit from free list

5

Potted Meat (No. 264)
2 heaped Tbs. potato salad with French dressing (No. 111) (20 g.)
Mixed salad, tomato, cucumber, lettuce
1 medium baked apple, no sugar (10 g.)

6

Jellied Consommé with mushrooms (No. 60)
Grilled kidneys, bacon and tomatoes
8 large chips (20 g.)
10 grapes and a piece of cheese (10 g.)

7

Fish Bonne Femme No. 212
2 egg-sized boiled potatoes (20 g.)
Cucumber and tomato salad with French dressing
1 small baked banana (No. 417) (10 g.)

8

Grilled lamb chop with herbs (No. 287)
2 heaped Tbs. mashed potatoes (20 g.)
Sliced green beans
1 small brickette ice cream (10 g.)

9

Fish Creole (No. 217) (6 g.)
1 heaped Tbs. boiled rice (10 g.)
Frozen Vanilla Mousse (No. 454) (11 g.)
2 heaped Tbs. fresh or frozen raspberries (3 g.)

10

Hot boiled ham with chopped green herbs
2 egg-sized boiled potatoes (20 g.)
Spinach
Baked Custard (No. 440) (10 g.) with fruit from the free list

11

Fillets of Fish with Lemon Sauce (No. 222) (10 g.)
2 heaped Tbs. mashed potato (20 g.)
Sliced green beans
Cheese and Celery

12

Grilled Lamb Patties (No. 290)
Grilled tomatoes
8 large chips (20 g.)
1 medium pear (10 g.)

13

Salmon Mousse (No. 233)
Cucumber salad
2 heaped Tbs. potato salad with French dressing (20 g.)
1 small ripe banana (10 g.)

14

Lamb Shashlik (No. 295)
2 heaped Tbs. boiled rice (20 g.)
1 large orange (10 g.)

40-gram Carbohydrate Menus

1

Grilled liver with mushrooms (No. 301)
8 large chips (20 g.)
4 heaped Tbs. green peas (10 g.)
Orange and Rhubarb Compôte (No. 433) using non-sugar sweetener (5 g.)
1 semi-sweet biscuit (5 g.)

2

Veal Blanquette (No. 320) (5 g.)
2 heaped Tbs. mashed potato (20 g.)
Brussels sprouts
Frozen Vanilla Mousse (No. 454) (11 g.) garnished with 6 large strawberries (4 g.)

3

Sole or Plaice Dieppoise (No. 240)
2 heaped Tbs. mashed potato (20 g.)
Lettuce salad with French dressing
Banana Mould (No. 420) using small bananas (20 g.)

4

Marinaded Steak No. 266 (3 g.)
2 heaped Tbs. mashed potato (20 g.)
Brussels sprouts
Fruit Salad using ¼ small banana, ¼ large orange, 7 grapes with non-sugar syrup (12 g.)
1 semi-sweet biscuit (5 g.)

5

Veal Parmesan (No. 326)
4 heaped Tbs. boiled noodles (20 g.)
Spinach
1 large orange (10 g.)
2 Semi-sweet biscuits (10 g.)

6

Sole or Plaice Voisin (No. 241)
2 egg-sized boiled potatoes (20 g.)
Sliced green beans
2 plain biscuits and cheese (10 g.)
1 medium apple (10 g.)

7

Fried Chicken and Almonds (No. 271) (5 g.)
2 heaped Tbs. boiled rice (20 g.)
Lettuce salad with French dressing
2 plain biscuits and cheese (10 g.)
5 grapes (5 g.)

8

Liver Pâté (No. 304)
2 exchanges bread and butter (20 g.)
Grapefruit and Beetroot Salad (No. 382) (5 g.)
Coffee Spanish cream (No. 462) (15 g.)

9

Chicken Paprika (No. 272) (3 g.)
2 heaped Tbs. boiled noodles (10 g.)
Brussels sprouts or spinach
Grilled grapefruit (No. 426), using a little less sugar (17 g.)

10

Roast Beef
2 small roast potatoes (20 g.)
Cauliflower with melted butter sauce
2 heaped Tbs. carrots (5 g.)
Chocolate Mousse (No. 438) (15 g.)

11

Poached Fresh Salmon or other fish
Sauce tartare (No. 117)
2 egg-sized boiled potatoes (20 g.)
Cucumber salad with French dressing
1 vanilla brickette (10 g.) with 1 exchange of fruit (10 g.)

12

Ham Mousse No. 279 (10 g.) (made with cream)
2 exchanges bread and butter (20 g.)
Lettuce salad with French dressing
1 large slice melon (10 g.)

13

Roast pork
Apple sauce made with 1 medium dessert apple, no sugar (10 g.)
2 small roast potatoes (20 g.)
Brussels sprouts
Egg jelly (No. 463) made with sugar substitute (2 g.)
Garnish with 8 grapes (8 g.)

14

Grilled Gammon rasher, tomatoes, mushrooms
8 large chips (20 g.)
Chocolate ice cream (No. 446) (20 g.)

Eating Out

It is simple if the patient has learnt to judge quantities of the controlled foods by sight.

A choice can be made from the following foods found in most menus.

First course. Grapefruit (no sugar) or clear soup.

Eggs. Boiled, poached, scrambled, omelette (count any bread or toast).

Fish. Fried in batter (leave the batter), grilled with lemon.

Meats. Roasts (only thin gravy) or grills.

Vegetables. Plain cooked in amounts from the diet, or from the free list (page 105). Salad and French dressing or lemon juice or vinegar.

Puddings. Fresh fruit in amounts allowed in the diet or have cheese instead with bread or biscuits in amounts allowed.

Beverages. See exchange lists, pages 107–8.

Packed Meals

If bread sandwiches are used most of the carbohydrate allowance will be used up in the bread. For example a 30-gram carbohydrate meal can have sandwiches made with 2 slices of a thin-cut sliced large loaf, that is, one 'round' of sandwich. Any of the carbohydrate-free fillings can be used such as cooked meats, chicken, cheese, canned salmon or sardine, egg, and salad vegetables.

An alternative is to use some starch-reduced rolls or crisp-bread (see exchange list) instead of the bread and use the remaining carbohydrate for fruit or a milky drink, see exchange lists.

CHAPTER 6

Over-weight

Why people get fat

AUTHORITIES agree that obesity is due to habitually eating more food than the body needs to supply the energy expended. The ratio of food intake to energy expended is wrong for that particular individual.

Sometimes this is simply because the family pattern of eating is a generous one, in which case several members of the same family will probably be overweight. Portions are probably larger than needed and second helpings the general rule.

Sometimes unhappy and frustrated people turn to food as a comforter.

Why some people seem able to eat large amounts of food and not put on weight while others on a comparatively small intake quickly become obese is not yet completely understood. What seems certain is that the rate of using up energy is an individual affair and the control of appetite is too. Some people, in fact, seem to need very little fuel to run their bodies.

How to Lose Weight

Losing weight is achieved by being more active and by eating less. This sounds simple but in our present society it is difficult to carry out. Less energy is needed to do most jobs today, yet good food has never been so plentiful and varied, and people now have more money and time for cooking and eating. Many of us have not yet learned to adjust eating habits to our new way of life.

Losing weight needs:

1. A great deal of determination to stick to the diet until results are achieved.

2. Organization of one's day to allow time for regular

exercise, e.g. allowing time to walk instead of using the bus or car.

3. A willingness to find out something about foods and how a wise selection can cause weight-loss without adversely affecting health.

4. Sympathy and cooperation from friends and relatives. The fact that a person is on a diet seems to bring out the worst in others, who try to undermine the reducer's determination by pressing on them unwanted food, saying being thin doesn't suit them, and so on.

It is sometimes a good idea not to tell anyone about the diet – just alter your eating habits without being conspicuous and one fine day people will realize that your surplus fat has gone and you look much better.

How the Normal Diet is Modified

Many diets have been devised for reducing weight including the low-calorie, low-carbohydrate, low-fat, high-protein, and many more. The one which has proved to be the most useful over a long period is the low-calorie diet. Because calories are restricted it is also a low-carbohydrate and low-fat diet, these two being the main sources of calories in any diet. The low-calorie diet also has the advantage that it is nearer to a normal pattern of eating than any of the other diets and thus easier to carry out.

The two main modifications to the normal diet are to eat smaller portions of food than many people are in the habit of having and to reduce the quantities of foods which are a concentrated source of energy. They are those with a high calorific value, and which provide little in the way of protein, minerals and vitamins, all essential in any healthy diet. These concentrated energy foods are:

ALL SUGARS, honey, syrup, treacle, and foods containing large amounts of these, e.g. jam, cakes, biscuits, chocolate, and sugar confectionery.

MOST FATS, which means cutting down on the amounts

of fried foods and pastry. Moderate amounts of butter or margarine (½–1 oz. (1–2 level Tbs.) total daily) are usually advised because of the vitamins they contain, and children should continue to have their cod-liver oil for the same reason. Oils, cooking fat, lard, and dripping are all restricted in quantity.

ALCOHOL. The quantity likely to be drunk at a time is more important than the calorific value per ounce. Thus a pint of beer or cider or a double of spirits will provide more calories than a glass of wine or sherry.

The following table gives the average calorific value for common measures of the different drinks. In theory these can be taken as exchanges for other foods but in practice they are a poor alternative because they make no useful contribution to the nutritive value of the diet, other than the calories which are what the slimmer should avoid. Thus to cut down on the consumption of alcohol is essential for slimmers.

½ pt (284 ml.) beer	70–90 calories
½ pt strong ale	210
½ pt stout	100
½ pt cider	100–120
A single brandy, whisky, gin, rum, vodka	75
3 Tbs. (½ small glass) dry sherry	50
sweet sherry	57
½ wine glass Burgundy, Beaujolais, Chianti, Medoc	60
Graves	63
Champagne	63
Sauternes	78
3 Tbs. (½ small glass) port	68

Fitting in with Family Meals

Special cooking is not needed except perhaps for providing an alternative to the pudding course, for example fruit stewed with saccharin, or raw fruit, or other puddings such as custards and milk pudding with saccharin.

Cooking Methods are Important

Frying and other methods using much fat are excluded. Grilling and oven-frying are used instead.

Simple methods of cooking should be the general rule as these usually produce food with a lower calorie value than complex methods using a large number of ingredients and processes.

Do not use recipes which contain a lot of fat, oil, and cream, such as sauces made with butter and cream, rich cream soups, puddings with much fat and sugar, pastries, cakes with elaborate decorations of sugar and butter icing.

This does *not* mean an end to good cooking and pleasant meals. Indeed the enjoyment in eating a simple meal not overloaded with creams, fats, and sugars is often much greater than that derived from the richest and most elaborate banquet.

Useful Special Foods

Non-Sugar Sweeteners. These are listed on page 99 and all are suitable for a reducing diet except Sorbitol which has a calorific value similar to that of sugar.

Proprietary 'Slimming' Foods. There are many low-carbohydrate, low-calorie, starch-reduced and 'slimming' foods on the market, the majority of them more expensive than normal foods and many of them of the same calorific value. There is no reason why the weight-watcher should not use them as part of a calorie-controlled diet provided the calories are counted.

There is no such thing as a 'slimming food'. It is the total daily calorie consumption which makes a diet 'slimming' or 'fattening', thus there are slimming and fattening diets but foods are low or high-calorie rather than 'slimming' or 'fattening'. Obviously the most useful foods for a slimming diet are the low-calorie ones.

Among the proprietary foods, substitutes for bread can be a trap for the unwary. This is because two or more pieces of, for example, starch-reduced bread may be a substitute for one slice of ordinary bread, but, if they are spread with butter or jam, the two will take twice as much and you can easily end up eating more, not fewer, calories.

Diabetic fruit squashes, if sweetened with saccharin and not Sorbitol, have a lower calorific value than ordinary squashes.

Diabetic jams, marmalades and canned fruits often contain Sorbitol and have the same calorific value as ordinary ones, while diabetic chocolate often has a higher calorific value than ordinary chocolate.

Before using any of these foods read the label and note the calorie content. If it isn't given, don't use the food. Compare the calorific values per piece with that given in the exchange tables pages 122–5.

Tips Other Dieters Have Found Helpful

1. Before starting a diet, try to find out why you are overweight. Keep a faithful diary of everything you eat and drink for a week and check it by the *Meal-pattern for a Good Diet* (page 18).

2. Eat more frequent very small meals. If you let yourself get really hungry it is easy to eat at one meal a slimmer's allowance for a whole day.

3. Avoid monotony, ring the changes on all the low-calorie foods listed on pages 120–1.

4. Collect interesting low-calorie or low-carbohydrate recipes and swop them with other dieters.

5. Look at yourself frequently in a full-length mirror.

6. Look to the future and remind yourself frequently why you want to lose weight.

7. Find a fellow dieter or someone else to give you sympathy and encouragement if you can't get it from family and friends.

8. Keep yourself busy. Idle people eat to fill in time.

9. When people start talking about eating and discussing favourite foods, you start talking about some of the good low-calorie or low-carbohydrate recipes you have collected.

10. Give yourself occasional luxury fruits, meats, or fish from the list of foods on pages 120–21.

11. When you give a party include unusual and exciting dishes which fit in with your diet.

12. Start a meal with a soup or low-calorie drink, to begin filling the stomach.

13. Chew thoroughly.

Foods Usually Allowed

Beverages. Tea and coffee with saccharin for sweetening, soda water, milk (amounts controlled), unsweetened fruit juices, vegetable juices, unsweetened mineral waters. Alcohol should be reduced in amount (ask about this). Dry wines have the lowest calorie content. Bottle cordial or squashes if sweetened with saccharin or saxin.

Bread. Amounts controlled. For exchanges see page 125.

Cereals and pasta. Amounts controlled.

Cheese. Amounts usually controlled. Low-fat cheeses like cottage cheese are the best.

Condiments and garnishes. All allowed *except* sweet pickles and chutneys, thick bottled sauces and salad dressings (Dietade salad dressing and Dietade French dressing are allowed). Use permitted ones freely to make foods appetizing.

Eggs. Cooked any way except fried, or with butter or cream or in starch-thickened sauces.

Fats, oils, and cream. Amounts restricted. Usually ½–1 oz. (1–2 level Tbs.) butter or margarine allowed daily for its vitamin content.

Fish. Any cooked without fat or starch-thickened sauces.

Fruit. Amounts of some fruits may be controlled but it is very important to use fruit in place of high-calorie, high-carbohydrate puddings. Avoid dried fruits like dates, raisins, etc., and fruits canned with sugar (Sorbitol must also be counted for calories). Dietade and Alfonal fruits, see exchange list.

If to be cooked, sweeten with a sugarless sweetener not containing Sorbitol (see page 99).

Meat, game, and poultry. Lean meat of any kind in permitted amounts (see page 124), cooked without fat (not pies and sausages). Stewing, baking, and grilling are the best methods of cooking.

Milk. Usually not more than ½ pt. (1 c.) whole milk or 1 pt. (2 c.) skimmed milk allowed daily, though some diets allow 1 pt whole milk. Dried skimmed milk or condensed whole unsweetened evaporated milk may be substituted for some of this. (*Exchanges*: 2 oz. (4 heaped Tbs.) dried skimmed milk equals 1 pt (2 c.) liquid skimmed milk. 4½ fl. oz. condensed whole unsweetened (evaporated) equals 1 pt (2 c.) liquid skimmed.)

Puddings. Restricted. Carbohydrate and calorie values are given for most recipes in this book.

Some low-calorie recipes are Nos. 404, 411, 413, 417, 423, 426, 431, 463, 466, 471, 476, 478.

Sauces and gravies. Use is restricted. Calorie values given in most recipes.

Soups and stews. Any stock. Low-calorie soups are useful to start a meal and help prevent overeating (see Nos. 43–7, 55, 60, 74).

Clear meat soups such as consommé are not high-calorie but frequently have the effect of stimulating the appetite and are not the best choice.

Sugars. Only sugar substitutes allowed (see page 99). Also see caution about Sorbitol and calorie values.

Vegetables. Free List. The following usually allowed as desired if cooked without fats or starchy sauces.

Asparagus, Brussels sprouts, cabbage, cauliflower, celery, chicory, cucumber, egg plant or aubergine, spinach beet, spinach, kale, broccoli, mustard and cress, watercress, turnips, radish, lettuce, mushrooms, sweet peppers, sauerkraut, French beans and runner beans, marrow and pumpkin, gherkins, tomatoes, spring greens, endive, corn salad.

Be careful of the amounts of these eaten: Beetroot, carrots, onions, parsnips, peas, broad beans, pulses, potatoes.

Meal-Pattern for the 1,000-Calorie Reducing Diet

It helps to have meals at regular intervals, to eat slowly, and to enjoy flavours.

Daily Allowance. ½ pt (1 c.) full cream milk (190 cals.) or 1 pt (2 c.) skimmed milk (200 cals.), ½ oz. (1 level Tbs.) butter or margarine (106–113 cals.).

On Waking. Tea with milk from allowance (no sugar).

Breakfast. Fruit exchange (50 cals.). Egg or exchange (90 cals.). Bread or exchange (70 cals.) with butter from allowance. Tea or coffee with milk from allowance (no sugar).

Mid-morning. Tea or coffee with milk from allowance (no sugar) *or* Bovril, Oxo or Marmite.

Midday. Unthickened soup (optional). Meat or exchange (140–150 cals.). Large portion green or root vegetable (not beetroot, parsnip or potatoes) *or* salad. Fruit exchange (50 cals). Tea or coffee with milk from allowance (no sugar).

Tea. Tea or coffee with milk from allowance (no sugar). Bread or exchange (70 cals.). Salad, Marmite, tomato or paste.

Evening. Meat or exchange (140–150 cals.). Green vegetable or salad. Fruit exchange (50 cals.). Bread or exchange (70 cals.). Tea or coffee with milk from allowance (no sugar).

Bedtime. Remainder of milk plain or in tea (no sugar) *or* one of the other permitted beverages, see page 120.

Anti-Flatulence Diet

Over-weight people suffering from heart condition may be recommended to have small meals at two-hourly intervals. As the large amounts of fibre in fruit and vegetable tend to cause flatulence it is better to use well-cooked and sieved or mashed vegetables and fruit.

Calorie Exchange Lists

These calorie exchange lists are to help you plan your own varied diet and still keep it within the 1,000 calorie limit.

Fruit Exchanges to give approximately 50 calories each. All fruit is prepared and served without added sugar. For non-sugar sweeteners, see page 99. Fruit frozen without sugar can be substituted for fresh fruit.

Apple	1 medium
stewed	6 tablespoons
Apricots, fresh	3 large
dried	6 halves
Avocado pear	1 medium
Banana	1 very small
Cherries	20
Currants, dried	1 level tablespoon
Damsons	12
Dates	4
Figs, fresh or dried	1
Gooseberries, ripe	15
Grapes	15
Greengages	4
Melon	1 large slice
Nectarines	2
Olives	4 large
Oranges	1 large
juice, fresh	8 tablespoons
Peaches, fresh	1 medium
dried	2 halves
Pears	1 large
Pineapple, fresh	2 heaped tablespoons diced
Plums	5 medium
Prunes	4 medium
Raisins	1½ level tablespoons
Raspberries	7 heaped tablespoons
Strawberries	17 large
Sultanas	1½ level tablespoons
Tangerines	3

Canned Fruit Juices

Unsweetened grapefruit	¼ pint (½c.)
Sweetened grapefruit	6 tablespoons
Pineapple	6 tablespoons
Tomato	Average portion
Sweetened orange	6 tablespoons
Unsweetened orange	8 tablespoons

Canned Fruit Dietade and Alfonal canned fruits in water (except Dietade Pineapple Crush) give approximately 45 calories per 7 oz. (198 g.) can. They may be used in place of fresh fruit, adding non-sugar sweeteners. Half a 7 oz. can of Dietade crushed pineapple gives 50 calories.

Free List

Average portions of the following are allowed provided they are served without sugar or Sorbitol; blackberries, currants (black, red or white), grapefruit, green gooseberries, lemons or juice, and rhubarb.

Many fruits can be purchased frozen without sugar and this is the best way of preserving home-grown fruit for reducing diets. Use in place of fresh fruit with non-sugar sweeteners.

NOTE: any recipe using fruit and which gives not more than 50 calories per portion may be used as a fruit exchange.

Breakfast Exchanges. Exchanges for one standard boiled egg (90 calories)

Bacon, lean, grilled	1 rasher
Cottage cheese, low-fat	⅔ of a 4 oz. carton
Yogurt, Ski brand	½ carton
Haddock, steamed, poached or grilled	1 small portion
Ham, lean, boiled	1 thin slice
Herring, baked, grilled or steamed	1 small
Kipper, grilled or boiled	1 small

Meat Exchanges. Instead of 2 oz. (one small portion) lean cooked or canned meat, game or poultry you can have one of the following (140–150 calories)

Cheese (except cream)	1 small portion
cottage (low-fat)	1 small carton (4 oz. size)
Egg, boiled or poached	1 large
Fish, white, steamed, poached, grilled or baked	1 medium portion
Kidney, grilled	1
Liver, grilled	2 thin slices

Pilchard, canned	1 small
Salmon, canned	1 small portion
Salmon or trout, fresh, grilled or baked	1 small portion
Sardine, canned	1 large
Sausage, grilled	1
Shellfish	1 large portion

Bread Exchanges. Instead of 1 slice of brown or white bread (1 oz.) you can have one of the following (70 calories)

Bread, 'Nimble' sliced	2 slices
'Cambridge Formula'	2 thick slices
'Slimcea'	2 slices
Crispbread, starch-reduced Energen	2½ pieces
Rolls, starch-reduced Energen	2½ rolls
Biscuits, semi-sweet e.g. Marie, Nice	2 biscuits
Cream-crackers	3 biscuits
Ryvita	2 biscuits
Potato, boiled	1 small
mashed	3 heaped Tbs.
Rice, boiled	2 heaped Tbs.
Parsnips, boiled, mashed	3 heaped Tbs.
Peas, canned, processed	3 heaped Tbs.
Beans, cooked haricot, butter or baked beans	3 heaped Tbs.
Lentils, boiled	2½ level Tbs.

Menus

These have been compiled from the exchange lists and calculated recipes and will provide approximately 200 calories to be used as exchanges for the midday meal on page 122; or 260 calories, which forms an exchange for the evening meal.

A look at the calculated recipes will show that simple methods of serving and cooking food are the best for reducing diets, for, as soon as recipes begin combining foods to make complex dishes, the calorific value begins to go up.

200-Calorie Menus as Exchanges for the Midday Meal

With any meal, tea or coffee with milk from the allowance but no sugar can be included. Alternatively use one of the permitted beverages listed on page 120.

1

Egg and yogurt mould (No. 194)
Large mixed salad from free list with permitted dressing
4 medium prunes stewed without sugar and with lemon or orange rind to flavour

2

Grilled Lamb Chops with herbs (No. 287)
Grilled tomatoes and mushrooms
Boiled cauliflower
8 large strawberries, fresh or frozen, dressed with 4 Tbs. fresh orange juice

3

A small portion soused fish (No. 243) with full portion of salad
½ grapefruit sprinkled with 1 level Tbs. sugar and grilled

4

Eggs mimosa (No. 195) with large portion of spinach
1 very small banana

5

Veal mould (No. 325)
Tomato, cucumber and lettuce salad with permitted dressing
1 large orange

6

A small portion of pressed chicken (No. 275), without sauce
Asparagus tips and lettuce salad with permitted dressing
1 large slice melon

7

A small portion of lean, cold ham
Tomato and Sweet Pepper Salad (No. 392)
Lettuce
1 fruit exchange

8

A small portion American fried cabbage (No. 338)
1 grilled sausage
Fruit from the Free List

9

Potted meat (No. 264)
Garnish of gherkin and tomato
Chicory or endive salad with permitted dressing
½ medium apple stewed with 2 chopped dates for sweetening

10

1 poached egg on a bed of spinach
½ portion stuffed oranges (No. 432)

11

2 portions lamb cutlets in aspic (No. 288)
Shredded sprouts and celery salad with permitted dressing
5 medium plums, ripe, or stewed and sweetened sugar substitute

12

Stuffed tomatoes (No. 364)
Baked mushrooms
Green beans
1 small boiled potato
Baked apple (sugar substitute)

13

Chicken and mushroom salad (No. 373)
1 small banana

14

Crab salad (No. 376), small portion crab
1 tangerine and 10 grapes

260-Calorie Menus as Exchanges for the Evening Meal

A drink can be included as for the 200-calorie menus.

1

Fish bonne femme (No. 212)
Tomato and lettuce salad with permitted dressing
1 small boiled potato
15 grapes

2

A small portion lean roast beef
3 heaped Tbs. mashed potato
Large portion cauliflower
Cinnamon apples (No. 411)

3

Sole or plaice Dieppoise (No. 240)
1 small boiled potato
French or runner beans
1 large pear

4

Casserole of veal (No. 321)
3 heaped Tbs. mashed potato
Spinach
1 large orange

5

Rice and Fish Mould No. 229
Garnish lemon wedges and gherkins
Lettuce and tomato salad with permitted dressing
1 slice bread
1 medium apple

6

A small portion hot boiled bacon or ham, lean
1 small boiled potato
Generous helping sauerkraut
Cider Jelly (No. 476)

7

Fish casserole (No. 213)
2 heaped Tbs. boiled rice
Spinach
A large slice of melon

8

A small portion lean roast lamb
Mint sauce (sugar substitute)
3 heaped Tbs. mashed potato
Brussels sprouts
Apple Snow (No. 413) (variation)

9

A small portion grilled fresh salmon
Grilled tomatoes
Lettuce and cucumber salad with permitted dressing
1 small boiled potato
1 very small baked banana (No. 417)

10

2 thin slices liver grilled as Shashlik with tomatoes and mushrooms (No. 307)
3 heaped Tbs. mashed potatoes
French or runner beans
A fruit exchange

11

A small portion roast chicken
Garnish asparagus spears and baked tomato
1 small boiled potato
Boiled chicory
½ portion baked bananas and prunes (No. 418)

12

A medium portion grilled fish garnished with lemon and gherkins
Grilled mushrooms
Lettuce or endive salad
3 heaped Tbs. mashed potato
½ portion Gooseberry and Banana Compôte (No. 423)

13

Rabbit stew (No. 309)
Portion mixed vegetables from the free list
1 small boiled potato
Salad of 8 large strawberries, fresh or frozen, with 4 Tbs. fresh orange juice

14

2 small grilled lamb cutlets
Garnished watercress and grilled tomatoes
3 heaped Tbs. mashed potato
Green vegetable
Lemon snow (No. 478) (without cream)

Eating Out

If it is impossible to refuse a dish in someone else's home, take only a small portion and compensate by eating less at the next meal or next day.

Soups. Clear soups.

Hors d'œuvre. Meats, fish, eggs, grapefruit, melon, radishes, tomato juice, tomato salad, cocktail onions, gherkins, celery sticks.

Eggs. Boiled eggs, omelettes.

Fish. Grilled with lemon. Fried in batter (leave the batter).

Meats. Grills and roasts.

Vegetables. No potatoes, any green vegetables (plain cooked), salads with vinegar and a dash of oil or lemon juice.

Puddings. Raw fruit and cheese, or cheese and biscuits.

Beverages. 1 small glass of dry wine or dry sherry or dry vermouth diluted with soda water and with a piece of lemon.

Sandwich Meals

Breads. As the amount is usually restricted it is better to use starch-reduced rolls or crispbread. The rolls can be hollowed out and filled, or carry the filling separately in cartons.

Fillings to use. Meat, fish, eggs, or cheese. Mince or chop and use sauce to moisten.

Alternative. Hard-boiled eggs with salad vegetables. Pieces of cheese to eat with fruit, or starch-reduced crispbreads. Lean grilled chop or cutlet, to eat with salad vegetables. Leg of cooked chicken. Rolled sliced cold meats to eat in the fingers. Fish or meat cakes, or hamburgers. Cartons of flavoured cottage cheese.

Salad vegetables. Radishes, cucumber, tomatoes, watercress, lettuce, celery, carrot, chicory.

Fruit. Any fresh, raw fruit from the list (pages 122–4). Nuts.

Beverages. Hot soups. Tea or coffee with milk from the allowance, no sugar.

A suitable meal would consist of:

2–4 starch-reduced rolls with filling, or 2 crispbreads.
1 hard-boiled egg or alternative.
Portion of raw vegetables.
Fresh fruit.
Hot or cold beverage.

CHAPTER 7

Diseases of the Cardio-Vascular or Circulatory System

THESE diseases include atheroma and arteriosclerosis, angina pectoris, congestive heart failure, coronary heart diseases, thrombosis, myocardial infarction, and hypertension.

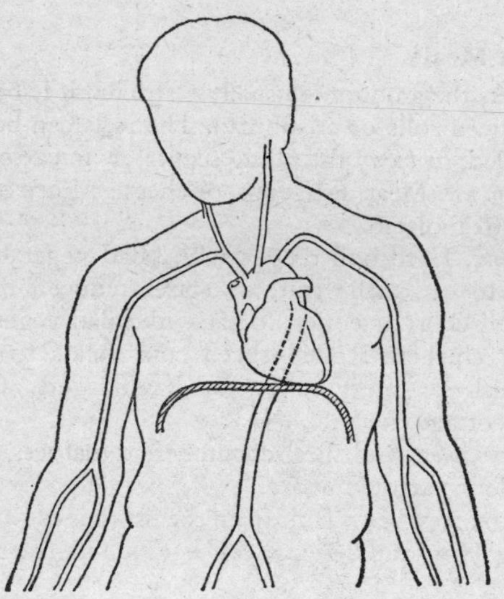

The main parts of the circulatory system

The circulatory system is the transport system of the body. It carries food from the intestines and oxygen from the lungs to all parts of the body to keep them nourished. In addition it carries away from the tissues waste products which are finally eliminated through the kidneys and in expired air.

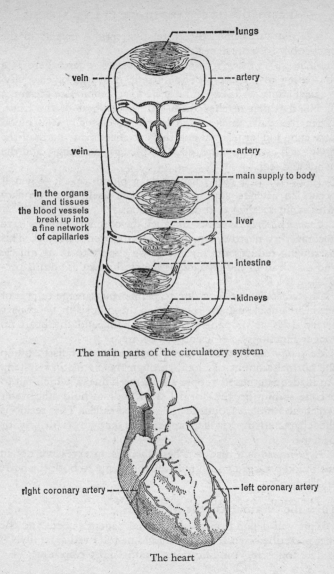

lungs
vein
artery
vein
artery
main supply to body
in the organs and tissues the blood vessels break up into a fine network of capillaries
liver
intestine
kidneys

The main parts of the circulatory system

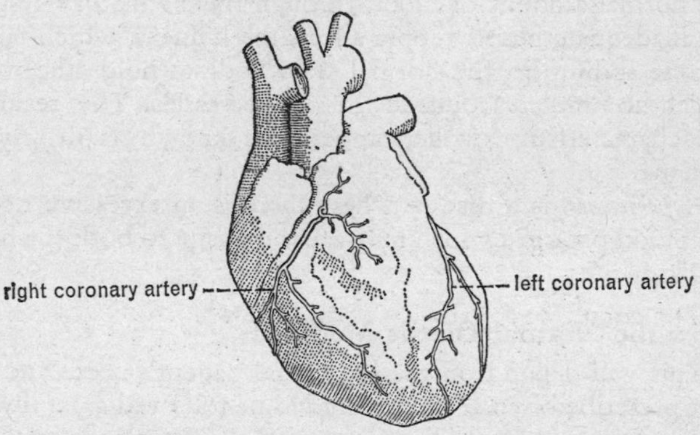

The heart

It is not surprising, therefore, that serious defects in the circulatory system affect the whole body.

Atheroma and arteriosclerosis are diseases where there is a thickening in the walls of the arteries and loss of elasticity. Normal artery walls expand readily to accommodate the surge of blood which reaches them with every beat of the heart. When the walls thicken and lose their elasticity, the blood flow is no longer normal and this can affect many parts of the body such as the heart itself, the kidneys, the lungs, and the hands and feet.

Thrombosis is a clot forming in a blood vessel. When it occurs in arteries supplying the heart itself, the coronary arteries, it is called coronary thrombosis.

Coronary heart disease occurs when the coronary arteries have become very narrow, usually owing to arteriosclerosis. This narrowing reduces the normal blood supply to heart muscle and may lead to the characteristic pain known as angina pectoris.

Myocardial infarction is due to permanent damage to part of the heart muscle usually following a thrombosis in a coronary artery. It is accompanied by severe pain, and the heart no longer functions as efficiently as before.

Congestive heart failure occurs when the heart fails to pump the normal amount of blood through the circulatory system. An inadequate blood supply affects the kidneys, which fail to excrete sodium in the normal way. Sodium holds the water which accumulates outside the blood vessels. The result is the characteristic swollen appearance known as dropsy or oedema.

Hypertension is a disease where there is an excessive rise in the blood pressure which may cause damage to both the heart and kidneys.

How the Normal Diet is Modified

This will depend on the individual patient's needs and the diet prescribed by the doctor should be followed carefully.

The following modifications are the most common:

1. A reduction in the calorie intake for all patients who are over-weight. This is because carrying extra weight about puts an additional strain on the heart. A low-calorie diet is given on page 121.

2. A reduction in the quantity of food eaten at any one meal. Digesting large meals puts an added strain on the circulatory system. Five or six small meals are usually found to be better than three large ones, and a light evening meal is always advisable, that is, have dinner at midday and only a light high tea or supper in the evening.

3. For oedema, and sometimes for high blood pressure, the amount of salt in the diet is restricted. This helps the elimination of fluid and relieves the condition. See the low-sodium diet (page 134).

4. When there is arteriosclerosis, atherosclerosis, and thrombosis, the total solid-fat content of the diet will probably be restricted and the use of oil advised instead. Some doctors prescribe large quantities of oil such as corn or safflower, in quantities larger than would be used in normal cooking. Eggs may be forbidden on account of the high cholesterol content of the yolk. See the 'Modified Fat Diet', page 147.

5. Any foods which cause distension and indigestion should be avoided. It will be seen from the diagrams on pages 44 and 130 that part of the stomach lies just below the apex of the heart and distension of the stomach by gases or large meals can interfere with heart action.

A patient may have one or more of the above modifications made to the diet and it is impossible to give all the likely permutations. Before using any of the diets outlined here it is most important to consult your doctor and make sure the diet is suitable.

Three addresses worth noting. The Chest and Heart Association, Tavistock House North, Tavistock Square, London WC1; or 65 North Castle Street, Edinburgh, EH2 3LT; or 28 Bedford Street, Belfast BT2 7FJ. The Association publishes a booklet *Diets for Heart Patients* which may be purchased from these addresses.

THE LOW-SODIUM DIET
(LOW-SALT OR SALT-FREE)

Prescribed for patients with oedema and sometimes for high blood pressure.

The purpose of this diet is to restrict the amount of fluid in the body. Restricting the amount of water that you drink does not help, but restricting the amount of sodium that you eat helps greatly because sodium holds back the fluid in the body.

All foods contain sodium in varying amounts, but common salt (sodium chloride), contains the most – hence the diet may be called by the doctor, 'low-salt' or 'salt-free'.

A label on food saying 'No added salt' does not mean it is necessarily suitable for all the diets, as the food may contain sodium in some other form.

Sodium occurs in bicarbonate of soda, baking powder, cake and pudding mixtures, self-raising flour, Scofa bread and flour, and many other preparations which contain bicarbonate of soda or baking powder. Many people also use bicarbonate (even washing soda is not unknown) in cooking vegetables.

How the Normal Diet is Modified

Various degrees of salt restriction may be prescribed, the most common being to forbid the use of all salt at table and all foods with a high sodium content (see list), and to allow little or no salt in cooking. A more strict control allows no salt at all in cooking, and foods allowed are selected from those with a very low salt content. The latter diet is seldom used for very long periods, as it is so unpalatable to most people; also, modern medical treatment is making the use of very restricted diets less necessary.

NOTE. Your doctor will say which modification is needed and his instructions should be followed carefully.

Foods with a High Sodium Content

Beverages. Bournvita, cocoa powder, Horlicks, most tinned tomato juice, beer, and all powders for making milk drinks.

Biscuits. Cream-crackers, digestive and water, Macvita, Ryvita, Vita Wheat, all savoury and cocktail biscuits.

Bread. All breads unless specially made as 'salt-free'. All shop scones and buns.

Cakes. All unless specially made salt-free.

Cereals and pasta. Most breakfast cereals, salted porridge and pasta if cooked with salt in the water. Ravioli, gnocchi, and other special pasta also; rice cooked in salted water.

Cheese. All cheeses.

Condiments and garnishes. All commercial pickles, commercial sauces and chutneys, French mustards, horseradish sauce, tomato paste (except Cirio brand).

Eggs. When cooked with added salt.

Fats, oil, and cream. Salted butter and margarine, bacon fat.

Fish. Bloaters, kippers, smoked haddock, salt herrings, shell fish, tinned fish, fish paste, roll mops, smoked cods' roe, smoked salmon and eel, golden fillets, fish fingers, and other prepared fish, fresh or frozen.

Fruit. Olives, candied peel, crystallized fruits, dried fruits other than prunes unless in small amounts.

Meat. Bacon, ham, sausages, tinned meat and poultry, shop-cooked meats and pies, meat pastes, pickled meats, pressed beef, salt pork, tongue, jellied veal, brawn.

Milk. Milk has a fairly high sodium content and therefore the amount allowed is usually controlled.

Nuts. All salted nuts, peanut butter.

Preserves. Golden syrup and treacle, mincemeat, lemon curd.

Puddings. All commercial packet and tinned puddings. Home-made ones unless specially made for the diet. Junket and milk puddings.

Sauces, soups, and stocks. All commercial sauces (except Dietade), soup cubes, Marmite (except the special salt-free one), Bovril, Oxo, bouillon cubes, meat extracts, canned and packet soups, gravy powders, home-made soups with added salt.

Sugar and sugar confectionery. Golden syrup and treacle, milk chocolate, cream toffees, liquorice.

Vegetables. All cooked in salted water, frozen vegetables with added salt, tinned vegetables unless specially made for a low-salt diet (Dietade).

Fitting in with Family Meals

A low-salt diet does entail more home cooking than most other diets. Most people find salt restriction a great hardship, and the family will probably not be willing to eat completely unsalted food, especially vegetables, sauces, and made-up dishes. There are two ways of dealing with this problem:

1. Cook the food without salt, remove the diet portion, and salt the rest before serving.
2. Cook and serve unsalted and let the family salt their own food at table.

If the patient is allowed salt substitutes (see page 139), these may be added before serving or at table.

Since food cooked without salt tends to be uninteresting in flavour you will find it a help to use spices, herbs, and other flavourings, perhaps more than you are accustomed to do. It is important to use all possible means to make the diet palatable for the patient, otherwise there is always the danger that he will lose interest in the dull food, eat insufficient, and become undernourished. On the other hand don't overdo the flavouring and give the patient indigestion. A list of suitable flavourings will be found on page 137.

Cakes, pastry, and puddings made with unsalted butter or margarine and with special sodium-free baking powder and plain flour are not very different from ordinary ones and you will probably find that the family accepts them quite happily.

When using any of the special foods listed on page 138, it is wiser to use them only for the patient as many of them are more expensive than normal foods.

Cooking Methods are Important

OUT: A heavy reliance on salt and on bottled sauces (except Dietade) as the main seasoning.

IN: The use of other permitted sauces and seasonings (see

full list, page 140) to make interesting flavours and help disguise the lack of salt. Here are some examples:

Pork. Apple sauce, sage and onion stuffing with unsalted breadcrumbs and no added salt, grilled, fried, or baked apple slices, fried, roast, or boiled onions, garlic, spiced apple sauce (No. 97), curry.

Lamb. Unsalted onion sauce (Nos. 82 and 88), redcurrant jelly, unsalted dill or fennel sauce (No. 92), mint sauce (No. 104), mint stuffing with unsalted breadcrumbs (No. 154), garlic, rosemary, curry, pineapple, ginger.

Beef. Unsalted home-made horseradish sauce (No. 102), roast onions, mustard, marjoram, nutmeg, onion, sage, thyme, bay leaf, sweet peppers, mushrooms, curry.

Liver. Fried or grilled apple rings, fried onions, grilled or fried mushrooms and tomatoes.

White fish. Parsley butter made with unsalted butter (No. 99), lemon, unsalted Italian tomato sauce (No. 106), curry, unsalted mustard sauce (No. 86), paprika pepper, bay leaves, mushrooms, marjoram, dill, fennel.

Veal. Lemon rind and juice, rosemary, bay, ginger, marjoram, curry, redcurrant jelly, sweet pickled fruit (No. 153) (home-made without salt).

Potatoes. Serve boiled ones with plenty of unsalted butter and chopped mint, chives, or onion or parsley, and other herbs for flavouring. Add mace or nutmeg, chopped green peppers.

Poultry. Curry, thyme, rosemary (put a sprig inside a roast chicken instead of stuffing), paprika pepper, mushrooms, sage, parsley, cranberry sauce.

French and runner beans. Marjoram, unsalted butter, nutmeg, unsalted French dressing (No. 114).

Broccoli. Lemon juice and pepper.

Cabbage. Unsalted mustard sauce (No. 86), unsalted dill sauce (No. 92), unsalted butter and lemon juice with sugar.

Carrots. Parsley, unsalted butter and pepper, mint, nutmeg, glazed Vichy carrots (No. 337).

Cauliflower. Nutmeg and unsalted butter.

Peas. Mint, mushrooms, parsley, onion, green peppers, unsalted butter and pepper.

Tomatoes. Basil, marjoram, onion, sugar, French dressing without salt (No. 114).

Asparagus. Lemon and unsalted butter and pepper.

Marrow. Ginger, mace, chopped fried onion.

Other changes in cooking methods:

OUT: The use of self-raising flour and packet cake and pudding mixtures and most 'convenience' foods (see list, page 135).

IN: The use of plain flour and special baking powder (see page 139) and home-made foods except those in the list below.

OUT: Adding bicarbonate of soda when cooking vegetables.

IN: The use of quick cooking by methods which retain colour in vegetables without the use of soda (see No. 329).

Special Foods for Low-Sodium Diets (*For addresses of manufacturers, see Appendix*)

CAUTION. Ask your doctor whether it is necessary and desirable for you to use these foods. Most of them are more expensive than normal foods.

Edosol (Trufood). A low-sodium synthetic milk powder. This is a help in diets where the amount of ordinary milk allowed is restricted to that used in beverages and you want to use milk for puddings and other cooking. It is also useful for increasing the protein content of the diet without adding to the salt content.

Casilan (Glaxo). This is a low-sodium, high-protein powder made from milk; if the patient has been recommended to have a high-protein diet this is a useful way of giving it without extra sodium.

Dietade foods. This firm make special low-sodium foods such as tomato ketchup (approx. 14 mg. sodium per oz.), salad cream (approx. 6 mg. sodium per oz.), canned baked beans and canned processed peas, mint flavoured (both approx. 5 mg. of sodium per oz.).

Unsalted bread. If this is prescribed it can be made at home (see Nos. 515 and 516). It can also be bought from most bakeries if you place a regular order. In London the Co-operative stores will get it to order; Harrods and Selfridges both sell it.

Rakusen's Unsalted Matzo Biscuits.

Kosher Margarine and Unsalted Butter. Obtainable from most grocers.

Salt-free Ryvita. Available in 3-lb. cartons direct from the manufacturer (see Appendix).

Salt-free Marmite. Obtainable in 4-oz. and 8-oz. jars.

Potassium Glutamate. A substance which brings out flavour in food and so helps disguise the lack of salt. Ask your doctor if you may have it. (Obtainable from chemists.)

Salt substitutes. Selora (Bayer products), which can be used in cooking or at table if your doctor says you may use it. Ruthmol (British Ethical Proprieties Ltd) and Therasal (Thomas Kerfoot and Co. Ltd) are also salt substitutes, but all three of these contain potassium chloride, which you may not be allowed to have.

Sodium-free baking powder. Any chemist will make this up for you. Store in a screw-topped jar and use half as much again as with ordinary baking powder.

Potassium bicarbonate	38·8 g.
Starch	28·0 g.
Tartaric acid	7·5 g.
Potassium bitartrate	56·1 g.

Foods Usually Allowed

CAUTION. Check this list with your doctor or dietitian and do not add to it without asking.

Beverages. Black tea and coffee or use milk from the allowance, or Edosol, lemonade, fruit squashes, fresh or tinned fruit juices, tonic and soda water, wines and spirits as allowed by the doctor. Use Edosol for night-cap drinks made with, for example, arrowroot (see No. 21), or enriched gruel (No. 22). (Up to one teaspoon of Ovaltine may be allowed daily; ask about this.)

Biscuits. Rakusen's unsalted Matzo biscuits (also used in

place of bread) or home-made biscuits using ingredients from this list, with no salt, salt-free baking powder and fats, and plain flour. See recipes for almond biscuit (No. 534), lemon biscuit (No. 541), shortbread (No. 547), jumbles (No. 540).

Bread. Unsalted bread may be the only one allowed; ask the doctor. Home-made yeast bread with the salt omitted is suitable (see No. 516). Scones and baking powder breads may be made with plain flour, no salt, unsalted butter or margarine and special baking powder (see page 139). Salt-free Ryvita. See recipe for quickbread (No. 518).

Cakes. Home-made (not packet mixes) without salt and using plain flour, special baking powder, and other ingredients from list of foods allowed. See Victoria sandwich (No. 575), and Madeira cake recipe variations (No. 560). When eggs are restricted those used in cakes should be counted too. Yeast cakes and sweet buns and any recipe without salt and with permitted ingredients from this list are also good.

Cereal and pasta. Serve cereals with milk from allowance, Edosol milk, or fruit juices. Shredded and Puffed Wheat, Puffed Rice. Plain flour only, Matzo meal, rice, spaghetti and other pastas boiled in unsalted water, ravioli, etc., home-made without added salt. Sago, semolina, tapioca, cornflour, custard powder, arrowroot, oatmeal porridge cooked without salt.

Cheese. Home-made cottage cheese, but it needs plenty of herbs and curry or paprika pepper to make up for the lack of salt, and must be made from naturally soured milk, not with rennet.

Condiments and garnishes. Pepper, curry powder (in small amounts), paprika pepper, vinegar, lemon juice, mustard (bottled French mustard has salt added); see recipe for home-made French mustard (No. 114). Herbs fresh or dried, horse-radish fresh and Heinz dried, salt substitutes if allowed, Dietade tomato ketchup and bottled salad cream, salt-free Marmite, spices, mushrooms, mustard and cress, potassium glutamate if allowed. Have a special condiment tray for the patient with salt substitute and home-made French mustard or chutney, pepper, and vinegar on it. Wine and sherry added to meat dishes before serving help flavouring. See also flavouring suggestions on page 137.

Eggs. As allowed by the doctor. They may be limited to one or two daily including eggs used in cooking. Two-thirds of the sodium is in the whites, so three yolks become equivalent in sodium content to one whole egg. Cook in any way, but omit salt and use salt-free baking powder, butter, or margarine. For thickening puddings and sauces, two egg yolks are equivalent to one whole egg. Use the whites to make meringues (No. 563), angel cake (No. 548), or fruit soufflé (No. 407) for the family.

Fats, oils, and cream. Unsalted butter and margarine (kosher), cooking fat, lard, oils, double cream, home-made dripping. Unsalted butter does not keep as well as salted, so be careful to store it in a cold place and use it up fairly quickly.

Fish. Fresh fish in moderation, home cooked in any way as long as the salt is left out and unsalted butter or margarine used. Fresh cod's roe and herring roe. Fried fish if the batter has no salt in it or if the fish only is eaten.

Fruit. All except olives, candied peel, dried fruit (dates and prunes allowed).

Meats. In moderation. Fresh beef, veal, lamb, pork, liver, poultry, sweetbreads, tripe, home cooked in any way so long as no salt is used and all butter or margarine is unsalted. Rabbit has the lowest sodium content of all meats.

Milk. Fresh liquid milk may be restricted to $\frac{1}{2}$ pt daily or less, for drinking and cooking. Edosol and Casilan are usually allowed in addition.

Nuts. All unsalted nuts allowed.

Preserves. Any except lemon curd and mincemeat.

Puddings. All must be home-made (but not packet mixes) without salt and with special baking powder (page 139), plain flour, and unsalted fat. When eggs are restricted those used in puddings must be counted too. Plain jellies, fresh, canned frozen, and stewed fruit. Suitable puddings are: bread puddings using unsalted bread, and other salt-free ingredients, fruit pies, flans and jam tarts using pastry made with plain flour and unsalted fats, fruit charlottes using salt-free bread-crumbs and salt-free butter, fruit crumble (No. 410) using plain flour and salt-free butter or margarine. Sponge pudding (No. 504), milk puddings with milk from the allowance, or Edosol milk, and unsalted butter or margarine.

Sauces and gravies. Home-made with unsalted ingredients. See basic sauces (No. 88) with unsalted fat and plain flour for the roux. Use herbs, spices, and vinegar for the seasoning. Dietade tomato ketchup and salad cream, unsalted gravy browning. See also chutney recipe (No. 150), relish recipe (No. 151). Other well-flavoured sauces are Nos. 96–100, 102, 106–7, 110, 119.

Soups and stocks. Unsalted bone and vegetable stock, unsalted Marmite. Soups tend to be very unpalatable without salt and most patients would prefer to go without. Serve fruit juices instead, fresh fruit cocktails, or hors d'œuvre with ingredients from list.

Sugars and sugar confectionery. Honey and all other sugars except syrup and treacle. Glucose, barley sugar, all boiled sweets, marshmallows, Turkish delight, peppermints.

Vegetables. All (except beetroot, spinach, and raw celery), fresh cooked without salt or soda and with unsalted butter or margarine. Unsalted sauces, Cirio's tomato purée and peeled whole tomatoes, Heinz strained peas, Dietade tinned peas and beans. (Read the labels.)

Meal-Pattern

On waking. Tea (using milk from the allowance or Edosol) or fruit juice.

Breakfast. Permitted cereal (with milk from allowance) or Edosol or fruit juice. Egg from allowance or meat or fish from the list or Dietade beans on toast or grilled or fried tomatoes and mushrooms. Salt-free bread and butter or margarine, with preserves from the list. Tea or coffee with milk from the allowance or Edosol.

Mid-morning. Beverage.

Midday. Fruit juice, grapefruit or melon, or home-made unsalted soup. Small portion meat or fish from the list. Vegetables. Pudding from the list. Tea or coffee as breakfast.

Tea. Tea as before. Salt-free bread and butter with preserves from the list and lettuce or tomato. Home-made cakes, biscuits, using ingredients from the list.

Evening.

CAUTION. Many patients who need a low-salt diet will have difficulty in digesting anything but a light evening meal.

Small amount of fish or meat dish. Vegetables or salad or fresh or stewed fruit. Salt-free bread and butter or margarine. Home-made cake or biscuit.

Bedtime. Any beverage from list. Use Edosol milk if necessary.

Eating Out

The choice is restricted because of the wide use of salt in normal cooking.

First course. Fruit juice, melon, grapefruit, fruit cocktail.

Eggs (if allowed). Boiled, or poached on toast without butter.

Fish. Fried in batter (leave the batter), grilled with lemon.

Meats. Roast or poultry (no gravy), grilled steak or chop or chicken.

Vegetables. Baked potatoes or chips, grilled tomatoes, undressed salads (or ask the waiter to leave salt out when he makes French dressing).

Puddings. Canned and stewed fruit, jellies, plain and fruit. Raw fruit, fruit salad, baked apple.

For other items see permitted foods, page 139.

Sandwich Meals

Breads. Salt-free breads if necessary, scones with sodium-free baking powder, Matzo biscuits, salt-free Ryvita.

Spreads. Salt-free butter or margarine if prescribed.

Sandwich fillings. Salt-free Marmite filling, cucumber, tomato, lettuce. Egg, meat, or fish in amounts allowed.

Sweet course. Jam or honey on salt-free bread, home-made biscuit or cake, barley sugar, marshmallow, Turkish delight.

Extras. Nuts – any unsalted ones. Fruit – any raw or cooked carried in a container.

Beverages. Tea, coffee, permitted milk, lemonade, fruit squashes and fruit drinks, tonic or soda water.

A suitable meal would consist of:

2 or more substantial sandwiches, with permitted amounts of egg, meat, or fish.

1 or more sweet sandwiches or an alternative of cake, biscuit, or sweet.

Any fruit.

Beverage.

Dinner Menus

As patients should be careful not to overeat, two courses are probably sufficient, or three very small ones, e.g. half the normal portion.

1

Braised liver (No. 299)
Roast potatoes
Brussels sprouts
Caramel oranges (No. 430)

2

Tomato and salt-free Marmite soup (No. 73)
Soused fish and salad (No. 243)
Matzos and salt-free butter
Apple flan with salt-free pastry

3

Grilled pork chop
Spiced apple sauce (No. 97)
Glazed onions (No. 347)
Sauté potatoes
Tomato, lettuce, and watercress to garnish
Fruit meringue (No. 398)

4

Fresh tomato juice
Grilled lamb cutlets rubbed with ground ginger before cooking
Grilled pineapple
Fried potatoes
Stewed pears
Caramel sauce (No. 131 or 132)

5

Orange and grapefruit cup (No. 431)
Roast beef with mixed roast vegetables (e.g. potatoes, onions, carrots)
Home-made horseradish sauce (No. 102) *or* fresh-grated horseradish
Fruit in jelly (No. 464)

6

Fruit soup (No. 59)
Hungarian fish stew (No. 226)
Potatoes mashed with salt-free butter and parsley
Lettuce salad with salt-free dressing (No. 110) or Dietade dressing
Lemon cream (No. 481)
Jumbles (No. 540)

7

Tomato juice jelly (No. 362)
Fish with garlic (No. 219)
Salad
Salt-free rolls (No. 515)
Peach flan

8

Fruit juice
Fillet of sole with mushroom sauce (No. 105)
Sauté potatoes
Grilled tomatoes
Pear condé (No. 495)

9

Grilled grapefruit (No. 426)
Stew (No. 267) with low-sodium dumplings (No. 156)
Broccoli with lemon juice and pepper
Fruit juice custard (No. 397)
Almond biscuit (No. 534)

10

Rabbit stew (No. 309)
Baked jacket potatoes with pepper and unsalted butter
Vichy carrots (No. 337)
Fruit salad with double cream

11

Tomato juice
Tripe soubise with salt-free Marmite (No. 316)
Boiled potatoes with plenty of unsalted butter
Fresh fruit in lemon jelly (No. 467)
Biscuit (No. 541)

12

Fruit cocktail (No. 395)
Veal stewed with sherry (No. 328)
Fried potatoes
Swedish apple cake (No. 416) (made with salt-free crumbs and butter)

13

Liver Shashlik (No. 307)
Fried apple and fried potato
Steamed salt-free sponge (No. 504)
Jam sauce (No. 143)

14

Squab hot-pot (No. 296)
Dietade peas
Blackcurrant jelly with green grapes and cream (No. 465)

High Tea or Supper Menus

NOTE. See caution on page 143.

1

Cold lean roast pork with chutney (No. 150)
Sliced tomatoes dressed with sugar, oil, and vinegar
Salt-free bread and butter
Victoria sandwich (No. 575)

2

Creamed fish (No. 216)
Mashed potatoes (No. 349 c)
Fried tomatoes
Fresh fruit salad
Biscuit (No. 541)

3

Chicken and mushroom salad (No. 373)
Salt-free crispbread with salt-free butter
Ripe banana
Biscuit (No. 534)

4

Turbot bonne femme (No. 212)
Lettuce salad with salt-free dressing (No. 114)
Melba toast with salt-free butter
Orange and grapefruit cup (No. 431)

5

Fried fresh cod's roe (No. 210) with lemon
Salt-free bread and butter
Jellied apple (No. 412)

6

Liver pilaf (No. 305) with fried mushroom and tomato
Salad of grapes and tangerines (No. 427)

7

Cold roast veal with sweet pickled pears (No. 153)
Sliced tomatoes
Matzos and salt-free butter
Fresh stewed or canned greengages *or* yellow plums, with sliced banana

8

Curried sweetbreads (No. 312)
Home-made chutney (No. 150)
Boiled rice
Raw fruit
Madeira cake (No. 560)

9

Meat jelly made with rabbit (No. 281)
Orange salad (No. 387)
Melba toast and salt-free butter
Jam tart with salt-free pastry and cream

10

Fish with pineapple sauce (No. 221)
Salt-free crispbread and salt-free butter
Orange and rhubarb compôte (No. 433)
Biscuit (No. 547)

11

Grilled beef patties (No. 262)
Grilled mushrooms and tomatoes
Salt-free bread *or* crispbread, and butter
Baked apples stuffed with nuts and jam (No. 414)

12

Cold steamed trout with horse-radish sauce (No. 102)
Matzos and salt-free butter
Grapefruit and prune salad (No. 424)

13

Dietade pea soup (No. 68)
Salt-free Melba toast and butter
Raw fruit
Victoria sandwich (No. 575)

14

Fried fresh soft roes on salt-free toast with pepper and lemon
Stuffed oranges (No. 432)

Celebration Meals

1

Cold poached trout with lemon wedges
Grilled spring chicken
Lettuce salad (ask waiter to leave salt out of dressing)
Game chips
Raw fruit

2

Melon and ginger
Grilled fillet or rump steak
Chipped potatoes
Lettuce salad (ask waiter to leave salt out of dressing)
Fresh fruit salad or jellied fruit and cream

DIET WITH MODIFIED OR LOW ANIMAL-FAT CONTENT

Sometimes prescribed for arteriosclerosis, atherosclerosis and thrombosis, see pages 130–33.

How the Normal Diet is Modified

The normal diet is modified by reducing the amount of fats such as meat fat, milk, cream and butter, margarine, cooking fat, lard, cheese, and egg-yolk, and using some oils instead, the best being corn oil, safflower, sunflower seed oil, soya bean oil, and fish oils.

The total amount of animal fat to use will be prescribed by the doctor.

It is usual to restrict the amount of butter or margarine, the number of eggs, and the amount of whole milk. Restricting butter or margarine means less vitamin A and D in the diet. Liberal amounts of fruit and vegetables such as green vegetables, carrots, and tomatoes, or fruit such as apricots and prunes, will supply carotene, and liver is a low-fat meat very rich in vitamin A. A liberal use of herrings, fresh or preserved (e.g. 1 lb. a week), will provide vitamin D.

Cod-liver oil or halibut-liver oil will provide vitamins A and D.

When the patient has been advised to take large quantities of oil these can be given as a pre-meal drink, either mixed with fruit juice or with tomato juice, plain or as a cocktail, No. 71.

Cooked vegetables dressed with oil, seasoning, and a dash of vinegar or lemon juice can be served as hors d'œuvre or salad. Potato salad dressed while warm absorbs a lot of oil. Many fried foods, especially potatoes and bread, absorb considerable quantities of oil but be careful not to let it get smoking hot or the oil will change composition and be less beneficial.

Some patients may be instructed to reduce the intake of sugar. No sugar will be allowed in tea, coffee or other drinks, and jam, jelly, honey and other foods containing a lot of sugar will only be allowed in moderation.

Fitting in with Family Meals

There should be no difficulty about this as foods cooked with oil are very palatable and should be enjoyed by all the family.

The rest of the family can have additional butter or margarine on their bread, melted as a sauce for vegetables and in the form of cream on fruit and puddings. It would be a wise precaution to see that any children in the family have cod-liver or halibut-liver oil to make sure they have enough vitamins A and D.

Cooking Methods are Important

OUT: All cooking with ordinary solid fats such as butter, margarine, dripping, cooking fat, and lard.

IN: Cooking with oil in amounts allowed by the diet or with special margarine, if allowed (see page 150).

If you have not been accustomed to using oil in cooking you will find it a big improvement in frying and also in such operations as grilling when the oil can easily be brushed over foods before cooking. When frying, do not allow the oil to smoke.

For cakes, puddings, and pastry a different technique is sometimes needed. The general method with cakes is to beat eggs, oil, and sugar together and add to the dry ingredients. Cakes which normally have melted fat as an ingredient can have oil substituted without altering the method. See Nos. 486, 517, 553 and 554, 565, 568, 570.

For sauces the oil is used to make a roux in the same way as with solid fat, but slightly less is usually needed.

Proportions for sauces

1 tablespoon of oil to 2 level tablespoons of flour to ½ pt (1 c.) liquid *or*

1 tablespoon of oil to 1 level tablespoon of cornflour to ½ pt liquid.

See also No. 79.

NOTE. Where oil is given in fl. oz. measure it like milk. 10 fl. oz. equals ½ pt or 1 fl. oz. oil equals approx. 2 tbs.

Special margarine (if allowed) can be used in any recipe to replace ordinary butter or margarine.

Useful Special Foods (*For addresses of suppliers see Appendix.*)

Liquid skimmed milk is usually prescribed in place of full-cream milk. It can be bought in crown-stoppered bottles from many dairies, but if not available skim at home (unless the diet is very low fat) or use Alfonal milks (see below).

Instant dried skimmed milk may be used in place of the liquid skimmed milk; it is often easier to obtain, and can be stored more easily. When reconstituted it can be used in place of whole liquid milk in beverages and all cooking. It can be added in dry form to flour when making cakes and puddings and then water can be used as the mixing liquid.

Machine-skimmed sweetened condensed milk may be used in place of liquid milk for puddings and sweet beverages. Alfonal separated milk may be prescribed by the doctor and is available in tins as a liquid milk or as evaporated milk and can be used in place of ordinary milk for all purposes.

Oils. Those usually recommended as being the best for this diet are safflower oils, sunflower seed oil, corn oil and soya bean oil. Peanut oil is also frequently allowed. These are usually sold by grocers and chemists under the proprietary name of the manufacturer, but the name of the oil should also appear on the label.

Mayonnaise made with corn oil by Alfonal.

Cheese Spread made with skimmed milk cheese, the cream of the milk being replaced by corn oil (Alfonal).

Margarine with a high percentage of permitted oils, e.g. Alfonal, Flora and Blue Band.

Cod-liver oil (from the chemist). A certain amount of this may be prescribed. It contains vitamins A and D lacking in most other oils.

Foods Usually Allowed

Beverages. Skimmed milk or special milks (e.g. Alfonal) in tea and coffee. Fruit juices, soft drinks, wines, spirits, beers, and cider (ask about these). Canned or fresh vegetable juices.

Biscuits. Plain (e.g. water), made with oil (see No. 545), or with special margarine, without fat (see Nos. 539, 543, and 546), and any recipe using other permitted ingredients.

Breads. Any kind.

Cakes. Fatless ones, e.g. angel cake (Nos. 548 and 549), meringues (Nos. 562 and 563), sponges (Nos. 569 and 573) (if whole eggs allowed), Pavlova (No. 564), raisin cookies (No.

546), gingerbread (No. 557), treacle loaf (No. 525); cakes made with oil, e.g. fruit cakes (No. 553 and 554), queen cakes (No. 565), sponge sandwich (No. 570), Genoese sponge (No. 568). Cakes made with special margarines if allowed (see page 150). Use any recipe which has other permitted ingredients.

Cereals and pasta. Any kind. Use oil for making sauces for spaghetti, etc.

Cheese. Low-fat cottage cheese (No. 161) and Alfonal cheese spread usually allowed freely.

Condiments and garnishes. Any allowed.

Eggs. Sometimes excluded or restricted to one daily, including those in cooking. Egg whites allowed freely (see cake and pudding section).

Fats, oils, and cream. Those allowed are usually chosen from corn oil, sunflower seed oil, soya bean or safflower oil, or cod-liver oil and there may be a prescribed amount of oil to be taken daily. Special margarines may be allowed (see page 150). Peanut butter usually allowed. Butter and cream and the total amounts of fat may be restricted; follow the doctor's advice.

Fish. Any usually allowed. Oil usually advised for the cooking.

Fruit. Any allowed.

Meat. Lean beef, lamb, veal, poultry in amounts prescribed, and either baked, grilled, boiled, or stewed, using oil for cooking. The following meats will probably be excluded because of their high fat and/or cholesterol content; pork, sausages, bacon, liver, sweetbreads, brains, goose, duck, canned luncheon meats and chopped pork.

Milk. Skimmed or special milk (see pages 149–50).

Nuts. Usually allowed, but make sure.

Preserves. Any except lemon curd and mincemeat.

Puddings and pastry. Pastry made with oil (see No. 486) or with special margarine (if allowed). Steamed puddings with oil (see Nos. 501 and 502), fatless puddings, e.g. water ices, sherbets (Nos. 456–60), jellies (Nos. 464–71) and meringues (Nos. 562 and 563), skimmed milk puddings (No. 493), fruit whips (No. 408), fruit in any way.

Sauces and gravies. Fatless (Nos. 120–9) or made with permitted oils and fats (see recipes). Salad creams, mayonnaise, and French dressing made with oil (see Nos. 113–17) may be allowed if the total fat in the diet is not restricted (ask about this).

Soups and stocks. Any fat-free stocks, consommé, cream soups made with oil sauce and skimmed milk (Nos. 76 and 77), or a fatless sauce, yeast and meat extracts.

Sugar and sugar confectionery. Any sugars. Boiled sweets, fondants, jellied sweets, marshmallows.

Vegetables. Any fresh, frozen, or tinned. Sauces made with oil or other permitted fat (see recipes).

Meal-Pattern

On waking. Fruit juice or tea, with permitted milk.

Breakfast. Any cereal with permitted milk or fruit juice. Cold meats (in amounts prescribed), kippers, fish kedgeree, grilled fish, or poached haddock. Bread and permitted fats, preserves. Tea or coffee, with permitted milk.

Mid-morning. Any beverage allowed.

Midday. Soup or hors d'œuvre from the list allowed. Meat or fish (usually not more than 3 oz. meat allowed, but more of fish if desired), vegetables. Sweet or cheese from the list.

Tea. Any beverage allowed. Small portion of permitted cake or biscuits.

Evening. Meat (in amounts prescribed) or fish, vegetables or salad. Fresh fruit, sweet from the list, pastry, or cake made with oil.

Bedtime. Beverage from the list.

Eating Out

Choose simple dishes rather than complex ones where the ingredients are unknown.

Soups. Consommé or clear soups, fruit juices or tomato juice, or vegetable juice.

Hors d'œuvre. Melon, grapefruit, fruit cocktail, fish, and vegetables which are usually dressed with oil and vinegar or oil mayonnaise.

Fish. Fried fish, grilled fish with lemon.

Meat. Roast (without gravy), grills, cold meats, beef, lamb, veal, poultry.

Vegetables. Any except fried or roast or ones like creamed spinach or any vegetable which is served with a sauce.

Puddings. Stewed or fresh fruit, baked apples, plain jelly, plain meringues, water ices, and sherbets.

For other items see permitted list of foods, pages 150–52.

Sandwich Meals

Breads. White, brown, or wholemeal breads, soft rolls, hard rolls, finger rolls, French bread, Vienna bread, cottage loaves, brown rye bread, rye and wheat crispbread, pumpernickel, oatcake.

Spreads. Fats from the allowance (see also fatless diet, page 102).

Sandwich fillings. Permitted cheese, meat, fish (see No. 527), eggs if not restricted, salad vegetables with oil mayonnaise and salad oil dressings.

Alternatives to sandwiches. Turnovers and pasties made with oil pastry. Cold fishcakes cooked in oil (see also reducing diet, page 129).

Sweet course. Permitted cakes and biscuits, tarts and turnovers with oil pastry, permitted puddings in cartons.

Fruits. Any kind.

Beverages. Any from the list.

A suitable meal would consist of:

2 substantial savoury sandwiches with permitted cheese, meat, or fish filling, or alternatives (see above).

1 item from the sweet course.

Fresh fruit.

Beverage.

Lunch, High Tea, or Supper Menus

CAUTION. Slimmers and those on a restricted sugar intake should have raw fruit instead of the puddings, or substitute a pudding from the low-calorie diet (page 121); only use these menus if the ingredients fit in with your diet prescription.

1

Crab salad (No. 376)
Bread or roll (No. 517)
Fresh fruit

2

Fish kedgeree (No. 227)
Lettuce salad
Compôte of prunes and cider (No. 435)

3

Creamed veal in potato nest (No. 322)
Green peas
Stuffed oranges (No. 432)

4

Fish casserole (No. 213)
Mashed potatoes with oil (No. 349)
Port wine jelly (No. 471)

5

Potted meat (No. 264) with
Endive, beetroot, and watercress salad
Crusty rolls
Fresh fruit

6

Stewed kidney (No. 285)
Mashed potatoes with oil (No. 349 g)
Waldorf salad (No. 394)

7

Veal mould (No. 325)
Tomato and sweet pepper salad (No. 392)
Rolls
Fresh fruit

8

Swiss salad (No. 391)
Rolls or bread
Jellied apples (No. 412)

9

Cod à la boulangère (No. 206) using oil
Baked tomatoes
Fruit meringue (No. 398)

10

Fried cod's roe (No. 210) with lemon wedges
Tomato and cucumber salad with oil dressing
Toast
Fresh fruit

11

Cottage cheese salad (No. 378) with tangerines
Bread or rolls
Pears in red wine sauce (No. 434)

12

Scalloped scallops (No. 236)
Mashed potato (No. 349 g)
Grilled tomatoes
Fresh fruit in cider jelly (No. 476)

13

Lamb cutlets in aspic (No. 288 or 289)
Potato salad (No. 390)
Tomato salad (No. 393)
Fruit purée dessert (No. 405)

14

Chicken and mushroom salad (No. 373)
Rolls
Gooseberry and banana compôte (No. 423)

Dinner Menus

1

Tomato bouillon (No. 70)
Sole aux crevettes (No. 239)
Potato purée with oil (No. 349 g)
Strawberry flan with oil pastry (No. 486)

2

Low-fat spinach soup (No. 76)
Oven-fried fish (No. 204) with wedges of lemon
Baked or grilled tomatoes
Mashed potatoes with oil (No. 349 b)
Lemon water ice (No. 457) *or* sherbet (No. 458)

3

Low-fat asparagus soup (No. 76)
Sole or plaice voisin (No. 241)
Sauté potatoes (oil)
Grapefruit and beetroot salad (No. 382)
Angel cake (No. 548 or 549)

4

Tomato juice frappé (No. 72)
Roast chicken with oil (No. 276)
Roast potatoes with oil (No. 356)
Carrots and brussels sprouts
Ripe pears with caramel sauce (No. 132)

5

Jellied consommé
Fish creole (No. 217)
Sauté potatoes with oil
Lettuce salad, oil dressing
Pineapple sherbet (No. 456)

6

Bouillon (packet or canned)
Skillet of beef and beans (No. 265)
Boiled rice
Snow custard (No. 444)
Fruit salad with cider (No. 406)

7

Shrimp and orange cocktail (No. 208)
Grilled lamb chops with herbs (No. 287)
Mashed potatoes (No. 349 b)
Grilled tomato
Cauliflower and parsley sauce made with oil (No. 79)
Port wine jelly (No. 471)

8

Consommé
Veal stewed with sherry (No. 328)
Baked potato
Spinach
Tangerine flan with oil pastry (No. 478)

9

Orange and grapefruit cup (No. 431)
Roast lamb with rice stuffing (No. 294)
Carrots and peas
Crème de menthe jelly (No. 470)

10

Onion soup (No. 67)
American meat loaf (No. 258)
Oil roast potatoes (No. 356)
Broccoli with lemon
Fruit meringue (No. 398)

11

Mixed vegetable soup (No. 46)
Ragoût of kidney (No. 284)
Boiled potatoes
Braised celery
Apple tart with oil pastry (No. 486)

12

Prawn cocktail (No. 209)
Baked chicken and pineapple (No. 268)
Roast potatoes with oil (No. 356)
Green peas
Mango fool (No. 429)
Raisin cookies (No. 546)

13

Tomato juice cocktail (No. 71)
Fried chicken with almonds (No. 271)
Sauté potatoes
Apple snow (No. 413) with meringue (No. 562)

14

Purée of green pea soup (No. 76)
Marinaded steak (No. 266)
Potatoes fried in oil
Watercress
Grapefruit and prune salad (No. 424)

Celebration Meals

1

Consommé
Cold lobster and rémoulade sauce (No. 116)
Lettuce salad
Boiled potatoes or potato salad
Water ice (Nos. 456–60) *or* fresh fruit
Coffee

2

Hors d'œuvre from list of permitted food (restaurant ones are usually oil-dressed)
Grilled entrecôte steak
Chips (usually oil-cooked)
Lettuce salad and French dressing
Raspberries or strawberries with liqueur *or*
Fresh fruit
Coffee

CHAPTER 8

Diseases of the Kidneys and Urinary Tract

THE function of the kidneys is to remove waste products from the blood and then excrete them in the form of urine. The urine is formed in the glomerulus of the kidney. It is very dilute and contains many substances the body does not want to eliminate. During its passage through the tubules water is reabsorbed to concentrate the urine and also the minerals, sugar, and other

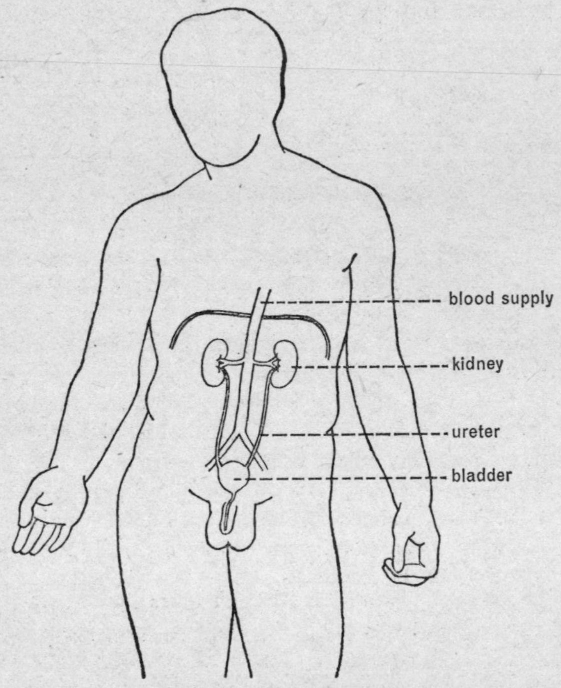

The kidneys and urinary tract

substances the body still requires. Finally the urine passes out of the kidney to the bladder for elimination from the body.

In addition to the large amounts of water in urine, there are waste products from the normal and abnormal breakdown of

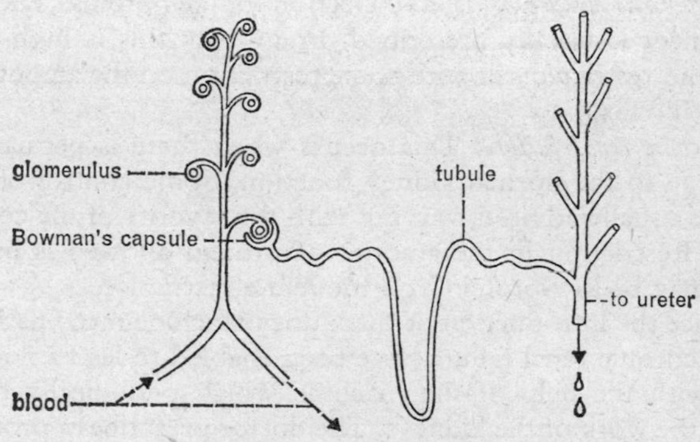

The main part of the kidney

protein in metabolism. In certain kidney diseases these products are retained by the body and hence the restriction of the amount of protein in the diet.

The kidneys are also an important means whereby the body gets rid of excess acid, by excreting an acid urine.

Many minerals, including sodium, are also eliminated in urine and where this mechanism fails, as in salt retention, a low-sodium diet may be necessary.

As the kidneys depend on a normal blood supply to enable them to function properly, an inefficient blood supply (e.g. in cardiac failure) means inefficient kidneys, and oedema (water retention) frequently results.

Diet is an important part of the control of many kidney diseases. It will vary with the form the disease takes and with the special needs of the patient. The doctor's prescription must, therefore, be carefully followed. The diet may control either the amount of protein (low or high), or the amount of salt, or fluid, or a combination of these.

Nephritis is due to inflammation in the glomerulus of the kidney. The diet prescribed may be fluids only, or a low-protein diet or a low-sodium diet (page 134); or fluids may be restricted.

Nephrotic syndrome is a collection of symptoms. Dietary treatment is usually prescribed. Frequently this is high-protein and restricted salt with some restriction on the amount of fluid allowed.

Chronic renal failure. This occurs when there is permanent damage to the normal kidney function. Some control of the diet is usually advised, varying with the severity of the condition. Restriction in the amount of protein allowed is usual, and may be low-protein or a moderate restriction.

Since the introduction of the kidney machine many patients with chronic renal failure have been enabled to lead a normal life with the help of the machine which periodically takes over the work of the kidneys. The doctor prescribes a protein-controlled diet for each individual patient.

THE LOW-PROTEIN DIET

How the Normal Diet is Modified

Foods contributing most protein to the normal diet are: meat, fish, poultry, eggs, milk, cheese, bread, and cereals. These, therefore, have to be restricted to very small portions.

Fruit and vegetables are freely allowed and a good intake of fat and sugar to provide energy.

Sometimes the salt is restricted as well as protein; no salt may be allowed at table or in cooking, and salty foods are restricted, as in a low-sodium diet (see page 134).

Fitting in with Family Meals

If the patient is simply on a low-protein diet, there is no difficulty, as the restriction is mainly one of the size of the portions of normal foods providing protein.

Some low-protein diets do, however, have to continue for a long time and can become very monotonous. In these cases an occasional specially designed meal such as those given in the menus on pages 166–8 will be appreciated. If these are used for family cooking additional protein will be needed for the rest of the family, especially children and teenagers, but this can be supplied by giving a milk drink or milky soup, a pudding made with milk, or biscuits and cheese as well as or instead of the pudding.

Foods Usually Allowed

Beverages. Tea and coffee using milk from the allowance, fruit drinks, lemonade, orangeade, vegetable juices. The total amounts of fluid allowed may be restricted.

Biscuits. Usually not more than one small portion of either biscuits or cake allowed per day.

Breads. Only in amounts prescribed by the doctor (see exchange list, page 163).

Cakes. See biscuits.

Cereals, starches, and pasta. Breakfast cereals, wheat-flour, and pasta, only in amounts allowed by the doctor. Allowed as desired are arrowroot, cornflour, rice, tapioca, sago, and potato flour.

Cheese. Only in amounts prescribed by the doctor (see exchange list, page 164). Probably none allowed if salt is restricted.

Condiments and garnishes. Any allowed except when salt is restricted.

Eggs. Only in amounts prescribed by the doctor (see exchange list, page 164). For low-sodium diets, no salt to be added in cooking.

Fats, oils, and cream. All allowed except cream and peanut butter.

Fish. Any kind but only in amounts prescribed (see exchange list, page 164). The low-sodium diet must omit tinned fish, kippers, bloaters, roll mops, and other pickled fish, smoked salmon, and trout.

Fruit. Any kind. Dried fruit restricted in low-sodium diets.

Meat, game, and poultry. Any kind but only in amounts prescribed (see exchange list, page 164). The low-sodium diet must omit bacon and ham, canned meats, sausages, pickled and salted meats.

Milk. Only in amounts prescribed by the doctor (see exchange list, page 164).

Preserves. Any except lemon curd and peanut butter.

Puddings and pastry. If using milk or eggs these must be taken from the prescribed daily allowance. Wheat-flour also allowed only in prescribed amounts. Avoid puddings containing bread unless this is taken from the day's allowance. Those allowed freely include all stewed fruits, raw, canned, frozen, or baked fruits, fruit salads (see recipe section), water ices (Nos. 457 and 459).

Sauces and gravies. Any made without eggs or milk unless these are taken from the day's allowance. Salt may be restricted.

Soups and stocks. Clear vegetable soups and stocks. If fluids are restricted soups are usually not allowed.

Sugars and sugar confectionery. Any sugars allowed including treacle, syrup, and honey. Boiled sweets.

Vegetables. Any kind except peas, dried beans, lentils, split peas, baked beans, broad beans, unless as exchanges (see list, page 165).

Meal-Pattern

CAUTION. This is to include only the daily amounts of food allowed by the doctor's prescription.

On waking. Tea (with milk from the day's allowance and fluid from the day's allowance).

Breakfast. Fruit, fresh or stewed, or a small glass of fruit juice. Cereal or bread from day's allowance. Tea or coffee (as early morning).

Mid-morning. Tea or coffee with milk from the day's allowance. 1 plain biscuit.

Midday. Meat, poultry, fish, or egg dish from the day's allowance. Permitted vegetables and potato. Pudding from the permitted list (see page 162).

Tea. Bread from allowance with butter, jam, jelly, honey, or made into sandwiches using tomato, lettuce, cucumber, dates, or banana.

Evening. Bread (from allowance) and butter and preserves or a main dish using food from the day's allowance. Fruit, fresh, stewed, or tinned. Tea or coffee (as early morning).

Bedtime. Beverages from day's allowance of fluids and milk.

Quantities of Food Allowed

These will be prescribed by the doctor and will vary with the patient's needs. It is important not to exceed the amounts.

Use the exchange list to build up a diet to suit the patient's taste.

Generous amounts of butter (2 oz. (4 level Tbs.)), sugar (3 oz. (6 level Tbs.)), and boiled sweets are usually allowed.

Protein Exchanges

These are conveniently based on exchanges for the three main types of food controlled: (1) milk; (2) bread and cereals; (3) meat, fish, eggs, and cheese, and certain vegetables such as lentils and beans which are used instead of meat by vegetarians.

Cereal Exchanges for 1 oz. bread. All the following foods contain approximately the same amount of protein (2·2 g.) as 1 oz. bread.

Bread and Breakfast Cereals

Bread	1 slice of a thin-cut large sliced loaf or 1½ slices of a small sliced loaf
Cornflakes	½ pt (1 cup)
Oatmeal porridge	4 level tablespoons
All-Bran	2 level tablespoons
Puffed wheat	3 heaped tablespoons

Rice Krispies	½ pint (1 cup)
Shredded wheat	¾ of a piece
Weetabix	1½ pieces

Biscuits

Cream-crackers	3 biscuits
Water biscuits	2 biscuits
Ryvita	3 biscuits
Vitawheat	3 biscuits

Milk Exchanges. All the following foods contain approximately the same amount of protein (9·0 g.) as 10 fl. oz. or ½ pt milk (1 c.).

Sweetened condensed or evaporated whole milk	¼ pint (½ cup)
Condensed sweetened skimmed milk	¼ pint (½ cup)
Instant dried milk	2 heaped tablespoons

Meat Exchanges. It is the usual practice to take 1 egg (standard size) as the basis for this exchange. All the following foods contain approximately the same amounts of protein (7·0 g.) as 1 egg.

Cheese

Cheddar and similar cheeses	1 oz. or 1 inch cube
Cottage cheese	½ small carton

Meats

Cooked meat, including offal	1 small thin slice
Cooked poultry or game	1 small thin slice
Cooked bacon	1 rasher
Fish	1 small thin fillet

Vegetables used as a Meat Substitute

Peas, boiled or canned	4 heaped tablespoons
Butter beans, boiled or canned	3 level tablespoons
Haricot beans, boiled	3 level tablespoons
Baked beans	4 level tablespoons
Lentils, boiled	$3\frac{1}{2}$ level tablespoons
Split peas, boiled	$3\frac{1}{2}$ level tablespoons
Broad beans, boiled	2 level tablespoons

Nuts (Shelled)

Almonds, Peanuts	1 oz.
Brazils, Walnuts, Cobs	2 oz.
Fresh coconut	6 oz.
Chestnuts	10 oz.

A typical low-protein diet contains a daily allowance of 40 g. of protein containing some milk ($\frac{1}{2}$ pt, 1 c.), bread, and meat.

A typical moderate-protein or 'restricted' protein diet is a daily allowance of about 60 g. of protein made up of the three main groups. It may allow one pint (2 c.) of milk daily. (By comparison a high-protein intake is 100–150 g. daily.)

Lunch, High Tea, or Supper Menus

CAUTION. The actual size of portion will have to be adjusted to the patient's daily allowance as prescribed by the doctor.

Those on a restricted sodium intake will need to omit salt from the recipes and any bacon used in them. For foods allowed in the low-sodium diet see page 139, and for suggestions for flavouring, page 136.

The menus are intended for the convalescent or chronic patient and not for the very sick, who wouldn't want to eat them anyway.

1

Herring fishcake (No. 224)
Lemon wedges
Grilled or baked tomatoes
Celery, apple, and raisin salad
Dressing (No. 109 or 113)

2

Pineapple and lettuce salad (No. 389)
Bread from allowance
Butter
Few grapes and small piece of cheese from allowance

3

Stuffed tomatoes on toast (No. 364)
Sauté potatoes
Fresh fruit salad

4

Mushroom risotto (No. 169)
Celery and sprout salad (No. 372)
Canned peaches

5

Tomato jelly (No. 362)
½ hard-boiled egg
Lettuce salad
Bread from allowance
Fresh fruit

6

Apple and cheese savoury (No. 164) (½ portion)
Bread from allowance
Raspberry water ice (No. 459)

7

Carrot and apple salad (No. 370)
Bread from allowance
Ripe banana

8

Cauliflower with bacon sauce (No. 344)
Mashed potatoes
Stuffed oranges (No. 432)

9

Chicory polonaise (No. 336)
Mashed potatoes
Fresh fruit

10

Vegetables au gratin (No. 330) (method 2)
Sauté potatoes
Baked apple sweetened with black treacle

11

Fish kedgeree (No. 227, variation)
Fresh fruit

12

Beef and lettuce salad with mustard sauce (No. 368)
Lemon sago (No. 497) with fruit salad

13

Potato and bacon cakes (No. 353)
Italian tomato sauce (No. 106)
Lettuce salad
Canned apricots

14

Vegetable ragoût (No. 331)
Bread from allowance, butter
Grapefruit and tangerine salad

Dinner Menus

1

Fish shape (No. 223)
Tomato sauce (No. 106)
Lettuce salad and French dressing
Stuffed stewed apple (No. 415)

2

Lamb or liver risotto (No. 169)
Tomatoes grilled or as salad
Dried fruit compôte (No. 421)

3

White fishcakes (No. 225) with lemon wedges
Celery, lettuce, and raisin salad with French dressing or low-protein dressing (No. 109)
Pineapple and orange mould (No. 436)

4

Stuffed cabbage leaves (No. 343)
Mashed carrots
Jellied apples (No. 412)

5

Steamed chicken and rice (No. 277)
Lettuce salad
Cinnamon apples (No. 411)

6

Asparagus with melted butter
Chestnut stew (No. 339)
Brussels sprouts
Caramel oranges (No. 430)

7

Tomato flan (No. 361)
Baked bananas and prunes (No. 418)

8

Hamburgers (No. 253) in brown sauce (No. 96)
Mashed potatoes (no milk)
Grilled tomato
Spinach
Grapefruit and prune salad (No. 424)

9

Beef mould (No. 260) ($\frac{1}{2}$ portion)
Brown sauce (No. 96)
Carrots and brussels sprouts tossed in butter
Fruit salad with cider (No. 406)

10

Tomatoes à la Provence (No. 363)
Sauté potatoes
Gooseberry and banana compôte (No. 423)

11

Baked stuffed potatoes (No. 348)
American fried cabbage (No. 338)
Lemon water ice (No. 457) with fresh or frozen raspberries

12

Fried potatoes and cheese (No. 350)
Lettuce salad
Fruit purée dessert (No. 405)

13

Grapefruit
Squab hot-pot (No. 296)
Brussels sprouts or cabbage
Blackcurrant water ice (No. 459)

14

Pommes de terre au lard (No. 352)
Waldorf salad (No. 394)
Grapes with tangerine (No. 427)

Celebration Meals

1

Asparagus with melted butter sauce
Chicken liver risotto (No. 169)
Lettuce salad with French dressing
Fresh peaches

2

Globe artichoke with French dressing
Small portion of vol-au-vent
Mixed salad with French dressing
Water ice (No. 459)

Eating Out

Hors d'œuvre. Fruit juices, tomato juice, vegetable juices, vegetables dressed with oil and vinegar.

Fish and meat. Very small portions of any of them.

Vegetables. Any except peas, beans, or lentils and those with a milk or egg sauce.

Pudding. Fruit salad, stewed fruit, fresh fruit, plain and fruit jellies, water ices, and baked apple.

For other items see list of permitted food, page 161.

Sandwich Meals

Breads. Only in amounts prescribed by the doctor (see exchange list, page 163).

Fillings. Meat, fish, eggs, cheese. Only from the day's allowance.

Sweet course. Boiled sweets, fruit, or permitted pudding in containers.

Fruit. Raw of any kind in generous amounts.

Salad vegetable. Also in generous amounts with permitted salad dressing and use them for fillings for sandwiches as well.

Beverages. Any from the list.

NOTE. Some of the dishes from the high-tea and supper

menus could be part of the carried meal, e.g. potato and bacon cakes, herring fish cakes, tomato jelly.

THE HIGH-PROTEIN RESTRICTED-SALT DIET

How the Normal Diet is Modified

By giving generous amounts of protein-rich foods such as eggs, meat, and fish, and by restricting the amount of salt in cooking and at table.

For details see low-sodium diet (page 134).

Because so many foods rich in protein have a high sodium content it is difficult to have a diet of ordinary foods which achieves both objectives.

The way out of the difficulty is to use generous amounts of Casilan (Glaxo) and Edosol (Trufood), both high-protein, low-sodium powders. The low-sodium diet (page 134) would be suitable if these two powders were used for additional milk drinks and milk puddings, to add to all sauces, and to provide additional sauces using salt-free butter and margarine for the roux.

CHAPTER 9

Undernutrition

A SPECIAL diet is not usually prescribed just because people are below their ideal weight but because health has been impaired owing to an excessive loss of body tissue due to undernutrition.

The condition can arise in a variety of ways and the treatment is often difficult. Usually the patient has a very small appetite, which in itself can have various origins, including medical or psychological, such as worry, strain, and even the desire to gain attention. There may be a disease of the intestine which prevents normal absorption of food or a wasting disease which calls for a large intake of food to rebuild the destroyed tissues. Or it may be that the patient has been eating a diet of poorly chosen foods which fail to supply the right nourishment for normal health. This can be due to pronounced food aversions or cranky diets, or just not understanding what constitutes a good basic diet. It can happen to people who eat out a lot and haven't learned to choose wisely from the restaurant menu or how to supplement its defects with what they eat at home, or it can happen in the home where food provided is not a good choice nutritionally.

How the Normal Diet is Modified

If the patient has a good appetite the good normal diet (see page 15) should be adequate. More often the appetite is poor, and then it is necessary to stress the concentrated foods and to give small, frequent meals to ensure an adequate day's total.

Bulky foods are best avoided. Chief among these are:

Raw salads, raw fruits, soup or any other dishes containing a lot of liquid, and large amounts of vegetables.

The concentrated foods are:

Sugar, cheese, dried and evaporated milk, eggs, bread, chocolates, raisins, cream, preserves, fats and oils.

The most concentrated form in which to give the essential vitamin C of fruit and vegetables is in rose-hip syrup or blackcurrant syrup or purée.

Drinking with meals is best avoided by people with small appetites, but if they do want a drink give them high-calorie drinks such as glucose or alcohol.

A small amount of alcohol taken before a meal frequently acts as a stimulant to the appetite as does a small helping of fairly concentrated consommé.

Fitting in with Family Meals

Family meals should be planned to contain normal good food of an easily digested kind, with emphasis on low bulk and high nutritive value.

In addition, encourage the patient to have between-meals snacks either of a fortified fluid (see Nos. 1–13) or of tea or coffee accompanied by thin bread and butter generously spread, and sometimes made into cheese or egg sandwiches; or give a piece of fruit cake or chocolate or raisins.

Popular foods, especially concentrated ones, should be served as often as possible and in as many ways as possible to avoid monotony.

Vegetables may be sieved or put in the electric blender to reduce the bulk and have butter, margarine, or cream added to them.

Any preserves that are popular should be given generously on bread or toast and as sauces for puddings.

Advice to relatives. Try to create a happy relaxed atmosphere at meal times and avoid argument, quarrelling, nagging, and fussing.

Good cooking and service of food. It is very important to get the highest nutritive value, to avoid making it indigestible, and to make it look enticing. For tips on these, see pages 20–24.

Useful Special Foods

In order to increase the nutritive value without adding bulk, there are various preparations which can be usefully added to normal food. This is a great help with a difficult patient with a small appetite who refuses to eat any extra food.

The preparations must be used with care so that too much does not spoil the food and tire the palate or cause digestive difficulty. It is better to use a little and often.

(*For names and addresses of manufacturers see Appendix.*)

Full-cream dried milk to enrich ordinary milk for cooking or in beverages in the proportions of 2 oz. (4 heaped Tbs.) full-cream dried milk to 1 pt (2 c.) liquid milk (use one of the proprietary baby foods sold by chemists).

Instant dried skimmed milk can be used in the same way for those who cannot tolerate extra fat.

Complan (Glaxo) is made from dried milk with vitamins and minerals added. It can be used in beverages and added to other foods. The manufacturer issues a booklet of recipes.

Prosol (Trufood) is a good source of protein and calcium and also supplies vitamins of the B complex and can be used in beverages and added to other foods. The manufacturer issues a booklet of recipes.

Casilan (Glaxo) is a very concentrated source of protein and calcium and can be used to fortify milk for cooking and beverages. The manufacturer issues a book of recipes.

Glucose (from chemist) can be used for sweetening and is less sickly than ordinary sugar. It needs to be dissolved in warm liquid.

Marmite adds B vitamins, sometimes difficult to provide when a person has a small and difficult appetite.

Wheat germ (from chemists and Health Food Stores) provides B vitamins and can be added to breakfast cereal and used in cooking for coating foods and adding with flour or with breadcrumb mixtures.

Blackcurrant syrup and rose-hip syrup are rich in vitamin C and provide this vitamin in a more concentrated form than the bulky fruits and vegetables. Use with water as a drink or in Nos. 11 or 26, 142, 399, 450, 459, 465, 508.

Concentrated Foods for a Person with a Small Appetite

(The choice of foods from this list will vary with the needs of the individual patient, and the doctor should be consulted.)

Beverages. All are allowed. Fortified milk drinks are good between meals (see Nos. 2–13, 17 and 18). A glass of dry wine as an aperitif before a meal helps the appetite.

Biscuits. All are allowed and sweet biscuits have a high calorie value.

Breads. All suitable. Butter toast while hot, as it takes more. Spread all bread liberally. Add dried milk and eggs to home-made breads.

Cakes. All allowed. Serve cake at dinner meals to eat with fruit salad or stewed fruit or as an extra with the coffee.

Cereals and pasta. All are good. Serve breakfast cereals with plenty of sugar and cream, while wheat-germ may be added to increase the vitamin and mineral intake. Add cream, egg, or butter to rice and semolina and other cereal puddings to enrich them. If pasta are popular use them freely.

Cheese is concentrated milk so use as much as possible of any kind the patient likes.

Condiments and garnishes. All allowed, and all are a most important aid to making food attractive and appetizing.

Eggs. Use as many as possible, especially in baking and in puddings, where they increase the nutritive value without adding a lot of bulk, e.g. use them for thickening sauces and soups and adding to milk puddings, or make a variety of custards and omelettes (see also Nos. 14–18, 58, 100, 139, 170–200, 440–3, 463, 479, 568, 575).

Fats, oils, and cream. All allowed and as much as can be tolerated. Use freely in cooking.

Fish. Any kind allowed. To increase the calorie value serve white fish with sauces containing butter, eggs, or cream (see Nos. 98–101, 220, 233, 235, 238).

Fruit. Every kind. Dried fruits are more concentrated than fresh. Provide raisins and dates for eating between meals and use them in cakes and puddings. Instead of raw fruit, use juices rich in vitamin C, e.g. blackcurrant syrup, rose-hip syrup, orange juice, guava juice. Add glucose to stewed fruit and serve with cream.

Meat, game, and poultry. Any kind allowed. Liver and kidney have a specially high nutritive value. Serve thickened gravies and sauces with all meats. Some high-calorie recipes are Nos. 248, 261, 269, 271, 279, 292, 294, 304, 306, 310, 320, 324, 327.

Milk. Use as much as possible in cooking and beverages and, for the very small eater, fortify it with dried milk, Prosol, Casilan, or Complan (see No. 1 e).

For those who can tolerate fat, use milk to which extra cream has been added. Keep a special jug of this mixture for the patient and give the normal milk to the family.

Nuts. All allowed and are good, though somewhat expensive, additions. Peanuts and peanut butter are concentrated, of a high nutritive value, and comparatively cheap. Because of a high cellulose content whole nuts are not well tolerated by everybody.

Preserves. All allowed. Always serve when bread and butter is eaten and use for puddings or in sauces; see Nos. 143 and 146 for puddings and pastry.

Puddings. Milk pudding using fortified milk, cream, and eggs, ice cream, jellies made with cream and egg, sponge puddings with a sauce, egg custard. Other high-calorie puddings are Nos. 402, 416, 419, 420, 437, 439, 445–8, 450–4, 461, 482, 485, 492, 494–6, 498, 508–9.

Sauces and gravies. Serve with meat, fish, puddings, and vegetables and as often as possible. Serve mayonnaise and French dressing with salad; cream or evaporated milk with puddings, or jams or syrup sauces or blackcurrant or rose-hip syrup.

Soups and stocks. These rate as bulky foods and are probably best avoided. If used, the best are small amounts of real meat consommé, which serve as an appetite stimulant before a meal.

For high-tea and supper meals, cream soups are best. Add eggs, cream, or milk to increase the calorie value.

Sugars and sugar confectionery. As much as possible, use glucose as well as sugar to sprinkle on puddings and stewed fruit. Chocolate is especially good. Use it for sauces and cakes as well. Give sweets at the end of a meal rather than between times when they are inclined to take away the appetite.

Vegetables. All are allowed. Vegetables tend to be bulky and for those with small appetites the best are potatoes (with fat, eggs and milk added to them), e.g. fried, sauté (see also Nos. 349–53).

Meal-Pattern

On waking. Milky tea.

Breakfast. Sweetened fruit juice. Cereal sprinkled with wheat germ and with cream and sugar, or a high-calorie porridge (No. 157). Egg or fish. Hot buttered toast and marmalade. Tea or coffee.

Mid-morning. Milky tea or coffee with cream and sugar or a fortified milk drink. Biscuits or bread or toast and butter and preserves.

Midday. Fruit juice or glass of dry wine as aperitif. Meat or fish dish with thick gravy and sauce. Vegetables and potatoes or pasta or rice with butter or margarine or thickened sauce. Pudding and/or biscuits and cheese. Tea or coffee. Sweets or chocolate.

Tea. Bread and butter and jam, or scones with butter and jam. Cake or biscuits.

Evening. Fruit juice or glass of dry wine as aperitif. Meat, fish, egg, or cheese dish with vegetable; or salad with mayonnaise or French dressing. Bread and butter or cream soup with toast. High-calorie pudding or cake. Tea or coffee.

Bedtime. Milk drink (fortified) and biscuits or sandwiches.

Daily Allowance of Basic Foods

Milk. At least 1 pt (2 c.) plus some dried skimmed milk and/or evaporated milk.

Butter or margarine, 2 oz. (4 level Tbs.) daily.

Meat, fish, eggs, or cheese. At least 2 good portions for main meals daily. Use additional eggs and cheese in cooking.

Vegetables and fruit. As in the basic menu plan (page 175).

Bread. At least ½ lb. (8 slices thin-cut large loaf) a day.

Sugar. 2 oz. (4 level Tbs.) or more.

Eating Out

Most restaurant menus are full of high-calorie foods, and choice should not be difficult.

Sandwich Meals

Breads. Any cut thinly and generously spread with butter and other spreads. Protein-enriched breads are good.

Concentrated savoury fillings. Cheese grated and mixed with mayonnaise, eggs mashed with mayonnaise and cream, home-made herring and liver paste (Nos. 303–4, 533), liver sausage, cold meats, peanut butter.

Alternatives. Pieces of cheese or hard-boiled egg to eat with a slice of bread. Sausage rolls made with cheese pastry, and sardine rolls the same. Pasties with meat filling.

Sweet courses. Breads containing dried fruits and nuts generously spread with butter, sponge cake, shortbread biscuits, chocolate biscuits, chocolate and sweets, fruit cake, baked custards. Milky jelly and cream in carton plus sweet biscuits.

Fruit. Small portion of fresh fruit.

Extras. Nuts or dried fruits.

Beverages. Milk drinks with sugar.

A suitable meal might consist of:

2 sandwiches with recommended fillings.
1 of the alternatives.
1 or more from the sweet course.
Fresh fruit and nuts or dried fruits.
Beverage.

Lunch, High Tea, or Supper Menus

1

Cream of chicken soup (No. 54)
Egg and yogurt mould (No. 194) with lettuce salad
Bread and butter
Cheese and biscuits

2

Creamed sweetbreads (No. 310)
Hot buttered toast
Fruit compôte with glucose and sweet biscuits

3

Scrambled eggs à la Romaine (No. 193)
Bread and butter
Grapefruit and date salad (No. 425) with cream and biscuits

4

Lentil soup (No. 62)
Ham roll salad (No. 384)
Bread and butter
Chocolate and/or sweet biscuit

5

Poached eggs mornay (No. 188)
Mashed potatoes
Bread and butter
Chocolate, nuts, and grapes

6

Quiche Lorraine (No. 167)
Watercress
Bread and butter
Ice cream with blackcurrant syrup sauce (No. 142)

7

Dairy soup (No. 57)
Salmon mousse (No. 233)
A little green salad
Bread and butter

8

Omelette à la crème (No. 179)
Bread and butter
Fruit salad and cream
Sweet biscuit

9

Herring fishcakes (No. 224)
Rémoulade sauce (No. 116)
Tomato salad (No. 393)
Bread and butter
Cheese and biscuits

10

Liver pâté (No. 304)
Small portion of green salad
Thin bread and butter
Apple trifle (No. 506) with cream

11

Cream of pea soup (No. 77)
Fish with pineapple (No. 221)
Small portion of salad
Bread and butter
Chocolate or biscuit

12

Scalloped egg and ham (No. 196)
Grilled or baked tomato
Bread and butter
Dried fruit compôte (No. 421) with cream
Lemon biscuits (No. 541)

13

Herring salad (No. 383)
Bread and butter
Caramel oranges (No. 430) with cream and almond fingers (No. 536)

14

Grilled lamb patties (No. 290)
Boiled potatoes with cheese sauce (No. 81)
Grilled tomato
Grapes
Shortbread (No. 547)

Dinner Menus

1

Small portion of consommé
Mixed grill with tomato, mushroom, and chips
Pavlova cake (No. 564) with cream and fruit

2

Glass of dry sherry
Fried liver and bacon
Sauté potatoes
Macédoine of vegetables (No. 332)
Lemon cheese meringue (No. 485)

3

Small portion of consommé
Liver provençale (No. 306)
Baked stuffed potato (No. 348)
Tossed lettuce salad
Banana and blackcurrant sundae (No. 450)

4

Orange juice with glucose
Poached white fish with Hollandaise sauce (No. 101)
Creamed potatoes (No. 349)
Tomato garnish
Ice cream (No. 454)
Hot chocolate sauce (Nos. 133–5)

5

Grapefruit and blackcurrant juices
Boiled skate and brown butter sauce (No. 98)
Boiled potatoes
Grilled or baked tomatoes
Steamed canary pudding (No. 498)
Marmalade sauce (No. 143)

6

Small grilled grapefruit (No. 426)
Salmon mayonnaise
Potato salad (No. 390)
Bread and butter
Charlotte Russe (No. 509)

7

Glass of dry sherry with stuffed olives
Rice and fish mould (No. 229) with egg and lemon sauce (No. 100)
Green peas dressed with butter
Stewed fruit with glucose
Whipped cream
Chocolate and nuts

8

Small glass Beaujolais
Bacon baked with cider (No. 246)
Boiled potatoes
Purée of brussels sprouts
Apple flan or tart with cream

9

Grapefruit juice with glucose
Roast pork
Roast potatoes
Mashed carrots and parsnips mixed
Watercress garnish
Baked banana and prunes (No. 418) with cream

10

Small portion of consommé
Roast shoulder of lamb with rice stuffing (No. 294)
Redcurrant jelly
Roast potatoes
Green peas and carrots dressed with butter
Peach Melba (No. 451) (with ice cream No. 454)

11

Orange juice and glucose
Steamed chicken with noodles and cream sauce (No. 269)
Prune whip (No. 409)
Almond biscuits (No. 534)

12

Small portion fish cocktail (No. 207)
Veal blanquette (No. 320)
Creamed potatoes (No. 349 b, d, or e)
Mashed carrots
Chocolate mousse (No. 439)

13

Fruit cocktail (No. 395)
Navarin of lamb (No. 292)
Carrots Vichy (No. 337)
Coffee Spanish cream (No. 462)

14

Small glass consommé
Veal flan (No. 324)
Purée of spinach
Fruit mousse with cream (No. 402)
Jumbles (No. 540) or sweet biscuits

CHAPTER 10

Fevers and Infections

THESE include influenza, tonsillitis and other throat infections, pneumonia, bronchitis, tuberculosis, measles, chickenpox, scarlet fever, typhoid fever, and any other disease where the temperature is raised above normal for any length of time.

The Effects of Fevers on the Human Body

The body's needs for energy, protein, and other nutrients is increased by a rise of body temperature.

In the healthy body there is a constant wearing out of tissues which have to be replaced to maintain good health, but in fevers this loss is two or three times the normal amount. The wastage cannot be repaired unless the diet contains plenty of protein-rich foods such as milk, cheese, eggs, meat, and fish.

In addition, there is an increased need for vitamins, especially vitamin C, which has been shown to have important healing properties.

There is a loss of water and salt due to profuse sweating, and plenty of fluids are needed to prevent dehydration. Digestion is frequently impaired and normal meals now frequently cause discomfort such as diarrhoea and abdominal distension.

The appetite also is frequently poor, and there may be nausea and vomiting.

Modern drugs have the effect of controlling most fevers and infections in a very short time and so the long debilitating period of fever is becoming rare. Nevertheless, some dietary treatment is usually advised in the early stages of the infection, and there are some fevers which still cannot be controlled by drugs. Unless the diet is adequate in these cases there will be severe tissue wastage and a lengthy convalescence.

How the Normal Diet is Modified

In the early stages give fluids only, not more than 6–8 fl. oz. ($\frac{3}{4}$ c.) at a time, at approximately two-hourly intervals to give about 6 pints (12 c.) throughout the twenty-four hours. (See fluid diet, page 25.)

Most of these fluids should have a high-protein and high-vitamin content. If the patient has a sore throat take care to see that the fluids are not too acid or highly seasoned. Salt is important as much is lost during sweating. It can be added to savoury fluids and to lemonade drinks. Very sweet fluids are not usually popular and can cause gastric upsets.

As the patient improves and appetite returns, some solids are gradually added to give a semi-solid or soft diet (page 31). Then the patient graduates to the light diet (page 38), and finally the normal diet (page 15).

To avoid overtaxing the digestion it is important to do this slowly. The first solids usually added are bread and butter, milk pudding, and custard, which replace some of the liquid feeds, and then the complete semi-solid or soft diet follows.

Fluids Usually Acceptable in Early Stages of a Fever

The amounts often recommended are 3–4 qts (12–16 c.) daily, but ask the doctor about this.

Home-made lemonade (No. 25), plain or with soda water, soda water, canned fruit juices with soda water, syrup fruit juices (bottled) with soda water, blackcurrant juices (bottled) with soda water, iced tea with lemon (No. 19), barley water (No. 20), fresh fruit juices sweetened with rose-hip syrup or blackcurrant syrup to add vitamin C, canned vegetable juices chilled. If you have a juice extractor make apple and lemon juice (No. 29), and home-made vegetable juices.

When this stage has been passed the full fluid diet (page 25) is given.

CHAPTER II

Anaemia

THERE are many different kinds of anaemia with a wide variety of causes.

Nutritional anaemia is due to a deficiency in the diet, which may be a deficiency of iron or protein, vitamin C, or other nutrients. It is most likely to occur when people have a poorly chosen diet of inadequate and infrequent meals. Or it may occur when the diet is insufficient to make good the blood losses occurring in menstruation and pregnancy.

In anaemia the red blood cells are either deficient in number or deficient in composition. Their function is to transport oxygen from the lungs to the tissues, where it is used for burning carbohydrates and fats to give energy. Thus, defective red blood cells mean poor energy production, with the result that an anaemic person is lacking in energy and vitality and quickly tires with any effort.

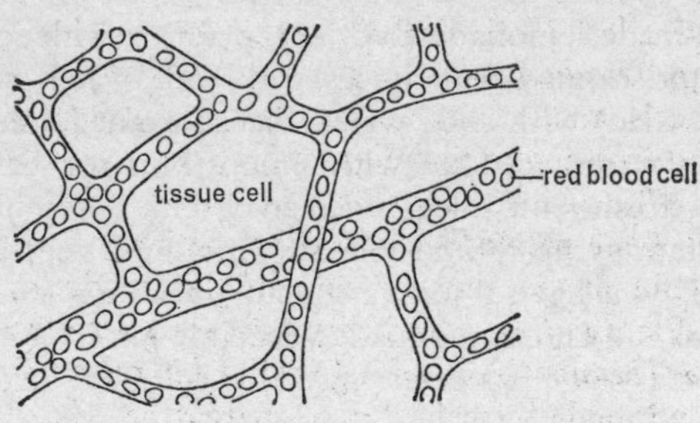

Capillary network showing red blood cells passing through. This is where food and oxygen pass into the cells and waste products pass out to the blood to be carried away to the kidneys and other organs of elimination.

(OXYGEN + FOOD = ENERGY)

Why the Diet is Important

It is true that anaemia is usually more effectively and cheaply treated by means other than diet (e.g. iron tonics), yet most doctors prescribe an improvement in diet as an aid to the treatment and as a means of bringing about a permanent cure. Anaemic people frequently suffer from general malnutrition, and to re-establish good eating habits is usually a help.

How the Normal Diet is Modified

Encouraging the patient to have a good normal diet (see page 15) is the most important step, with, in addition, emphasis on the foods which experience has shown to be especially valuable in treating anaemia. These are foods which are rich sources of either protein, iron, or vitamins, or all three together.

Where the appetite is poor, less bulky foods should be used and small, frequent meals served. Sometimes the patient dislikes the very foods she most needs, and in that case guile is needed to disguise them, combined with a wide and varied use of anything she does like.

Special cooking is not necessary, as all foods for this diet are suitable for the rest of the family.

Foods for Diets in Anaemia

Beverages. Use any kind. A small glass of alcoholic beverage before meals acts as an appetite stimulant for many. Milk drinks and fruit juices make good between-meals drinks.

Breads. White bread is fortified with iron, calcium, and vitamins, but if the patient has a small appetite and eats only two or three thin slices a day the contribution made by bread will be small. Plenty of meat and eggs are the alternative.

Cakes and biscuits. True sponge cakes and others using plenty of eggs and made with butter or margarine. Use dried fruits and black treacle for variety.

Cereals and pasta. Breakfast cereals with added iron and protein are the best; add milk, egg, and cheese to other cereal dishes. If the patient has a small appetite it is probably better to omit the breakfast cereal and serve an egg and a slice of bread and butter instead.

Cheese. Use freely for the same reasons as milk (see below).

Condiments and garnishes. Use any which will help to tempt the appetite of the small eater and give pleasure to the others.

Eggs. Egg yolk especially should be used freely, so if you are doing any special cooking for the patient use egg yolks only and the whites for family cooking. Give at least one egg a day as an egg dish and use more in cooking. If the patient dislikes eggs on their own use extra in cooking. In addition to cakes and puddings use them in sauces and soups (see Nos. 58, 83, 100, 101).

Fats, oils, and cream. Butter, cream, and margarine are the best to use because they contain vitamins A and D.

Fish. Useful as an additional source of protein, and oily fish give additional vitamins. Canned fish is very valuable, so that, if the patient likes sardines, herrings, and canned salmon, use them freely.

Fruit. Most useful are citrus fruits, loganberries, raspberries, redcurrants and blackcurrants, apples, apricots, peaches, pineapple, prunes, raisins, and strawberries. Use some fresh, canned, or frozen, and some dried. Fruit juices and purées are good for those who can't take the whole fruit.

Meat. This is one of the most important sources of iron in the average diet, liver, heart, kidney, and brain being the best. Corned beef and fresh beef are also very good. The first three can be mixed with other meats in stews, casseroles, meat loaves, and rissoles, galantines, and suchlike to disguise the flavour (see Nos. 249, 251, 254–60, 305). People who eat little or no meat should have plenty of eggs, bread, and vegetables to compensate.

Milk. A good intake is important (at least 1 pt (2 c.) daily). It is not an iron-rich food but it is a rich source of other nutrients needed. If milk is disliked as a beverage, use plenty in cooking, especially the concentrated, dried, and evaporated milks.

Preserves. Home-made ones with a high fruit content are the best, e.g. a thick dried apricot or dried peach jam. Treacle is a good alternative.

Puddings. Concentrate on those using milk, eggs, and the fruits from the list. Use butter, margarine, and cream for the fat because of their vitamins. Make pastry with butter or margarine.

Sauces and gravy. Any are suitable. Sauces made with concentrated tomato paste are especially good. Use good stocks or meat cubes, the liquid from cooking vegetables, or yeast extracts, for savoury sauces. Use egg yolks for thickening whenever possible and margarine, butter, or cream for the fats.

Soups and stock. A small amount of concentrated meat consommé acts as an appetite-stimulant for many. Other soups are generally bulky and filling and are best avoided if the patient has a small appetite.

Sugars and sugar confectionery. Use sparingly, as too much sugar dulls the appetite for more important food. Black treacle contains appreciable amounts of iron and calcium and, if liked, can be used freely in cooking and in place of jam on bread, and even on breakfast cereals and puddings. Make gingerbread and other cakes with it also (see Nos. 525 and 558). Treacle toffee is the best choice, or sweets made from dried fruits (see No. 422). Cut down on sweet chewing between meals and have appetizing drinks or snacks instead.

Vegetables. Leeks, mustard and cress, radishes, spring onions, broccoli tops, and endive are specially valuable, together with cabbage, brussels sprouts, cauliflower, kale, green lettuce, asparagus, tomatoes, turnip tops, and watercress. Purées and vegetable juices should be used when whole vegetables are unsuitable.

Meal-Pattern for the Anaemic Person with a Small Appetite

On waking. Fruit juice or milky tea.

Breakfast. Either an egg dish or a small portion of breakfast cereal with prunes, apricots, peaches, blackcurrant purée, or black treacle. Bread or toast and preserves if desired. Milk or cream. Tea or coffee.

Mid-morning. Egg nog, milk drink, tea, or coffee, with a sandwich or roll with egg or meat filling.

Midday. Small portion of fruit juice. As large a portion of meat as can be eaten. Potatoes and other vegetable or salad. A small portion of any from the pudding or fruit list. Coffee or tea.

Tea. Tea or coffee. Egg or meat-filled sandwiches and cake or biscuits from the list.

Evening. Meat or egg dish, cold meats, egg, or sardines. Small portion of bread or toast. Salad or fresh fruit. Tea or coffee.

Bedtime. Milk drink, biscuit.

Sandwich Meals for the Anaemic Person with a Small Appetite

Breads. Any white bread cut thinly, milk twists, cottage loaves, cream-crackers, water biscuits, protein-enriched breads.

Concentrated fillings. Eggs, mashed with mayonnaise. Home-made liver pâté (No. 303 or 304) or liver sausage, liver galantine (No. 259), cold meats, sardines.

Alternatives. A hard-boiled egg to eat with bread or plain biscuits, beef hamburgers in a soft roll, leg of chicken with tomato, sausage roll with cheese pastry, sardine rolls, pasties with meat filling.

Sweet course. Small piece of sponge, dried fruit, or sweets.

Fruit. Small portion of fresh fruit or a tomato.

Beverages. Any milk ones are best.

A suitable meal would consist of:

1 or more sandwiches.
1 from the alternatives.
Small portion from the sweet course.
Small portion of fresh fruit.
Beverage.

Lunch, High Tea, or Supper Menus

1

Corned beef hash (No. 251)
Lettuce salad
Egg jelly (No. 463) and black-currant syrup

2

Liver pâté with toast (No. 303)
Fresh fruit salad and cream
Sponge cake

3

Devilled kidney (No. 282)
Mashed potatoes
Celery and cheese

4

Scalloped brains (No. 278)
Creamed potatoes
Grapefruit and orange cup (No. 431)
Bread and butter

5

Potted meat (No. 264)
Mixed salad
Bread and butter
Cold baked apple and cream

6

Ham custard (No. 192)
Bread and butter
Fresh or frozen raspberries and cream

7

Cheese soufflé (No. 183)
Brown bread and butter
Fresh fruit

8

Liver sausage or beef galantine (No. 259)
Endive and beetroot salad
Bread and butter
Sponge cake

9

Kidney omelette (No. 174)
Tangerine and cottage cheese salad (No. 378)
Bread and butter

10

Liver terrapin (No. 308) on toast
Grilled tomatoes
Cheese and dates

11

Beef galantine (No. 259)
Lettuce salad
Bread and butter
Milk jelly (No. 472) with Melba sauce (No. 146)

12

Salmon mousse (No. 233)
Cucumber salad
Bread and butter
Fruit flan and cream

13

Stuffed tomato salad (using corned-beef stuffing)
Bread and butter
Rum omelette (No. 177)

14

Sole Dieppoise (No. 240)
Mashed potatoes
Watercress
Biscuits and cheese
Raw orange

Dinner Menus

1

Fresh orange juice
Grilled beef patty (No. 262)
Green peas
Apricot fool (No. 396)

2

Grapefruit
Steak and kidney pie
Brussels sprouts
Orange baked custard (No. 443)

3

Canned or fresh vegetable juice
Meat loaf (No. 258) (using some liver amongst the meat)
Tomato sauce (No. 108)
Green beans
Banana and ice cream with blackcurrant sauce (No. 450)

4

Tomato juice cocktail (No. 71)
Marinaded steak (No. 266)
Duchess potatoes (No. 349 e)
Blackcurrant jelly and grapes (No. 465)
Cream

5

Orange and grape cocktail (No. 395)
Liver Shashlik (No. 307) with rice
Zabaglione (No. 200)
Macaroons (No. 543)

6

Grapefruit and blackcurrant juice
Braised lambs' tongues (No. 280)
Green peas
Chocolate mousse (No. 438)

7

Small cup of consommé
Veal flan (No. 324)
Lettuce salad
Ice cream and Melba sauce (No. 146)

8

Melon cocktail (No. 395)
Meat balls with noodles (No. 248) (use some liver)
Cherry flan and cream

9

Fresh orange juice
Stewed kidney (No. 285)
Mashed potatoes (No. 349)
Celery and cheese

10

Tomato juice
Salmon loaf (No. 232) with
Parsley sauce (No. 80) or anchovy sauce (No. 91)
Green peas
Prune whip (with evaporated milk, (No. 409)

11

Grapefruit juice with honey
Braised beef with prunes and wine (No. 249)
Boiled potatoes
Crème au caramel (No. 441)

12

Vegetable juices
Goulash (No. 252)
Small portion cabbage
Apricot flan (add rose-hip syrup to the glaze)

13

Fresh orange juice
Bacon baked with cider and treacle (No. 246)
Boiled potatoes
Biscuits, cheese, and watercress

14

Cold consommé
Mixed grill
Chips
Watercress
Grilled tomato
Treacle gingerbread (No. 558)
Whipped cream

CHAPTER 12

Gout

Gout is a disease which affects the bones and soft tissues of the body. It occurs most commonly in males and its most marked effect is frequently seen in the joints of the big toes, which become swollen, inflamed, and very painful. Swelling of the affected parts is caused by deposits of sodium urate.

Gout is due to a fault in metabolism which seems, in many people, to be an inherited defect. It is known that acute attacks are frequently brought on by over-eating, especially of rich and fatty foods, and that a change in dietary habits is generally beneficial. If the patient is obese, weight reduction is usually considered of prime importance.

Dietary treatment is usually advised during severe attacks (see page 193). Whether it is recommended afterwards usually depends on the frequency and severity of the attacks. Sometimes more moderate eating and drinking habits accompanied by weight reduction are all that are required. When the symptoms and pain become chronic a diet is frequently prescribed (see page 193).

How the Normal Diet is Modified

In acute attacks the diet prescribed is usually a light one (see page 193) with plenty of non-alcoholic fluid. Fluid is important to help to prevent urates from being deposited in the kidneys and causing damage. The patient may be too ill to eat and the diet will then be fluids only. Foods known to aggravate the condition are usually excluded; otherwise the patient has what he feels he can eat.

Foods usually excluded are: Meat in general, but especially liver, sweetbreads, heart, kidney, brains, meat extracts, consommé, meat soups, gravies, and sauces made with meat stock. Fish in general, but especially fish roes, mussels, anchovies, sardines and herrings, whitebait, sprats and smelts. Whole-grain cereals, such as wholemeal bread and wheat breakfast cereals, wheatgerms, oatmeal, and rolled oats. Vegetables: beans, peas, asparagus, cauliflower, mushrooms, and spinach.

In place of meat, plenty of milk, eggs, and cheese are given.

Sometimes people with gout are overweight. Then it is usual to give a low-calorie diet as well. Chronic cases are advised to have good normal diet (see page 193), with moderate amounts of meat and fish (2 oz. daily) and either the omission of, or else the restriction of, the foods listed above as especially likely to aggravate the condition. A moderate fat-intake is usually recommended and plenty of non-alcoholic fluid.

Fitting in with the Family Meals

The diet need not entail special cooking, but careful menu planning is needed.

As liver, kidneys, and herring are nutritionally such valuable foods, it is a pity to exclude them from the diet for the rest of the family. Either use them when the patient is away for that meal or give him some alternative which is quickly prepared, e.g. an omelette, or turn his vegetables into an au gratin dish (see No. 330) or polonaise (see Nos. 335 and 336) or dishes such as Nos. 350 or 351.

Recipe books written specially for vegetarian cookery are a help in giving variety to a diet for gouty people.

Foods Usually Allowed (*For after an acute attack has passed and in the mild stages*)

Beverages. Plenty of all kinds except alcohol, which should only be given if the doctor allows. Not Bovril, Oxo, or Marmite.

Breads. White breads, buns, rolls, and scones made with white flour. Wholemeal should be limited to one portion daily.

Cakes and biscuits. Any made with white flour. None at all if on reducing diet.

Cereals and pasta. Any allowed. Whole-grain cereals, such as wheat breakfast cereals, wheatgerm, oatmeal, and rolled oats, should be limited to one small portion daily.

Cheese. Any kind. Use as a replacement for the meat which is restricted.

Condiments. Any, in moderate amounts.

Eggs. As many as possible, in place of meat and fish and as a main course (see recipes).

Fats, oils, and cream. In moderate amounts. Avoid frying whenever possible.

Fish. When allowed is usually limited to 2–3 oz. (small portion) daily or per meal as an alternative to meat. Any kind is used except herring, mackerel, scallops, fish roes, anchovies, sardines, smelts, sprats, whitebait, and mussels. Avoid fried fish and do not serve with rich sauces.

Fruit. Any kind as much as liked.

Meat, game, and poultry. When allowed, usually limited to 2–3 oz. (small portion) daily or per meal. Any kind except liver, sweetbread, heart, kidney, goose, partridge.

Milk. Use as much as possible in beverages and in cooking; evaporated milk and dried milk are also useful. Skimmed milk may be advised in low-calorie diets.

Nuts. Any allowed.

Preserves. All allowed unless on a reducing diet.

Puddings. Any allowed but only small portions of pastry and suet puddings, and none at all in the low-calorie diet.

Sauces and gravies. Avoid those made with meat stock or Bovril, Oxo, or Marmite. Any which have a lot of fat (e.g. mayonnaise, hollandaise) should be taken in very small amounts.

Soups and stocks. Vegetable stocks only (see No. 40) and soups made without meat or meat stock. Not Bovril, Oxo, or Marmite. See Nos. 53, 57, 59, 75, and 77. (Read the labels of packets and tinned soups before using.)

Sugars. All allowed unless on a reducing diet.

Vegetables. Any kind, as much as liked, except for beans,

peas, asparagus, cauliflower, mushrooms, and spinach, which should be taken occasionally in small portions only.

Meal-Pattern 1 (*For Acute Attacks*)

Sometimes milk and fluids are all the patient can take, otherwise the following is a typical meal-pattern:

On waking. Tea or fruit juice.

Breakfast. Fruit juice. Breakfast cereal from list with milk and sugar. Toast or bread and butter with preserves. Tea or coffee.

Mid-morning. Beverage of choice (*not* alcohol).

Midday. Cheese or egg dish with vegetables or salad. Stewed fruit. Tea or coffee.

Tea. Biscuits or cake, tea.

Evening. Cream of vegetable soup. Cheese or egg sandwiches, or bread and cheese with celery or tomatoes. Fresh fruit or fruit salad.

Bedtime. Milk drink and biscuits.

Water. A daily total of 4 pints (8 c.) or more should be taken as water or as other fluids, e.g. soft drinks, mineral water, barley water, or milk according to the patient's preference.

Meal-Pattern 2 (*For Chronic Cases or after an Acute Attack*)

CAUTION. Check this list with your doctor or dietitian.

On waking. Tea or fruit juice.

Breakfast. Fruit or fruit juice. Breakfast cereal from the list with milk and sugar. Egg, toast or bread and butter, and preserves. Tea or coffee.

Mid-morning. Beverage of choice (*not* alcohol).

Midday. Fruit, egg, cheese, or vegetable hors d'œuvre. 2 oz. (small portion) meat, fish, or poultry from list. Vegetables. Pudding from list or cheese. Tea or coffee.

Tea. Biscuit and cake. Tea.

Evening. Cream of vegetable soup. Cheese or egg sandwiches or egg salad or cooked dish with bread and butter. Stewed or fresh fruits.

Bedtime. Milk drink and biscuits.

In addition. Plenty of water to drink. 3 pints (6 c.) or more, some as fruit or vegetable juices.

Daily Allowances of Basic Foods for Meal-Pattern 2

1–2 pt (2–4 c.) milk
2 oz. (small portion) meat, fish, or poultry
2 eggs and 2 oz. (2 inch cube) cheese

Reducing Diet. The 1000-calorie diet (page 121) will be suitable, but ask your doctor first.

Sandwich Meals

Breads. Any white bread, soft white rolls, hard white rolls, finger rolls, French bread, Vienna bread, milk twists, cottage loaves, cream-crackers, water biscuits, or starch-reduced rolls if on a reducing diet.

Sandwich fillings. Cheeses of all varieties including cottage cheese. Egg fillings (see Nos. 527 and 528).

Alternatives to sandwiches. Hard-boiled eggs (plain or stuffed). Pieces of cheese to eat with bread and butter or biscuits and salad vegetables. Pasties and turnovers with egg, cheese, and/or vegetable filling. Celery sticks stuffed with cheese, stuffed tomatoes.

Raw vegetables. Radishes, cucumbers, tomatoes, watercress, lettuce, celery, carrots, chicory.

Sweet course. Sweet sandwich fillings, small portion pastry or cake, dried fruits. Sweets: a portion of stewed or canned fruit in a carton.

Fresh fruit. Instead of or in addition to sweet course.

Extras. Nuts of any kind.

Beverages. Tea, coffee, cocoa, fruit drinks and squashes, soup from the permitted list (see page 191).

A suitable meal would consist of:
2 or more sandwiches with egg or cheese filling.
Use items from the list of alternatives for variety.
Portion of raw vegetables and one of fresh fruit or nuts.
Beverage.

Eating Out

Frequently a problem, especially if the sufferer has to attend many official or business lunches or dinners. Avoid the foods listed on page 190, and take only one course containing meat, fish, game, or poultry.

If this causes embarrassment ask for very small portions and leave some so that the total in several courses does not add up to more than one normal one. Avoidance of overeating is important in preventing further attacks.

If a bottle of mineral water is ordered as well as the wine, something is always at hand for an alternative drink and helps to avoid excessive consumption of alcohol.

If the patient is the host, choosing a meal from foods allowed to the gouty patient can produce a very good meal, and the guests will benefit from one less bout of excess eating.

Choose from the following foods:

First course. Melon, artichokes, grapefruit, fruit cocktail, cream of vegetable soup, egg dishes.

Fish. Small portion as alternative to meat. Grilled or poached salmon, with butter and lemon. Grilled or poached sole, plaice, halibut, turbot, cod, haddock.

Meat. Small portion grilled (not liver or kidney), roast (not goose or partridge). Veal and ham pie, pork pie, Cornish pasties, sausage rolls.

Vegetables. Potatoes cooked any way, carrots, cabbage, brussels sprouts, celery, tomatoes, lettuce, watercress, endive.

Puddings. Any on the menu,

For other items see permitted food list (page 191).

Diet for Chronic Gout or after an Acute Attack

NOTE. The size of portion must be restricted to that allowed in the diet prescription for the individual patient.

Lunch, High Tea, or Supper Menus

1

Cheese soup (No. 53)
American tomato and egg salad (No. 366)
Bread and butter
Apple and nuts

2

Tomato soup (No. 77)
Quiche Lorraine (No. 167)
Fresh fruit

3

Soufflé omelette (No. 180) with tomato sauce (No. 108) and bacon rolls
Lettuce salad
Stewed pears with caramel sauce (No. 131 or 132)

4

Vegetable juices
Ham custard (No. 192)
Toast
Biscuits and cheese
Fresh orange

5

Potato and watercress soup (No. 69)
Stuffed egg salad (No. 197)
Bread and butter
Banana

6

Cream of celery soup (No. 77)
Macaroni cheese with ham (No. 165)
Pineapple and orange mould (No. 436)

7

Cream of carrot soup (No. 77)
Eggs mornay (No. 188)
Tomato garnish
Grapefruit and date salad (No. 425)

8

Tomato flan (No. 361)
Cheese and biscuits
Fresh pear

9

Cucumber soup (No. 55 or 56) (use vegetable stock)
Cheese soufflé (No. 183)
Canned peaches with Melba sauce (No. 146)

10

Tomato juice cocktail (No. 71)
Chestnut stew (No. 339)
Jellied apples (No. 412)

11

Gnocchi (No. 357) with tomato sauce (No. 108) and cheese
Lettuce salad
Caramel oranges (No. 430)

12

Minestrone (No. 65)
Bacon omelette (No. 172)
Roll and butter
Stuffed stewed apple (No. 415)

13

Onion broth (NO stock) (No. 45)
Fricassée of eggs (No. 199)
Blackcurrant jelly and grapes (No. 465)

14

Potato and watercress soup (No. 69)
Eggs lyonnaise (No. 198)
Celery
Cheese
Dates

Dinner Menus (*If preferred, have cheese and biscuits instead of sweet*)

1

Fillets of sole au gratin (No. 220)
Waldorf salad (No. 394)
Jam omelette (No. 176)

2

Fish kedgeree (No. 227)
Apple, cucumber, and cottage cheese salad
Zabaglione (No. 200)
Macaroons (No. 543)

3

Tomato and sweet pepper salad (No. 392)
Creamed veal in potato nest (No. 322)
Chocolate mousse (No. 438)

4

Grapefruit
Tripe au gratin (No. 315)
Carrots and potatoes
Apple flan

5

Chicken pilaf (No. 273)
Grapefruit and beetroot salad (No. 382)
Lemon cheese meringue (No. 485)

6

Stuffed tomatoes (NO meat or fish) (No. 364 or 379)
Scalloped brains (No. 278)
Creamed potatoes (No. 349)
Orange mousse (No. 399)

7

Navarin of lamb (No. 292)
Carrots Vichy (No. 337)
Fresh fruit salad and cream
Cheese and biscuits

8

Veal olives (No. 319)
Creamed potatoes (No. 349)
Lettuce salad
Crème au caramel (No. 441)

9

Hard-boiled egg with tomato sauce (No. 106)
Parisian salad (No. 388)
Steamed canary pudding (No. 498)
Marmalade sauce (No. 143)

10

Tomato juice cocktail (No. 71)
Moussaka (No. 261)
Celery and sprout salad (No. 372)
Fruit meringue (No. 398)

11

Fish soufflé (No. 184)
Egg and lemon sauce (No. 100)
Cabbage, celery, and cheese salad
Refrigerated peach flan (No. 490)

12

Spaghetti Bolognese (No. 263)
Celery and cheese
Fresh fruit

13

Omelette fines herbes (No. 171)
Roll and butter
Swedish apple cake (No. 416)
Biscuits and cheese

14

Cucumber soup (No. 55 or 56) (use vegetable stock)
Pressed chicken (No. 275)
Orange salad (No. 387)
Charlotte russe (No. 509)

Celebration Meals

1

Hors d'œuvre, choosing from vegetable and egg dishes
Fish or meat vol-au-vent
Mixed salad
Peach Melba (No. 451) or other ice pudding *or* cheese or Welsh rarebit

2

Melon
Minute steak
Potato purée
Lettuce salad
Charlotte russe (No. 509) *or* crème au caramel (No. 441) *or* cheese and celery

CHAPTER 13

Diseases of Childhood

WHEN children are sick they usually lose their appetites to some extent and become faddy feeders. This does not matter for a short time but, in any illness which is prolonged, failure to eat will not only delay healing but will hinder normal growth and development. Any devices to coax children to eat the right foods at this time are worth trying.

Tips Others Have Found Useful

1. Concentrate on familiar and well-liked foods, as far as the diet will allow. If a strange food has to be given, try to make it look as like the familiar as possible or serve it with a very popular food.

2. Make food attractive to look at by using coloured food and pretty dishes.

3. Individual portions appeal more than a helping from a big dish and cook more quickly. Individual jellies and cold sweets set more quickly.

4. Avoid stodgy and lumpy food, and food which is difficult to handle and chew. Serve it cut into convenient-sized pieces.

5. Remove all bones from fish and serve it in a colourful sauce, e.g. tomato, anchovy, parsley.

6. Serve only small portions and allow second helpings if needed.

7. Serve meals at regular times.

8. Drinking straws are often a help in getting children to take fluids and also help to avoid spilling.

9. Milk is more attractive if served in tall pretty glasses with a little flavouring or colouring and a straw.

10. If children refuse to eat, don't let them see you are worried about it.

11. Children with a preference for savoury things will take milk flavoured with Marmite or meat extract or dried milk added to soups and broth.

12. Use plenty of milk in cooking, either liquid, dried, or evaporated. As the last two are concentrated, a lot can be given in a small bulk. It can be used not only in all kinds of puddings, but also in soups, gravies, mashed vegetables; the milk powders can be added dry with the other dry ingredients to cakes and steamed or baked puddings.

13. If children dislike eggs by themselves, use them in cooking. Choose puddings made with egg, add eggs to mashed potatoes, milk puddings, sauces, and make savoury supper dishes with eggs, e.g. Nos. 171–5, 178–81, 188–93, 195–9.

14. If refusal to eat cooked vegetables is the trouble, try raw salads and salad fillings for sandwiches or give very small amounts of three or more different vegetables on the plate to make it look interesting, colourful, and tempting.

15. If they need concentrated sources of vitamin C such as blackcurrant syrup and rose-hip syrup and do not like it as drinks, use it in or with puddings, e.g. Nos. 399, 450, 465, 508.

16. If a special diet is needed, explain why to older children as they are more likely to cooperate than if merely told it is doctor's orders, or good for them.

17. Make sure hot food will stay hot for as long as the child takes to eat it; for slow feeders insulated plates are a help.

18. Small children who have just learnt to feed themselves will probably need help again when they are ill, but do not continue this longer than is necessary.

THE LIQUID OR FLUID DIET FOR CHILDREN

This is basically the same as for adults, see pages 25–31, but the quantities will naturally vary. The following are quantities that are likely to be taken at different ages (check with your doctor).

Full fluid diet six times a day

Age	*Amount per feed*
2–5 yrs	4–5 fl. oz. ($\frac{1}{2}$ c.)
5–8 yrs	8–10 fl. oz. ($\frac{3}{4}$ c.)
8–14 yrs	10 fl. oz. (1 c.)

THE SEMI-SOLID OR SOFT DIET AND LIGHT DIETS FOR CHILDREN

These are usually the same as for adults (see pages 31–8), except that for small children soups would be omitted from the basic menu and tea and the evening meal suggested in the meal-pattern on pages 34–5 would be combined into a high-tea meal taken at about 4.45–5.0 p.m.

Fruit juice or milk drinks would be given between meals if needed.

CONDITIONS AFFECTING THE MOUTH AND THROAT

Sore throat, tonsillitis, mumps, swollen glands, or any disease which makes chewing and swallowing difficult and painful.

How the Normal Diet is Modified (*Check this with your doctor*)

As with adults, a good normal diet is important, the main change being one of consistency. Any normal foods are usually allowed provided they are soft enough to be easily swallowed without chewing or without hurting when swallowed. If the throat is sore, highly seasoned foods, vinegar, lemon, salad dressings, and acid fruits and juices such as orange, grapefruit, or blackcurrant should be avoided. The normal diet is resumed as soon as possible.

Popular foods with most children will be:

Soft ice creams (No. 445–8 and 454–5), ginger ale, water ices (Nos. 459 and 460), cold milk shakes with ice cream, sherbet (No. 460), apple, pear, or apricot juices, clear jellies made with fruit juices (No. 464). When the throat is sore all drinks are usually preferred cold. Feeds are given every two hours.

Add these foods as the healing progresses:

Milky soups (No. 77), minced meat, mashed potatoes, lightly cooked eggs, sieved vegetables, cereal milk puddings with fruit purées.

Meal-Pattern for a Child Recovering from a Sore Throat

On waking. Chilled milk or fruit juice.
Breakfast. Lightly cooked egg. Milk drink or creamy milk gruel.
Mid-morning. Milk shake.
Dinner. Minced meat with mashed potatoes and sieved vegetable. Ice cream with fruit purée.
Tea. Milky vegetable soup (sieved). Jelly.
Bedtime. Milk drink.

GASTRIC AND DUODENAL ULCERS

As for adults (see pages 49–59).

DIARRHOEA

This is a common complaint with children and has a variety of causes. Because of the very watery stools a great deal of fluid is lost from the body. Beverages therefore play an important part in the treatment.

In acute stages only boiled water may be given, but when the worst symptoms subside grated raw apple or stewed sieved apple and fruit juices with glucose added are given in frequent small amounts. Sweetened yogurt with black-currant purée is also added and yeast extract drinks and skimmed milk.

When the convalescent stage is reached the diet given is a low-residue one (see page 50).

The appetite needs tempting and it is no good trying to give the child unpopular, unfamiliar foods. It is most important that all foods should be very fresh and should be handled and stored in a hygienic manner (see page 23).

General recommendations given for adults (see page 50) also apply to feeding children, except that the meal-pattern needs modifying for young children as given below.

Meal-Pattern for Small Child Recovering from Diarrhoea

using foods allowed; see page 52 (check this with your doctor)

On waking. Fruit juice.

Breakfast. Milk with porridge or cereal. Bread and toast or butter or margarine and preserves. (1 egg or 1 oz. (25 g.) bacon added when more convalescent.)

Mid-morning. Yogurt sweetened with fruit juice or milk.

Midday. Meat or fish or thick milky soup. Vegetables. Pudding.

Tea. Milk drink or milk sweet. Bread and butter or margarine or preserves or sandwiches with cheese or egg. Plain cake or biscuit.

Bedtime. Milk or milk drink.

ATONIC CONSTIPATION

(Check this with your doctor)

For young children add the following to their normal diet:

Fruit juices (prune and orange), tomato juice, fruit purées or prunes, apricots, apple sauce, vegetable purées, whole-grain cereals.

Older children as for adults (see page 75).

Meal-Pattern for a Diet for Constipation in Young Children

On waking. Glass of prune or orange juice.

Breakfast. Shredded Wheat or Weetabix with milk, cream, and sugar. Wholemeal bread and butter with jam, marmalade, and honey. Milk.

Also one of the following: egg, chopped bacon, or ham (1–2 tablespoons), steamed, grilled, or creamed flaked fish (1–2 tablespoons), flaked herring, sardine, and herring roes (1–2 tablespoons).

Mid-morning. Milk drink.

Dinner. Meat, liver, fish. Potatoes and vegetable purée. Stewed fruit and milk and tomato juice or fruit juice.

Tea. Wholemeal bread made into sandwiches with one of the following: Raw fruit or salad vegetables. Biscuits made with rolled oats, oatmeal, or wholemeal flour. Milk.

Bedtime. Milk.

FEVERS AND FEVERISH COLDS

Influenza, tonsillitis, infectious diseases, measles, chickenpox, bronchitis, pneumonia.

Why the Diet is Important

Whenever there is fever the body loses protein, which is the main constituent of all cells. This causes loss of weight and wastage of muscles and other tissues, and, in the case of children, growth is not normal. The object of the diet is to give food which is as nourishing as possible in a form the child can digest. This is given at frequent intervals, as not much will be taken at any one time.

How the Diet is Modified (*Check this with your doctor*)

In the early stages milk and fruit juices form the basis of the diet and are given at two-hourly intervals.

Milk. With fruit-flavoured syrup as used for milk shakes, egg nog (Nos. 14–18), ice cream (Nos. 445–8), jelly creams (Nos. 472–5), cream soups (No. 77), semolina or rice pudding or arrowroot pudding. Soups Nos. 53, 54, 57, 58. Proprietary starch foods, e.g. Bengers', Farex. Sugar and glucose added to all liquids.

As the child recovers and appetite returns add:

Steamed lamb cutlets (No. 297), white fish, chicken, cheese, minced beef or lamb, cooked egg dishes, liver, bacon, chopped vegetables, and fresh fruit.

Some bread and cereal should be added too, but not served instead of the other foods.

When the appetite is poor the milk used should be a fortified one, e.g. made with 1½ pts (3 c.) of fresh milk, 1½ oz. (4 level Tbs.) Casilan (Glaxo), and 1 egg. Use this sweetened and flavoured or made into soup with tomato juice or chicken broth.

Meal-Pattern for a Child Who is Recovering

Breakfast. Fortified milk with porridge or cereal. Scrambled egg or bacon. Bread and butter or toast.

Mid-morning. Orange or blackcurrant juice.

Dinner. Meat, or fish, or grated cheese. Vegetables. Custard or cereal pudding made with fortified milk. Fresh or stewed fruit.

Tea. Fortified milk with tea to flavour and colour. Egg, cheese, or sardine sandwich. Cakes or fruit.

Bedtime. Fortified milk with cereal. Biscuits or cake.

TYPHOID FEVER (ACUTE STAGES)

(*Check this with your doctor*)

Give milk, cereals, ice cream, plain chocolate. Then give a *low-fibre diet* (see page 50) using the following foods:

Scrambled egg, steamed white fish, pounded chicken, calves' foot jelly, custards and junkets, finely puréed stewed fruit, broths, pounded brains, creamed potatoes, milk puddings. These foods are given at regular meal times. Give plenty of fresh fruit juices as well.

JAUNDICE AND CIRRHOSIS

The diets are the same as for an adult low-fat diet (see page 84). (*Check this with your doctor*.)

Extra protein is usually needed by the child and the high-protein milks are suitable, for example: 1 pt (2 c.) skimmed fresh milk mixed with 1 oz (2½ level Tbs.) Casilan (Glaxo), or 1 pt (2 c.) water mixed with 4 oz. (¾ c.) dried skimmed milk powder. These are used for sweet drinks with as much glucose added as the patient can tolerate.

Meal-Pattern for the Younger Child

Breakfast. High-protein or skimmed milk flavoured with tea or coffee and sugar. Fruit or cereal. Toast with butter from the allowance and marmalade. Boiled or scrambled egg, lean ham, poached haddock, baked beans.

Mid-morning. High-protein milk flavoured to taste, with sugar.

Dinner. Lean meat, chicken, liver, white fish, omelettes. Vegetables or salad. Raw or cooked fruit, milk pudding, baked or steamed sponge.

Tea. High-protein milk with 1 teaspoon of Bournvita or Ovaltine. Skimmed milk soup. Toast or rusks and jelly, or jam with sponge cake and stewed fruit.

Bedtime. Milk.

Daily allowances. 1–1½ pts (2–3 c.) skimmed milk, at least some of it with Casilan or dried skimmed milk as above.

After-meal sweets. Barley sugar, acid drops, boiled sweets, marshmallows. These can also be used with puddings. Glucose and fruit juices should be given freely.

OVER-WEIGHT

Why Diet is Important

Fat children are conspicuous and different, and this is liable to lead to behaviour difficulties. They cannot compete with others in games, and the obese teenage girl is at a disadvantage in looks and dress when compared with others. Also the fat child is very likely to grow into the over-weight adult.

Restricting foods is difficult if the family eating pattern is one of overeating, and there are many overweight members of the family. Children tend to imitate the eating habits of their elders.

Foods Usually Allowed (*Check this with your doctor*)

Beverages. The milk allowance may be taken as a beverage flavoured with weak coffee or tea.

Also allowed are fruit juices, unsweetened, or sweetened with saccharin, and diabetic fruit squashes. Marmite, Bovril, and Oxo all allowed.

Biscuits. Starch-reduced only.

Breads. Any kind but not more than the day's allowance, as prescribed.

Cereals. 1 oz. (1 slice) of bread at breakfast or tea can be replaced by $\frac{1}{2}$–$\frac{3}{4}$ oz. ($\frac{1}{2}$–$\frac{3}{4}$ c.) non-sugared cereal, served with the milk allowance or fresh fruit juice.

Cheese. All allowed in generous amounts. Many children enjoy eating it without bread or biscuits.

Fats. Butter $\frac{1}{2}$–$\frac{3}{4}$ oz. (1–1$\frac{1}{2}$ level Tbs.) daily. Avoid frying.

Eggs. Cooked any way except fried.

Fish. Any kind, boiled, poached, steamed, or grilled.

Fruit. Raw fruit or stewed with saccharin or saxin. Dietade canned fruits in water (see page 106).

Meats. Any kind of lean meat, game, or poultry.

Milk. Not more than 1 pt. (2 c.) of full cream milk or 2 pts (4 c.) of skimmed. Possibly some evaporated, e.g. 2–3 tablespoons of evaporated milk instead of $\frac{1}{4}$ pt ($\frac{1}{2}$ c.) fresh in jellies or on stewed fruit.

Preserves. Use Marmite and meat and fish pastes instead.

Puddings. Milk junkets, milk jellies, fruit juice jelly with saccharin, fresh fruit.

Sauces and gravies. Unthickened wherever possible, or low-calorie ones (see recipes).

Vegetables. Green vegetables and salad, as much as desired. Small helpings of root vegetables, not more than 4 oz. (1 medium) potatoes daily.

Meal-Pattern for a Reducing Diet for a Child (*Check this with your doctor*)

Breakfast. Milk from the allowance with a dash of tea but no sugar. Bread 1–2 oz. (1–2 slices) or amounts prescribed.

Butter ¼ oz. (½ level Tbs.) or amounts prescribed. Piece of fish or 1 egg or 1 rasher lean bacon.

Mid-morning. Milk, ⅓ pt (⅔ c.)

Dinner. Half portion meat or fish, 1 small potato. Small portion of root vegetables. Large portion green vegetables or salad. Pudding ¼ pt (½ c.) milk as junket or jelly with saccharin or saxin to sweeten, plain fruit jelly, or a helping of fresh or cooked fruit sweetened with saccharin.

Tea. ¼ pt (½ c.) milk-flavoured tea but no sugar. 1–2 oz. (1–2 slices) bread or amounts prescribed. ¼ oz. (½ level Tbs.) butter or margarine or amount prescribed. Marmite or paste, lettuce, tomato. Fresh fruit.

Supper. ¼ pt (½ c.) milk flavoured with cocoa and sweetened with saccharin. Half portion meat or fish or 1 egg or 1 inch cube of cheese or 1 sardine. Green salad if desired. 1 oz (1 slice) bread or as prescribed. ¼ oz. (½ level Tbs.) butter or margarine or as prescribed. Apple or orange or fruit jelly.

NOTE. For a very young child the supper meal will be taken at teatime, and at bedtime they should have: skimmed milk with a small teaspoon of Ovaltine or Bournvita, or a portion of skimmed milk jelly, or junket. 1 slice of bread with butter or margarine from the allowance.

Daily allowances (check these with the doctor's prescription): Butter or margarine ½ oz. (1 level Tbs.). Skimmed milk 1¼ pt (2 ½ c.) or whole milk 1 pt. (2 c.). Bread 4 oz (4 slices).

School Dinner

Dinners. If the child cannot come home to dinner, his mother should go and see the head, explain the position, and find out whether it is better for the child to take a packed lunch or whether the staff are willing and able to see the child has a suitably modified meal. Permission to take fruit from home instead of having the pudding course may be the best solution, providing that those in charge of the child see that he does not have pudding as well.

From the child's point of view, the best course is that which makes him least conspicuous and different from the others. Going home for dinner is the best solution provided that some of the other children also do so.

Instead of spending pocket-money on sweets encourage the child to buy apples or oranges. Ice cream is a better choice than sweets, a small ice cream giving about 80 calories (apple 40), while only 1 oz. sweets gives 93 calories, a 2-oz. bar of milk chocolate 167 and 3 biscuits 168 calories.

Sandwich Lunches for the Over-weight Schoolchild

Bread. As the total amount is restricted use starch-reduced rolls and crispbread.

Fillings. These can either be put in the hollowed-out rolls or carried separately in tubs.

Alternatives to sandwiches. Hard-boiled eggs with salad vegetables, pieces of cheese to eat with fruit, salad vegetables, or starch-reduced rolls. Lean grilled chops or cutlets (veal or lamb) to eat with salad vegetables, leg of cooked chicken, rolls of cold sliced meat to eat in fingers, fish or meat cakes with salad vegetables, hamburgers, or cartons of flavoured cottage cheese.

Raw vegetables. Radishes, cucumber, tomato, watercress, lettuce, celery, carrots, chicory.

Sweet course. Portion of low-carbohydrate jelly or baked custard or other sweet (see recipes).

Fruit. Fresh fruit from the list.

Beverages. Diabetic squashes, weak tea or coffee.

A suitable meal would consist of:

4 starch-reduced rolls, 2 filled and 2 to be eaten with one or two of the alternatives suggested above.

Raw vegetable.

Sweet course.

Fruit and a few nuts.

Beverages: diabetic or home-made low-calorie squashes or diluted fruit juices.

Foods Over-weight Children tend to be fond of and which should be Excluded from the Family Diet for their Sake

Fried foods

Puddings. Steamed, or pastry puddings and dumplings, Yorkshire pudding.

Cakes and biscuits. All except biscuits which are starch-reduced.

Sweets. All.

Bread and potatoes. Only in prescribed amounts.

Sugar. Use saccharin occasionally, but it is better to train the child not to like very sweet things.

Encourage the child to spend pocket-money on fresh fruit rather than on sweets, ice cream, and biscuits.

DISEASES OF THE KIDNEY

Restricted-Protein Diet

Frequently salt is not allowed in cooking, but the details of the diet are the same as those for the adult. See page 160.

The meal-pattern is the same as for the adult, but needs adjusting for the younger child as given below.

Meal-Pattern for Younger Children on a Low-Protein Diet

(*Check this with your doctor*)

Breakfast. Fruit and sugar, porridge or Shredded Wheat. Bread or toast with butter or margarine and marmalade or honey. Milk in tea.

Mid-morning. Fruit juice with sugar.

Dinner. Chicken, rabbit, white fish in amounts prescribed. Potatoes and other vegetables. Stewed fruit with milk to drink or on the pudding.

Tea. Bread, scones, buns in amounts prescribed. Jam or honey. Tomatoes or salad. Fish or egg or cheese, in amounts prescribed. Milk in tea.

Bedtime. Fruit juice.

NOTE. The quantities of the protein-rich foods will be controlled by the doctor's prescription.

Low-Sodium Diet for a Child (*Check this with your doctor*)

This may be prescribed for some months in the case of kidney disease. Low-sodium milk (Edosol), is used, as the child must have milk. The rest of the diet is the same as the foods allowed to adults (see page 134). The young child needs a modified meal-pattern as below:

Meal-Pattern for Younger Children on a Low-Sodium Diet

Breakfast. Porridge or fruit. Unsalted bread and butter or margarine. Egg or white fish, tomatoes, fishcake. Tea with Edosol milk.

Mid-morning. Sweetened fruit juice or Edosol milk.

Dinner. Meat, chicken, white fish, omelette. Vegetables cooked without salt. Edosol milk pudding. Stewed fruit with cream, pancake, bread-and-butter pudding, batter pudding, or jam or fruit tart with cream, all made without salt.

Tea. Tea with Edosol. Unsalted bread toasted with unsalted butter or margarine and jam or marmalade. Special biscuits. Fruit.

Supper. Edosol milk flavoured with drinking chocolate. Fish and chips, poached egg, omelette, shepherd's pie, cottage pie, lamb cutlets, or home-made soup, all cooked without salt.

Extras. Honey, jam, marmalade, glucose sweets.

NOTE. For the very young child, supper and tea will be combined at teatime and only a drink taken at bedtime.

DENTAL CARIES

How the Normal Diet is Modified

Three factors are important:

1. General good nutrition (see page 15).

2. Restriction in amounts of sticky foods containing sugar and starch which cling round the teeth (for example, certain types of sweets, biscuits, and cakes). If these are eaten the teeth should be cleaned by brushing or rinsing the mouth with water or by eating a piece of raw fruit or vegetable afterwards.

3. By attending to the consistency. Every meal should have something requiring chewing to give jaw and gum exercise. Biscuits and other sweet things which require chewing and contain ingredients which don't stick to the teeth are allowed (see recipes Nos. 544–5).

When sweet things are given have them at meal times and not between.

UNDERNUTRITION

Causes of undernutrition in children are similar to those for adults, see page 170.

Sometimes a child refuses to eat certain foods as a means of manipulating the adult. This frequently happens when a child feels he or she is not getting the attention and affection expected from the adult. The most effective way of regaining attention is to be difficult at meal times, especially by refusing to eat a food to which the adult attaches great importance. It is important not to let the child see that you are concerned by his refusal to eat and not to coax or bully. When the child sees his behaviour is not having any effect he will soon start to eat normally again.

It is very important to see that undernourished children have an adequate breakfast and that when they have between-meal snacks, these are nourishing ones such as a milky drink.

If the child has an aversion to a nutritionally important food, then it is important to increase the consumption of substitutes. For example, if a child refuses to eat green vegetables, he will often eat an alternative such as an orange, or take a drink of blackcurrant syrup.

An undernourished child needs a high-calorie diet, therefore all foods should be as concentrated as possible to avoid too much bulk. See the diet for adults, page 170.

ANAEMIA

The treatment is the same as for the adult. See page 182.

CHAPTER 14

Diet in Old Age

A HEALTHY, active, old person does not need any special diet. Familiar foods and eating habits are very important to their happiness and well-being. It is unwise to suggest changes unless there are very compelling reasons.

The good normal diet for old age is the same as for adults (see page 15).

There are, however, various circumstances which bring about changes in old people's eating habits, gradually leading to poor nutrition and a decline in health.

Among the causes are loneliness and unhappiness, which frequently lead to a disinclination to prepare proper meals. Old men who have not been used to doing their own catering frequently deteriorate in health when there is no one to look after them. The loss of teeth or poor dentures or removal of dentures for eating frequently lead to changes in eating habits, which are usually for the worse.

If these adverse circumstances can be righted and a better diet obtained, marked improvement frequently follows. The old person loses the apathy of the malnourished and becomes lively and happy again.

Frequent attacks of indigestion will sometimes mean that certain important foods are omitted from the diet and no substitutions made.

Financial difficulties are another frequent cause of trouble. Rising costs of fuel and other expenses can lead to less being spent on food, and because it is difficult for the old to change their eating habits they tend to go without rather than to eat different and cheaper foods.

In many cases they do not know how to adapt to reduced finances.

Shopping and food-storage difficulties can also lead to a

poor diet. The difficulty of buying small enough amounts of perishable foods is a very real one unless shopkeepers are sympathetic.

Foods for Feeding the Aged

Beverages. Any which are liked, alcohol in moderation. A little is good because it acts as a comforter.

Breads, cakes, and biscuits. Any kinds, but they should not form too large a part of the diet.

Cereals. Any allowed. The use of some whole-grain, e.g. breakfast cereal, helps to prevent constipation.

Cheese. Mild Cheddar and processed cheeses grated or melted in sauces or soups are best. Cottage cheese is easy to eat and digest. Of all the protein-rich foods, cheese is best value for money.

Condiments. Well-flavoured foods are enjoyed by old people, but don't overdo it or indigestion may result.

Eggs. 3 to 5 weekly cooked any way. If they are hard-boiled it is advisable to mash them before serving.

Fats, oils, and cream. All in moderation. Margarine, butter, and cream are best because of the vitamins they contain.

Fish. Boned fish is safest, or canned. Soft roes make good snack meals and salmon, herring, and sardine provide vitamins A and D as well.

Fruit. Fresh oranges or orange juice. Mashed ripe banana and soft fruits. Stewed or canned fruit, fruit juices, rose-hip syrup.

Meat, game, and poultry. Any except the very fat meats, such as pork, and rich poultry like goose and duck.

Milk. One of the most important foods. At least 1 pt (2 c.) daily for drinking and cooking. Evaporated or condensed milks give concentrated alternatives but skimmed milks are best avoided as they lack the vitamins found in the cream.

Old people who refuse to take milk drinks will often take milk puddings and soups made with milk or will use evaporated milk on cereals and puddings instead of cream.

Preserves. Any kind they like.

Puddings and pastry. Milk puddings, jellies, ice cream, stewed fruits, custard, light sponge puddings are best. Avoid rich pastry and suet puddings.

Sauces and gravies. Avoid the very fatty ones. Otherwise give any kind they like.

Soups. Any kind they like.

Sugar and sugar confectionery. Any kind they like, but not too many sweets eaten between meals.

Vegetables. Potatoes and a green vegetable should be included every day together with any other kind they like.

Daily Allowance of Basic Foods

Milk. 1 pt (2 c.) or more. Not less than ½ pt (1 c.).

Eggs. 1 daily if possible, at least 3 a week.

Meat, fish, and cheese. A good helping of at least one of these daily.

Vegetables and fruits. Potatoes and at least one other vegetable or instead of the second vegetable have one orange or one tomato or a dose of rose-hip syrup or blackcurrant juice or purée.

Fats. 1 oz. (2 level Tbs.) of margarine or butter and some additional fat for cooking.

Bread. 2 to 3 slices, or more if the person is active and not obese.

Meal-Pattern for Old People

On waking. Tea.

Breakfast. Cereal with milk and sugar *or* egg, bacon, or fish dish. Bread with butter or margarine and marmalade. Beverage.

Mid-morning. Beverage and biscuits or bread and butter.

Midday. Meat with potatoes and vegetable or salad. Pudding. Beverage.

Tea. Bread and butter. Cake or biscuit. Tea.

Evening. Cheese or egg snack, cold meat and salad, or sandwiches made with any of these. Tomato or orange. Bread and butter with preserves. Beverage.

Bedtime. Milk drink and biscuits or a sandwich.

Special Diets and the Aged

The treatment for many of the degenerative diseases of the old frequently includes dietary changes. Long-established habits make it difficult to get the cooperation of the patient unless his desire to get better is sufficiently strong to overcome his natural dislike of change.

In hospital they will often cooperate to please the charming nurse or the dietitian, and at home to please those who are caring for them, or because they want to get well and become independent again.

Special diets are basically the same for the aged as for younger people and details are given in the previous chapters.

Some modification to their diet is, however, necessary when the old suffer from disabilities, and the following suggestions for dealing with these difficulties have been found helpful.

Chewing Difficulties

It is surprising the amount of chewing that can be done with hard old gums. But certain modifications in the consistency of foods are advisable.

Cheese. Should be grated because if swallowed in lumps it is very likely to cause discomfort. Moistened with a little bottled sauce or salad dressing, it will hold together for sandwich fillings. Melted in sauces and in soups is another good way of giving it. Cheese dishes are usually soft in texture and a good substitute for meat.

Meat. Is better minced and mixed with gravy or sauce to moisten it and make it easier to swallow. The sauces should be well flavoured and varied to avoid monotony. Canned and packet soups made thick can serve as quick sauces and diluted tomato purée is another easy one. Tender meat from stews, braises, or roasts can be chopped finely and mixed with the gravy.

Fish. May need flaking and mixing with sauces as for the

meat. Where the eyesight is poor it is wiser to remove bones. For the old person living alone fillets of fish are the best buy, or canned fish where the bones are softened.

Eggs. Are easy to eat if lightly cooked, but hard-cooked ones should be mashed or chopped.

Fruit. Is too difficult raw except for mashed fruit, soft fruits, and banana, but stewed, pulped, or puréed fruit and fruit juices should be consumed frequently. Rose-hip syrup is good, as the old person often likes its sweetness.

Vegetables. Tend to be excluded because of chewing and digesting difficulties and this leads to vitamin deficiency. They are easy to eat if chopped finely, mashed, or sieved, and should be eaten every day. The canned infant purées are often a good solution to this problem.

Puddings such as milk puddings, jellies, ices, and light sponge puddings are the easiest for old people to deal with.

Indigestion and Flatulence

These troubles are frequently due to an inability to chew properly and once this has been taken care of, as suggested above, the trouble will probably disappear. Sometimes simply eating smaller meals more frequently helps.

The ability to digest does, however, tend to decline with age and it is frequently advisable to reduce the intake of foods known to cause discomfort and flatulence.

The following are other suggestions which have been found helpful, though it must be borne in mind that foods which cause indigestion differ with individuals.

Cheese. Swallowing lumps of cheese without chewing, or eating very ripe cheese, sometimes causes trouble and leads old people to say that they can't digest cheese. This is a pity, as cheese is an excellent food for the old.

If it is used as already suggested for those who can't chew properly, most people will then have no more trouble.

Meats. Very fatty meats like pork, goose, and duck are usually best avoided, and so are heavily salted and pickled meats. Simple methods of cooking with the minimum amount of frying and moderate seasoning are the best.

Fish. Usually an easily digested food, fish is often made less so by cooking methods, especially bad frying, which produces a fatty, indigestible result. An improvement in cooking techniques by substituting grilling or baking for frying are the remedies. Salted, heavily smoked, soused, and pickled fish sometimes have to be avoided as well.

Fruit. The omission of fruit from a diet on the grounds of indigestion is a fairly common occurrence. Unless fairly large amounts of potatoes and vegetables are eaten instead, this can lead to vitamin C deficiency. The best way to give fruit in these cases is either to mash soft, ripe fruit or use it stewed, canned, or sieved, served with milk pudding or breakfast cereal. Fruit juices, rose-hip syrup, or blackcurrant syrup are good alternatives.

Vegetables. Unfortunately the most commonly eaten vegetables (cabbage, Brussels sprouts, broccoli, cauliflower) are frequently found to produce flatulence and this tends to cause old people to eat inadequate amounts of them. Freshly cooked, boiled, or mashed potatoes are valuable if eaten regularly. Mash them with milk and butter or margarine and season well.

Spinach, cooked and chopped or sieved, is usually easily digested and so are skinned tomatoes. Other vegetables usually well tolerated are cooked and chopped carrots, garden or frozen peas, and cooked beetroot, as long as it is not doused in vinegar. Boiled onions can often be easily digested and their flavour enjoyed while fried ones might cause great discomfort.

Puddings. Rich pastry and steamed suet puddings are best avoided.

Sugar, preserves, and sweets. Excessive consumption of very sweet foods, especially between meals, is best avoided. Sometimes only sieved jams or jellies are advisable.

Fats, oils, and cream. Intolerance of fats is a frequent disability in old age, and a moderate fat intake (page 84) is frequently advised. Avoiding fried foods and any cooking methods using a lot of fat (pastries, rich sauces, suet) is usually all that is needed. Butter and margarine are the best fats to use for general purposes.

Sauces and gravies. Old people enjoy well-flavoured food and sometimes use bottled sauces with a heavy hand to make dull food more palatable. As the vinegar and spices in these sometimes cause trouble it is better to improve the flavour of food during cooking rather than resort to these devices.

Condiments. Very highly seasoned food can produce indigestion, but is frequently popular with old people. A moderate use of condiments is important to make food palatable for those with a declining sense of taste.

Managing on a Small Income

The fact that the wrong economies can lead to a diet of cheap food regardless of nutritional needs means that those managing on a small income frequently eat an inadequate diet and become malnourished and ailing. To know which foods are good value nutritionally is important to old and young.

A portion of either meat, fish, or eggs should be eaten at least once a day in addition to milk and some vegetable and fruit. These, together with bread and margarine and other foods added for variety and to satisfy the appetite, should be regarded as essentials in the diet.

Milk. Very good value nutritionally. All old people should try to have 1 pt (2 c.) a day for drinking and cooking.

Cheese. One of the cheapest sources of protein – much cheaper than meat.

Meats. Nutritionally, the cheap cuts are as good as the more expensive but are more trouble to cook. The easiest to manage are minced meat (lean if possible) and chops from neck of lamb which cook easily (by grilling, baking, or stewing). Corned beef is an excellent meat and can now be bought in small tins; when opened it can safely be left in a cold larder for two days. The following foods are also easy and economical:

Fish. Cheap fish is as good nutritionally as dearer kinds. A herring, boned and steamed or grilled, is excellent value.

Eggs. Eggs are such a valuable food that at least 3–5 a week should be bought. Fresh eggs are an excellent gift to take to an old person.

Fruit. A bottle of rose-hip syrup is probably the best investment for vitamin C. Oranges are also good value.

Vegetables. Potatoes freshly cooked and used frequently are always important in low-cost diets. Cheap green vegetables and carrots should be used when possible, and onions for their flavour. Potatoes and green vegetables eaten daily can take the place of fruit, or, if the person does not like green vegetables, a tomato a day instead.

Bread. Ordinary white bread is the best value for money.

Puddings. Puddings are not essential in a diet but give pleasure to those with a sweet tooth. The best are milk and cereal puddings or custards with stewed fruits when available from the garden, or when plentiful and cheap. For those who like a savoury end to a meal, bread or plain biscuits with cheese (grated if chewing is difficult) is more economical than pudding.

Cakes and biscuits. Luxury foods such as cakes and biscuits should not be bought at the expense of other food, except as a treat. They are good items to take as gifts to old people who are known to be fond of them.

Sugars, preserves, and sweets. Nutritionally these are extras to give variety to the diet and the cheapest palatable ones are the best buy.

Fats, oils, and cream. Margarine is best value for money. Home-made dripping is the most economical fat for frying.

Soups. Soups are comforting in cold weather and can be made very cheaply at home. If soups are bought, packet ones are probably the best, as it is not necessary to use the whole packet at once. They and the tinned ones can be made to go further by diluting with a meat cube and water, or with water saved from cooking vegetables. Meat cubes and water with chopped raw vegetables cooked in it, or mashed cooked ones added, with some rice or oatmeal for thickening, make a good economical dish.

Old People Living Alone

If you have an elderly relative or friend who insists on living alone but no longer has the ability or facilities to cook properly, it is a problem to know how to help them to eat enough of the right foods to maintain good health.

'Meals on wheels' are an answer to this difficulty but they are available to comparatively few people. Many local authorities have arrangements for extensive welfare services for old people. Details of these can be obtained from your town hall.

Ready prepared and canned foods are usually too expensive for the old age pensioner to buy. Their solution to the feeding problem is too much bread, biscuits, sweets, and cups of tea.

The deficiencies which occur in such a diet are chiefly shortage of protein (usually obtained from meat, fish, eggs, cheese, and milk) and vitamin deficiency, due to the absence of vegetables and inadequate amounts of fruit as an alternative.

Gifts to old people can be selected to help remedy these deficiencies, for example, a gift of eggs. A boiled egg a day helps to make up for the lack of proper meals. If they like canned milk, give them small tins of evaporated or condensed milk to go with breakfast cereal or to make cocoa and other milk drinks. Ordinary Cheddar cheese or boxes of varied-flavoured processed cheese is another good gift as are the small-sized cans of luncheon meat, chopped ham, Spam, and corned beef, provided their hands are strong enough to use a can opener. Likewise, the small tins of baby food give an excellent variety of very suitable foods for the aged. To overcome the lack of vegetables, take any fresh fruit you know they will eat; otherwise give them a bottle of rose-hip syrup, which is often popular because of its sweetness. Anything which can be used to make hot drinks, such as bottled blackcurrant juice, yeast extract, and proprietary drinks of various kinds, may also be helpful.

Recipes

CONVERSION TABLES

Table of Handy Measures

The cup used in the recipes is a half pint or 10 fluid ounce size (approx. 300 millilitres). (An American cup is 8 fluid ounces.)

1 tablespoon equals 15 millilitres.
1 teaspoon equals 5 millilitres.
1 pint is 20 fluid ounces. (An American pint is 16 fluid ounces.)
1 pound is 16 ounces.
1½ level c. flour hold 8 oz.
1 level c. castor or granulated sugar holds 8 oz.
1 level c. fresh breadcrumbs holds 3 oz.
1 level c. syrup or treacle holds 14 oz.
1 level c. fat holds 8 oz.

To Convert to Metric

The table below shows equivalent metric weights and measures together with approximate equivalents which can be used to convert quantities given in the recipes to metric quantities. These approximations are sufficiently accurate to produce good results, but they may alter the carbohydrate and calorie values per portion.

British	Metric	Approximate quantities for recipe conversion
1 ounce	28·35 grams	25–30 grams
1 pound	453·6 grams	500 grams or ½ kilogram
1 fluid ounce	28·41 millilitres	25–30 millilitres
1 pint	568·2 millilitres	5 decilitres or ½ litre
1 inch	2·54 centimetres	2½ centimetres

Temperatures

	°F.	°C.
Tepid water	80	30
Simmering	185	85
Boiling	212	100
Freezing	32	0

Oven Temperatures

°F	°C
250	120
275	135
300	150
325	163
350	177
375	190
400	205
425	218
450	232
475	246
500	316

ABBREVIATIONS

Abbreviations Used in Recipes

oz. = ounce or ounces
fl. oz. = fluid ounce or ounces
lb. = pound or pounds
pt = pint or pints
tsp. = teaspoon or teaspoons
Tbs. = tablespoon or tablespoons
c. = cup or cups
qt = quart or quarts

NOTE. A fluid ounce is a volume measure and has been used for the liquids needed in some recipes. Many kitchen measures are marked in fluid ounces as well as pints.

NOTES ON THE RECIPES

Wherever possible the carbohydrate and calorie content has

been indicated. The figures used for these estimations have been taken from *The Composition of Foods* by McCance and Widdowson (1960) (composition per ounce).

When it is not practicable to calculate the recipes exactly, for example because of the number of alternative ingredients, an indication has been given of its carbohydrate and calorie value (i.e. low or high). Recipes specially adapted for low-sodium, low-protein, and gluten-free diets have also been indicated. Where a recipe can be adapted to suit a variety of diets, the necessary modification is given at the foot of the recipe under the heading 'Variation'.

BEVERAGES

1. Milk

These are the varieties of milk which can form the basis of drinks:

(*a*) *Whole, or full-cream, liquid milk* (ordinary bottled milk). The amount of cream varies considerably, those with most cream being the dearest. For most diets the cream is the least important part of milk. The milk may be raw, pasteurized, or sterilized, the last two being the safest to give to sick people.

(*b*) *Skimmed liquid milk*, which is obtainable from some large dairies, is ordinary milk which has been machine-skimmed (that is with the cream removed) and is cheaper than any of the whole milks. If a bottle of whole milk is allowed to stand and the top poured off carefully, the milk left will be sufficiently free of fat for all but the very strict low-fat diet.

(*c*) *Dried whole milk* forms the basis of most infant milks. When mixed with water it can be used as fresh liquid milk.

(*d*) *Instant dried skimmed milk* is equivalent to fresh skimmed when mixed with water.

NOTE. Both the dried milks may be added dry to fruit juices and other beverages and whisked in with the rest of the ingredients.

(*e*) *Enriched or fortified milks* are all suitable for using as a basis for drinks, sauces, milk puddings, and cooking in general whenever it is desirable to increase the protein and calorie content of the diet.

(i) *Enriched whole milk.* Warm the fresh milk and sprinkle the powder on top. Either whisk until smooth, shake well in a screw-top jar, or mix with an electric blender.

Proportions: 1 pt. (2 c.) milk to 2 oz. (4 heaped Tbs.) instant dried skimmed or full-cream milk powder, or Prosol (Trufood) or 1 oz. (2½ level Tbs.) Casilan (Glaxo).

Sugar, glucose, honey, syrup, or treacle may be added for sweet beverages, allowing ½ oz. (1 level Tbs.) or more according to taste. Glucose must be dissolved in warm liquid before being added. Cream may be added if it is allowed the patient.

(ii) *Enriched skimmed liquid milk.* This is primarily used for high-protein, low-fat, low-calorie diets. Instead of liquid skimmed milk, 2 oz. dried skimmed milk powder (4 heaped Tbs.) can be dissolved in 1 pt (2 c.) of warm water.

Proportions: 1 pt (2 c.) liquid skimmed milk with: 2 oz. dried skimmed milk powder (4 heaped Tbs.), 1 oz. Casilan (2½ level Tbs.) or 1oz. milk powder and ½ oz. Casilan.

Alternative Mixtures when only powder is used.

Proportions to add to 1 pt (2c.) water: 4 oz. dried skimmed milk powder (¾ cup), 2 oz. dried skimmed milk powder (4 heaped Tbs.) and 1 oz. Casilan (2½ level Tbs.), or 3 oz. dried skimmed milk powder (½ c.) and ½ oz. Casilan.

2. Milk Drinks

Quantities: Allow 6–8 fl. oz. (¾ c.) of liquid for each drink.

Any of the milks in No. 1 (*a–e*) may be used for these drinks. A day's supply of fortified milk may be made at a time and stored in the refrigerator. Any of the following flavours may be used, adding sweetening to taste:

3. Blackcurrant

8 fl. oz. (¾ c.) milk 1–1½ Tbs. of blackcurrant syrup. Serve cold.

Ice cream may be added for high-calorie diets in which fat is allowed.

4. Apricot Shake

6 fl. oz. (½ c.) milk. 2 oz. apricot purée from fresh, canned, or frozen fruit (¼ c.) .

5. Banana Milk Shake

8 fl. oz. (¾ c.) milk. 1 small ripe banana (2 oz. skinned).

Mix in the electric blender or with a rotary whisk.

6. Honey Prune Shake

6 fl. oz. (½ c.) milk. Honey to sweeten. 2 fl. oz. (4 Tbs.) unsweetened prune juice from stewed prunes. 1 tsp. lemon juice and a pinch of salt.

7. Strawberry Shake

6 fl. oz. (½ c.) milk. 2 oz. sieved strawberries from fresh, canned, or frozen fruit (¼ c.). Sugar if necessary.

8. Milk Possett

½ pt. (1 c.) milk. ½–1 oz. syrup, treacle, or honey (½–1 level Tbs.). Heat milk and stir in the sweetening. Serve hot.

9. Malted Milk

½ pt (1 c.) milk. 1 oz. malt extract (1 level Tbs.). Heat milk and stir in the extract. Serve hot.

10. Coffee

Flavour to taste with soluble coffee or strong black coffee and serve hot or cold. If ice cream is allowed, add it to the cold drinks.

11. Fruit Juice Drinks

To 8 fl. oz. (¾ c.) of the basic milk drink add 1 or more Tbs. fruit juice, purée or syrup. Serve cold.

12. Loganberry Drink

Quantities for 1

⅛ pt (5 Tbs.) milk
½ oz. glucose (1 level Tbs.)
½ egg
½ oz. instant dried milk powder (1 heaped Tbs.)
2 oz. canned loganberries (¼ c.)

Put ingredients into the electric blender and mix until smooth. Alternatively mix with a rotary egg-whisk. If necessary, strain to remove pips. Chill before serving.

One portion. Carbohydrate 40 g. Calories 255.

13. Iced Coffee

Quantities for 1

$\frac{1}{8}$ pt. (5 Tbs.) black coffee
$\frac{1}{2}$ oz. sugar (1 level Tbs.)
1 Tbs. cream
$\frac{1}{4}$ pt ($\frac{1}{2}$ c.) milk, plain or enriched
1 oz. (2 level Tbs.) ice cream

Make the coffee, sweeten and cool. Add the milk and then chill. Add the cream or ice cream just before serving.

One portion (using plain milk). Carbohydrate 28 g. Calories 242.

14. Vanilla Egg Nog

Quantities for 1

1 egg
1–2 level tsp. sugar
8 fl. oz. ($\frac{3}{4}$ c.) hot or cold milk, plain or enriched
A few grains of salt
Vanilla essence to taste
1 tsp. sherry or brandy (optional)
Grated nutmeg (optional)

Beat egg and sugar thoroughly and add the milk. Add the flavourings to taste.

One portion (plain milk, no sherry). Carbohydrate 19 g. Calories 272.

15. Hawaiian Egg Nog

Quantities for 1

1 egg
Pinch of salt
$\frac{1}{4}$ pt ($\frac{1}{2}$ c.) canned pineapple juice
Extra sugar if liked
Pinch of nutmeg

Separate yolk and white. Beat yolk well and stir in the cold juice. Beat the egg white stiffly and stir it in. Pour into a large glass and sprinkle with nutmeg.

One portion (no extra sugar). Carbohydrate 19 g. Calories 162.

16. Orange Egg Nog

Quantities for 1

1 small egg
½ oz. sugar (1 level Tbs.)
6 oz. (½ c.) orange juice, chilled

Whip egg and sugar until frothy. Add orange juice and beat again. Serve at once.

One portion. Carbohydrate 31 g. Calories 214.

17. Banana Egg Nog

Quantities for 1

1 egg
2 oz. peeled banana (1 small)
¼ pt (½ c.) single cream
2 Tbs. milk
½ oz. Casilan (1¼ level Tbs.) *or* 1 oz. milk powder (2½ level Tbs.)
½ oz. sugar (1 level Tbs.)
Vanilla essence

Put all the ingredients into the electric blender and mix until smooth. Alternatively, beat with a rotary whisk. Serve cold.

One portion. Carbohydrate 38 to 43 g. Calories 549 to 671.

18. Chocolate Egg Nog

Quantities for 1

1 egg
8 fl. oz. (¾ c.) milk, plain or enriched
⅛ oz. cocoa (½ level Tbs.)
¼ oz. sugar (½ level Tbs.)

Separate white and yolk. Make cocoa in the usual way with the milk and sugar. Add the egg yolk and whisk. Beat whites and fold in. Serve hot.

One portion. Carbohydrate 20 g. Calories 288.

19. Iced Tea with Lemon

Method 1. Strain hot strong tea into glasses one-third full of ice cubes. Add sugar and lemon juice to taste and a thin slice of lemon per glass. This usually gives a clearer drink than method 2.

Method 2. Make average or weakish tea. Strain. Add sugar and lemon juice to taste. Cool and chill in the refrigerator. Serve with a slice of lemon.

If you are going to use a lot of iced tea this is the better method, as it will keep some time in cold storage and is ready for instant use.

Variations. Substitute some orange juice for the lemon and an orange slice on top. Fresh mint leaves are a pleasant addition.

20. Barley Water

Quantities for ¾ – 1 pt. (1½–2 c.). *Cooking time* 2 hrs

- 2 oz. pearl barley (4 level Tbs.)
- 1 qt (4 c.) water
- Rind and juice of 2 lemons
- Sugar to taste

Wash the barley and put in a pan with the water and thinly peeled lemon rinds. Cover and simmer gently 2 hrs. Strain, sweeten to taste, cool, and add lemon juice.

Variation. Add milk to taste instead of the lemon juice.

21. Arrowroot Drink

Quantities for 1

- 1 level tsp. arrowroot
- 1 Tbs. water
- ½ pt (1 c.) milk, plain or enriched
- Sugar to taste

Blend arrowroot gradually with the water. Bring the milk to the boil, pour on to the arrowroot, mix, and return to the pan. Bring to the boil, stirring all the time. Sweeten to taste and serve hot or chilled.

Variation. If skimmed milk is used, this is suitable for a low-fat diet.

22. Enriched Gruel

This is a very thin porridge with sugar, dried milk, and cream added. Any cereal can be used to make the porridge, e.g. oatmeal (strained afterwards), patent groats, and other infant cereals, semolina, or ground rice.

Quantity: Allow 6 oz. (½ c.) thinned porridge per portion, preferably made with milk. A portion of the family porridge can be thinned for this.

Add: ½ oz. glucose (1 level Tbs.)
½ oz. full-cream dried-milk powder (1¼ level Tbs.)
Cream to taste, if allowed

Variations. Use Edosol or Casilan for low-sodium diets and dried skimmed milk for low-fat diets (omit cream).

Proportions for Rolled Oat Gruel

Quantities for 1

½ oz. rolled oats (⅛ c.)
½ pt (1 c.) water or milk
Salt (omit for low-sodium diets)

Cook for the time recommended on the packet. Sieve, sweeten, and enrich as above.

23. Vegetable Juices

These may be bought in small cans. Chill before serving. Fresh vegetable juices may be prepared in an electric juice extractor. Alternatively, make vegetable stock by boiling chopped vegetables in water to cover for 20 minutes and then straining and seasoning to taste. Serve hot or cold.

24. Tomato Yogurt

Mix equal quantities of tomato juice and yogurt. Beat to blend well and season to taste with salt and pepper. If liked, add onion, celery or garlic salt, or paprika pepper and a little Worcestershire sauce. It is better if the tomato juice and yogurt are both chilled before mixing.

25. Lemonade or Orangeade

Method 1

4 lemons or 3 lemons and 1 orange
2 pts (4 c.) boiling water
4 oz. sugar (½ c.)

Wash lemons and slice. Put in a jug with the sugar. Pour over the boiling water, cover, and leave to infuse until cold. Strain and serve cold with ice.

Method 2 (for electric blender).

2–3 lemons, 2 oranges and 1 lemon, or 1 orange and 2 lemons.

Wash fruit and cut into about 8 pieces. Put in the blender with water to cover and mix for a few seconds until just broken up. Strain at once. Dilute to taste and add as much sugar or liquid glucose as possible (dissolve glucose powder in warm water).

Variations. 1. Make either of these without sugar and use to make a long drink from very sweet blackcurrant syrup or rose-hip syrup. This makes a drink very rich in vitamin C. 2. For *low-calorie and low-carbohydrate diets* make either of the above and sweeten with saccharin or Saxin instead of sugar.

26. Glucose Sweetened Fruit Juices

Use fresh fruit juices or unsweetened canned ones. The addition of some lemon juice brings out the flavour and enables more glucose to be added. Powdered glucose needs to be dissolved in warm liquid, so use a little of the fruit juice to do this and, when cold, add remaining juice.

Alternatively, make a thick glucose-and-water solution and use this for sweetening.

27. Recipes for the Juice Extractor

An electric juice extractor makes it possible to produce a wide variety of fresh fruit and vegetable juices in the home. Manufacturers provide recipe booklets. The following are a few mixtures which most people will like.

28. Fruit and Parsley Juice

Quantities for 1

½ oz. parsley (handful)
1 small orange, peeled
1 apple
⅛ lemon, peeled
½ banana, peeled

The banana may be mashed separately and added to the juices just before serving.

29. Apple and Lemon

Quantities for 1

8 oz. apple (2 medium)
¼ peeled lemon
Sugar or glucose to taste

30. Celery and Tomato

Quantities for 1

4 oz. celery (2 large sticks)
6 oz. tomatoes (3 medium)
⅛ peeled lemon
Sugar and salt to taste

31. Carrots and Orange

Quantities for 1

8 oz. carrots (2 medium)
1 peeled orange
Sugar to taste

32. Cocktail

4 oz. carrots (1 medium)
4 oz. apples (1 medium)
4 oz. celery (2 large sticks)
½ peeled lemon

33. Recipes for an Electric Blender or Liquidizer

Any of the recipes Nos. 1–26 are suitable, but the following are specially designed for this form of mixing. Put all the ingredients in the goblet together and switch on. The electric blender mixes ingredients more smoothly and faster than is possible by any hand method.

34. Tomato Milk Drink

Quantities for 1

2 tomatoes (4 oz.)
⅛ pt (5 Tbs.) water
½ oz. milk powder (1¼ level Tbs.)
½ level tsp. celery salt

Suitable for a low-calorie or low-fat diet if skimmed milk powder is used.

One portion. Carbohydrate 9–10 g. Calories 63–91.

35. Tomato Cheese

Quantities for 1

¼ pt (½ c.) chilled tomato juice
2 oz. cottage cheese (¼ c.)
Pinch of celery salt
Additional salt to taste

Suitable for a low-calorie or low-fat diet.

One portion. Carbohydrate 9 g. Calories 126.

36. Banana and Pineapple

Quantities for 1

2 oz. peeled ripe banana (1 small)
½ oz. milk powder (1¼ level Tbs.)
¼ pt (½ c.) canned pineapple juice

Suitable for a low-fat diet if skimmed milk powder is used.

One portion (no sugar). Carbohydrate 36–37 g. Calories 271.

37. Orange and Milk

Quantities for 1

6 fl. oz. (½ c.) orange juice
1 oz. milk powder (2½ level Tbs.)
¼ oz. (½ level Tbs.) sugar, glucose, or honey

Suitable for a low-fat diet if skimmed milk powder is used

One portion. Carbohydrate 35–38 g. Calories 187–276.

38. Cheese and Banana

Quantities for 1

¼ pt (½ c.) milk, plain or enriched
2 oz. cottage cheese (¼ c.)
3 oz. (1 medium) peeled ripe banana
¼ oz. brown sugar (½ level Tbs.)

Suitable for a low-fat diet if the milk is skimmed.

One portion. Carbohydrate 17 g. Calories 189.

39. Chocolate Banana Milk Shake

Quantities for 1

¼ pt (½ c.) milk
½ oz. milk powder (1¼ level Tbs.)
¼ oz. caster sugar (½ level Tbs.)
⅛ oz. cocoa (½ level Tbs.)
2 oz. peeled banana (1 small)
½ oz. (2 level Tbs.) desiccated coconut (optional)

Place all ingredients in the electric blender and mix until smooth. Alternatively, beat with a rotary egg whisk. Serve hot or cold.

One portion. Carbohydrate 32–33 g. Calories 230–260.

SOUPS AND STOCKS

40. Vegetable Stock

Cooking time. 20–30 mins. (5–10 mins. pressure cooking). Use any mixture of vegetables, such as the outside leaves of cabbage, cauliflower stalks, outside celery stalks and leaves, green tops of leeks, watercress stalks, mushroom stalks and peelings, onion peelings and skins, and any other vegetable trimmings available. Chop or shred them fine, and add boiling water to barely cover. Add a few bacon rinds, a bouquet garni, a few peppercorns, and one or two cloves. Cover and cook. Strain and use.

41. Bone Stock

Cooking time. 2–3 hrs (¾ hr pressure cooking). Use any kind of bones. Chop them and put in a pan with water to cover. Bring to the boil and skim. For each pt of water add 1 onion, 1 carrot, and a bouquet garni. Cover and simmer slowly. Strain and, when cold, remove the fat from the top.

42. Beef and Vegetable Soup

Quantities for 4. *Cooking time* 20 mins.

2 carrots, shredded
1 stalk celery, chopped
1 sliced onion, chopped
½ oz. (1 level Tbs.) butter
¾ pt (1½ c.) stock
¼ pt (½ c.) tomato juice
4 oz. lean beef, minced (½ c.)
Salt and pepper to taste
Chopped parsley

Melt the butter and add the vegetables. Cover and cook gently for about 5 mins. without browning. Add stock, tomato juice, and the beef and bring to the boil. Simmer gently, stirring frequently for about 10 min. or until the vegetables are cooked. Season to taste and serve with chopped parsley. The cooked soup may be put into an electric blender to make a smooth mixture. Thin down with milk afterwards if necessary.

One portion (without milk). Carbohydrate 5 g. Calories 100.

43. Broths

Stock to use. Stock from boiled meat, boiled chicken carcass, meat and bone stock, bone stock, meat or yeast extract and water, bouillon cubes and water.

Quantities. Allow 1½ pt (3 c.) stock for 4 portions. *Cooking time.* Will vary with the ingredients. Average 10–20 mins. *Ingredients* to allow for 1½ pt stock.

44. Cabbage Broth

½ lb. cabbage
2 oz. cooked or smoked sausage, sliced (add just before serving)

For method, see No. 48.

One portion. Carbohydrate 7 g. Calories 63.

45. Onion Broth

3 large onions (¾ lb.)
1 oz. breadcrumbs (3 level Tbs.)
A little yeast extract or grated cheese
Pinch of sugar
Salt and pepper

For method, see No. 48.

One portion. Carbohydrate 10 g. Calories 46.

46. Julienne Soup

1 small carrot (2 oz.)
1 small turnip (3 oz.)
1 small leek (2 oz.)

For method, see No. 48.

One portion. Carbohydrate 4 g. Calories 19.

47. Carrot and Rice Soup

2 carrots (6 oz.)
½ oz. rice (1 level Tbs.)
Chopped parsley

For method, see No. 48.

One portion. Carbohydrate 12 g. Calories 43.

48. Pasta or Rice Soup

1 oz. vermicelli, noodles, macaroni, or rice

One portion. Carbohydrate 8 g. Calories 34.

Method for Nos. 44–8. Peel or otherwise prepare the vegetables and slice them very thinly or grate them coarsely. Bring the stock to the boil, add the chosen ingredients, and boil gently until they are cooked. Season to taste, adding chopped parsley or other herbs as desired. Serve very hot.

49. Sieved Vegetable Broth

Sieve the vegetables and return them to the soup.

Any combination of vegetables may be used, or vegetables plus pasta or cereals. Breadcrumbs or semolina may be used to make thickened broths, using ½–1 oz. to 1 pt liquid.

50. A Bread-and-cheese Broth

May be made by putting thin slices of stale French bread into the soup plates, pouring on boiling seasoned stock, and serving grated cheese separately.

51. Brain Soup

Quantities for 4. *Cooking time* ½ hr

8 oz. calf's brain
½ oz. (1 level Tbs.) butter
½ oz. plain flour (1½ level Tbs.) *or* ¼ oz. cornflour (¾ level Tbs.)
½ pt (1 c.) milk
1½ pts (3 c.) vegetable or chicken stock
1 egg yolk
1 Tbs. cream or evap. milk
Salt and pepper
1 Tbs. chopped parsley or chives

Soak the brains in cold water until all the blood is removed. Gently remove the skin and any fibre. Put brains in just enough warm water to cover, bring to the boil, and simmer 10 mins., drain, and slice. Make a sauce with the butter, flour, and milk. Add stock and sliced brains, simmer a few minutes. Mix egg yolk and cream in a small basin and pour a little of the stock into this. Mix well and pour back into the soup which should not be boiling at this stage. Heat and stir for a few minutes without boiling. Season to taste. Sprinkle with the chopped parsley or chives and serve at once.

One portion. Carbohydrate 9 g. Calories 143.

52. Calf's Foot Soup (*Low carbohydrate, low-calorie*)

Quantities for 4. *Cooking time* 3 hrs (1 hr pressure cooking)

1 calf's foot cut in pieces
4–5 sticks celery sliced
1 small onion
1 sprig parsley
1 sprig thyme
3 pts (6 c.) water (2 pts (4 c.) pressure cooker)
Salt and pepper
Chopped parsley or cooked vegetables to garnish

Wash the pieces of calf's foot. Put all the ingredients in a pan, and simmer gently for 3 hrs or pressure cook for 1 hr. Strain, re-heat, and season to taste. Serve with the chosen garnish.

53. Cheese Soup

Quantities for 4. *Cooking time* 15 mins.

1 oz. (2 level Tbs.) butter
1 oz. plain flour (3 level Tbs.) *or* ½ oz. cornflour (1½ level Tbs.)
1 pt (2 c.) chicken stock
½ pt (1 c.) milk
1 level tsp. Marmite
2 level Tbs. grated cheese
2 Tbs. single cream
Salt and pepper
Parsley to garnish

Make a roux with the butter and flour. Add chicken stock and milk and boil gently for 10 mins. Add the Marmite and stir until blended. Remove from the heat and add cheese and cream, whisking until smooth. Season to taste and garnish with parsley.

One portion. Carbohydrate 11 g. Calories 225.

54. Cream of Chicken Soup

Quantities for 4. *Cooking time* 1¼ hrs (½ hr pressure cooking)

1 chicken carcass
1 carrot, peeled
1 onion, peeled
Sprig of parsley
1¼ pts (2½ c.) water
½ pt (1 c.) thin white sauce (No. 79)
Salt and pepper
1–2 oz. (2–4 Tbs.) finely chopped cooked chicken meat or giblets
chopped parsley

Put the chicken carcass, vegetables, sprig of parsley, and water in a pan and simmer 1¼ hrs, or ½ hr pressure cooking. Strain. Stir in the sauce, season to taste and add the chicken meat or giblets (sieved if necessary), and the chopped parsley. Re-heat.

One portion. Carbohydrate 8 g. Calories 125.

Variation. Just before serving, add one egg yolk mixed with 2–3 Tbs. cream.

55. Cucumber Soup (*Low-fat*)

Quantities for 4. *Cooking time* ½ hr

1 lb. cucumber, sliced (1 large)
1 oz. onion (1 small)
Piece of bay leaf
1 pt (2 c.) fatless stock, well flavoured
Salt and pepper
Chopped parsley

Cook the cucumber, onion, bayleaf, and stock until the vegetables are tender. Remove bay leaf. Sieve, or put in the electric blender. Re-heat and season to taste. Serve with chopped parsley.

One portion. Carbohydrate 4 g. Calories 19.

56. Creamed Cucumber Soup

Quantities for 4. *Cooking time* 1 hr

1 lb. cucumber (1 large)
2 oz. onion (1 small)
1¼ pts (2½ c.) stock
Salt and pepper
2 egg yolks
¼ pt (½ c.) yogurt
Paprika pepper

Peel and slice the cucumber and onions. Simmer in the stock until soft. Sieve and re-boil. Season to taste. Remove from the heat. Mix the egg yolks with the yogurt and add to the soup. Stir and re-heat but do not boil. Serve hot, sprinkled with paprika pepper.

One portion. Carbohydrate 6 g. Calories 95.

57. Dairy Soup

Quantities for 4. *Cooking time* 15–20 mins.

- 2 oz. butter or margarine (4 level Tbs.)
- 2 oz. dried skimmed milk powder (4 heaped Tbs.)
- ½ level Tbs. plain flour *or* ¼ level Tbs. cornflour
- ¼ level tsp. dry mustard
- ¾ pt (1½ c.) warm water
- 2 oz. processed Cheddar cheese (2 slices)
- Salt and pepper
- 1 oz. chopped watercress *or* lettuce (1 c.)

Method 1. Melt the fat and remove from the heat. Stir in the milk powder, flour, and mustard. Mix well and gradually add the warm water, stirring until smooth. Bring to the boil, stirring constantly, and cook for a few minutes. Add the cheese and melt without boiling. Season to taste. Add the cress or lettuce and heat for another 5 mins.

Method 2. Put the milk powder, flour, mustard, and water into the electric blender and mix until smooth. Pour into a pan, stir until boiling, and cook a few minutes. Add the fat and cheese and heat without boiling until the cheese is melted. Mix until smooth, Season to taste, add the cress or lettuce and heat for another 5 mins.

NOTE. If a naked flame is used for cooking, it is advisable to make this soup in a double boiler as it tends to catch easily.

One portion. Carbohydrate 10 g. Calories 230.

58. Egg Broth

Quantities for 4

- 2 pts (4 c.) meat stock or broth
- 4 eggs
- Salt and pepper to taste
- 2 oz. bread, toasted (2 slices)
- Chopped parsley (optional)

Method 1. Heat the broth or stock to boiling point. Beat the egg until very light. Remove stock from the heat and pour the egg into it, whisking well to keep from curdling. Season and serve at once with fingers of toast. Add chopped parsley if allowed.

Method 2. Heat the broth or stock and season to taste. Break the egg into a heated soup plate and pour on the boiling soup. Stir round to mix egg before eating. Serve with fingers of toast and chopped parsley if allowed.

Method 3. Heat broth or stock and season to taste. Poach the egg in it and lift the egg out on to the soup plate. Sprinkle with chopped parsley and pour the soup over. Serve with fingers of toast.

One portion. Carbohydrate 10 g. Calories 137.

59. Fruit Soups (*low-fat*)

Quantities for 3–4. *Cooking time* depends on fruit

8 oz. fruit
1 pt (2 c.) water
Sugar to taste
Flavouring to taste
Cornflour, arrowroot, or potato starch to thicken

The sharper fruits like black and redcurrants, raspberries, and blackberries are the best to use and they should be fresh, as canned ones are rather too sweet. Frozen fruit may be suitable depending on the kind and the amount of sugar added. Apple flavoured with lemon rind also makes a good soup. Boil the fruit in the water until reduced to a pulp. Strain and measure the liquid. Sweeten and flavour to taste and thicken with cornflour, arrowroot, or potato starch in the proportion of ½–1 level Tbs. to 1 pt liquid. Blend thickening with a little cold water and add to the hot soup. Stir until it thickens and comes to the boil. Serve hot or cold. If cold, use the smaller amount of thickening, and sprinkle the top with caster sugar to prevent a skin forming during cooling.

60. Jellied Consommé with Mushrooms (*low-fat*)

Quantities for 4. *Cooking time* 15–20 mins.

4 oz. small mushrooms
½ pt (1 c.) water
1 tsp. wine vinegar
¼ oz. gelatine (1 level Tbs.)
½ pt (1 c.) consommé (canned is suitable)
Soya sauce
Worcester sauce
Salt and pepper to taste

Wash mushrooms, remove the stems, and chop them finely. Leave small mushrooms whole, cut others in pieces. Heat water and vinegar, add seasoning, and poach the mushrooms until tender, about 15–20 mins. Lift out and put in individual serving dishes. Dissolve the gelatine in the hot liquid, add consommé, salt and pepper, and sauces to taste. When well blended pour over the mushrooms and leave to set. Chill before serving.

One portion. Carbohydrate a trace. Calories 5.

61. Kidney Soup

Quantities for 4. *Cooking time* 2 hrs

8 oz. ox kidney
1 oz. (2 level Tbs.) fat
1 small onion sliced
1 oz. plain flour (3 level Tbs.)
2 pts (4 c.) stock
Small piece turnip, diced
1 small carrot, diced
Small piece celery, chopped
Sprig of parsley
1 bayleaf
Pinch of ground mace
Salt and pepper

Wash and skin the kidney. Cut in small pieces, removing the core. Heat the fat and fry the kidney quickly. Lift out and fry the onion and flour until well browned. Let the pan cool a little and then add the stock, bring to the boil. Add rest of ingredients with about ½ level teaspoon of salt. Cover and boil gently 2 hrs. Strain and return soup to pan. Chop a few pieces of kidney and return to the soup. Season to taste and serve.

One portion. Carbohydrate 21 g. Calories 190.

62. Lentil Soup

Quantities for 4. *Cooking time* 2 hrs

1 oz. dripping or oil
1 carrot diced
1 onion sliced
1 turnip diced
2 pts (4 c.) stock
3 or 4 bacon rinds
7 oz. lentils (¾ c.)
A pinch of dried thyme or a little chopped savory
1–2 level tsp. salt
Pinch of pepper
½ pt (1 c.) milk
Chopped parsley

Heat the fat and fry the carrot, onion, and turnip in it for a few minutes. Add remaining ingredients except for the milk. Cook until the lentils are tender. Sieve, or cool and put it into the electric blender. Re-heat, thin down with milk, taste for seasoning, and serve.

One portion (in electric blender). Carbohydrate 35 g. Calories 290.

63. Liver Soup No. 1

Quantities for 4. *Cooking time* 35 mins.

8 oz. liver
1 oz. plain flour (3 level Tbs.) *or* ½ oz. cornflour (1½ level Tbs.)
1 oz. (2 Tbs.) fat or oil
4 oz. chopped mushrooms (1 c.)
2 pts stock
Salt and pepper
2 Tbs. diced carrot
1 Tbs. chopped parsley

Remove skin and tubes and cut the liver in small dice. Toss in flour and fry lightly in the hot fat together with the mushrooms. Add stock, salt and pepper, and carrot, cover, and simmer until the liver is tender (about 30 mins.). Taste for seasoning and serve sprinkled with parsley.

64. Liver Soup No. 2 (*low-fat*)

Quantities for 4. *Cooking time* 15–20 mins.

4 oz. liver
1¼ pt (2½ c.) well seasoned stock
1 onion, chopped
Few mushroom stalks, chopped
Small piece carrot, chopped
½ bayleaf
Sprig thyme
Salt and pepper
Ground mace or nutmeg
Gravy browning
Chopped parsley
1 level Tbs. cornflour (optional)

Wash the liver in warm water. Put liver, stock, vegetables, and herbs in a pan and bring to the boil. Simmer gently for 15–20 mins. or until the vegetables are cooked. Take care not to over-cook the liver and make it hard or the soup will be granular. Remove the herbs and rub the meat through a sieve or put into the electric blender. Return to the pan to re-heat and season with salt and pepper and a little ground mace or nutmeg. If a thicker soup is required add cornflour blended with a very little water. Colour to taste with gravy browning. Add chopped parsley to taste.

One portion (in electric blender). Carbohydrate 4 g. Calories 58.

65. Minestrone

Quantities for 4. *Cooking time* ¾ hr

1 lb. mixed vegetables including some green and some onion
1 oz. (2 level Tbs.) fat
2 pts (4 c.) stock
1 level Tbs. tomato paste
1 oz. (¼ c.) broken macaroni
Salt and pepper to taste
2 oz. (½ c.) grated Parmesan cheese

Prepare the vegetables and slice or dice. Melt the fat and cook the vegetables in it slowly for 10–15 mins. with the lid on the pan and without browning, stirring occasionally. Add the stock and tomato and bring to the boil. Add macaroni and some salt and pepper and boil until the vegetables are cooked. Taste for seasoning. Serve the cheese separately.

One portion (without cheese). Carbohydrate 12 g. Calories 170.

66. Mushroom Soup

Quantities for 4. *Cooking time* ½ hr

8 oz. mushroom
1½ pts (3 c.) water or chicken stock)
1 slice onion chopped
2 oz. (4 level Tbs.) butter
1 oz. plain flour (3 level Tbs.) *or* ½ oz. cornflour (1½ level Tbs.)
Salt and pepper
4 Tbs. cream
4 Tbs. milk
Lemon juice
Grated nutmeg
Chopped parsley

Wash and chop the mushrooms including the stalks. Add to the hot stock or water together with the onion. Boil for 20 mins. and then sieve, or cool and put into the electric blender. Melt butter and mix in the flour. Cook 1–2 mins. and then add the mushroom liquid. Stir until it boils and boil for a few minutes. Season to taste, and add milk and cream and a little lemon juice and grated nutmeg to taste. Serve at once with parsley to garnish.

One portion (in electric blender). Carbohydrate 10 g. Calories 132.

67. Onion Soup (*low-fat*)

Quantities for 4. *Cooking time* 20 mins.

8 oz. onion (2 medium)
1 pt (2 c.) stock
3 level Tbs. dried skimmed milk
Salt and pepper

Slice the onion finely and boil in the stock until tender. Sieve the soup. Beat in the dried milk. Alternatively, cool the soup a little, add dried milk, and put all into the electric blender. Re-heat and season to taste.

One portion (in electric blender). Carbohydrate 7 g. Calories 42.

68. Dietade Pea Soup (*low-sodium*)

Quantities for 3–4. *Cooking time* 5 mins.

1 can Dietade processed peas ($15\frac{1}{2}$ oz., 439 g.)
Edosol milk or Casilan
2–3 Tbs. wine or cider
2–3 Tbs. double cream

Rub the peas and liquid from the can through a sieve or put in the electric blender with a little Edosol milk powder. Heat and then dilute with water to give the desired thickness. Add wine and cream just before serving.

69. Potato and Watercress Soup

Quantities for 4. *Cooking time* ½ hr

½ oz. (1 level Tbs.) fat or dripping
1 lb. potatoes sliced (4 medium)
2 oz. leek or onion sliced (1 small)
2 bacon rinds
1 pt (2 c.) water
2 oz. (½ c.) watercress chopped
1–2 level tsp. salt
Pinch of pepper
½ pt milk

Heat the fat and stew the vegetables and bacon rinds in it with the lid on the pan for 10–15 mins. without browning. Add water and watercress and cook until the vegetables are tender. Remove the bacon rinds and sieve the soup or put in an electric blender. Add the milk and re-heat; season to taste.

One portion (in electric blender). Carbohydrate 25 g. Calories 167.

70. Clear Tomato Bouillon (*low-fat*)

Quantities for 4. *Cooking time* 15–20 mins.

½ pt (1 c.) tomato juice
1½ pts (3 c.) fatless stock
½ level Tbs. chopped onions
¼ bayleaf
1 clove
¼ level tsp. celery seed
¼ level tsp. peppercorns
Good pinch sugar
Salt to taste

Put all ingredients in a pan and simmer for 15–20 mins. Strain, season to taste. Serve hot.

One portion. Carbohydrate 4 g. Calories 23.

71. Tomato Juice Cocktail (*low-fat*)

Quantities for 4

½ pt fresh or canned tomato juice (1 c.)
1 Tbs. vinegar
1 Tbs. lemon juice
½ tsp. Worcester sauce
1 tsp. grated or finely chopped onion
¼ level tsp. celery salt
2 level tsp. sugar
¼ bayleaf

Mix all ingredients together and leave to stand in a cool place for 15 mins. Strain through muslin or a fine nylon or plastic strainer. Chill and serve in small glasses.

One portion. Carbohydrate 3 g. Calories 15.

72. Tomato Juice Frappé

Quantities for 4

1 pt (2 c.) tomato juice
Worcester sauce
Salt and pepper

Season the juice to taste with salt and pepper and Worcester sauce or make a tomato juice cocktail (see No. 71). Pour into the freezing tray and freeze to a mush, stirring once. Mash up with a fork before serving in small glasses.

One portion. Carbohydrate 7 g. Calories 30.

73. Tomato and Marmite Soup No. 1 (*low-sodium*)

Quantities for 4. *Cooking time* A few mins.

½ pt unsalted tomato juice (fresh or Cirio brand, but read the label)
1 good tsp. salt-free Marmite
½ pt water
Paprika pepper
Good pinch sugar
Salt substitute, if allowed
Chopped parsley
Pepper

Mix the tomato juice, Marmite, and water, bring to the boil, and simmer for a few minutes. Season well with pepper, paprika pepper, sugar, and salt substitute, if it is allowed. Garnish with parsley.

One portion. Carbohydrate 5 g. Calories 20.

74. Tomato and Marmite Soup No. 2

Quantities for 4. *Cooking time* A few mins.

½ pt (1 c.) tomato juice fresh *or* canned
1 good tsp. Marmite
½ pt (1 c.) water
Salt and pepper
Chopped parsley
1 oz. grated cheese (3 level Tbs.)

Bring to the boil and simmer for a few minutes, seasoning to taste. Serve with chopped parsley and grated cheese if liked.

One portion. Carbohydrate 7 g. Calories 61.

75. Quick Cream of Vegetable Soup (*using an electric blender*)

Quantities for 4

Approx. 1 lb. vegetables 1 pt (2 c.) milk

This can be made and served very quickly, which means maximum flavour and food value are retained.

Manufacturers of blenders recommend several ways of making such soups, the simplest of which is to cook the prepared vegetables in a little butter or oil until they are almost tender, as for making any vegetable soup, then put them into the blender goblet with a little cold milk and mix to a purée. Heat the rest of the milk and use to dilute the purée to the desired consistency. Heat, season to taste, and serve. No thickening or binding is necessary.

This is one of the best methods for making both spinach and mushroom soups.

76. Low-Fat Vegetable Soup

Quantities for 4. *Cooking time* ¾ hr

¾ pt (1½ c.) liquid	Seasoning
½ pt (1 c.) vegetable purée (see below)	Cereal, breadcrumbs *or* potato for thickening

The hot purée is added to the hot liquid and the whole seasoned and thickened to taste with blended plain flour in the proportions of ½ oz. (1½ level Tbs.) to 1 pt (2 c.) liquid, cornflour ¼ oz. (¾ level Tbs.), semolina ½ oz. (1 level Tbs.), or stale breadcrumbs or potato powder sprinkled in until the desired thickness is reached. Boil for a few minutes to cook the thickening. Mashed potato may also be used for thickening or instant potato powder sprinkled in.

For liquids use skimmed milk which can be fresh or dried, vegetable stock, fat-free meat stock, or stock left from boiling vegetables for the purée or from canned vegetables.

Make the purée by cooking the prepared vegetables in a little water and then sieving or putting in an electric blender.

Vegetables to use:

Spinach, fresh, frozen, or canned, or canned purée.

Asparagus, fresh or canned.

Celery, fresh or canned, cooked with a little onion.

Mushroom, 4 oz. plus some mushroom stock to make up the ½ pt purée.

Potato, with onion, leek, or watercress cooked with the potato.

Green pea, fresh, frozen, or canned plus mint and a little sugar. Use 4 oz. shelled peas plus some stock.

Tomato, fresh or canned, plus sugar, bayleaf, and onion.

Carrot, fresh or canned plus a little onion and sugar.

Garnishes. Chopped green herbs, chopped hard-boiled egg white, croutons of toast, and chopped lean ham.

77. Cream of Vegetable Soup

Quantities for 4. *Cooking time* ¾ hr

1 pt (2 c.) thin white sauce made with milk (No. 79)
½ pt (1 c.) thick vegetable purée
Salt and pepper to taste
Other flavourings such as paprika and nutmeg to taste
2 Tbs. chopped parsley or watercress

To make the purée the vegetables should be cooked in the minimum amount of water and then sieved or put in an electric blender. Make up to ½ pt with some of the vegetable water if necessary. Canned vegetables may be used and also strained canned vegetables which are very useful for making small amounts of soup. Do not combine sauce and purée until just before serving, otherwise the mixture may curdle. Add hot purée to hot sauce and season to taste. Add parsley or watercress. To increase the protein content of the soup make the sauce with fortified milk (No. 1 (*e*)).

Vegetables to use:

Celery. Use outside pieces of one large head of celery with 1 small onion or canned celery with a little cooked onion.

Tomato. Canned, fresh, or bottled tomatoes and ½ level tsp. sugar and a little paprika pepper.

Pea. 12 oz. fresh or frozen green, canned garden, or processed with some sugar or mint, or alternatively soak and cook 6 oz. of dried peas.

Spinach. 12 oz. spinach.

Carrot. 1 lb. carrots (4 medium), 1 slice onion.

Add sugar and nutmeg.

Artichoke. 1 lb. Jerusalem artichokes and 1 slice onion.

Swede. 1 lb. swede and 1 slice onion.

Asparagus. Use 8 oz. asparagus and make up purée with cooking water or use canned asparagus and the liquid.

Variation using an electric blender. Blend the raw vegetables with cold milk using less vegetable, as there is no waste. Use this liquid to make a thin sauce by the roux method (see No. 79). (Not suitable for tomato soup.) For extra flavour the onion in the recipe may be kept back and fried gently in the fat before making the roux.

78. Vichyssoise (*high calorie*)

Quantities for 4. *Cooking time* 45 mins.

1 lb. leeks (four)
2 oz. (4 level Tbs.) butter
3 medium potatoes (¾ lb.)
Salt and pepper
1 pt (2 c.) chicken stock
¼ pt (½ c.) double cream
Chopped chives

Chop the white part of the leek, melt butter, and cook leeks slowly in this without browning. Peel potatoes, cut in cubes, and add to the leeks with water barely to cover. Add seasoning and simmer 15 mins. Add the stock and cook until the potatoes are soft. Rub through a sieve, or put in electric blender, add the cream, and sprinkle with chives. Serve hot or chilled.

One portion (in electric blender). Carbohydrate 25 g. Calories 375.

SAUCES

79. White Sauces

Quantities for 4. *Cooking time* About 15 mins.

Proportions. For 1 pt (2 c.) of milk with salt and pepper and flavourings to taste use the quantities given below.

Thin Sauce

1 oz. (2 level Tbs.) butter or margarine *or*
1 Tbs. oil

1 oz. plain flour (3 level Tbs.) *or* ½ oz. cornflour (1½ level Tbs.)

One portion. Carbohydrate 12 g. Calories 177.

Medium or Flowing Sauce

1½ oz. (3 level Tbs.) butter or margarine *or*
2 Tbs. oil

1½ oz. plain flour (4½ level Tbs.) *or* ¾ oz. cornflour (2 level Tbs.)

One portion. Carbohydrate 15 g. Calories 217.

Thick or coating sauce

2 oz. (4 level Tbs.) butter or margarine *or*
2 Tbs. oil

2 oz. plain flour (6 level Tbs.) *or* 1 oz. cornflour (3 level Tbs.)

One portion. Carbohydrate 18 g. Calories 258.

A thin sauce is used for soups where very slight thickening is needed, flowing sauce is the usual sauce-boat consistency, and coating is for masking food. Melt the fat or heat the oil in a small pan. Add flour and mix well, cooking very gently until it looks mealy (roux). Remove from the heat and gradually add the milk, stirring and beating well to make smooth. Return to the heat and stir until it boils. Boil gently 5 mins. or cook 10–20 mins. over boiling water. Add seasonings to taste.

80. Parsley Sauce

Add 1 oz. (½ c.) chopped parsley.

81. Cheese Sauce

Add a pinch of dry mustard to the roux and 3–4 oz (1 c.) grated cheese to the finished sauce and allow the cheese to melt without boiling. Broken-up processed cheese may be used instead of grated. Use more cheese for a stronger flavour.

One portion. Add 90–120 calories to basic recipe.

82. Onion Sauce

Add two chopped boiled onions (½ lb.) or dried onion to taste.

One portion. Add 2 g. carbohydrate and 7 calories to the basic recipe.

83. Egg Sauce

Add 2–3 chopped hard-boiled eggs.

One portion. Add 50–70 calories to the basic recipe.

84. Dutch Sauce

Add two egg yolks (don't boil after this) and a squeeze of lemon juice or a few drops of vinegar.

One portion. Add 50 calories to the basic recipe.

85. Caper Sauce

Add 1 level Tbs. chopped capers, 4 level Tbs. vinegar.

86. Mustard Sauce

Add 1 level Tbs. mustard mixed with a little vinegar.

87. High-Protein Sauce

Blend one of the following with the milk: 1½ oz. (4 level Tbs.) Casilan, 2 oz. (4 heaped Tbs.) dried skimmed milk powder, 2 oz. full cream dried milk powder, 2½ oz. Prosol. Or sprinkle 3 oz. (1 level c.) Complan into the finished sauce.

88. Low-sodium Sauce

Use Edosol milk, salt-free butter or margarine, and omit salt when flavouring.

89. Gluten-free Sauce

Use cornflour for thickening or wheat-starch instead if preferred (same proportions).

90. Sweet Sauce

Instead of salt and pepper, 1 oz. sugar (2 level Tbs.).

One portion. Add 28 calories to the basic recipe.

91. Anchovy Sauce

Add anchovy essence to taste and a little lemon juice (not suitable for the low-sodium diet).

92. Fennel or Dill Sauce

Add 4 level Tbs. chopped fresh fennel or dill or infuse the dried seed in the stock before making the sauce. Add vinegar and sugar to taste.

93. Béchamel Sauce

Quantities for 4. *Cooking time* 20 mins.

1 pt (2 c.) milk
1 shallot or small onion (2 oz.)
Small piece of carrot
Small piece of celery
A piece of bayleaf
5 peppercorns
2 oz. (4 level Tbs.) butter or margarine
2 oz. (6 level Tbs.) plain flour
or
1 oz. (3 level Tbs.) cornflour
Salt
4 Tbs. single cream

Put milk, prepared vegetables, and seasonings into a pan. Bring to the boil, remove to a warm place and infuse 5 mins. Strain. Make a roux with the fat and flour, add milk, blend, and cook 5–10 mins. Just before serving add the cream.

One portion. Carbohydrate 20 g. Calories 300.

Variations (*low-sodium diet*). Omit the salt and use Edosol milk and salt-free butter or margarine.

94. Thin Gravy (*low-fat, low-carbohydrate, low-calorie*)

Pour off all the fat from the roasting tin but retain the juices. To do this hold the pan in a cloth at one corner and tilt so that the gravy runs down to the opposite corner. Wait a moment or two for the sediment to settle and the fat to collect on top, then pour very slowly and gently and the fat will run off leaving the juices behind. The drippings left are then reheated in the roasting pan with or without added stock. Season to taste. Stir well to incorporate with the sediment in the pan. When it is important to remove all the fat (in the low-fat diet), pour the juices into a basin and remove any more fat that rises by blotting it up with clean kitchen paper towels. Then finish as before, using fat-free stock.

95. Thick Gravy

Pour off as before, except for about 2 Tbs. of the fat. Add two level Tbs. of flour or ½ level Tbs. cornflour, mix well, and cook until it begins to brown. Add 1 c. stock. Stir until it boils and cook for a few minutes, season to taste, strain, and serve.

Variation (gluten-free diet). Replace the flour with 1½ level Tbs. of cornflour or wheat-starch. Some people prefer to make all their gravies with cornflour instead of flour, whether necessary for the diet or not.

96. Brown Sauce

Quantities for 4. *Cooking time* 30–50 mins.

- 2 oz. (4 level Tbs.) fat or 1 oz. (2 Tbs.) oil
- 6 oz. onions (2 medium), sliced
- 4 oz. carrots (2 medium) sliced
- 2 oz. (6 level Tbs.) plain flour *or*
- 1 oz. (3 level Tbs.) cornflour
- 1 pt (2 c.) stock
- ¼ bayleaf
- Sprig parsley
- Salt and pepper

Heat the fat and fry the onions and carrots until lightly browned. Add the flour, stir and cook for about 15 mins. until the flour is light brown. Remove from the heat and cool a little. Add stock gradually, stirring well. Heat until it boils, add bayleaf and parsley, and simmer for ½ hr. Strain, re-heat, and season to taste.

Variations (gluten-free diet). Use cornflour or wheat-starch instead of flour. *Low-sodium diet.* Use salt-free stock and omit the salt. Use salt substitute if allowed.

97. Spiced Apple Sauce (*low-fat, low-sodium*)

Quantities for 4

- ½ pt (1 c.) apple sauce
- 1 level Tbs. honey
- ½ level tsp. nutmeg
- Cinnamon to taste
- Ginger to taste

Combine all the ingredients thoroughly and serve either hot or cold.

One portion. Carbohydrate 16 g. Calories 61.

98. Brown Butter Sauce (*low-sodium*)

Quantities for 4

4 oz. (½ c.) unsalted butter
½ level Tbs. chopped parsley
½ Tbs. vinegar

Melt the butter in a small saucepan. Cook it gently until it browns. Then add the parsley and vinegar and pour quickly over the food.

One portion. Carbohydrate a trace. Calories 57.

99. Parsley Butter or Maître d'Hôtel Butter

Quantities for 4

2 oz. (4 level Tbs.) butter
1 Tbs. chopped parsley
Salt and pepper
Few drops lemon juice

Warm the butter to soften but not melt it. Work the other ingredients into it. Cool and then mould into small pats to put on the meat or fish just before serving.

One portion. Carbohydrate a trace. Calories 57.

Variation (*low-sodium diet*). Use unsalted butter and omit salt.

100. Egg and Lemon Sauce

Quantities for 4. *Cooking time* 10 mins.

1 oz. (2 level Tbs.) butter or margarine
1 oz. plain flour (3 level Tbs.) *or* ½ oz. cornflour (1½ level Tbs.)
¼ pt (½ c.) milk
½ pt (1 c.) fish stock
1 egg yolk
2 Tbs. cream
Salt and pepper
Juice of ½ lemon

Make a sauce by the roux method, using the butter, flour and fish stock and cook 5 mins. or longer. Add the egg yolk, cream, and lemon juice just before serving and cook until it thickens. Do not allow to boil after this. Serve hot.

One portion. Carbohydrate 8 g. Calories 159.

Variations. 1. Use a fortified milk for a high-protein diet (see No. 1e). 2. *Low-sodium diet.* Omit the salt and use salt-free butter or margarine and Edosol milk.

101. Hollandaise Sauce

Quantities for 4

4 oz. ($\frac{1}{2}$ c.) butter	2–3 Tbs. boiling water
2 egg yolks	$\frac{1}{2}$ level tsp. salt
1 Tbs. lemon juice	Few grains cayenne pepper

Divide the butter into three portions. Put one in a double boiler with the egg yolks and lemon juice and cook over the hot water, stirring with a small wire whisk until the butter is melted. Add the second piece of butter, continue heating and as the mixture thickens add the third piece of butter. Add the boiling water and cook for one minute. Season. Should the mixture curdle, add 2 Tbs. double cream or 2 Tbs. boiling water drop by drop.

One portion. Carbohydrate a trace. Calories 276.

102. Horseradish Sauce

Quantities for 4

2 level tsp. dry mustard	1 tsp. wine vinegar
$\frac{1}{4}$ c. grated horseradish (1 oz.)	$\frac{1}{8}$ pt yogurt ($\frac{1}{2}$ small pot)
Pinch of paprika pepper	Salt to taste

Mix the mustard, horseradish, and paprika pepper. Add the vinegar and yogurt and beat until well mixed. Serve cold.

One portion. Carbohydrate 2 g. Calories 25.

Variation (*low-sodium diet*). Omit the salt and use $\frac{1}{8}$ pt double cream in place of the yogurt. If fresh horseradish is not available, Heinz dried horseradish is salt-free.

103. Lemon Sauce

Quantities for 4. *Cooking time* 15–20 mins.

3 egg yolks	$\frac{1}{2}$ pt (1 c.) warm stock
Juice of 1 lemon	Salt and pepper

Beat the yolks and lemon juice together until thick and light. Put over hot water and gradually beat in the stock, stirring until it thickens and is light and fluffy. Season to taste and serve at once. Suitable for meat, fish, or vegetables.

One portion. Carbohydrate a trace. Calories 53.

104. Mint Sauce

Quantities for 4

$\frac{1}{8}$ pt (5 Tbs.) chopped fresh mint
$\frac{1}{2}$ oz. (1 level Tbs.) sugar
$\frac{1}{4}$ pt ($\frac{1}{2}$ c.) vinegar

Mix ingredients together and allow to stand 2 hrs before using.

One portion. Carbohydrate 4 g. Calories 15.

105. Mushroom Sauce

Quantities for 4

1 pt (2 c.) brown sauce (see No. 96) (variations according to diet)
2 oz. button mushrooms

Wash and chop the mushrooms and stalks and add to the sauce and cook 5 mins. If larger mushrooms are used, skin as necessary and use the trimmings and coarse stalks for making the brown sauce.

One portion. Carbohydrate 11. Calories 186.

106. Italian Tomato Sauce

Quantities for 4. *Cooking time* About $\frac{1}{2}$ hr

2 Tbs. olive oil
2 onions finely chopped (4 oz.)
Small tin of tomato paste ($2\frac{3}{4}$ oz.)
Pinch of thyme
1 pt (2 c.) water
Salt and pepper

Heat the oil in a small pan and fry the onions for 5 mins. Add the tomato paste and cook for a few minutes, stirring all the time. Add the thyme and water, cover, and simmer gently for about 25 mins. or until of the desired thickness. Season to taste. Strain if necessary.

One portion. Carbohydrate 2 g. Calories 84.

Variation (*low-sodium diet*). Use Cirio brand tomato paste (read the label) and omit the salt.

107. Sweet Pepper and Tomato Sauce

Quantities for 4. *Cooking time* about $\frac{1}{2}$ hr

2 sweet peppers, green or red (4 oz.)
8 oz. tomatoes, fresh or canned (4 medium)
2 Tbs. water
2 medium gherkins
1 Tbs. wine vinegar
Salt and pepper

If fresh peppers are used, remove the seeds and stalks. Cut up small. Skin and chop fresh tomatoes, if used. Put peppers, tomatoes, and water in a pan and simmer until reduced to a pulp. Slice the gherkins thinly and add with the vinegar. Season to taste and serve hot.

One portion. Carbohydrate 4 g. Calories 16.

Variation (low-sodium diet). Omit the gherkins and use fresh tomatoes or Cirio brand of unsalted tomatoes.

108. Quickly Made Tomato Sauce

Quantities for 4. *Cooking time* 15–20 mins.

1 oz. (2 level Tbs.) butter
1 small onion, chopped
1 oz. (3 level Tbs.) flour
½ pt (1 c.) stock
¼ pt (½ c.) milk
½ bay leaf
2 Tbs. tomato paste (2 oz.)
Salt and pepper
Pinch sugar

Heat the butter in a small pan and fry the onion in it gently until it is tender but not browned. Add the flour and mix and cook until it goes mealy. Gradually add the stock and milk and stir until smooth. Add bay leaf and tomato and boil gently for about 8 mins. Strain, re-heat, add seasoning to taste, and serve hot.

One portion. Carbohydrate 8 g. Calories 111.

109. Boiled Salad Dressing (*low-protein, gluten-free*)

Quantities for 4. *Cooking time* 10 mins.

1 oz. (3 level Tbs.) cornflour
½ pt (1 c.) water
¼ oz. (½ level Tbs.) sugar
Salt and pepper
Mustard to taste
½ oz. (1 level Tbs.) butter or margarine or 1 Tbs. oil
Vinegar or lemon juice to taste

Blend the cornflour, water, and seasonings. Heat and stir until it boils and boil to thicken. Cook for a few minutes longer. Add the fat and cool (oil to be added after cooling). Add the vinegar or lemon juice to taste.

One portion. Carbohydrate 8 g. Calories 90.

110. Dried Milk Dressing (*low-fat*)

Quantities for 4

½ level tsp. salt	¼ level tsp. sugar
½ level tsp. dry mustard	1 Tbs. water
Pinch of pepper	1 Tbs. vinegar or lemon juice
1 oz. dried skimmed milk powder (2½ level Tbs.)	

Mix all the ingredients together and beat until smooth.

One portion. Carbohydrate 4 g. Calories 25.

Variation (*low-sodium diet*). Omit the salt and use Edosol powder instead of the dried skimmed milk powder.

111. Yogurt Dressing (*gluten-free, low-carbohydrate*)

Quantities for 4

1½ Tbs. lemon juice	¼ tsp. made mustard
¼ level tsp. salt	¼ pt (½ c.) Yogurt

Mix the lemon juice and seasonings and gradually add the yogurt, mixing until well blended. Chill, in the refrigerator if possible, for ½ hr.

One portion. Carbohydrate negligible. Calories 24.

112. Boiled Dressing (*low-fat, gluten-free*)

Quantities for 4

1 oz. cornflour (3 level Tbs.)	Few grains cayenne pepper
1 level tsp. salt	½ pt (1 c.) skimmed milk
1 level tsp. mustard	4 Tbs. vinegar or lemon juice or to taste
½ level Tbs. sugar	

Mix the dry ingredients together and add the milk slowly. Cook over boiling water until the mixture thickens. Add vinegar or lemon juice to taste. Cool.

One portion. Carbohydrate 15 g. Calories 70.

113. French Dressing No. 1

Quantities for 4

3 Tbs. oil	Pinch of sugar
Pinch of pepper	1 Tbs. vinegar, wine, tarragon, or other herb vinegar
1 level tsp. dry mustard	

Mix the oil, seasonings, and sugar and add the vinegar. Stir before using as it separates on standing.

One portion. Carbohydrate a trace. Calories 100.

114. French Dressing No. 2 (*low-sodium*)

Quantities for 4

1 level tsp. sugar
½ level tsp. dry mustard
¼ level tsp. paprika pepper
Dash of pepper
Salt substitute if allowed
4 Tbs. oil
2 Tbs. vinegar
2 Tbs. water

Mix the dry ingredients with the oil and then add vinegar and water. Store in a bottle and shake before using.

One portion. Carbohydrate 9 g. Calories 136.

115. Mayonnaise

Quantities for 4

1 egg yolk
½ level tsp. salt
¼ level tsp. mustard
A few grains cayenne pepper
1 Tbs. lemon juice or vinegar
¼ pt (½ c.) oil

Mix egg yolk, salt, mustard, and pepper, and ½ Tbs. lemon juice or vinegar. Beat well with a rotary beater or wire whisk. Add the oil ½ tsp. at a time and make sure it is well blended before adding more. When a quarter of the oil has been used start adding the rest 1 Tbs. at a time. When all the oil has been used, add the rest of the lemon juice or vinegar to make it the desired consistency.

One portion. Carbohydrate a trace. Calories 293.

116. Sauce Rémoulade

Quantities for 4

¼ pt (½ c.) mayonnaise
½ level Tbs. French mustard
½ level Tbs. chopped gherkins
½ level Tbs. capers
1 level tsp. chopped herbs (parsley, chervil, tarragon)
¼ tsp. anchovy essence

Mix thoroughly and use with cold meat, poultry, fish, and lobster.

One portion. Carbohydrate a trace. Calories 293.

117. Sauce Tartare

Quantities for 4

- $\frac{1}{4}$ pt ($\frac{1}{2}$ c.) mayonnaise
- 1 level Tbs. chopped gherkins or capers
- $\frac{1}{2}$ level tsp. finely chopped onion

Mix well.

One portion. Carbohydrate a trace. Calories 293.

118. Fish Cocktail Sauce (*low-fat, low-carbohydrate, low-calorie*)

Quantities for 4

- 2 Tbs. tomato ketchup
- 1 tsp. Worcester sauce
- 1 tsp. lemon juice
- 1 tsp. grated horseradish
- Cayenne pepper
- Salt

Blend the ingredients and mix with the fish. Serve on a bed of finely shredded tender lettuce.

One portion. Carbohydrate and calories negligible.

119. Tomato Juice Dressing (*low-fat, low-calorie, low-carbohydrate*)

Quantities for 4

- $\frac{1}{4}$ pt ($\frac{1}{2}$ c.) tomato juice
- 2 Tbs. lemon juice or vinegar
- 1 Tbs. finely chopped chives
- Salt and pepper
- Mustard to taste
- $\frac{1}{4}$ oz. honey (1 level tsp.)
- Chopped parsley, Grated horseradish } optional

Combine in a screw-topped jar and shake before using.

One portion. Carbohydrate 3 g. Calories 13.

Variation (*low-sodium diet*). Omit the salt and use salt-free tomato juice.

120. Low-fat Sauces

These must all be thickened by the blending method instead of by making a roux.

After the portion for the diet has been removed, butter, margarine, or cream may be added to the remainder for the rest of the family.

Quantities for 4

Proportions. For 1 pt (2 c.) of liquid, with salt and pepper and flavourings to taste, use the quantities given below:

Thin Sauce

2 level Tbs. plain flour (⅔ oz.) *or*
1 level Tbs. (⅓ oz.) cornflour, arrowroot, custard powder, or potato starch, or special wheat-starch.

One portion (using flour). Carbohydrate 11 g. Calories 112.

Medium Sauce

3 level Tbs. plain flour (1 oz.) *or*
1½ level Tbs. (⅔ oz.) cornflour, arrowroot, etc.

One portion (using flour). Carbohydrate 13 g. Calories 120.

Thick Sauce

6 level Tbs. plain flour (2 oz.) *or*
3 level Tbs. (1 oz.) cornflour, arrowroot, etc.

One portion. Carbohydrate 18 g. Calories 145.

Method. Mix the thickening with a little cold liquid. Heat the remainder of the liquid and, when boiling, pour into the blended mixture. Return to the pan and stir until it thickens. Boil for 5 mins. or longer, with flour and cornflour, otherwise just bring to the boil.

Suitable liquids. Skimmed milk (fresh or dried), vegetable stock, water from boiled vegetables, or liquid from canned vegetables, tomato juice, canned vegetable juices, fat-free stock, Marmite, Bovril, Oxo.

121. Brown Sauce

Use a good vegetable stock, vegetable juices, or a fat-free meat stock. Thicken with cornflour and add gravy browning for colour.

122. For Vegetables

Use the liquid from boiled vegetables, or vegetable stock, or the liquid from canned vegetables. Season with salt and pepper and add chopped parsley. Dried skimmed milk or its equivalent may be added to increase the protein value.

123. Celery Sauce

Add ½ pt (1 c.) celery purée to 1 pt (2 c.) vegetable or milk sauce.

124. Mushroom Sauce

Add 2 oz. (½ c.) chopped mushrooms to 1 pt (2 c.) vegetable or milk sauce. Fish stock and fat-free meat stock may also be used. Boil for a few minutes to cook the mushrooms. If mushroom trimmings or stalks are available use them to make the stock.

125. Parsley Sauce

Add 4 Tbs. chopped parsley to 1 pt (2 c.) white or vegetable sauce. For serving with fish, use fish stock or milk to make the sauce and add a little lemon juice.

126. Tomato Sauce

Use a little fresh or canned tomato juice or tomato paste diluted to taste (about 2 Tbs. paste to 1 pt (2 c.) stock). Cook a slice of onion and a piece of bayleaf in the sauce for flavouring. Season with salt, pepper, and sugar.

Alternatively, a little tomato paste can be added to a white or vegetable sauce.

127. Sharp Sauce (*for fish*)

To 1 pt (2 c.) sauce made with fish stock add 1 level tsp. dry mustard mixed with the juice of a lemon.

128. Anchovy Sauce

Add 2–4 tsp. anchovy essence to 1 pt (2 c.) sauce made with milk or fish stock or with some of each.

129. Caper Sauce

Add 2 Tbs. chopped capers and 1 Tbs. of the vinegar to 1 pt (2 c.)sauce.

SWEET SAUCES

130. Apricot Sauce (*low-fat*)

Quantities for 4

Soak 4 oz. (¾ c.) dried apricots overnight and then cook them with 1 oz. sugar (2 level Tbs.) Sieve them or pulp in the electric blender, and thin if necessary. Serve cold. Lemon juice may be added to taste.

One portion. Carbohydrate 20 g. Calories 80.

131. Caramel Sauce No. 1

Quantities for 4. *Cooking time* about 10 mins.

2 oz. sugar (4 level Tbs.)
2 Tbs. water
1 pt (2 c.) milk
1 oz. plain flour (3 level Tbs.)
or ½ oz. cornflour (1½ level Tbs.)
¾ level tsp. salt
Vanilla essence to taste

Use less flour if it is to be served cold. Boil the sugar and water together in a small heavy pan, until toffee coloured. Blend the flour with a little of the cold milk and heat the rest. Dissolve the caramel in the hot milk, pour into the blended flour, stir, and return to pan. Boil until it thickens. Add salt and vanilla.

One portion. Carbohydrate 28 g. Calories 176.

Variation (*low-fat diet*). Use skimmed milk.

132. Caramel Sauce No. 2 (*low-fat*)

Quantities for 4. *Cooking time* 5 mins.

4 oz. (½ c.) sugar
¼ pt (½ c.) water

Use a small strong saucepan, cook the sugar and half the water in it, stirring until the sugar dissolves, and then boil hard without stirring until it turns a light brown. Remove the pan from the heat. Cool, and add the rest of the water and heat and stir until the caramel dissolves.

One portion. Carbohydrate 30 g. Calories 112.

133. Chocolate Sauce No. 1

Quantities for 4. *Cooking time* 10 mins.

1 oz. plain flour (3 level Tbs.) *or* ½ oz. cornflour or arrowroot (1½ level Tbs.)
¼ level tsp. salt
2 level Tbs. cocoa
1½ oz. sugar (3 level Tbs.)
1 pt (2 c.) milk
Vanilla

Mix flour, salt, cocoa, and sugar to a smooth paste with a little cold milk. Boil the rest of the milk and when boiling pour on to the blended mixture. Return to the pan and stir until it boils and thickens. Boil for a few minutes, add vanilla, and serve hot. If required cold, use less thickening and sprinkle the top of the finished sauce with caster sugar to prevent a skin forming as it cools.

One portion. Carbohydrate 23 g. Calories 171.

134. Chocolate Sauce No. 2

Quantities for 4

4 oz. plain chocolate	Flavouring, e.g. vanilla,
¼ pt. (½ c.) evaporated milk	rum, brandy, or liqueur

Break the chocolate in pieces and melt over hot water (not boiling), add the evaporated milk, and beat until thick and smooth. Flavour to taste and serve hot or cold (see above).

One portion. Carbohydrate 19 g. Calories 210.

135. Chocolate Sauce No. 3

Quantities for 4

2 oz. drinking chocolate (½ c.)	Top of milk, single cream, *or*
2 Tbs. water	evaporated milk
1 tsp. vanilla	

Mix chocolate and water. Bring to the boil, stirring all the time. Add vanilla and dilute with the milk or cream. Use hot or cover with a sprinkling of caster sugar to prevent skin forming, and leave to cool.

136. Cream

The amount of fat in cream varies. Single cream contains 18 per cent fat, double cream 48 per cent, canned cream 23 per cent. For whipping there should be about 25 per cent fat, so double cream needs diluting with about half as much single cream. Double cream can be whipped but gives a very thick solid result and easily turns to butter.

Calorie values: single cream, 62 per oz.; double cream 131 per oz.

137. Evaporated Milk in place of Whipped Cream

This is more economical than using cream and has a lower fat and higher protein content. When whipped, it gives almost double the volume obtained with an equivalent amount of cream, so less may be used.

Chill the cans of milk in the refrigerator, preferably overnight. It will then whip up easily into a thick, light cream and can be used in place of cream in any recipe.

138. Fluffy Custard Sauce

Quantities for 4

½ pt (1 c.) milk	1 oz. sugar (2 level Tbs.)
2 egg yolks	Vanilla essence

Heat the milk. Beat the yolks and sugar and add the hot milk gradually, whisking all the time. Add the vanilla. Place the sauce in the top of a double boiler or put in a basin over a pan of boiling water. Whisk until very frothy.

One portion. Carbohydrate 11 g. Calories 125.

139. Egg Custard Sauce

Quantities for 4. *Cooking time* 10–15 mins.

1 pt (2 c.) milk	½ oz. sugar (1 level Tbs.)
2 eggs or 4 yolks	Flavouring to taste

Heat the milk to just below boiling. Beat the eggs and sugar together slightly and pour in the hot milk, stirring well. Put the sauce in the top of a double boiler or in a basin over a pan of boiling water. Cook until the custard thickens slightly, or coats the back of the wooden spoon used for stirring. Stir frequently to keep the custard smooth. Flavour to taste and serve hot or cold.

CAUTION. Remove from the heat as soon as cooked, otherwise the sauce will curdle.

One portion. Carbohydrate 4 g. Calories 208.

Variation. For a trifle, when the cold custard needs to be thicker than this, use 3 eggs to the pt.

140. Low-fat Custard Sauce

Make a custard powder sauce with skimmed milk, following the usual method. If eggs are allowed make egg custard sauce (No. 139) using skimmed milk.

141. Fruit and Jam Sauces (*low-fat, gluten-free, low protein*)

Quantities for 4. *Cooking time* 10 mins.

- 1 pt (2 c.) liquid (see Nos. 142–5)
- ⅔ oz. cornflour, arrowroot, custard powder, gluten-free flour, *or* potato flour (1½ level Tbs.)
- Sugar to taste
- Lemon juice or other flavourings to taste

NOTE. For a sauce to be served cold, use only half the amount of thickening.

Blend the cornflour (or alternative), smooth with a little of the liquid. Boil the remainder and pour into the blended mixture, mix well, return to the pan, and stir until it boils. Custard powder and cornflour need to be cooked for a few minutes, the others need only be brought to the boil.

Potato flour (fecule) makes the best sauces. It is imported and sold in packets in the same way as cornflour. If the sauce is to be served cold, sprinkle a little sugar evenly over the top and leave to cool undisturbed when the sugar will prevent a skin forming. Use any of the following flavourings:

142. Fruit Juice Sauce

Use 1 pt (2 c.) of any fruit juice with 1 Tbs. lemon juice. Concentrated syrups like blackcurrant should first be diluted with water. Many other real fruit syrups are now obtainable or can be made from fresh, canned, or frozen fruits.

143. Jam or Marmalade

Use 1 pt (2 c.) of water and ½ c. (4 oz.) jam or marmalade and 2 tsp. lemon juice.

144. Lemon Sauce

Use the rind and juice of 2 lemons. Heat the finely grated lemon rind in the water. Add the juice just before serving.

145. Orange Sauce

Rind and juice of 2 oranges in the same way as for the lemon sauce. Add 1 Tbs. marmalade with the juice.

146. Melba Sauce (*low-fat*)

Quantities for 4

½ pt (1 c.) raspberry purée from fresh or canned raspberries (about 1 lb.)
2 level tsp. cornflour or potato flour
1 oz. sugar (2 level Tbs.)
Lemon juice to taste

Thicken the purée with blended cornflour or potato flour, sweetening the fresh raspberries and adding lemon juice to taste. When cooked, cool and store in a covered jar in the refrigerator and use as required on milk puddings. Some people prefer to make a thicker purée and omit the cooking and thickening.

One portion. Carbohydrate 26 g. Calories 101.

147. Mock Whipped Cream (*low-fat*)

Quantities for 4

4 fl. oz. (8 Tbs.) cold water
1 Tbs. lemon juice
1 oz. sugar (2 level Tbs.)
3 oz. dried skimmed milk powder (½ c.)
Vanilla or other flavouring

Place the water and the lemon juice in a bowl. Sprinkle on the milk powder and sugar and beat until thick and light. Beating by hand may take ten or more minutes. Flavour to taste. Use within half an hour as it does not keep well. It makes a big bowl of cream.

One portion. Carbohydrate 18 g. Calories 98.

148. Syrup or Honey Sauce (*low-fat*)

Quantities for 4. *Cooking time* 1 min.

4 oz. syrup or honey (½ c.)
½ pt (1 c.) water
Rind and juice of 1 lemon *or* a pinch of ground ginger

Cook the syrup or honey and water together in a small saucepan. Add the lemon or ginger. Serve hot.

One portion. Carbohydrate 45 g. Calories 168.

149. Syrup Cream (*low-fat*)

Quantities for 4

1 egg white (1 oz.)
Pinch of salt
1 heaped dessertspoon golden syrup (1 oz.)

Whip the egg white and salt until stiff. Melt the syrup and bring to the boil. Pour syrup into egg white, whisking well until the mixture is thick like whipped cream. Serve in place of cream in a low-fat diet.

One portion. Carbohydrate 6 g. Calories 24.

ACCOMPANIMENTS AND CONDIMENTS

150. Low-Sodium Apple Chutney (*for cold or hot meats, curries, etc.*)

1 lb. onions (4 medium)
5 lb. cooking apples (2½ kg.)
2 level tsp. ground ginger
2 tsp. pickling spices tied in muslin
1 pt (2 c.) vinegar
1½ lb. (3 c.) sugar

Mince the onions and cook for 20 mins. in very little water. Core and mince the apples. Add to the onions, together with ginger and spices and cook ½ hr or until tender, adding some of the vinegar. Add the rest of the vinegar and the sugar and cook until thick. Pot and tie down when cold. It keeps very well.

Variation. If dried fruit is liked in chutney, add some chopped dates.

151. Low-Sodium Apple Relish (*as a sauce with cold or hot meats*)

1 small onion chopped
1 level Tbs. cornflour
8 oz. apple (2 medium), peeled and grated
2 oz. red jam (2 level Tbs.)
1 oz. brown sugar (2 level Tbs.)
1 level tsp. paprika pepper
1 level tsp. curry powder *or* mustard
2 Tbs. vinegar
Salt substitute if allowed

Blend the cornflour with ¼ pt cold water and put it in a pan with all the other ingredients, except the salt substitute. Bring to the boil and simmer 5 mins. Add salt substitute to taste and use hot or cold. Keeps several days or a week or more in the refrigerator.

152. Home-made French Mustard for the Low-Salt Diet

3 level Tbs. mustard
½ level tsp. sugar
¼ level tsp. pepper
1½ tsp. vinegar (malt *or* tarragon)
1½ tsp. oil

Mix mustard to a stiff paste with a little cold water. Add the other ingredients and mix well. Keeps very well.

153. Sweet Pickled Fruit (*for cold meats*)

4 lb. fruit, e.g. pears, peaches, plums, or Morello cherries
1 pt (2 c.) vinegar
2 lb. (4 c.) brown or white sugar
3-in. stick cinnamon
4 pieces root ginger
6 cloves

Prepare the fruit, removing the skin of pears and peaches, and the stones and cores of all fruit. Cut large fruits in half. Boil the other ingredients for 10 mins. with the lid on the pan. Remove spices and add fruits. Simmer until almost tender but still firm. Drain and pack loosely in warmed jars. Boil the liquid to reduce it and make it syrupy. Pour over the fruit and seal down. Keep several weeks before using. If required it will keep several years.

154. Mint Stuffing for Lamb

8 oz. stale breadcrumbs (2⅔ c.)
½ c. chopped fresh mint
4 level Tbs. chopped onion
3 oz. (6 level Tbs.) margarine or dripping
3 level Tbs. chopped parsley
1 level tsp. salt
Pinch of pepper
1 level Tbs. sugar

Fry the onion in a little of the fat and mix all the ingredients together.

Low-sodium diet. Use unsalted breadcrumbs and margarine.

155. Veal Forcemeat

2 oz. fresh breadcrumbs (⅔ c.)
1–2 oz. suet (3–6 level Tbs.)
1 Tbs. chopped parsley
1 level tsp. dried thyme *or* savory
½ level tsp. grated lemon rind
Pinch of mace
½ level tsp. salt
¼ level tsp. pepper
1 egg
Milk to mix

If stuffing fairly fatty meat, use only 1 oz. of suet. Grate fresh suet or use packet suet. Wash, dry, and chop the parsley and grate the lemon rind finely. Mix all the ingredients together, binding with the beaten egg. Use milk only if needed.

Whole recipe (2 oz. suet). Carbohydrate 44 g. Calories 818.

156. Dumplings (*salt-free*)

Quantities for 4. *Cooking time* 15–20 mins.

- 4 oz. plain flour (¾ c.)
- ½ level tsp. special baking powder (see page 139)
- 1 oz. grated fresh suet (4 level Tbs.)
- 1 level tsp. chopped parsley, chives, or other fresh herbs
- Water to mix

Sift the flour and baking powder and add the suet and herbs. Mix to a very soft dough with cold water. Shape into dumplings by rolling in the hands, and steam or boil separately from the meat which is being cooked to go with it.

One portion. Carbohydrate 22 g. Calories 166.

157. High-Calorie Porridge

Quantities for 1

- 6 oz. (1 portion) porridge (cooked weight), using approximately 1 oz. of oats or rolled oats
- ¼ oz. glucose (½ level Tbs.)
- ½ oz. dried milk powder, full cream if possible (1¼ level Tbs.)
- ½ oz. wheat germ (2 level Tbs.)
- Cream if allowed

Make the porridge and add the other ingredients, mixing to blend well. Serve cream separately or mix it in.

One portion (no cream). Carbohydrate 35 g. Calories 206.

158. Yorkshire Pudding (*gluten-free*)

Quantities 12 individual puddings. *Cooking time* about 20 mins. *Temperature* 450 °F. No. 8.

- 2 oz. (6 level Tbs.) special wheat-starch
- 2 level tsp. Casilan
- Pinch of salt
- 2 eggs
- Milk to mix

Sift together the wheat-starch and Casilan. Beat eggs and salt and then stir in the starch. Add sufficient milk to bring the batter to a creamy consistency. Grease the tins liberally and put in the oven to heat. Beat batter for 5 mins. and then pour into the warm tins and bake at once in a hot oven until well risen and browned. Serve at once.

159. Yorkshire Pudding (*gluten-free, without Casilan*)

Quantities 12 individual puddings. *Cooking time* about 20 mins. *Temperature* 450 °F. No. 8.

4 oz. wheat-starch (¾ c.)	2 eggs
½ level tsp. salt	6 fl. oz. (12 Tbs.) milk

Heat a little fat in the bottom of the bun tins or deep patty tins. Sift wheat-starch and salt into a basin and make a well in the centre. Break in the eggs and add half the milk. Stir from the centre, gradually working in all the flour and adding the remainder of the milk to make a thin batter. Beat thoroughly. Pour into hot tins and bake in a hot oven until well risen and browned. Serve at once.

CHEESE DISHES

160. Cheese

Cheese is an important item in many diets, especially in high-protein and low-carbohydrate diets.

There is not a great deal of difference in nutritional content between one cheese and another, except for the following

Cream cheese is made from cream and is equivalent to eating butter, that is, has a high fat content.

Cottage cheese is made from sour milk and has more water in it than most.

Curd cheese is really the same thing as cottage cheese, though the name is often used for a skimmed-milk cottage cheese to distinguish it from one containing some cream.

Dutch Edam has a lower fat content than most.

Norwegian Mysost is low in sodium and calcium content, and contains carbohydrate.

For people on a low-carbohydrate diet serve cheese without bread or biscuits but with fresh fruit, salad vegetables, or pickles.

Cheese should be cooked slowly to avoid making it tough, stringy, and indigestible. Grated cheese is the best to use, either Parmesan or dry Cheddar. Diced processed cheese is also suitable.

161. Home-made Cottage Cheese

It is useful to be able to make this at home for someone who is on a low-fat or a low-sodium diet. Milk which has been pasteurized, scalded, or sterilized will not sour. See if your dairy can supply you with some raw milk. You can make the low-fat variety from skimmed milk and rennet, but not the low-sodium one, as rennet contains salt. The low-fat one can also be made from spray-dried skimmed milk powder, using 1½ times the usual amount of powder to water and 1½ times the usual amount of rennet.

When the curd has formed, either by souring or the use of rennet, put the basin of curd over hot water and heat until curd and whey separate out. Scald a piece of muslin, wring out, place in a strainer, and pour the curd and whey carefully in the centre. Gather the ends together to make a bag, tie with string, and hang up to drip for twenty-four hours. Remove the curd and mash and flavour as desired, either sweet or savoury.

162. Baked Rice and Cheese

Quantities for 4. *Cooking time* 40 mins. *Temperature* 350 °F. No. 4.

8 oz. rice (1 level c.)
¼ pt (½ c.)medium white sauce (see No. 79)
Salt and pepper
2 oz. grated cheese (½ c.)

Cook the rice very gently in water until tender and all the water is absorbed (about 15 mins.). Do this in the oven. Make the sauce, add the cheese, and stir until it melts. Season to taste. Combine rice and sauce and heat in slow oven for 20 mins. Serve with meat or fish or by itself as a supper savory.

One portion. Carbohydrate 53 g. Calories 320.

163. Cheese Custard

Quantities for 4. *Cooking time* ½–¾ hr. *Temperature* 350 °F. No. 4. (3 mins. pressure cooking)

4 eggs beaten slightly
½ pt (1 c.) milk
½ oz. (1 level Tbs.) butter
2½ oz. grated Parmesan cheese (½ c.)
Pinch of salt
Pinch of cayenne and paprika peppers
1 level tsp. prepared mustard

Heat milk and butter together and then mix all ingredients thoroughly. Grease individual moulds, and pour in the mixture. For baking, put in a pan of hot water and bake in a slow oven until set. For pressure cooking, cook for 3 mins. and let the pressure reduce slowly. Turn out and serve with fingers of toast.

One portion. Carbohydrate 2 g. Calories 227.

164. Apple and Cheese Savoury

Quantities for 4

4 medium dessert apples
1 oz. grated cheese (1 level Tbs.)

Peel, core, and slice the apple across in four thick slices. Put in the grill pan and sprinkle on cheese. Put under the grill until the cheese melts. Serve hot.

One portion. Carbohydrate 10 g. Calories 70.

165. Macaroni Cheese with Ham

Quantities for 4. *Cooking time* ¾ hr. *Temperature* 375 °F. No. 5.

4 oz. macaroni (1 c. cut)
1 pt (2 c.) cheese sauce (No. 81)
2 oz. cooked chopped ham (¼ c.)
Buttered breadcrumbs (No. 521)

Boil one quart of water in a large pan with one level Tbs. salt. Add the macaroni and boil, without a lid, until just tender but still with some firmness. Drain in a colander, pour boiling water through. Put macaroni and ham in layers in a pie-dish and pour over the cheese sauce. Cover with buttered breadcrumbs and bake in a moderate oven to brown the top, or cook under the grill. Serve hot.

One portion. Carbohydrate 40 g. Calories 578.

166. Cheese Pudding

Quantities for 4. *Cooking time* ½–¾ hr. *Temperature* 375 °F. No. 5.

½ oz. (1 level Tbs.) butter or margarine
½ pt milk
3 oz. fresh breadcrumbs (¾ c.)
1 level tsp. salt
¼ level tsp. pepper
1 level tsp. made mustard
4 oz. grated cheese (1 level c.)
3 eggs

Grease a 2-pt pie-dish or other baking dish. Heat milk and fat and pour over the breadcrumbs. Leave to soak for a few minutes. Add remaining ingredients, including the egg yolks. Beat egg whites stiffly and fold into the mixture. Pour into the dish and bake until risen and lightly browned. Serve at once.

One portion. Carbohydrate 15 g. Calories 317.

167. Quiche Lorraine

Quantities for 4. *Cooking time* 1 hr. *Temperature* 450 °F. No. 8 then 375 °F. No. 5.

Pastry
4 oz. flour (¾ c.)
2 oz. (4 level Tbs.) fat
Filling
2 eggs
½ level tsp. salt
Pinch pepper
½ pt (1 c.) hot milk
2 oz. grated cheese (⅔ c.)
3 rashers bacon, grilled
½ oz. (1 level Tbs.) butter

Roll pastry to line 7–8 in. flan ring or sandwich tin. Bake blind in a hot oven for 15–20 mins. Beat eggs and season slightly, add milk and cheese and the chopped cooked bacon and butter. Pour into the pastry case and bake in a moderate oven 30–40 mins. or until the filling is set. Serve hot or cold.

One portion. Carbohydrate 26 g. Calories 500.

168. Sweetened Cottage Cheese (*low-fat*)

Beat or sieve the skimmed milk cottage cheese to make it smooth. Add sugar and vanilla to taste. Place in a mound in individual dishes and sprinkle with cinnamon. Surround with stewed fruit or fruit purée. Alternatively put a layer of fruit purée in the bottom of the dish and the cheese on top. Sprinkle with cinnamon as before.

169. Risotto

Quantities for 4. *Cooking time* 20–30 mins.

- 2 oz. (4 level Tbs.) fat
- 4 oz. chopped onion (1 medium)
- 8 oz. rice (1 c.)
- 1½ pt (3 c.) stock
- 4 oz. chopped mushrooms (1 c.) liver, lean lamb, or tomatoes (½ c.)
- Salt and pepper
- 2 oz. grated cheese (½ c.)

Use a heavy pan and fry the onion in the fat until it begins to brown. Add the rice and cook for 2 mins. longer. Add a quarter of the stock and cook for 15–20 mins., or until the rice is tender, adding the rest of the stock gradually. All should be absorbed by this time. Add the fried or grilled mushrooms, liver, lamb, or tomato a few minutes before serving. Season to taste. Serve the grated cheese separately.

One portion (with liver). Carbohydrate 52 g. Calories 451.

Variation (*low-protein diet*). Use either meat or cheese reduced to the amounts allowed in the diet.

EGG DISHES

170. Eggs

Egg-whites are used frequently in diet cookery, especially for low-fat diets. It is better not to use raw ones too often, and it will be seen that most of the recipes in this book use a method which cooks the whites lightly. Cakes and puddings made with whites need to be cooked more slowly at a lower temperature than when whole eggs are used, otherwise the products tend to be tough and unpalatable. Never try to cook an egg-white custard in a pressure cooker.

The yolks may be used up in family cooking, to make omelettes, scrambled eggs, and custards, and for thickening sauces. Two yolks plus 1 Tbs. water can be taken to equal one whole egg. If the yolks are not to be used until the next day, add the water, cover, and keep in the refrigerator.

171. French Omelette

Quantities for 4. *Cooking time* 2 mins.

8 eggs	¼ level tsp. pepper
1 level tsp. salt	1 oz. (2 level Tbs.) butter

Cook in one large pan or make four small individual omelettes. Beat the eggs just enough to mix them and add the seasonings. Melt the butter in the pan and, when it is just beginning to brown, add the eggs. Keep a good heat under the pan. As soon as the underside of the omelette begins to set, lift the edges with a knife and tilt the pan to let the uncooked mixture run underneath. Continue this until the omelette is almost set but still moist on top. Fold over away from the handle end and turn out on to a hot plate. Serve at once.

One portion. Carbohydrate nil. Calories 241.

Variations:

172. Bacon Omelette

Fry 2 lean chopped rashers of mild bacon in the pan before adding the egg. Add 4 level Tbs. chopped parsley to the egg.

One portion. Add 43 calories to No. 171.

173. Cheese Omelette

Mix 2 oz. grated cheese (½ c.) with the egg.

One portion. Add 60 calories to No. 171.

174. Kidney Omelette

Fry 4 chopped sheep's kidneys in 2 oz. (4 level Tbs.) butter and spread on the omelette before rolling up.

One portion. Add 142 calories to No. 171.

175. Mushroom Omelette

Chop 4 oz. (1 c.) mushrooms and fry in the butter before adding the eggs. A little more butter will probably be needed.

176. Jam Omelette

Omit salt and pepper. Spread with 4 Tbs. hot jam before rolling up.

One portion. Add 20 g. carbohydrate and 74 calories to No. 171.

177. Rum Omelette

Omit the salt and pepper. Turn on to a hot plate, sprinkle with sugar, and pour over 4 Tbs. hot rum. Set light to it and baste the omelette with it.

178. Golden Omelette

Quantities for 4. *Cooking time* 5 mins.

4 slices bread (4 oz.)	8 eggs
4 oz. (4 level Tbs.) butter	Salt and pepper

This may be cooked in one large pan or in four lots in an omelette pan. Remove the crusts from the bread and cut it in small cubes. Fry crisp and light brown in the hot butter. Beat the eggs and add seasoning. Pour over the bread and cook until just set. Fold over and serve at once.

One portion. Carbohydrate 7 g. Calories 352.

179. Omelette à la crème (*Mushroom Omelette with Cheese Sauce*)

Quantities for 4. *Cooking time* 15 mins.

4 oz. (1 c.) chopped mushrooms	4 Tbs. double cream
2 oz. (4 level Tbs.) butter	8 eggs
¾ pt (1½ c.) cheese sauce (No. 81)	Salt and pepper

Wash mushrooms and chop coarsely. Stew them in ½ oz. butter in a small pan until they are tender. Add cream to the cheese sauce and keep hot. Make the omelette from the seasoned eggs, adding the mushrooms during cooking. Fold on to a hot heat-resisting dish and pour the sauce over. Brown lightly under the grill.

One portion. Carbohydrate 16 g. Calories 655.

180. Soufflé Omelette

Quantities for 4. *Cooking time* 15 mins.

4 eggs	1 oz. (2 level Tbs.) butter
4 Tbs. water	Chopped parsley
½ level tsp. salt	Sauce if desired
Pinch pepper	

Separate yolks from whites and beat the yolks and water until thick and lemon-coloured. Beat the whites stiffly. Melt the butter in the pan, using 1 large pan or cook in 4 individual lots. Fold egg whites into yolk and pour into the pan. Cook very slowly for about five minutes until set underneath. Put in a moderate oven or under a slow grill for 8–10 mins. until the top looks dry but is not shrunken. Fold in half and turn on to a hot dish. Sprinkle with chopped parsley and serve with the sauce poured over, e.g. tomato, cheese, or mushroom.

One portion. Carbohydrate nil. Calories 160.

181. Spanish Omelette

Quantities for 4. *Cooking time* about 15 mins.

6 eggs
1 level tsp. salt
Pinch pepper
4 Tbs. chopped parsley
2 oz. (4 level Tbs.) fat
8 oz. (1 c.) mixed cooked diced vegetables

Any vegetables may be used, including some raw tomato and raw sweet red pepper. Beat the eggs, add seasoning, and parsley. Heat the fat in a small frying pan and toss the vegetables in it. Pour the eggs over the vegetables and cook, without stirring, until the egg is brown underneath. Place in the oven or under the grill to set the top lightly. Fold over and serve at once.

One portion. Carbohydrate 3 g. Calories 222.

182. Soufflés

Quantities for 4

1 oz (2 level Tbs.) butter or margarine *or* 1 Tbs. oil
1 oz. plain flour (3 level Tbs.)
¼ pt (½ c.) milk
3 eggs or 3 yolks and 4 whites
Flavouring, see below

Make a thick sauce with the fat, flour, and milk. Separate yolks and whites and beat the yolks with one Tbs. cold water. Add to the sauce together with the flavouring. Beat whites stiffly and fold in. Pour into the prepared dish. Bake or steam. Serve at once.

One portion. Carbohydrate 7 g. Calories 174.

Steamed Soufflé. Grease a 1 pt soufflé dish or deep round casserole. Cut a double piece of greased greaseproof paper or a strip of aluminium foil to tie round the dish and project two inches above the top. Place a circle of greased paper in the bottom and cut a square piece for the top. Put in the soufflé mixture and put the greased square on top. Steam gently for ¾ to 1 hr or until firm to the touch. Remove paper and string, turn out on to a hot dish and pour the sauce round.

Baked Soufflé. Grease a 1 pt soufflé dish or four small ones. Prepare paper or foil to tie round as above. Pour in the mixture and bake in a moderate oven, 375 °F. No. 5, until risen and brown, 20–30 mins. for a large one, 15–20 mins. for small ones. Serve at once, in the dish, and serve the sauce separately.

183. Cheese Soufflé

3 oz. finely grated cheese (1 c.)
Pinch of salt
Nutmeg, mustard, and cayenne pepper

One portion. Add 90 calories to No. 182.

184. Fish Soufflé

4–6 oz. (½–¾ c.) finely flaked or puréed cooked fish. Season with a pinch of salt and pepper and 1 Tbs. lemon juice. Serve with parsley sauce (No. 80) or anchovy sauce (No. 91).

One portion. For the fish add 36 calories to recipe No. 182.

185. Chocolate Soufflé

Dissolve 1 oz. (25 g.) grated chocolate in milk before making the sauce. Add 1 oz. sugar (2 level Tbs.), pinch of salt, and one tsp. vanilla. Serve with chocolate sauce (No. 133, 134, or 135), flavoured with a little rum.

One portion. Add 11 g. carbohydrate and 67 calories to recipe No. 182.

186. Vanilla Soufflé

Add 2 oz. sugar (4 level Tbs.), a pinch of salt, and 1 tsp. vanilla. Serve with jam sauce (No. 143) or custard sauce (No. 139).

One portion. Add 56 calories to No. 182.

187. Lemon Soufflé

Add a pinch of salt, finely grated rind of one lemon and 2 oz. sugar (4 level Tbs.). Serve with Melba sauce (No. 146) or a purée of fresh raspberries.

One portion. Add 56 calories to No. 182.

188. Poached Eggs Mornay

Allow $\frac{1}{8}$ pt (5 Tbs.) cheese sauce (No. 81) for each egg. Place the very lightly poached eggs in a heat-proof serving dish. Cover with cheese sauce and put under a hot grill for just a few seconds to colour the top. It must on no account be left long enough to become tough and stringy.

Per egg. Carbohydrate 8 g. Calories 216.

189. Eggs Crécy

Quantities for 4. *Cooking time* 20–30 mins.

1 lb. carrots (4 medium)
Salt and pepper
1 oz. (2 level Tbs.) butter or margarine
1 pt (2 c.) Béchamel sauce (No. 93)
4 eggs
Chopped parsley

Peel or scrape and slice the carrots. Boil until tender, mash with the butter and seasoning. While the carrots are cooking make the Béchamel sauce. Arrange the carrots in the bottom of four hot dishes. Keep hot. Poach the eggs, drain, and put on top of the carrots. Pour the sauce over and sprinkle with chopped parsley.

One portion. Carbohydrate 26 g. Calories 473.

190. Eggs Raymond

Quantities for 4. *Cooking time* 10–15 mins. *Temperature* 375 °F. No. 5.

1 oz. (2 level Tbs. butter)
4 Tbs. shelled shrimps
4 Tbs. double cream
4 eggs
Salt and pepper
4 oz. grated cheese (1 c.)

Use individual shallow fireproof baking dishes and melt the butter in them or use one large dish. Spread the shrimps evenly over the bottom and spoon over the cream. Break in the eggs, season with salt and pepper, and sprinkle the cheese on top. Bake in a moderate oven until nearly set and then brown very lightly under the grill.

One portion. Carbohydrate 1 g. Calories 332.

191. Egg in a Nest

Quantities for 4. *Cooking time* 2–3 mins. *Temperature* 375 °F. No. 5.

4 eggs
4 oz. toast (4 slices)
2 oz. (4 level Tbs.) butter
Pinch of salt

Separate white and yolk, keeping the 4 yolks intact and separate. While making the toast, beat the white stiff with a pinch of salt. Heap on the hot toast, make a nest in the centre of each, and drop in the yolk. Cook in the oven for about 2 mins. Place the butter in the centre and serve hot.

One portion. Carbohydrate 15 g. Calories 273.

192. Ham Custard

Quantities for 4. *Cooking time* 1 hr. *Temperature* 350 °F. No. 3.

4 oz. ham, minced or chopped ($\frac{1}{2}$ c.)
3 eggs
$\frac{3}{4}$ oz. cornflour ($2\frac{1}{2}$ level Tbs.)
$\frac{3}{4}$ pt ($1\frac{1}{2}$ c.) milk
Salt and pepper
1 oz. bread (1 slice)

Grease a $1\frac{1}{2}$-pt pie-dish or other baking dish. Separate the yolks and whites of the eggs, putting the whites in a basin with a pinch of salt. Mix the cornflour with a little of the cold milk. Heat the remainder and then pour into the cornflour. Stir, return to the pan, and cook and stir until it boils; cook 3–5 mins. Add the ham and the egg yolks. Mix well and season to taste. Beat the whites until stiff and fold into the other mixture. Pour into the baking dish. Cook in a slow oven until set. Toast the bread and cut into fingers. Serve with the mould.

One portion. Carbohydrate 14 g. Calories 300.

193. Scrambled Eggs Romaine

Quantities for 4. *Cooking time* 10–20 mins.

2 lb. spinach
4 Tbs. cream
Salt and pepper
1 oz. (2 level Tbs.) butter
8 eggs
8 Tbs. milk
2 oz. grated Parmesan cheese ($\frac{2}{3}$ c.)

Boil spinach, drain well, and chop. Put back in the pan and dry off. Add the cream, season well, and keep hot. Beat eggs, season, and add the milk. Melt the butter in a small pan and scramble the eggs and milk, well seasoned. Arrange the spinach in a flat mound on four hot plates. Put the scrambled egg in the centre and sprinkle with cheese. Serve at once.

One portion. Carbohydrate 8 g. Calories 428.

194. Egg and Yogurt Mould

Quantities for 4

- 4 eggs, hard-boiled
- 1 tsp. Worcester sauce
- Pinch paprika pepper
- 3 anchovy fillets, chopped
- ½ pt (1 c.) chicken stock
- ¼ oz. gelatine (½ level Tbs.)
- Salt and pepper
- ¼ pt (½ c.) yogurt
- Slice of anchovy fillet to garnish
- Parsley or chervil

Separate yolks and whites. Sieve yolks and chop whites finely. Dissolve gelatine in the stock. Mix the yolks with the Worcester sauce, paprika pepper, anchovy fillets, and stock. Season to taste. Chill. When just beginning to set, beat in the yogurt and add the egg whites. Pour into a shallow serving dish and leave to set. Unmould. Garnish with anchovy fillets and parsley or chervil. Serve with a salad.

One portion. Carbohydrate 2 g. Calories 122.

195. Eggs Mimosa

Quantities for 4 *Cooking time* 20 mins.

- 1 pt (2 c.) medium white *or* Béchamel sauce (No. 93)
- 8 eggs
- 4 slices toast *or* ½ lb. mashed potatoes, *or* ½ lb. parsnips *or* 1 lb. spinach
- Parsley to garnish

Make the sauce and hard-boil the eggs. Prepare the toast or cook and mash the vegetables to make a small bed on each plate. Keep hot. Separate whites and yolks of the eggs. Chop the whites and re-heat in the sauce. Mash the yolks or put through a sieve. Pour sauce on to the toast or bed of hot vegetables. Sprinkle the mashed yolks over the top and garnish with parsley.

One portion.	With toast, carbohydrate	25 g.	Calories 312
	with potato	20 g.	310
	with parsnips	17 g.	274
	with spinach	7 g.	149

196. Scalloped Eggs and Ham

Quantities for 4. *Cooking time* 30 mins. *Temperature* 400 °F. No. 6.

4 oz. cooked ham, minced or chopped (½ c.)
¾ oz. (1½ level Tbs.) butter or margarine
¾ oz. flour (2½ level Tbs.)
1 level tsp. dry mustard
½ pt (1 c.) milk
Salt and pepper
2 eggs, hard-boiled
Topping
1 oz. fresh breadcrumbs (3 level Tbs.)
½ oz. (1 level Tbs.) butter or margarine

Melt the ¾ oz. fat and add the flour and mustard. Stir and cook until it looks mealy. Add the milk and stir until it boils. Boil 3 mins. and season to taste. Melt the ½ oz. fat in a small pan and add the breadcrumbs. Stir until they are well coated. Slice the eggs and mix with the sauce and the ham. Put in a baking dish and sprinkle the crumbs on top. Bake about 20 mins. or until heated through and brown on top. Serve hot.

If preferred, cook in individual dishes, when the cooking time will be less, but more topping probably needed, to cover the larger surface.

One portion. Carbohydrate 11 g. Calories 323.

197. Stuffed Eggs

Hard-boil the eggs, cut in half and remove yolks, mash with the chosen filling and put back in the whites. Decorate by piping or with parsley or other garnish.

Fillings:

1. Grated cheese, mustard, and melted butter.
2. Minced ham and chopped parsley.
3. Anchovy essence and lemon juice.
4. Grated cheese and Marmite.
5. Cooked minced chicken or veal with mayonnaise.

198. Eggs Lyonnaise

Quantities for 4. *Cooking time* 20 mins.

4 hard-boiled eggs
½ pt (1 c.) onion sauce (No. 82)
Salt and pepper
2 oz. grated cheese (½ c.)

Slice the eggs and heat them in the sauce. Place them in a fireproof dish and cover with the cheese. Place in oven or under grill to melt cheese. Serve hot.

One portion. Carbohydrate 8 g. Calories 260.

199. Fricassée of Eggs

Quantities for 4. *Cooking time* 20 mins.

½ pt (1 c.) brown sauce (No. 96
4 hard-boiled eggs
4 rashers streaky bacon
1 Tbs. chopped parsley

Make the sauce. Cut eggs in half and heat gently in the sauce. Remove bacon rinds, roll up rashers, and fasten on a skewer. Grill or bake until the outside is crisp. Put eggs and sauce in a hot dish, garnish with the bacon and parsley, and serve hot.

One portion. Carbohydrate 5 g. Calories 300.

200. Zabaglione

Quantities for 4. *Cooking time* about 10 mins.

3 egg yolks
1½ oz. sugar (3 level Tbs.)
¼ pt (½ c.) Marsala or Madeira wine

Put egg yolks and sugar in a quart-sized pudding basin. Beat with rotary whisk until thick and light. Add the wine and mix well. Place in a basin over a pan of boiling water and continue beating until the mixture has risen well and is thick. Pour into individual glasses and serve hot with small macaroons.

One portion. Carbohydrate 14 g. Calories 164.

FISH

201. Choice of Fish

Fish forms an important part of many diets because it is easy to digest and can be cooked in a wide variety of ways.

Most diets specify 'white fish' because it has very little fat in the flesh and this makes it easier to digest than the oily fish such as herring, salmon, fresh-water eels, trout, sardines, sprats, mackerel, and several others.

Varieties of white fish include: Sea bream, cat fish, cod, conger eel, dabs, flounder, haddock, hake, halibut, John Dory, ling, megrim, monk fish, mullet, plaice, pollack, pollan, saithe, skate, sole, stockfish, torsk, turbot, whiting, witch.

When oily fish is allowed it is important to use kinds such as herring, canned salmon, and sardines once or twice a week as these are an important source of vitamin D, which is not very plentiful in the average diet. If oily fish is cooked by methods other than frying or sousing most digestions can tolerate it. Poaching, steaming, and baking are the best methods for diet cooking.

202. Baked Fish

Quantities. ½ lb. steak *or* 6 oz. fillet per person. *Cooking time* 20–30 mins. *Temperature* 375 °F. No. 5.

Method 1. Prepare the pieces of fish and place in a shallow greased fireproof dish. Cover with a coating sauce which can be any of the following: cheese, tomato, parsley, anchovy, egg, mustard, pepperone and tomato, or tomato purée. Sprinkle the top with buttered breadcrumbs (No. 521). Bake in a moderate oven until the fish flakes easily when tested with a fork. Serve at once, preferably in the dish in which it has been cooked.

Method 2. Omit sauce and breadcrumbs. Brush fish with either oil, melted butter, or margarine, cover with a lid or piece of aluminium foil and bake as before. Serve a permitted sauce separately.

One portion. White fish. Carbohydrate nil. Calories 120.

Variations: 1. *Low-fat diet.* Use method 1, with unbuttered crumbs and a low-fat sauce (No. 120). 2. *Gluten-free diet.* Use either method if gluten-free breadcrumbs are used, and the sauce thickened with wheat-starch, or use Italian tomato sauce (No. 107). 3. *Low-sodium diet.* Use method 2 with oil, salt-free butter, or margarine. Serve with a low-salt sauce

(No. 88). 4. *Low-carbohydrate diet.* Use method 2, and serve with a low-carbohydrate sauce (Nos. 98, 99, 100, 101). 5. *Low-calorie diets.* Use method 2 and serve with lemon wedges.

203. Grilled Fish

Quantities. 4–6 oz. fillet *or* 1 steak *or* 1 small fish per person. *Cooking time* 5–25 mins. depending on thickness.

If small whole fish are being cooked, cut two or three deep gashes on either side to allow the heat to reach the centre. Brush white fish with oil or melted fat. Grill gently until brown one side, turn, and brown the other. The fish is done when the flakes separate easily, or, if there is bone, when the fish easily leaves the bone. Serve with lemon juice or melted butter, if allowed, and wedges of lemon.

One portion. (white fish). Carbohydrate nil. Calories 80–120.

Suitable sauces, provided they are allowed in the diet, would be egg and lemon sauce (No. 100), lemon sauce (No. 103), Italian tomato sauce (No. 106). See also suggestions in No. 202.

204. Oven-Fried Fish

Quantities. 1 steak *or* thick fillet per person.

Cooking time 10–20 mins. *Temperature* 400 °F. No. 6.

Clean and dry fish. Dip in seasoned flour, then in beaten egg, and finally in breadcrumbs. Heat sufficient oil in a baking tin to cover the bottom. When hot put in the fish, baste with oil, and cook uncovered.

Variations: 1. *Gluten-free diet.* Use dried gluten-free breadcrumbs. 2. *Low-sodium diet.* Use salt-free breadcrumbs.

205. Poached Fish

Quantities. Allow 1 thick piece of fillet or 1 steak per portion.

Cooking time 10–15 mins.

To each ½ pt (1 c.) of water used add:

¼ Tbs. vinegar	¼ bayleaf
½ level tsp. salt	1 small piece carrot
1 peppercorn	1 slice onion (optional)
1 sprig parsley	

Use a frying pan or shallow casserole for cooking and just

enough liquid to cover the fish (about ½ pt for 3–4 portions). Bring liquid and seasoning to the boil. Add fish and reduce heat to keep below boiling. This can be done in a slow oven or on top. Test with a fork at the thickest part and if the flakes separate easily it is done. Lift out with a fish slice on to a hot dish. Strain the liquid and use as stock for a permitted sauce.

Variations. Poach fish in milk (about ½ pt for 3–4 portions) or milk and water with any of the above flavourings. Use liquid for the sauce.

206. Cod à la Boulangère

Quantities for 4. *Cooking time* ½ hr. *Temperature* 400 °F. No. 6.

- 1½–2 lb. piece of cod
- 1 lb. potatoes (4 medium), parboiled
- 8 oz. small onions, parboiled
- 1 level tsp. salt
- ¼ level tsp. pepper
- 1 oz. butter or 2 Tbs. oil
- 2 Tbs. chopped parsley

Put the cod in a greased baking dish. Cut potatoes in thick slices or chunks. Arrange round the cod. Add the onion and sprinkle with the seasoning. Dot with the butter or sprinkle with the oil. Bake until the fish and potatoes are tender. Serve sprinkled with chopped parsley.

One portion. Carbohydrate 27 g. Calories 200.

207. Fish Cocktail

Quantities for 4

- ¼ pt (½ c.) tomato ketchup
- 1 tsp. Worcester sauce
- 1 Tbs. horseradish sauce (optional)
- ½ Tbs. lemon juice
- ½ level tsp. dry mustard
- ¼ pt (½ c.) double cream
- ½ lb. (1 c.) flaked cooked fish or shellfish
- 4 lettuce leaves
- Chopped parsley or other herbs

Combine all the ingredients except the fish and lettuce. When well blended, add the fish and mix in gently. Chill. Wash and shred the lettuce and put in individual glass dishes, or large wineglasses. Place the fish on top of the lettuce and garnish with parsley or herbs.

One portion. Carbohydrate 6 g. Calories 163.

Variations. Instead of the ketchup, a home-made salad dressing may be used to give a milder flavour.

Gluten-free diet. Use home-made sauces or ones from the list (see page 63).

208. Shrimp and Orange Cocktail

Quantities for 4

- 2 large oranges
- 7 oz. shelled cooked shrimps (1 c.)
- 2 Tbs. chopped cucumber or gherkins
- 2 Tbs. mayonnaise
- 2 oz. shredded lettuce
- Chopped parsley

Peel oranges, remove all membrane and pith, and divide in pieces the same size as the fish. Keep a few shrimps for garnishing and mix the rest with the oranges. Add the cucumber or gherkins and the mayonnaise. Line large glasses with shredded lettuce leaves and add the shrimp mixture. Garnish with remaining shrimps and some chopped parsley. Chill before serving.

One portion. Carbohydrate 5 g. Calories 88.

Variation (gluten-free diet). Use home-made mayonnaise or one from the list (see page 63).

209. Prawn Cocktail (*low-fat*)

Quantities for 4

- ½ pt (1 c.) tomato juice
- 2 Tbs. lemon juice
- 2 tsp. made mustard
- 2 tsp. Worcester sauce
- Celery salt to taste
- 2 Tbs. yogurt
- 4 oz. or ½ pt (1 c.) shelled cooked prawns

Mix all the ingredients together except the prawns. When smooth, add the prawns, put in deep glasses, and chill.

One portion. Carbohydrate 4 g. Calories 50.

Variations (gluten-free diet). Use sauce from the list (see page 63).

210. Fried Cod's Roe

Tie the roe in a thin cloth to keep it in shape. Put it into boiling water and cook for ½ hr. Lift it out in the cloth and leave until cold. Remove the cloth and cut the roe in ½ in.

slices. Dust with flour and fry in hot f well browned. Serve with wedges of

One portion (3 oz.). Carbohydrate 3 g.

211. Cod's Roe Pie (*also suitable for herri*

Quantities for 4. *Cooking time* 30 mins.

1 lb. cooked or canned roes
4 hard-boiled eggs
½ pt (1 c.) medium white sauce (No. 79) *or* cheese sauce (No. 81)

Topping
4 level Tbs. breadcrumbs
4 level Tbs. grated cheese *or*
1 lb. mashed potatoes (4 medium)

Slice the roes into a shallow baking dish. Cover with chopped egg and then the sauce. Top either with the breadcrumbs and cheese mixed together or with the mashed potato. Brown in the top of the oven or under the grill.

One portion. Carbohydrate 19–35 g. Calories 508–99.

Variation (*gluten-free diet*). Use gluten-free flour for the sauce and gluten-free breadcrumbs.

212. Fish Bonne Femme (*gluten-free, low-fat*)

Quantities for 4. *Cooking time* 15–20 mins. *Temperature* 375 °F. No. 5.

4 portions of fish, fillet *or* steak (about 1½ lb.)
Salt and pepper
4 oz. mushrooms, sliced
2 fl. oz. (4 Tbs.) dry white wine

Put the fish in a shallow baking dish and season well. Cover with the mushrooms and moisten with wine to come not more than halfway up the fish. Bake, uncovered, until the fish is tender. If liked, the liquid may then be thickened with potato flour or by reduction (fast boiling).

Variation. When fat is allowed, thicken the liquid with 2 Tbs. double cream and 1 egg yolk mixed together. Do not boil again.

Low-sodium diet. Omit the salt and sprinkle a little finely grated lemon rind on the fish.

One portion, (without thickening). Carbohydrate 1 g. Calories 133.

213. Fish Casserole (*low-fat*)

Quantities for 4. *Cooking time* 15–20 mins. *Temperature* 375 °F. No. 5.

1 lb. fillets plaice *or* sole
6 oz. tomatoes, skinned and chopped (3 medium)
4 oz. (1 c.) mushrooms, chopped
4 level Tbs. breadcrumbs
1 level tsp. grated lemon rind
Salt and pepper
½ pt (1 c.) fish stock, wine or cider

Mix the tomato with half the mushroom, the breadcrumbs, lemon rind, and seasoning. Spread on the fillets and roll up tightly. Pack close together in a casserole, cover with the rest of the mushroom, and add the liquid. Season well. Cover and cook for 20 mins. in a moderate oven.

One portion Carbohydrate 5 g. Calories 114.

Variations (*gluten-free diet*). Use gluten-free breadcrumbs.

Low-sodium diet. Omit salt, use substitute if allowed, and salt-free breadcrumbs.

214. Creamed Fish

Quantities for 4. *Cooking time* 30 mins.

1 lb. boiled or steamed or canned fish, flaked (2 c.)
¾ pt (1½ c.) medium thick Béchamel or parsley sauce (No. 93 or 80)
Salt and pepper
Paprika pepper (optional)
Lemon juice or anchovy essence, chopped green herbs, or a little grated onion
Toast or mashed potatoes
Parsley or tomato to garnish

Heat the fish in the sauce, seasoning to taste. Serve on toast or in a border of mashed potatoes. Garnish with parsley or tomato.

One portion. Carbohydrate 27–32 g. Calories 340–400.

Variations (*modified fat diet*). Make sauce with oil (see Nos. 79–92). (*Low-fat diet.*) Use white fish and make a fatless sauce (Nos. 120–9). Mash the potatoes with skimmed milk and season well.

215. Scalloped Fish

Fish, sauce, and flavourings as above, but put the mixture in individual scallop dishes, cover with buttered breadcrumbs (dry crumbs for low fat), and heat in a moderate oven.

216. Creamed Fish (*low-sodium*)

Quantities for 4. *Cooking time* 10–20 mins.

1 lb. white fish
2 oz. (4 level Tbs.) salt-free butter
2 oz. plain flour (6 level Tbs.)
1 pt (2 c.) milk (from allowance or Edosol)
2–4 Tbs. lemon juice
2–4 Tbs. tarragon vinegar
Pepper
Salt substitute (if allowed)
Chopped parsley or tomato to garnish

Steam the fish for 7–8 mins. or till cooked. Flake it. Make a sauce with the butter, flour, and milk. Cook 5 mins. and then add the lemon juice, vinegar, and flavourings. Add the flaked cooked fish and re-heat. Serve with the garnish.

One portion. Carbohydrate 19 g. Calories 350.

Variations. Add salt for other diets. *Low-fat diet.* Omit butter and make sauce with skimmed milk by the blending method. See No. 120.

217. Fish Créole

Quantities for 4. *Cooking time* 20 mins.

1 oz. (2 level Tbs.) fat
4 oz. onions chopped (1 medium)
2 oz. green sweet pepper, chopped (4 level Tbs.)
8 tomatoes, skinned (1 lb.)
4 oz. (1 c.) mushrooms, chopped
Salt and pepper
1½ lb. fillets of white fish

Heat the fat and fry the onions in it. Add the rest of the vegetables, and cook gently, stirring frequently until a soft pulpy sauce is formed. Season to taste. Poach, bake, or grill the fish and serve with the sauce.

One portion. Carbohydrate 6 g. Calories 206.

218. Fish Florentine

Quantities for 4. *Cooking time* about 30 mins. *Temperature* 375 °F. No. 5.

½ pt (1 c.) Béchamel sauce (No. 93)
4 oz. grated cheese (1 c.)
8 fillets of plaice or sole (1 lb.) *or* four portions any other white fish
4 Tbs. white wine or lemon juice
1½ lb. spinach or 2 small pkts frozen

Make the Béchamel sauce, add 1½ oz. of the cheese and allow to melt. While the sauce is cooking, season the fish and fold the fillets in three. Place in a greased baking dish and sprinkle with the wine or lemon. Cover and put in a moderate oven for 10 mins. or until cooked. Cook the spinach and drain well. Remove the cooked fish from the baking dish and pour off any liquid. Put in the spinach, then the fish on top and finally cover with the sauce. Sprinkle remaining cheese on top and brown in the top of a hot oven or under the grill. Serve at once.

One portion. Carbohydrate 25 g. Calories 555.

219. Fish with Garlic (*low-sodium*)

Quantities for 4. *Cooking time* 35 mins.

- 3 oz. (6 level Tbs.) salt-free margarine
- 8 oz. onions, chopped (2 medium)
- 1 clove garlic, finely chopped
- 1 Tbs. tomato paste
- Juice of 1 lemon
- 1 level tsp. paprika pepper
- ¼ level tsp. cayenne pepper
- ¼ level tsp. ground mace
- ⅛ level tsp. freshly ground black pepper
- 1 lb. cod fillet
- 2 Tbs. tarragon vinegar

Heat margarine in a saucepan. Add onion and garlic. Cover and allow to soften slowly. Remove lid and increase heat to brown lightly. Add tomato paste, ¼ pt water, and the lemon juice. Bring to the boil and simmer with lid half on for 10–15 mins. Add the pepper and mace. Wash, dry, and trim the fish into cutlets. Place in a greased fireproof dish, moisten with water and the tarragon vinegar, and poach for 15–20 mins. Arrange on a hot serving dish, with a good spoonful of the onion mixture over each piece of fish.

One portion. Carbohydrate 3 g. Calories 263.

Variation. Add salt for low-carbohydrate diet.

220. Fish au Gratin

Quantities for 4. *Cooking time* 30–40 mins.

- 1 lb. cooked white fish (2 c. flaked)
- ¾ pt (1½ c.) parsley sauce (No. 80)
- 1½ lb. freshly cooked mashed potatoes (6 medium)
- 1½-oz. grated cheese (6 level Tbs.)
- 3 level Tbs. dried bread-crumbs
- ½ oz. (1 level Tbs.) margarine

Mix fish and sauce and make sure it is well seasoned. Make a border with the mashed potato in a fireproof dish, pour the fish mixture into the centre and sprinkle with cheese and crumbs. Dot with margarine and brown under a hot grill or in a hot oven.

One portion. Carbohydrate 50 g. Calories 500.

Variation (*gluten-free diet*). Make the sauce with gluten-free flour and use gluten-free breadcrumbs.

221. Fish with Pineapple (*low-sodium*)

Quantities for 4. *Cooking time* 10 mins.

- 1 lb. fillets white fish
- 1 oz. (2 level Tbs.) salt-free butter
- 1 oz. cornflour (3 level Tbs.)
- ½ pt(1 c.) milk from allowance or use Edosol
- 8 oz. pineapple, crushed or chopped (1 level c.)
- ⅛ pt (5 Tbs.) double cream
- Pepper
- Chopped parsley

Poach, bake, or grill the fish. Make a sauce with the butter, cornflour, and milk. Cook for 5 mins. and add the pineapple and cream. Add pepper to taste. Pour over the fish and decorate with parsley.

One portion. Carbohydrate 20 g. Calories 327.

Variation. Add salt for other diets.

222. Fillets of Fish with Lemon Sauce

Quantities for 4. *Cooking time* 30 mins.

- Fish bones and trimmings for stock from 1½ lb. fillets of white fish
- 1 oz. (2 level Tbs.) butter or margarine
- 1 oz. plain flour (3 level Tbs.) *or* ½ oz. cornflour (1½ level Tbs.)
- ¼ pt (½ c.) milk
- Salt and pepper
- Juice of ½ lemon
- 1 egg yolk
- 2 Tbs. cream
- 2 Tbs. chopped parsley

Cover the fish trimmings with cold water and simmer for 20 mins. Strain. Roll thin fillets and fasten with cocktail sticks. Cut thick fillets in portions. Poach gently in a little of the stock. Lift out and place in a hot dish. Make sauce with the butter or margarine, flour, milk, and ½ pt of the fish stock. When cooked add the lemon juice, egg yolk, and cream and heat gently to thicken without boiling. Pour over the fish and decorate with the parsley. Serve at once.

One portion. Carbohydrate 8 g. Calories 280.

Variation. For those who can have shellfish, garnish the dish with ½ pt shelled shrimps or prawns.

223. Fish Shape

Quantities for 4. *Cooking time* 1¼–1½ hrs. *Temperature* 300 °F. No. 3.

2 oz. fresh breadcrumbs (⅔ c.)
2 Tbs. milk
12 oz. (1½ c.) fish, freshly cooked and flaked
2 oz. (4 Tbs.) melted butter or margarine
2–3 eggs
Salt and pepper

Combine the crumbs and milk. Add fish and melted fat and beat until very smooth. Beat eggs and add them together with the seasoning. If an electric blender is available put all ingredients in the goblet and beat smooth. Put in a greased mould, cover, and steam 1¼–1½ hrs. Or bake with the mould standing in a pan of water. Unmould and serve with a sauce suitable for the diet.

One portion. Carbohydrate 8 g. Calories 290.

224. Herring Fish Cakes (*low-protein*)

Quantities for 8 cakes. *Cooking time* Grilling 10 mins. Baking 15–20 mins. *Temperature* 450 °F. No. 8.

8 oz. freshly cooked herring
¾ lb. freshly cooked mashed potato (3 medium)
½ oz. (¼ c.) chopped parsley
Salt and pepper
1 egg
Breadcrumbs

Remove all skin and bones from the herring and mix fish with the potato. Add parsley and seasoning and bind with some of the egg. Spread out on a plate to cool. Shape into cakes. Brush with the rest of the egg mixed with a little water, and coat with crumbs. Bake in a hot oven or grill until brown.

Variation (*gluten-free diet*). Use gluten-free breadcrumbs for coating.

225. White Fish Cakes (*low-protein*)

Quantities for 8 cakes

8 oz. mashed potato (1 c.)
8 oz. cooked flaked fish (1 c.)
Salt and pepper
Pinch of mace or nutmeg
1 tsp. onion juice or a little onion powder
1 Tbs. chopped parsley
A little vinegar or lemon juice
1 egg
Breadcrumbs

Mix and cook as for herring fish cakes (No. 224).

226. Hungarian Fish Stew (*low-sodium*)

Quantities for 4. *Cooking time* 20 mins. *Temperature* 375 °F. No. 5.

1 lb. tomatoes, fresh or canned (4 medium)
2 oz. (4 level Tbs.) salt-free butter or margarine
4 oz. onions, sliced (2 small)
Pepper
½ level tsp. paprika pepper
Sugar
Salt substitute if allowed
1 lb. cod fillet
Chopped parsley

Skin and chop the tomatoes. Heat 1 oz. fat and fry the onions in it gently until tender. Add tomatoes and cook until soft, and the sauce well blended. Season to taste. Cut cod fillets in 4 portions and put in shallow greased dish, with the rest of the fat in bits on top. Cover with aluminium foil or a lid and bake about ten minutes or until cooked. Add any liquid to the tomatoes, and pour over the fish. Sprinkle with parsley and serve hot.

One portion. Carbohydrate 5 g. Calories 220.

227. Kedgeree

Quantities for 4. *Cooking time* 20 mins.

2 oz. (4 level Tbs.) butter or margarine
8 oz. raw rice (1 c.) or 4 c. boiled
1 lb. cooked flaked fish (2 c.)
2 hard-boiled eggs
Salt and pepper
Pinch of nutmeg
1 lemon
Parsley

Cook the fish and rice. Melt butter or margarine and stir in the fish and rice. Add seasoning and chopped egg white. Heat gently until thoroughly hot through. Pile on a hot dish. Rub the egg yolk through a sieve and sprinkle over the top of the kedgeree. Garnish with parsley and serve with wedges of lemon.

One portion. Carbohydrate 49 g. Calories 475.

Variations. For those who are allowed it use smoked fish, which makes a more tasty kedgeree. (*Modified-fat diet.*) Use 2 Tbs. oil instead of the butter or margarine. (*Low-protein diet.*) Use only 4 oz. fish.

228. Lobster Salad

The cooked lobster is split in half and the claws arranged round it together with halved or quartered lettuce hearts. Dressings used are simply vinegar or lemon juice (low-calorie or low-fat diets), or French dressing (No. 113–14), mayonnaise (No. 115). Low-fat dressing (No. 110 or 112) could also be used.

229. Rice and Fish Mould

Quantities for 4. *Cooking time* ½ hr

8 oz. fillet white fish
2 oz. rice (¼ c.)
1 egg, beaten
¼ pt (½ c.) milk
½ level tsp. salt
¼ level tsp. pepper
Good pinch of ground mace
Squeeze of lemon juice

Boil the rice. Mince the raw fish coarsely or chop it finely. Mix rice and fish with the other ingredients. Pour into greased individual moulds. Steam for ½ hr or until firm. Turn out and serve hot with a sauce, or cold with a salad.

One portion. Carbohydrate 15 g. Calories 144.

Variation (*low-fat diet*). Use skimmed milk.

230. Salmon au Gratin

Quantities for 4. *Cooking time* 20 mins.

¾ oz. margarine or 1 Tbs. oil
¾ oz. plain flour (2 level Tbs.)
About ½ pt (1 c.) milk
½ lb. tinned salmon, flaked
¼ oz. (⅛ c.) chopped parsley
Salt and pepper
1½ oz. (½ c.) grated cheese
½ oz. (2 level Tbs.) dried breadcrumbs

Melt the margarine or heat the oil. Add the flour, stir, and cook for a few minutes. Gradually add the milk to make a fairly thick, creamy sauce. Stir until it boils and cook for a few minutes. Add the parsley and salmon and season to taste. Pour into a fireproof dish. Sprinkle the cheese and breadcrumbs on top and brown under the grill or in a hot oven.

One portion. Carbohydrate 10 g. Calories 272.

Variation (*gluten-free diet*). Use ¾ oz. (2 level Tbs.), wheat-starch instead of the flour and use gluten-free breadcrumbs.

231. Cauliflower with Salmon Sauce

Quantities for 4. *Cooking time* ½ hr

1 large cauliflower	½ pt (1 c.) milk
2 oz. (4 level Tbs.) margarine or 2 Tbs. oil	Salt and pepper
	8 oz. canned salmon (227 g.)
2 oz. plain flour (6 level Tbs.)	Lemon juice
½ pt (1 c.) cauliflower stock	Chopped parsley

Divide the cauliflower in sprigs and boil in a little lightly salted water. Strain and keep the stock. Put cauliflower to keep hot. Make a sauce with the margarine or oil, the flour, milk, and seasoning and the cauliflower stock. Boil for 5 mins. and season to taste. Add salmon and lemon juice and re-heat. Pour the sauce over the cauliflower and sprinkle with chopped parsley.

One portion. Carbohydrate 15 g. Calories 290.

232. Salmon Loaf

Quantities for 4. *Cooking time* 45 mins. *Temperature* 375 °F. No. 5.

8 oz. canned salmon (227 g.)	½ level tsp. salt
¼ pt (½ c.) milk	Pinch of pepper
3 oz. (1 c.) fresh breadcrumbs	1 tsp. lemon juice
2 eggs	Pinch of ground mace

Strain the liquid from the salmon and keep it to add to a sauce to serve with the loaf. Mash the salmon, including skin and bone, as all is very soft. Heat milk and pour on to breadcrumbs. Soak one to two minutes. Add egg yolks and fish together with the flavourings and lemon juice. Beat egg whites stiff and fold in. Pour into a greased 1-lb. loaf-tin, or similar-sized baking dish. Bake in a moderate oven. Turn out on a hot dish and mask with a sauce such as parsley or tomato, Béchamel, or egg and lemon sauce.

One portion. Carbohydrate 15 g. Calories 180.

233. Salmon Mousse

Quantities for 4

- ¼ pt (½ c.) aspic jelly
- Cucumber or sweet red pepper for garnish
- 8 oz. fresh cooked or canned salmon (1 c. flaked)
- ⅛ pt (5 Tbs.) whipping cream
- Paprika pepper
- Salt and pepper
- Tarragon vinegar
- Worcester sauce
- Watercress

Chill a mould and then line with a layer of melted aspic jelly. Use meat aspic or recipe No. 289. Leave to set. Prepare decorations, dip in melted aspic, and decorate the set jelly in the mould. Leave to set. Mash or purée the salmon (in electric blender if possible). Whip the cream and mix with the salmon. Add ⅛ pt melted aspic and seasonings to taste. Spoon into the mould and leave to set. Unmould and garnish with watercress.

One portion. Carbohydrate 1 g. Calories 180.

234. Salmon Savoury

Quantities for 4. *Cooking time* 10 mins.

- 1 oz. (2 level Tbs.) fat
- 1 oz. flour (3 level Tbs.)
- ½ pt (1 c.) water
- 8 oz. canned salmon (227 g.)
- 1 Tbs. chopped parsley
- 2 tsp. vinegar
- Salt and pepper
- 4 slices toast

Make the sauce with the fat, flour, and water, and cook for a few minutes. Add the flaked salmon, herbs, and vinegar and season to taste. Put on the toast and place under the grill for two minutes. Serve immediately.

One portion. Carbohydrate 25 g. Calories 254.

235. Fillets of Sole or Plaice with Cream and Grapes (Veronique)

Quantities for 4. *Cooking time* 15–20 mins.

- 1 lb. fillet sole (8 fillets)
- Dry white wine
- 1 small onion, chopped (2 oz.)
- Sprig of parsley
- Salt and pepper
- 8 oz. grapes, skinned and pipped
- ½ pt (1 c.) double cream
- 1 oz. (2 level Tbs.) butter

Remove the dark skin from the fillets and put fish in a flat baking dish. Add dry white wine to cover, onion, parsley, salt and pepper, and cook gently until the flakes separate easily. Remove the fillets and keep hot. Put the liquid in a small pan and boil to reduce to half the volume. Strain and return to the pan with the grapes and cream. Bring to the boil and cook until it thickens, adding butter bit by bit. Mix until smooth and pour over the fillets.

One portion. Carbohydrate 12 g. Calories 550.

236. Scalloped Scallops

Quantities for 4. *Cooking time* 20 mins. *Temperature* 375 °F. No. 5.

4 level Tbs. breadcrumbs
8 scallops
Cayenne pepper and salt
Lemon juice
Chopped parsley
$\frac{1}{4}$ pt($\frac{1}{2}$ c.) medium white sauce (No. 79) *or* Béchamel sauce (No. 93)
1 oz. (2 level Tbs.) butter or margarine

Grease four deep scallop shells and strew in a few breadcrumbs. Put two scallops in each and sprinkle on a few grains of cayenne, a little lemon juice, and some chopped parsley. Cover the scallops with the well-seasoned sauce and sprinkle in more crumbs. Put small knobs of butter or margarine on top or sprinkle with a little oil and bake in a moderate oven. Serve hot.

One portion. Carbohydrate 5 g. Calories 167.

Variation (modified fat diet). Use a sauce made with oil (see No. 79).

237. Creamed Soft Roes

Quantities for 4. *Cooking time* 20 mins.

8 soft herring roes
$\frac{1}{4}$ pt ($\frac{1}{2}$ c.) milk
$\frac{1}{2}$ oz. plain flour ($1\frac{1}{2}$ level Tbs.)
Salt and pepper
Lemon juice
Chopped parsley
4 slices toast *or* $\frac{1}{2}$–1 lb. mashed or Duchess potatoes (No. 349)

Stew the roes gently in the milk until they are tender (10–15 mins.). Lift out and keep hot. Mix flour to a paste with a little cold water, add the hot milk, return to pan, and stir until it boils. Cook five minutes. Season well and add lemon juice to taste. Pour over the roes, which should be put on the toast or in a border of potatoes. Garnish with chopped parsley.

One portion. Carbohydrate 19–27 g. Calories 211–277.

Variation (gluten-free diet). Use ¼ oz. gluten-free flour in place of the ordinary flour and use gluten-free toast.

Canned roes. Make sauce as above, and heat the roes in it.

238. Sole Meunière à l'Orange

Quantities for 4. *Cooking time* 8–10 mins.

4 large fillets sole, skinned (1 lb.)
Salt and pepper
2 oz. (4 level Tbs.) butter
½ oz. flour (1½ level Tbs.)
1 large orange, peeled and sliced

Sprinkle the fillets with salt and pepper and then with flour to coat lightly. Heat half the butter in a pan and fry the fillets until lightly browned. Place on a hot dish. Arrange slices of orange on each fillet. Heat remaining butter until light brown and pour over the fish. Serve at once.

One portion. Carbohydrate 5 g. Calories 216.

239. Sole aux Crevettes (*low-fat, low-carbohydrate*)

Quantities for 4. *Cooking time* 10–15 mins. *Temperature* 375 °F. No. 5.

4 large or 8 small fillets sole (1 lb.)
Salt and pepper
White wine
1 pt (2 c.) shelled shrimps
Chopped parsley

Season the fillets and roll up. Poach gently in a baking dish in the oven with wine to moisten. Just before the fish is cooked, add the shrimps which may be fresh, canned, or frozen. Serve sprinkled with chopped parsley.

One portion. Carbohydrate a trace. Calories 144.

240. Sole Dieppoise (*low-fat, low-carbohydrate*)

Quantities for 4. *Cooking time* 10–15 mins. *Temperature* 375 °F. No. 5.

8 fillets sole (1 lb.)
Salt and pepper
White wine
2 doz. cooked mussels
½ pt (1 c.) cooked shelled shrimps
Chopped parsley

Season the fillets and roll up. Poach gently in a little white wine. This may be done in a shallow pan on top of the stove or in the oven as in No. 239. Just before the fish is cooked, add the mussels and shrimps and allow them to become hot, but do not cook for long. Serve sprinkled with chopped parsley.

One portion. Carbohydrate a trace. Calories 150.

241. Sole Voisin (*low-carbohydrate*)

Quantities for 4. *Cooking time* 30 mins. *Temperature* 375 °F. No. 5.

4 small sole, filleted (1 lb. fillets)	Italian tomato sauce (No. 106)
White wine	Salt and pepper

Make the sauce. Season the fillets and fold in half. Poach slowly in the oven with just enough wine to moisten. They will take 10–15 mins., depending on the thickness. If there is a little liquid left after cooking, add it to the tomato sauce and pour over the fish.

One portion. Carbohydrate 2 g. Calories 225.

242. Plaice or Sole Mornay

Quantities for 4. *Cooking time* ¾ hr

2 large plump sole or plaice (2 lb. or more)	2 oz. (4 level Tbs.) butter or margarine
1 pt (2 c.) milk and water *or* wine and water	2 oz. plain flour (6 level Tbs.) *or* 1 oz. cornflour (3 level Tbs.)
Parsley stalks	Lemon juice
Small piece of onion	6 oz. grated cheese (2 level c.)
Salt and pepper	

Skin and fillet the fish. Make a fish stock with the bones and skin, onion, and seasoning, and water to cover. Simmer 20 mins. Strain. Poach the fish in a very little of this stock for 10–12 mins. While the fish is cooking, make a sauce with the butter or margarine, flour, and ½ pt of the stock. Season to taste and add lemon juice and 2 oz. of the cheese. Allow the cheese to melt. Drain the fish and put a layer of cheese sauce in the bottom of the baking dish. Add the fillets, cover with the remaining sauce and sprinkle the top with the remaining cheese. Grill very gently, just to melt the cheese and brown nicely. On no account should the cheese be allowed to toughen.

One portion. Carbohydrate 15 g. Calories 500.

Variation. Fillets of any white fish may be treated in the same way.

243. Soused Fish Salad

Quantities for 4. *Cooking time* 20–30 mins. *Temperature* 375 °F. No. 5.

- 1½ lb. fillet of fish
- ½ pt (1 c.) vinegar
- ½ pt (1 c.) water
- 6 peppercorns
- ½ bayleaf
- ½ level tsp. mixed herbs
- ¼ level tsp. salt substitute (if allowed)
- 2 oz. (4 level Tbs.) chopped onion
- 1 small lettuce
- 8 oz. tomatoes (4 medium)

Wash and trim the fish. Put in a fireproof dish. Mix the vinegar, water, peppercorns, bayleaf, and onion. Pour this over the fish and bake in a moderate oven 20–30 mins. or until the fish will flake when tested. Allow to cool in the liquid. Prepare the lettuce and arrange on a dish. Drain the fish, place it on the lettuce, and garnish with slices of tomato. Strain the liquid in which the fish was cooked and serve as a salad dressing.

One portion. Carbohydrate 5 g. Calories 162.

244. Fillets of Plaice or Sole with Mushrooms

Quantities for 4. *Cooking time* 20 mins.

- 1 small tin mushrooms *or*
- 4 oz. fresh, stewed mushrooms
- 8 fillets sole or other white fish
- Milk
- Bayleaf
- 1 oz. (2 level Tbs.) butter
- 1 oz. flour (3 level Tbs.)
- Salt and pepper
- Lemon juice

Make a purée of the mushrooms, using a sieve or an electric blender. Place a little of the mixture on each fillet and fold over. Alternatively, make a sandwich of fillets and mushrooms. Poach in a very little milk with the bayleaf for flavouring. Lift out and keep hot. Remove the bayleaf. Use the milk, butter, and flour to make ½ pt white sauce (No. 250). Season and add lemon juice to taste. Pour over the fish.

One portion. Carbohydrate 10 g. Calories 212.

Variation (*low-sodium diet*). Use salt-free butter, fresh mushrooms, and omit the salt.

245. Steamed Stuffed Fillets

Quantities for 4. *Cooking time* 10 mins. or longer

4 large or 8 small fillets plaice *or* sole
2 oz. fresh breadcrumbs ($\frac{1}{2}$ c.)
2 hard-boiled eggs, mashed
Pinch grated lemon rind
Salt and pepper
2 oz. (2 Tbs.) melted butter
A little milk to moisten

Mix all the ingredients, except the fish, adding enough milk to moisten. Spread this on the fillets. Roll up tightly and pack close together or else fasten each with thread to keep it in shape. Steam over boiling water for 10 mins. or until the fish flakes when tested. Steaming may be done in a plate on top of a saucepan, covering the fish with greased paper and a saucepan lid. Serve with lemon or with a sauce.

One portion. Carbohydrate 7 g. Calories 274.

Variation (*gluten-free diet*). Use gluten-free crumbs.

MEAT AND POULTRY

246. Bacon Baked with Cider

Quantities 6–8 oz. per portion. *Cooking time* 30 mins. per lb. *Temperature* 400 °F. No. 6.

Piece of bacon 3 lb. or more
Black treacle
Cloves and about $\frac{1}{2}$ pt (1 c.) dry vintage cider

Soak the bacon 4–5 hrs. Put in cold water to cover. Bring to the boil and remove any scum which rises. Cover and simmer for half the required cooking time. Heat the oven for baking. Remove bacon from liquid and cut off the rind. Score the fat in a criss-cross fashion, using a short sharp knife and making a diamond pattern. Press a clove into the fat in each diamond. Place the meat in the roasting pan and trickle over the surface a large Tbs. of black treacle. Put the cider in the pan round the meat and bake in the oven for the remainder of the cooking time, basting frequently with the cider mixture. Serve with the basting liquid as an unthickened gravy.

247. Bacon Hot-pot

Quantities for 4. *Cooking time* 4 hrs or ½ hr pressure cooker 1 hr baking. *Temperature* 350 °F. No. 3.

- 6 oz. (1 c.) butter beans
- 1½ lb. piece of bacon
- 1 large onion, sliced
- 2 sticks celery, chopped
- ½ level tsp. mustard
- ¼ level tsp. pepper
- 2 oz. black treacle (2 level Tbs.)
- 1 pt (2 c.) stock

Soak the beans and bacon overnight in plenty of cold water. Drain, cut the bacon into four pieces. Put bacon, beans, and vegetables in a casserole. Mix mustard, pepper, and treacle with some of the stock and pour over the meat and vegetable together with enough of the rest of the stock to cover. Put on the lid and cook in a moderate oven for 3 hrs. Remove the lid and raise the pieces of meat to the top. Cook another hour to brown the meat and concentrate the stock. If the pressure cooker is used, cook beans and meat ½ hr then turn into a dish and bake 1 hr. Uncover as before. Serve from the casserole.

One portion. Carbohydrate 34 g. Calories 858.

248. Meat Balls with Noodles (*high-calorie*)

Quantities for 4. *Cooking time* 1 hr plus ½ hr to make the sauce

- 2 oz. stale bread (2 slices)
- 1 lb. lean beef
- ¼ onion or small piece garlic
- 2 Tbs. chopped parsley
- 1 oz. grated Parmesan cheese (3 level Tbs.)
- 1 level tsp. salt
- ¼ level tsp. pepper
- 2 small eggs, beaten
- 3 Tbs. oil
- 8 oz. noodles
- Italian Tomato Sauce (No. 106)

Soak the bread in cold water for 5 mins. Squeeze dry and mash well. Mince the beef finely with the onion. If garlic is used instead, chop it very finely. Mix the bread, meat mixture, parsley, cheese, seasoning, and egg together thoroughly. With wet hands shape into about 16 small balls. Make the tomato sauce. Heat the oil and brown the meat balls in it, shaking the pan frequently to keep the balls round. Drain off excess fat and pour in the tomato sauce. Cover and cook gently for about ¾ hr. Boil the noodles, drain, and arrange on a hot dish. Put the meat balls and tomato sauce in the centre.

One portion. Carbohydrate 60 g. Calories 600.

249. Braised Beef with Prunes and Wine

Quantities for 4. *Cooking time* 2½–3 hrs. *Temperature* 350 °F. No. 4.

1 oz. (2 level Tbs.) fat
2 lb. piece of lean beef (1 kg.)
Large piece of bacon rind *or* some lean scraps of bacon
8 oz. onions, chopped (2 medium)
8 oz. carrots, chopped (2 medium)
8 oz. (1½ c.) prunes
½ level tsp. salt
¼ level tsp. pepper
½ pt (1 c.) red wine
8 oz. noodles
Grated Parmesan cheese

Heat the fat in a deep saucepan or enamelled cast-iron casserole. Fry the meat in it until browned all over. Remove the meat. Put the bacon rind in the bottom of the pan and the vegetables and prunes on top. Add seasoning and wine and return the meat. Cover and cook very gently until the meat is tender. Just before dishing up, boil the noodles in salted water, drain, and arrange round the edge of a platter. Carve the meat and arrange slices in the centre of the noodles and put the vegetables, prunes, and sauce round it. Sprinkle the noodles with the cheese and serve.

One portion. Carbohydrate 75 g. Calories 836.

250. Casserole of Beef with Tomatoes

Quantities for 4. *Cooking time* 1½–2 hrs. *Temperature* 300 °F. No. 2.

1 lb. piece of steak (about 1 in. thick)
1 oz. (3 level Tbs.) plain flour
1 oz. (2 Tbs.) fat or oil
Salt and pepper
2 oz. onions, sliced (1 small)
½ pt (2 c.) cooked or canned tomatoes
A little chopped or dried marjoram
A pinch of sugar
Vegetables to garnish

Rub the flour, salt, and pepper into the meat. Heat the fat and brown the meat and then the onions. Put meat and onions in a casserole with the remaining ingredients. Cover and simmer until tender, adding a little water during cooking if it seems likely to dry up. Cut the meat into portions and serve on a hot dish with the gravy and some vegetables to garnish.

One portion. Carbohydrate 9 g. Calories 310.

251. Corned Beef Hash

Quantities for 4. *Cooking time* 10 mins.

- 12 oz. diced corned beef
- 1½ lb. diced cooked potatoes (6 medium)
- 1 oz. (2 Tbs.) fat or oil
- 1 small onion, sliced
- 2 Tbs. milk

Mix the meat and potatoes. Heat the fat and fry the onions in it until brown. Add the meat and potato and sprinkle the milk over it. Stir well and cook over a very low heat until it is brown underneath. Fold over, turn out, and serve hot.

One portion. Carbohydrate 33 g. Calories 360.

Variation. Add 4 oz. cooked diced beetroot to the mixture before cooking.

252. Goulash

Quantities for 4. *Cooking time* 2–3 hrs (20 mins. pressure cooking). *Temperature* 300 °F. No. 2.

- 1 oz. (2 Tbs.) fat or oil
- 1 lb. lean meat cut in 1-in. cubes
- 2 onions, sliced
- 2 level tsp. paprika pepper
- 1 level tsp. salt
- 2 Tbs. tomato paste
- Pinch of caraway seeds
- ¼ pt (½ c.) stock

Heat the fat and brown the meat in it. Remove the meat and brown the onions too. Add the rest of the ingredients. Cover and simmer gently for 2–3 hrs (or pressure cook 20 mins.). More stock may be needed during cooking. Serve with boiled potatoes or noodles if either of these are allowed in the diet.

One portion. Carbohydrate 3 g. Calories 386.

253. Hamburgers

Quantities for 8 hamburgers. *Cooking time* 15 mins.

- 8 oz. (1 c.) minced lean beef
- 4 oz. stale bread, soaked and squeezed (4 slices)
- Pinch of dried herbs
- 2 level tsp. salt
- ¼ level tsp. pepper
- ¼ level tsp. dry mustard
- 1 Tbs. Worcester sauce
- 1 oz. very finely chopped onion (2 level Tbs.) *or* some onion juice
- 1 egg (optional)

Mix all the ingredients together and form into 8 flat cakes.

Fry in shallow fat for 15 mins. or until cooked in the middle. Cover the pan with a lid or plate during the cooking.

One hamburger. Carbohydrate 7 g. Calories 96.

254. Basic Minced Meat Mixture for Loaves and Rissoles and Patties, etc.

Quantities for 4

1 lb. lean raw meat, beef, veal, lamb, pork, and some liver if possible
2 oz. (⅔c.) fresh breadcrumbs
1 level tsp. salt
1 egg
¼ level tsp. pepper
1 tsp. finely grated onion
¼ level tsp. ground mace

Remove fat and any gristle or stringy bits from the meat. For patients who can have only very tender meat, use the best cuts of beef. Any cut of the others is suitable. Mince the meat finely, putting it through two or three times if making a meat loaf or galantine, as the fine texture makes it hold together better, and slice more easily. Mix all ingredients together. Then finish in any of the ways listed below.

One portion. Carbohydrate 8 g. Calories 260.

255. Baked Meat Rissoles

Shape the mixture into 8 small flat cakes. Wrap each in a thin rasher of streaky bacon. Fasten with a toothpick and pack close together so that they keep each other in shape. Put in a baking dish and cook in a hot oven (450 °F., No. 8) for 20–30 mins. Gravy may be made in the pan afterwards, or serve with vegetables accompanied by a sauce.

256. Grilled Rissoles

Shape in 8 cakes ½–1 in. thick and grill for 10–15 mins. Brown them quickly and then finish more slowly.

257. Fried Rissoles

Shape as for grilling. Brown in a little hot fat or oil and then finish cooking more slowly, giving 10–15 mins. in all. Gravy may then be made in the frying pan.

258. Meat Loaf

Shape the mixture into a long narrow loaf, place in the

roasting pan with a little fat and a piece of silicone paper on top. Bake in a moderate oven (375 °F., No. 5) for about ¾ hr, removing the paper for the last 10 mins. to allow the top to brown. Make gravy in the pan or serve with some other permitted sauce. Cut in thick slices to serve.

259. Meat Galantine

Put the mixture in a greased basin or stone jar with straight sides. Cover with aluminium-foil lid and steam for 2 hrs or pressure cook ¼ hr. Turn out and roll in dry breadcrumbs. Slice when cold. Alternatively, the mixture may be shaped in a sausage shape, wrapped up in a neat parcel of aluminium foil, and steamed. Finish as before. If bacon is allowed in the diet, include a little minced mild cured bacon with the meat.

260. Beef Mould

Quantities for 4. *Cooking time* ¾–1 hr. *Temperature* 350 °F. No. 3.

1 lb. (2 c.) lean beef minced
4 oz. (½ c.) bacon or ham minced
2 oz. (⅔ c.) fresh breadcrumbs
2–3 Tbs. stock
Salt and pepper

Grease 4 individual pudding moulds. Mix all ingredients together thoroughly, adding a good sprinkling pepper and some salt if the bacon is not salty; press well into the mould. Cover with a lid of aluminium foil and steam or bake in a moderate oven. Turn out and serve hot with sauce or cold with salad.

One portion. Carbohydrate 8 g. Calories 350.

Variation (*gluten-free diet*). Substitute crumbs of gluten-free bread.

261. Moussaka

Quantities for 4. *Cooking time* 1 hr. *Temperature* 375 °F. No. 5.

2 oz. (4 level Tbs.) butter or margarine
12 oz. (1½ c.) minced raw beef
8 oz. onions, chopped (2 medium)
2 Tbs. chopped parsley
8 oz. tomatoes, coarsely chopped (4 medium)
Salt and pepper
1½ lb. potatoes, sliced thinly (6 medium)

4 Tbs. white wine
½ oz. (1 level Tbs.) butter or margarine
½ oz. (1½ level Tbs.) plain flour
½ pt (1 c.) milk
1 egg
1 oz. grated cheese (3 level Tbs.)

Grease an 8–9 in. cake tin or a straight-sided mould or fireproof dish. Heat the 2 oz. butter or margarine and fry the meat, onion, parsley, and tomatoes. Season well. Put a layer of potatoes in the bottom of the tin or mould, then a layer of meat mixture and continue like this until ending with a layer of potato. Sprinkle on the wine. Make a sauce with the ½ oz. butter or margarine, flour, and milk. Remove from the heat and add the slightly beaten egg and the cheese. Mix well and pour over the potatoes. Bake until the top is brown. Cut in wedges or squares for serving.

One portion. Carbohydrate 45 g. Calories 462.

262. Grilled Beef Patty (*low-fat*)

Quantities for 4. *Cooking time* 15–20 mins.

1 lb. rump or fillet steak
Salt and pepper

Remove excess fat and mince the meat. Season with salt and pepper and shape into 4 patties about 1 in. thick and 3 ins. diameter. Place on the grilling rack in the lowest position and grill with a medium heat, turning once. Serve at once.

One portion. Carbohydrate nil. Calories 200.

Variations (*low-sodium diet*). Omit the salt. Use potassium glutamate if allowed, or salt substitute. Or serve with Dietade tomato ketchup.

263. Spaghetti Bolognese

Quantities for 4. *Cooking time* 30 mins.

2 Tbs. oil
1 onion, chopped
12 oz. (1½ c.) raw minced beef
3 level Tbs. flour
2 level Tbs. tomato paste
Salt and pepper
¾ pt (1½ c.) stock
8 oz. spaghetti
3 oz. (1 c.) grated Parmesan cheese

Heat the oil and fry the onion in it until cooked but not brown. Add the meat and stir and fry for two minutes. Remove from the heat and add flour, tomato, and stock. Stir until it boils and simmer gently for about 10 mins. Season to taste. Cook the spaghetti in plenty of boiling salted water for 5 mins. or until it is just tender. Drain. Pile the spaghetti on a hot dish, put the sauce in the centre, and sprinkle with the cheese.

One portion. Carbohydrate 34 g. Calories 462.

264. Potted Meat (*low-fat*)

Quantities for 4. *Cooking time* 2½ hrs (½ hr pressure cooking)

8 oz. shin beef
1 knuckle veal, sawn in pieces
1 level tsp. salt
6 all-spice
6 peppercorns
A small piece of bayleaf

Cut the beef in small pieces, carefully removing all fat. Remove the meat from the knuckle of veal and cut it up. Put the meat and bones in a pan with the salt and enough water to cover (for pressure cooking use 1 pt water). Simmer 2½ hrs (½ hr pressure cooking), or until the meat is tender. Remove meat and bones and shred the meat. Pack into a basin or mould. Boil the liquid with the all-spice and peppercorns until it is reduced to about ½-pt. Strain over the meat and leave to set. Unmould, slice, and serve with salad.

265. Skillet of Beef and Beans

Quantities for 4. *Cooking time* 45 mins.

8 oz. lean frying steak
2 Tbs. oil
1 onion, chopped
8 oz. sliced green beans
2 sticks celery, sliced
1 level Tbs. cornflour
1 Tbs. Worcester or soy sauce
Liquid from the mushrooms
Stock
7½-oz. tin mushrooms (213 g.)
Canned or fresh cooked sweet red pepper to garnish
Boiled rice

Cut the meat in ½-in.-wide fingers. Brown in the hot oil, using a deep frying pan or shallow stew pan. Add the onion and cook 4–6 mins. Add beans and celery and mix. Combine the cornflour and sauces with ¼ pt liquid made up of mushroom liquor and stock. Add to the meat together with the mushrooms. Stir and cook until it thickens, adding more liquid as needed. Cover and cook until the beans are tender. Garnish with sweet red pepper and serve with boiled rice.

One portion (without the rice). Carbohydrate 7 g. Calories 200.

266. Marinaded Steak (*low-fat*)

Quantities for 4. *Cooking time* 2 hrs. *Temperature* 350 °F. No. 3. *Marinating* 2 hrs

- 1 lb. steak, cut in portions
- ½ oz. (1½ level Tbs.) flour
- ½ level tsp. salt
- ¼ level tsp. mustard
- ½ Tbs. vinegar
- 1 tsp. Worcester sauce
- ¼ pt (½ c.) water

Remove any fat and put the meat in a casserole. Mix the dry ingredients together and add the liquid gradually. Pour this over the meat and leave it to stand for 2 hrs, stirring occasionally. Cover and cook gently for 2 hrs.

One portion. Carbohydrate 3 g. Calories 212.

267. Beef Stew (*low-sodium*)

Quantities for 4. *Cooking time* 2 hrs or longer

- 1 lb. stewing steak
- 2 oz. (4 level Tbs.) lard
- 4 oz. onions, sliced (2 small)
- 4 oz. mushrooms, sliced
- 8 oz. carrots, sliced (2 medium)
- 4 oz. celery, sliced (4 stalks)
- 4 oz. tomatoes, sliced (2 medium)
- Sage, thyme, pepper, marjoram
- Salt substitute if allowed
- 2 oz. (6 level Tbs.) plain flour *or* 1 oz. (3 level Tbs.) cornflour

Trim off fat and cut steak into pieces. Fry steak brown in the lard, adding the onions towards the end of frying. Add the other vegetables and the minimum amount of water. Add seasoning and simmer until tender. Blend flour and cornflour with cold water. Use enough to thicken the gravy as desired. The less liquid used the better the flavour will be. Serve with salt-free dumplings as desired.

One portion (without the dumplings). Carbohydrate 15 g. Calories 460.

268. Baked Chicken and Pineapple

Quantities for 4. *Cooking time* 1 hr. *Temperature* 375 °F. No. 5.

4 portions of broiler chicken (2–3 lb.)
½ level tsp. dried rosemary
1 level tsp. salt
½ level tsp. pepper
6 shallots, sliced (6 oz.)
¼ pt (½ c.) canned unsweetened pineapple juice
¼ level tsp. ground ginger
Paprika pepper

Wash and dry the chicken. Combine rosemary, salt, and pepper, and rub into the chicken. Arrange skin-side-up in a shallow baking dish. Place sliced shallots round it. Combine pineapple juice and ginger. Sprinkle paprika over the chicken and pour in the pineapple juice. Bake uncovered until tender.

One portion. Carbohydrate 10 g. Calories 300.

269. Boiled or Steamed Chicken with Noodles

Quantities for 4. *Cooking time* ¾ hr

4 portions broiler chicken (2–3 lb.)
8 oz. egg noodles
1 pt (2 c.) Béchamel sauce (No. 93)
2 eggs
Juice of 1 lemon
Chopped parsley

Steam or poach the chicken for ½ hr or until tender. If steamed, boil the noodles in the water below the chicken. While cooking, make the sauce and just before serving add the egg and lemon juice, allowing it to heat until it thickens, but not to boil. Arrange chicken on noodles, or in a ring of noodles, and pour the sauce over the chicken. Garnish with chopped parsley.

One portion. Carbohydrate 65 g. Calories 565.

270. Chicken Casserole (*low-fat*)

Quantities for 4. *Cooking time* 1½–3 hrs. *Temperature* 300 °F. No. 2.

1 chicken, jointed (about 3 lb.)
8 oz. onions, sliced (2 medium)
8 oz. carrots, sliced (2 medium)
2 oz. celery, sliced (2 stalks) *or* 2 oz. mushrooms
2 level tsp. salt
¼ level tsp. pepper
¼ level tsp. ground mace
Cornflour
Rice
Chopped parsley

Remove any fat from the pieces of chicken and put them in a casserole with the vegetables, salt, pepper, mace, and enough cold water barely to cover. Cook gently until the chicken is tender, the time depending on the age. (It may be cooked on top or in the oven.) Thicken the stock with blended cornflour using 1–2 level Tbs. to 1 pt stock and serve the meat in a border of boiled rice. Sprinkle with plenty of chopped parsley.

One portion (without rice). Carbohydrate 6 g. Calories 210.

271. Fried Chicken and Almonds

Quantities for 4. *Cooking time* about 20 mins.

- 12 oz. freshly cooked chicken meat
- 2 oz. ($\frac{1}{3}$ c.) shelled blanched almonds
- 1 oz. (2 Tbs.) fat or oil
- 1 small onion or shallot, chopped
- 4 oz. mushrooms, sliced
- $\frac{1}{2}$ oz. ($1\frac{1}{2}$ level Tbs.) cornflour
- $\frac{1}{4}$ pt ($\frac{1}{2}$ c.) chicken stock
- 1 tsp. Worcester or soya sauce
- Salt and pepper

Cut chicken in small pieces. Heat fat or oil to cover the bottom of a deep sauté or frying pan. Fry the almonds until lightly browned and crisp. Remove and fry chicken, mushrooms, and onions until brown. Remove. Add cornflour to the pan and stir and cook for a minute or two. Add stock and stir until boiling. Add sauce and season to taste. Return the chicken and reheat, cooking a little longer if necessary.

One portion. Carbohydrate 5 g. Calories 275.

272. Chicken Paprika (*low-fat*)

Quantities for 4. *Cooking time* $\frac{3}{4}$–1 hr

- $2\frac{1}{2}$–3 lb. broiler in pieces
- 1 level tsp. salt
- 2 level tsp. paprika pepper
- $\frac{1}{4}$–$\frac{1}{2}$ pt ($\frac{1}{2}$–1 c.) chicken stock
- 1 small onion, chopped
- $\frac{1}{4}$ pt ($\frac{1}{2}$ c.) yogurt
- 2 Tbs. chopped parsley

Wash and dry the chicken. Sprinkle with 1 level tsp. salt and 1 level tsp. paprika pepper. Put in the grill pan, without the rack, and cook 5 mins. each side, or until well browned. Do not put too near the heat or it will scorch before browning. Put in a lidded pan with $\frac{1}{4}$ pt chicken stock, and the onion. Cover and simmer 30–40 mins. or until tender, adding more stock if needed. Lift out the chicken and keep hot. If excess liquid is present, pour off some, to leave about ¼ pt. Stir in yogurt and rest of salt and pepper. Heat slowly, stirring well, but do not boil. Pour over chicken and sprinkle with chopped parsley.

One portion. Carbohydrate 3 g. Calories 225.

Variation (*high-calorie, high-fat diet*). Fry the chicken in oil or butter instead of grilling. Cream could be used in place of the yogurt.

273. Chicken Pilaf

Quantities for 4. *Cooking time* 35 mins.

1 small onion, chopped
1 Tbs. oil
3 oz. rice (⅓ c.)
½ pt (1 c.) chicken stock
½ level tsp. salt
Pinch of pepper
Pinch dried thyme or fresh chopped thyme
1 oz. raisins (2 level Tbs.)
½ green sweet pepper, chopped
4 oz. diced cooked chicken (1 c.)
½ red sweet pepper, sliced

Fry the onion in the oil. Add the rice and cook gently for 5 mins., stirring continuously. Cool a little. Add stock, seasoning, raisins, and green pepper. Bring to the boil, cover, and simmer 25 mins. or until the rice is tender and all the liquid absorbed. Stir occasionally with a fork. Stir in the chicken gently, taste for seasoning, and serve garnished with the red pepper.

One portion. Carbohydrate 33 g. Calories 355.

274. Pot-Roasted Broiler

Quantities for 4. *Cooking time* 1½ hrs. *Temperature* 350 °F. No. 4.

1 chicken (about 3 lb.)
2 oz. (4 level Tbs.) butter
1 level tsp. salt
¼ level tsp. pepper

Wash and truss the chicken. Dry well in paper towels. Heat the butter in a casserole and fry the chicken brown all over. Sprinkle with salt and pepper and cover and cook gently until tender. Turn the chicken two or three times during cooking. Pour juice and butter over the chicken when serving.

275. Pressed Chicken

Quantities for 4

8 oz. (2 c.) diced cooked chicken
2 hard-boiled eggs, sliced
½ pt (1 c.) aspic (use chicken stock, gelatine, and seasoning)
Tartare sauce

Put the chicken and egg in layers in a mould. Pour in the cool well-seasoned aspic. Leave to chill. Unmould, slice thinly and serve with tartare sauce or with salad.

One portion (without sauce). Carbohydrate 1 g. Calories 162.

276. Roast Chicken with Oil

Cooking time 20-25 mins. per lb. *Temperature* 400-425 °F. No. 6-7.

Clean, wash, and dry the chicken. Season with salt and pepper. Place a small onion or a sprig of rosemary inside the bird and tie up. Put in a covered casserole or roasting pan, or wrap in aluminium foil and put in a roasting pan. Add a little water. Cook in a hot oven. 20 mins. before the end remove the covering, pour over 3 Tbs. oil, and put back to brown, uncovered. Serve with gravy or with a sauce made with oil. If necessary reduce the gravy by boiling hard or thicken as desired. See Nos. 94–5. If roast potatoes are wanted, cook them separately.

277. Steamed Chicken and Rice (*low-fat*)

Quantities for 4. *Cooking time* about 20 mins.

8 oz. rice (1 level c.)
1 pt (2 c.) stock *or* water
2 level tsp, salt
8 oz. (2 c.) cooked chicken diced
1 onion, very finely chopped
2 oz. mushrooms, chopped (½ c.)
2 oz. cucumber or celery chopped (½ c.)
Pepper
Chopped tomato *or* sweet red pepper (fresh or canned)
Chopped parsley

Bring the rice, water, or stock and salt to the boil in a casserole or heavy pan. Boil 5 mins. Add onion, mushroom, cucumber or celery and the chicken. Cover, and cook gently until the rice is done and all the liquid absorbed. Add pepper to taste and a little chopped tomato or sweet red pepper for colour. Sprinkle with chopped parsley and serve hot.

One portion. Carbohydrate 53 g. Calories 338.

278. Scalloped Brains

Quantities for 4. *Cooking time* ½–¾ hr

3 calves' brains or 4 sheep's
1 pt (2 c.) Béchamel sauce (No. 93)
Buttered crumbs (No. 521)
Chopped parsley to garnish

Soak brains 2 hrs in cold water, changing the water twice. Carefully remove skin, blood, and fibre. Wash again. Put the brains in enough salted water to cover and simmer for the required time (15 mins. sheep's, 20 mins. calves'). Drain and cut in pieces. While they are cooking prepare the sauce and crumbs. Heat individual fireproof dishes. Put in the brains, pour over the sauce and cover with crumbs. Brown under the grill or in a hot oven. Garnish with parsley.

One portion. Carbohydrate 31 g. Calories 582.

279. Ham Mousse

Quantities for 4. *Cooking time* 25–30 mins.

6 oz. (¾ c.) minced cooked lean ham or bacon
½ pt (1 c.) Béchamel sauce (No. 93)
Little made mustard
½ oz. gelatine (1 level Tbs.)
⅛ pt (5 Tbs.) stock
⅛ pt (5 Tbs.) double cream or evap. milk
1 egg white
Garnish of salad vegetables *or* rolls of ham

Mix ham, sauce, and mustard. Dissolve gelatine in hot stock. Add sauce and leave until cold but not set. Whisk cream or prepared evaporated milk (No. 137) and fold into the mixture. Whisk the egg white stiff and fold it in. Pour into a mould or soufflé dish and leave to set. Serve in the dish or unmould. Decorate with salad vegetables, or rolls of ham.

One portion (with cream). Carbohydrate 10 g. Calories 433. (With milk.) Carbohydrate 12 g. Calories 380.

Variation. Instead of all ham use 2 oz. ham and 4 oz. chicken or game.

280. Braised Lambs' or Sheep's Hearts

Quantities for 4. *Cooking time* 1¾ hrs

4 hearts
Veal forcemeat (No. 155)
1 oz. (2 level Tbs.) butter
2 med.-sized onions, sliced
½ pt (1 c.) stock

Cut all fat off the hearts and all gristle and blood vessels. Using scissors, cut the walls dividing the two sides of the heart to make one cavity for stuffing. Wash in running water and then soak in cold water for 30 mins. to remove all blood. Drain the hearts and wipe dry on paper towels. Fill with forcemeat and sew up the top of each heart with white cotton and a darning needle. Heat the butter in a saucepan and fry the hearts in it, until brown all over. Remove and fry the onion lightly. Return the hearts and add a few spoonsful of stock. Cover and cook gently 1½ hrs or until tender, adding more stock as needed to prevent burning. Remove the cotton before serving the hearts, with the onion and gravy poured over.

One portion. Carbohydrate 15 g. Calories 620.

281. Meat Jellies (*low-fat*)

Quantities for 4

- 12 oz. freshly cooked meat
- ¾ pt (1½ c.) fat-free stock
- ¾ oz. (1½ level Tbs.) gelatine
- Salt and pepper
- Squeeze lemon juice
- 3 Tbs. sherry (optional)

Remove all skin, fat, and gristle from the meat, which may be any kind, including a little lean ham. Mince or chop the meat finely. Dissolve gelatine in hot stock. Add lemon juice, sherry, meat, and seasoning to taste. Pour into individual moulds and leave to set. Unmould and serve.

One portion. Carbohydrate 6 g. Calories 220.

Variations. 1. Use half canned tomato juice and half stock or add a little tomato paste to the hot stock. 2. *Low-sodium diet.* Use rabbit for the meat and if allowed add potassium glutamate or salt substitute to the stock instead of salt. Some fresh tomato juice could be used for part of the stock, or Dietade tomato sauce.

282. Devilled Kidneys

Quantities for 4. *Cooking time* about 1 hr

- 8 sheep's kidneys
- 2½ oz. (5 level Tbs.) fat
- 1 large onion, chopped
- 1 carrot, chopped
- 1 oz. (3 level Tbs.) plain flour
- ¾ pt (1½ c.) stock
- Small piece bayleaf
- Sprig parsley
- 1 Tbs. made mustard
- 1 tsp. curry powder
- 1 Tbs. Worcester sauce
- 1 tsp. anchovy sauce

Remove fat and skin the kidneys. Cut out the core with a pair of kitchen scissors or sharp knife. Wash in warm water and dry on paper towels. Cut in half but not quite through and open out flat like a book. Heat 1 oz. fat and fry the onion and carrot in it until brown. Add the flour and stir and cook for about 15 mins. until it is light brown. Remove from the heat and gradually add the stock. Return to the heat and stir until it boils. Add the bayleaf and parsley and more water if it becomes too thick. Simmer for ½ hr. Strain, reheat, and add the mustard, curry, Worcester sauce, and anchovy. Add salt to taste. Keep hot. Fry the kidneys in the remaining fat. Put in serving dish and pour the sauce over.

One portion. Carbohydrate 10 g. Calories 310.

283. Grilled Kidney

Cooking time 5–10 mins.

Leave whole with some of their own fat for basting, or cut in half, brush with oil, and grill slowly. They are cooked when small beads of blood appear on the surface.

284. Ragoût of Kidneys

Quantities for 4. *Cooking time* 20 mins.

6 lambs' or 4 veal kidneys
Salt and pepper
1 oz. (2 level Tbs.) fat or 1 Tbs. oil
1 oz. plain flour (3 level Tbs.)
½ Tbs. finely chopped onion
¾ pt (1½ c.) stock
2 oz. mushrooms, sliced
¾–1 lb. (1½–2 c.) mashed potatoes

Skin and trim the kidneys and cut into slices. Sprinkle with salt and pepper. Heat the fat and fry the kidneys for 5 mins. Remove and keep hot. Brown the onion in the fat, add the flour, mix, and cook for a few minutes. Add the stock, stir until it boils and then add the mushrooms. Return the kidneys and cook a few minutes longer. Serve in a border of mashed potatoes.

One portion. Carbohydrate 26 g. Calories 270.

285. Stewed Kidney (*low-fat*)

Quantities for 4. *Cooking time* 10 mins.

8 lambs' kidneys
4 oz. lean gammon
1 pt (2 c.) stock
3 level Tbs. cornflour

2 level Tbs. tomato paste
Salt and pepper
2 Tbs. chopped parsley
Toast, mashed potato, boiled rice, or pasta

Remove fat, skin, and tubes from kidneys. Cut kidney and gammon into small pieces. Simmer gently in the stock 5 mins. Thicken liquid with the cornflour blended with a little cold water. Add the tomato paste, seasoning, and parsley. Serve on unbuttered toast or in a border of potatoes mashed with skimmed milk, or in a border of macaroni or spaghetti.

One portion (without toast, etc.). Carbohydrate 14–23 g. Calories 266–310.

Variation. Use a little red wine in place of some of the stock.

286. Baked Lamb Chops with Tomatoes and Cheese

Quantities for 4. *Cooking time* 1½ hrs. *Temperature* 300 °F. No. 2.

4 lamb chops about 1 in. thick
1 oz. (2 level Tbs.) fat
2 onions, sliced
¾ lb. canned tomatoes (340 g.)
½ level tsp. salt
¼ level tsp. pepper
1 level tsp. sugar
2 oz. grated cheese (½ c.)
2 oz. fresh breadcrumbs (½ c.)

Trim all surplus fat from the chops. Heat fat and brown chops in it. Place in a large shallow casserole in a single layer. Put several slices of onion on top of each chop. Pour the tomatoes round and add seasoning and sugar. Mix cheese and breadcrumbs and sprinkle thickly over the chops. Cover and bake slowly.

One portion. Carbohydrate 15 g. Calories 271.

Variation (*gluten-free diet*). Use gluten-free breadcrumbs.

287. Grilled Lamb Chops with Herbs (*low-fat*)

Quantities for 4. *Cooking time* 10–12 mins.

4 lamb chops or 8 small cutlets
1 level tsp. dried basil or rosemary
1 level tsp. marjoram
1 level tsp. dried thyme
1 level tsp. salt

Trim excess fat from the meat. Mix herbs and salt and rub into each side of the chops. Cover and chill 1 hr. Grill in the usual way for 10–12 mins. or until cooked to taste.

One portion. Carbohydrate a trace. Calories 80.

Variation (low-sodium diet). Omit the salt. Instead rub chops or cutlets with ground ginger before grilling.

288. Lamb Cutlets in Aspic (*plain*)

Quantities for 4. *Cooking time* 1 hr

4 cutlets from the best end of neck (1 lb.)
½ pt (1 c.) stock
1 bayleaf
2 peppercorns
¼ oz. (½ level Tbs.) gelatine
Salt and pepper to taste

Trim all fat from the cutlets. Put in a pan with the stock and simmer until meat is tender, about 20 mins. Remove cutlets to a shallow entrée dish, just big enough to hold them. Leave stock to cool. Skim the fat from the stock and reheat with the bayleaf and the peppercorns. When boiling, strain and add the gelatine. When dissolved, season to taste. Pour over the cutlets, and leave to set. Turn out of the mould and garnish with salad vegetables.

One portion. Carbohydrate a trace. Calories 70.

289. Lamb Cutlets in Aspic (*garnished*)

Quantities for 4. *Cooking time* ¾ hr

4 cutlets from best end of neck (1 lb.)
Vegetables or herbs for garnishing
Aspic jelly
½ oz. (1 level Tbs.) gelatine
½ pt (1 c.) boiling water
2 level tsp. sugar
½ level tsp. salt
2 Tbs. tarragon vinegar
2 Tbs. lemon juice
Hard-boiled egg, cucumber, tomato, and lettuce to garnish

Trim all fat from the cutlets. Bake in a moderate oven or steam for 30 mins. Press between two plates with weight on top. Leave to become cold and chill in the refrigerator. Prepare the vegetable garnish, which may be mint leaves, pieces of red sweet pepper, slices of olives, or small sprigs of chervil. Make the aspic by dissolving the gelatine in boiling water, and adding the other ingredients. Leave to cool and begin to thicken. Place the cutlets on a wire rack over the plate and pour some of the jelly over to coat them. Let it set. Arrange the garnish on top and gently pour over another layer of jelly. Leave to set. Serve with the finely chopped surplus jelly and a garnish of hard-boiled eggs, cucumber and tomato, and lettuce leaves.

One cutlet. Carbohydrate 32. Calories 80.

290. Grilled Lamb Patties

Quantities for 4. *Cooking time* 20–25 mins.

- 1 lb. lean lamb (no bone)
- ½ level tsp. salt
- ¼ level tsp. pepper
- 4 rashers streaky bacon

Put meat through mincer twice. Mix with the seasoning and shape into 4 cakes, about ½ in. thick. Wrap a rasher of bacon around each and secure with a cocktail stick, or tie with thread. Grill slowly, turning once.

One portion. Carbohydrate nil. Calories 325.

291. Haricot Mutton

Quantities for 4. *Cooking time* 2¼ hrs (20–25 mins. pressure cooking). *Temperature* 300 °F. No. 2.

- 2 lb. mutton or lamb (with bone)
- 1 oz. (2 level Tbs.) fat
- 4 oz. onion, sliced (1 medium)
- 8 oz. carrots, sliced (2 medium)
- 1 turnip, sliced
- 4 oz. (½ c.) haricot beans (soaked overnight)
- 1 level tsp. salt
- ¼ level tsp. pepper
- 1 Tbs. Worcester sauce or tomato or mushroom ketchup

Cut the meat in pieces for serving and trim off some of the surplus fat. Heat the 1 oz. fat and brown the meat in it. Add the vegetables and fry 1–2 mins. Add boiling water to cover (½ pt if pressure cooking). Add the strained beans and the salt and pepper. Cover and cook slowly 2 hrs or pressure cook for 20 mins. Add the sauce or ketchup and serve.

One portion. Carbohydrate 32 g. Calories 390.

292. Navarin of Lamb

Quantities for 4. *Cooking time* 2 hrs. *Temperature* 300 °F. No. 2.

1 oz. (2 level Tbs.) fat or 1 Tbs. oil
1 lb. lamb (without bone)
1 level tsp. salt
¼ level tsp. pepper
Good pinch of sugar
½ oz. plain flour (1½ level Tbs.)
¾ pt (1½ c.) water
Piece of garlic (optional)
8 small onions, peeled
1 lb. small potatoes (preferably new)

Remove excess fat and cut the meat in pieces weighing about 2 oz. Heat the 1 oz. fat or 1 Tbs. oil and fry the meat in it, adding seasoning and sugar during frying. When the meat is well browned, pour off excess fat, sprinkle in the flour, and cook until it begins to turn brown. Add the water, mix well, bring to the boil, and add the chopped garlic. Simmer for 1 hr on top or in the oven. Meanwhile, brown the onion in a little hot fat or oil. Drain well. Add to the meat together with the potatoes and simmer until the vegetables are tender, about ¾ hr. Before serving, skim off any surplus fat.

One portion. Carbohydrate 28 g. Calories 397.

Variation. Add 2 Tbs. tomato paste and a few peas or beans, with the onions and potatoes.

293. Ragoût of Lamb and Butter Beans

Quantities for 4. *Cooking time* 2 hrs

4 oz. (½ c.) butter beans, soaked overnight
2 lb. shoulder of lamb
1 level tsp. salt
½ level tsp. paprika pepper
2 Tbs. oil
6 shallots or small onions (3 oz.)
¾ pt (1½ c.) canned tomatoes
2 Tbs. chopped parsley
1 level Tbs. cornflour
¼ pt (½ c.) yogurt

Cut the meat off the bone, cut into 1-in. cubes, and sprinkle with the salt and paprika pepper. Heat the oil in a saucepan or casserole and fry the meat in it until brown. Add the beans, shallots, tomatoes, and parsley. Cover and simmer gently until the meat and beans are tender. Blend the cornflour with a little cold water and stir into the meat. Bring back to the boil and then stir in the yogurt. Serve at once.

One portion. Carbohydrate 25 g. Calories 420.

294. Roast Shoulder of Lamb with Rice Stuffing

Quantities ¾ lb. per portion. *Cooking time* 30 mins. per lb. *Temperature* 375 °F.–400 °F. Nos. 5–6.

Boned shoulder of lamb
1 clove
Stuffing
3 oz. rice (6 level Tbs.) boiled
2 oz. sultanas (2 level Tbs.)
4 rashers bacon, chopped
1 kidney, chopped
½ tsp. chopped rosemary
½ grated lemon rind
½ level tsp. salt
¼ level tsp. pepper
1 egg or 2 yolks
Gravy
2 level Tbs. plain flour
1 tsp. tomato paste
½ pt (1 c.) stock
Salt and pepper to taste

Cut the clove of garlic and rub a basin with it. Add the stuffing ingredients, mix together, and bind with egg or yolks. Stuff the lamb and sew up with coarse thread. Roast the shoulder. Meanwhile make a stock with the bones. When the meat is cooked, remove and keep hot. Pour off all except 2 Tbs. of the fat. Add the flour, mix well, cook a few minutes, and add stock and tomato purée. Stir until it boils, season to taste, and serve.

295. Lamb Shashlik (*low-fat*)

Quantities for 4. *Cooking time* 15 mins. *Marinading* 3–4 hrs

1 lb. lean leg of lamb (no bones)
Juice of 1 lemon
Tiny bit of garlic
Salt and pepper
4 tomatoes
4 oz. mushrooms

Remove all fat and cut the lamb into cubes about 1 in. in size. Put in a basin and pour over the lemon juice. Add the garlic, salt, and pepper, and stir well. Leave for 3–4 hrs. Thread on long thin skewers, alternating the meat with halves or quarters of mushrooms and tomatoes. Grill for about 15 mins.

One portion. Carbohydrate 2 g. Calories 223.

296. 'Squab' Hot-pot (*low-protein*)

Quantities for 4. *Cooking time* 2 hrs. *Temperature* 350 °F. No. 3.

1 lb. middle neck of lamb
8 oz. apple, peeled and sliced thinly (2 medium)
2 level tsp. sugar
½ tsp. ground mace
4 oz. (½ c.) onion, finely chopped
2 level tsp. salt
¼ level tsp. pepper
8 oz. potato, sliced thinly (2 medium)
¼ pt (½ c.) stock or water
Chopped parsley

Cut the meat in pieces and trim off as much fat as possible. Place a layer of apple at the bottom of the casserole or pie-dish. Sprinkle with half the sugar and mace and arrange the meat on it. Add onion, seasoning, and remaining apple, sugar, and mace. Cover with a layer of sliced potato and pour over the stock or water. Bake slowly. Serve sprinkled with chopped parsley.

One portion. Carbohydrate 20 g. Calories 316.

Variation (*low-sodium diet*). Omit the salt and use home-made salt-free stock or water.

297. Steamed Lamb Chop or Cutlets

Quantities allow 1–2 small cutlets or 1 chop according to appetite. *Cooking time* small thin cutlet, about 10 mins. Chop, 20 mins.

Trim all fat from the meat except for a very thin layer on the outside. Season with salt and a little pepper if allowed. Take a piece of aluminium foil or cooking parchment big enough to wrap the meat in with a good overlap. Put the meat in the middle and fold the edges of the wrapping to make a neat parcel. Have the edges of the foil or paper on top and keep this way up during cooking, so that the juices do not escape. Cook in the top of a steamer or on a plate over a pan of boiling water, using another plate or the saucepan lid as a cover. This way takes a little longer to cook than in a steamer. Remove meat from the paper and serve the juices as a sauce.

298. Lamb Stew (*low-fat*)

Quantities for 4. *Cooking time* 1–1½ hrs. *Temperature* 300 °F. No. 2.

- 1 lb. very lean lamb (1½–2lb. with fat and bone)
- ½–1 lb. potatoes, peeled and sliced thinly (2–4 medium)
- 2 carrots, scraped and sliced
- 3 sticks celery sliced
- 1 shallot sliced
- ½ level Tbs. salt
- Pinch pepper
- ½ pt (1 c.) water
- Chopped parsley

Remove bone and all visible fat from the meat. Cut in moderate sized cubes. Place meat and vegetables in layers in a casserole, seasoning each layer. Add the water, cover and simmer 1–1½ hr on top or in the oven until tender. Add chopped parsley to taste. If desired the liquid may be thickened with a little blended cornflour.

Variation. Use other lean meat, e.g. veal, and different combinations of vegetables.

One portion. Carbohydrate 25 g. Calories 330.

299. Braised Liver (*low-sodium*)

Quantities for 4. *Cooking time* ½–¾ hr

- 12 oz. liver, sliced
- 1 oz. plain flour (3 level Tbs.)
- ¼ level tsp. pepper
- 1 oz. (2 Tbs.) lard or oil
- 4 oz. onions, sliced (2 medium)
- 4 oz. tomatoes, skinned and sliced (2 medium)
- 6 oz. mushrooms
- ¼ pt (½ c.) stock
- Salt substitute if allowed

Coat the liver in the flour and pepper mixed. Fry the sliced onions in the fat and then fry the liver quickly. Add the other ingredients and simmer ½–¾ hr or until tender.

One portion. Carbohydrate 8 g. Calories 229.

300. Grilled Liver

Cooking time 5–10 mins.

Cut liver in slices and brush with oil, grill fairly slowly. It is cooked when small beads of blood appear on the surface.

301. Grilled Liver with Mushrooms

Quantities for 4. *Cooking time* 8 mins.

1 lb. calves' or lambs' liver sliced
4 Tbs. French dressing (No. 113)
2 tins mushrooms (7½ oz. (213 g.) size), drained

Brush the liver with dressing both sides and put in the bottom of the grill pan. Grill at moderate heat for 4 mins. Turn and grill 2 mins. Cover with the mushrooms and grill 2 mins. longer.

One portion. Carbohydrate 1 g. Calories 288.

302. Minced Liver in Tomato Sauce (*low-fat*)

Quantities for 4. *Cooking time* ½–¾ hr

8 oz. liver, sliced
¾ lb. tomatoes (6 medium)
1 small piece bayleaf
Salt and pepper
Pinch sugar
½ oz. cornflour (1½ level Tbs.)
1 lb. potatoes (4 medium)
1 Tbs. hot skimmed milk
Chopped parsley

Put potatoes to boil. Grill the liver slightly and then mince it. Sieve tomatoes or pulp them in the electric blender. There should be about ½ pt purée. Heat the tomato with the bayleaf, remove bayleaf, season to taste, blend cornflour with a little cold water and use to thicken the tomatoes. Add liver and reheat. Drain the potato and mash it with the milk and seasoning. Make a border of this on a hot dish, add the liver, and sprinkle with chopped parsley.

One portion. Carbohydrate 30 g. Calories 213.

Variations. For other diets use full-cream milk to mash the potatoes and add 1 oz. margarine or butter.

303. Liver Pâté *Recipe No.* 1 (low-fat)

Quantities for 4 or more. *Cooking time* 10–15 mins.

½ lb. liver (ox is suitable)
1 meat cube
½ level Tbs. gelatine (¼ oz.)
½ tsp. onion juice or grated onion
1 tsp. Worcester sauce
Salt and pepper to taste

Wash the liver and cook gently in water just to cover for about 7–10 mins., or until cooked through but not hard. Drain, keeping the stock. Remove any skin and tubes from the liver and mince it finely, sieve, or wait and put all the ingredients in the electric blender later on. Dissolve the meat cube in the hot stock. Add the gelatine and dissolve. Add the remaining ingredients and the liver; at this stage the whole lot may go in the electric blender to be made smooth. Pour into a mould and chill. Unmould and serve in slices with salad or with toast for an hors d'œuvre.

One portion. Carbohydrate 10 g. Calories 180.

304. Liver Pâté *Recipe No. 2*

Quantities for 6. *Cooking time* 1 hr. *Temperature* 350 °F. No. 3.

8 oz. calves' or lambs' liver
6 oz. mild fat bacon, pieces
¼ level tsp. pepper
¼ level tsp. ground mace or nutmeg
4 oz. thinly sliced mild streaky bacon (4 rashers)

Remove the rind from the bacon and mince the fat bacon and liver together twice. If a very fine pâté is required, put the liver and bacon through a sieve or in the electric blender. Add pepper and the mace or nutmeg. Mix very thoroughly. Line a small cake or loaf tin with the streaky bacon and pack in the mixture. Cover with greased paper or aluminium foil and bake in a moderate oven for 1 hr. Leave in the tin to cool. Turn out and slice.

One portion. Carbohydrate nil. Calories 246.

305. Liver Pilaf

Quantities for 4. *Cooking time* ½ hr

4 oz. (½ c.) rice
1 pt (2 c.) chicken or veal stock
2 oz. butter (4 level Tbs.)
2 level tsp. salt
½ level tsp. pepper
12 oz. sheep's or calves' liver
Vegetables to garnish

Wash and drain the rice. Prepare the stock. A chicken bouillon cube will do instead of chicken stock, but use less salt. Cut the liver into small pieces. Put the stock, 1 oz. butter, salt, and pepper into a pan, bring to the boil, and add the rice. Stir and cook slowly. This is best done either in the oven at 350 °F. (No. 3), or in the top of a double boiler. Cook until the rice is quite tender. Dish in a mound or pack into individual heated moulds and then turn out on the serving dish. Heat the remaining ½ oz. butter in a small frying pan and toss the pieces of liver in it until lightly browned and cooked. Pile on the rice and surround with a garnish of vegetables such as young green peas or baked or grilled tomatoes.

One portion. Carbohydrate 12 g. Calories 220.

Variations (*soft diet.*) Cook liver very lightly and then mince or chop it. (*Low-sodium diet.*) Omit the salt when cooking the rice and use home-made salt-free stock or salt-free Marmite stock. If salt substitute is allowed or potassium glutamate, add it to the rice just before dishing up.

306. Sheep's Liver with Onions or Liver Provençale

Quantities for 4. *Cooking time* ¾ hr

- 1 oz. (2 Tbs.) butter, oil, or lard
- 2 oz. bacon, coarsely chopped (2 rashers)
- 1 lb. onions, chopped (4 medium)
- 2 level Tbs. plain flour *or* 1 level Tbs. cornflour
- 2 level tsp. salt (less if bacon is salty)
- ¼ level tsp. pepper
- ½ pt (1 c.) brown stock
- 1 lb. sheep's liver, cut in small pieces
- 2 Tbs. chopped parsley

Heat the fat and fry the bacon. Lift out the bacon and fry the onions, stirring frequently until just beginning to brown. Sprinkle in the flour or cornflour and seasoning. Mix and cook for a minute or two. Add the stock and stir until blended and boiling. Add the liver and bacon. Cover and simmer gently for ½ hr. Dish up and sprinkle with chopped parsley.

One portion. Carbohydrate 12 g. Calories 330.

307. Liver Shashlik

Quantities for 4. *Cooking time* 10–15 mins. after ½ hr marinading

- 1 lb. liver cut in 1½-in. pieces
- 2 medium tomatoes, quartered
- 8 oz. small mushrooms
- Fresh bayleaves
- Oil
- Vinegar
- Salt and pepper
- Chopped parsley
- Juice of 1 lemon

Prepare the liver and vegetables. Take 8 long thin skewers or brochettes and thread the ingredients on in the following order: bayleaf, liver, mushroom, tomato, repeating until all is used up. Put in the bottom of the grill pan and brush with a very little oil. Moisten with a little vinegar and season with salt and pepper. Leave to marinate for ½ hr. Grill for 8–10 mins., turning once. Swill out the grill pan with a little stock or water. Boil hard in saucepan or grill pan to reduce the marinade. Add parsley and lemon juice and pour over the meat.

One portion. Carbohydrate 2 g. Calories 190.

Variation (low-sodium diet). Omit the salt.

308. Liver Terrapin

Quantities for 4. *Cooking time* 10 mins.

- 8 oz. raw liver, minced
- 2 eggs, hard boiled
- 1 oz. (2 level Tbs.) butter or margarine
- 1 oz. plain flour (3 level Tbs.)
- 1 level tsp. dry mustard
- ½ pt (1 c.) stock
- 1 Tbs. ketchup or smilar sauce
- Salt and pepper
- 4 slices toast (4 oz.)

Separate the egg yolks and whites, mash the yolks, and chop the whites. Melt the butter or margarine and add the flour and mustard. Stir and cook for 1–2 mins. Gradually add the stock. Stir until it boils and boil for 5 mins. Add the ketchup, raw liver, and egg yolk and heat well without boiling. Season to taste. Make the toast and serve the liver mixture on it. Decorate with chopped egg white. Serve hot.

One portion. Carbohydrate 27 g. Calories 493.

Variation (gluten-free diet). Use ½ oz. gluten-free flour (1½ level Tbs.) and gluten-free toast.

309. Rabbit Stew (*low-sodium*)

Quantities for 4. *Cooking time* 1½ hrs

- 1 lb. rabbit
- 2 oz. (¼ c.) onion chopped
- 2 oz. carrot chopped (1 small)
- ½ pt (1 c.) water
- ⅛ level tsp. mixed dried herbs
- 2 cloves
- 2 blades mace
- 1 oz. plain flour (3 level Tbs.) *or* ½ oz. cornflour (1½ level Tbs.)
- ⅛ pt (5 Tbs.) milk (from allowance or use Edosol)
- Pepper
- Salt substitute, if allowed
- Chopped parsley

Wash the rabbit and put it in a pan with the water and prepared vegetables. Add the herbs, cloves, and mace tied in a piece of muslin. Stew slowly for 1½ hrs. Mix the flour to a smooth cream with the milk and add it to the stew. Stir until it thickens and cook 3–4 mins. longer. Season to taste and serve sprinkled with chopped parsley.

One portion. Carbohydrate 8 g. Calories 148.

310. Creamed Sweetbreads

Quantities for 4. *Cooking time* 1–1¼ hrs

4 sweetbreads or 1 lb.
1 oz. (2 level Tbs.) butter or margarine
1 oz. plain flour (3 level Tbs.)
¼ pt (½ c.) milk
¼ pt (½ c.) stock from the sweetbreads
Salt and pepper
Lemon juice
Chopped parsley

Soak the sweetbreads at least 1 hr in cold water. Drain and put in the pan. Blanch by covering with cold water, adding a few drops of lemon juice and bringing slowly to the boil. Simmer 5 mins. for sheep's and 10 mins. for calves' sweetbreads. Plunge in cold water and then remove any gristle and skin. Put the blanched sweetbreads in 1 pt salted water and simmer gently until tender (about ¾–1 hr). Remove and keep hot.

Make a sauce by melting the fat, adding the flour, and cooking for a few minutes. Remove from the heat and add the liquid gradually. Return to the heat. Stir until it boils and boil for a few minutes. Season to taste, with salt, pepper, and lemon juice. Then reheat the sweetbreads in the sauce and serve with chopped parsley sprinkled over.

Variation. Serve with small fingers of crisp toast or triangles of fried bread and button mushrooms.

One portion (without the bread or mushrooms). Carbohydrate 8 g. Calories 309.

311. Braised Sweetbreads

Quantities for 3–4. *Cooking time* 1–1½ hrs. *Temperature* 375 °F. No. 5.

4 sweetbreads or 1 lb.
Mixed vegetables
¼ pt (½ c.) stock
Salt and pepper
Cornflour
Chopped parsley

Soak the sweetbreads for at least 1 hr in cold water. Drain and put in a pan. Blanch by covering with cold water, adding a few drops of lemon juice, and bringing slowly to the boil. Boil for 5 mins. for sheep's and 10 mins. for calves' sweetbreads. Plunge the sweetbreads into cold water and then remove any gristle and skin. Take a pan large enough to hold the sweetbreads in a single layer and slice or chop enough prepared mixed vegetables to make a layer 1 in. thick on the bottom. Season with salt and place the sweetbreads on top. Add enough stock barely to cover the vegetables. Put on the lid. Simmer gently for 45 mins. in the oven or on top of the stove. Lift out the sweetbreads and surround with the vegetables, sieved if necessary. Thicken the liquid with a little cornflour (1 level Tbs. to $\frac{1}{2}$ pt), season, and pour over the sweetbreads. Sprinkle with chopped parsley and serve hot.

312. Curried Sweetbreads

Quantities for 4. *Cooking time* 45 mins.

4 sweetbreads or 1 lb.
Lemon juice, Flour, Curry powder } for coating
1 oz. (2 level Tbs.) butter for frying
Sauce
1 oz. (2 Tbs.) fat or oil
1 onion, chopped
1 oz. plain flour (3 level Tbs.)
1 level Tbs. curry powder
$\frac{1}{2}$ pt (1 c.) stock
1 apple, chopped
1 small tomato, chopped
1 level tsp. brown sugar
$\frac{1}{2}$ level tsp. salt
Grated rind and juice of $\frac{1}{4}$ lemon
$\frac{1}{2}$ bayleaf
1 Tbs. mango chutney

Soak sweetbreads for at least 1 hr in cold water. Drain and put in a pan with cold water to cover, and a squeeze of lemon juice. Bring to the boil and simmer 5 mins. for sheep's and 10 mins. for calves' sweetbreads. Plunge in cold water and remove any gristle and skin. When cold, slice and coat with flour and curry powder. To make the sauce, fry the onion in the fat, add the flour and curry powder, and mix and cook 1–2 mins. Add the stock and stir until it boils. Add remaining ingredients and simmer 30 mins., adding more stock if needed. Strain and reheat. Melt the butter and fry the prepared sweetbreads until lightly browned. Serve with the curry sauce. Serve plain or with boiled rice.

One portion. Carbohydrate 16 g. Calories 343.

Variations (*low-sodium diet*). Omit the salt and use salt-free stock or salt-free Marmite and home-made chutney. Use potassium glutamate or salt substitute if allowed.

313. Stewed Sweetbreads (*low-fat*)

Quantities 1 sweetbread per person. *Cooking time* 1½ hrs

Cornflour	Skimmed milk
Salt and pepper	Chopped parsley

Soak the sweetbread in cold water for 1 hr to remove the blood. Strain, put in a small pan, and add fresh water to cover. Just bring to the boil for sheep's sweetbreads, simmer 10–12 mins. for calves', then plunge in cold water. Remove skin and fibre. Put in a pan with salted water barely to cover and simmer gently 1 hr. Lift out and keep hot. Measure liquid and allow 1–2 level Tbs. cornflour per pt. Blend cornflour with a little skimmed milk, add to stock, and stir until it boils. Boil for a few minutes and then return the sweetbreads to reheat. Sprinkle with chopped parsley.

Variation. For other diets thicken the liquid with less cornflour and add beaten egg yolk and cream just before serving.

314. Tripe and Egg Pie

Quantities for 4. *Cooking time* 1¼ hrs

1 lb. dressed tripe	¼ pt (½ c.) milk
1 large onion	¼ pt (½ c.) tripe stock
Salt and pepper	2 eggs, hard-boiled
½ lemon	1 lb. potatoes (4 medium)
1 oz. (2 level Tbs.) butter	1 Tbs. hot milk
1 oz. plain flour (3 level Tbs.)	1 oz. (2 level Tbs.) margarine

Cut the tripe into fingers and blanch by covering with cold water, bringing to the boil and cooking for two minutes. Strain. Put the blanched tripe in a saucepan and just cover with cold water. Add the onion, 1 level tsp. salt, and a squeeze of lemon juice. Simmer for 1 hr. Strain. Make a sauce from the butter, flour, milk, and tripe stock. Stir until it boils and cook for a few minutes. Season to taste. Add the tripe and the chopped onion (if allowed) and the sliced hard-boiled eggs. Put in a hot pie-dish. Mash the boiled potatoes with the hot milk and margarine and season well. Spread on top of the tripe and brown in a hot oven or under the grill.

One portion. Carbohydrate 30 g. Calories 400.

315. Tripe au Gratin

Quantities for 4. *Cooking time* 1¼ hrs

1 lb. dressed tripe	1 oz. plain flour (3 level Tbs.)
1 large onion	¼ pt (½ c.) milk
½ lemon	¼ pt (½ c.) tripe stock
Salt and pepper	2 heaped Tbs. breadcrumbs
1½ oz. (3 level Tbs.) butter	2 heaped Tbs. grated cheese

Cut the tripe into fingers and blanch by covering with cold water, bringing to the boil and cooking for 2 mins. Strain. Add cold water just to cover the blanched tripe and add 1 level tsp. salt, the onion, and a squeeze of lemon juice. Cover, bring to the boil, and simmer 1 hr. Make a sauce from the butter, flour, milk, and tripe stock. Stir until it boils, and cook for a few minutes. Add the tripe and the chopped onion (if allowed). Pour into a hot pie-dish. Melt the ½ oz. butter and stir in the crumbs to coat well. Then remove from the heat and add the cheese. Sprinkle this on top of the tripe and crisp under a hot grill but take care not to overcook the cheese.

One portion. Carbohydrate 12 g. Calories 304.

316. Tripe Soubise

Quantities for 4. *Cooking time* 1¾ hrs or less

1 lb. tripe	1½ oz. (3 level Tbs.) margarine or butter
1 pt (2 c.) water	1½ oz. plain flour (4½ level Tbs.)
1 onion, chopped	1½ pt (3 c.) milk
1 small piece carrot, chopped	2 tsp. Marmite
1 clove	Chopped parsley
Salt and pepper	

Put the tripe in cold water, bring to the boil, drain, and rinse. Scrape and remove any fat. Cut in pieces and put in the water with the vegetables, clove, and seasoning and simmer gently 1½ hrs, or until tender. (If the tripe is already almost cooked the time will be much less.) Drain off the liquid and remove clove. Make a sauce with the fat, flour, milk, and ¼ pt tripe liquid or enough to make a creamy consistency. Add Marmite and stir until dissolved. Taste for seasoning and pour over the tripe and sprinkle with chopped parsley.

One portion. Carbohydrate 15 g. Calories 300.

Variations (*low-sodium diet*). Omit salt and use salt-substitute if allowed. Use milk from the allowance or Edosol and special salt-free Marmite and fat. (*Low-fat diet.*) Omit fat and make sauce with skimmed milk. Blend the flour or 1 level Tbs. of cornflour and use this to thicken the liquid.

317. Sheep's Tongue and Tomato Mould

Quantities for 4. *Cooking time* 1½–2 hrs (pressure-cooking ¾ hr)

4 tongues, fresh or salted
2 bayleaves
2 small onions
½ pt (1 c.) canned tomato juice
½ oz. gelatine (1 level Tbs.)
¼ pt (½ c.) hot water
Salt and pepper to taste
Pinch grated nutmeg

If the tongues are salted, soak overnight in cold water. If fresh, soak for 1 hr or so. Put tongues in cold water to cover with 1 onion and 1 bayleaf and simmer until tender. Meanwhile, make the jelly by simmering the tomato juice, 1 bayleaf, and 1 sliced onion for 5 mins. Strain and add the gelatine dissolved in hot water. Season to taste with salt and pepper and nutmeg. Skin the tongues while hot, removing bones and any gristly bits from the roots. Cut in small pieces as for a brawn. Add tongue to tomato liquid and pour into a mould. Chill and then unmould, slice, and serve with salad.

One portion. Carbohydrate 5 g. Calories 360.

318. A Dish of Boiled Sheep's Tongues

Quantities for 4. *Cooking time* 2½ hrs

1 pt (2 c.) water
½ level tsp. salt
1 large onion, sliced
Bouquet garni
4 sheep's tongues
½ oz. (1 level Tbs.) butter or margarine
½ oz. (1 level Tbs.) lard
1 level Tbs. plain flour *or* ½ level Tbs. cornflour
1 pt (2 c.) hot stock from the tongues
Chopped parsley
4 small onions, peeled

Boil water and salt. Add the large sliced onion, bouquet garni, and then the tongues. Simmer gently 1½ hrs or until they are tender. Peel tongues and remove small bones. Melt the fats, add flour, stir, and cook until it turns yellow. Add the strained stock from cooking the tongues. Stir until it boils, add the tongues and the small onions and simmer ½ hr or until the onions are cooked. Sprinkle with chopped parsley.

One portion. Carbohydrate 17 g. Calories 418.

Variation. Add small onions to the tongue and stock about ½ hr before the end of cooking time. Then merely reheat tongue and onions in the sauce.

319. Veal Birds or Olives

Quantities for 4. *Cooking time* 1¼ hrs. *Temperature* 300 °F. No. 2.

- 1 lb. veal, thin slices of fillet or leg
- Veal forcemeat (No. 155)
- 1½ oz. butter or olive oil (3 Tbs.)
- 1 Tbs. chopped onion
- 1 oz. plain flour (3 level Tbs.)
- ¾ pt (1½ c.) stock
- 1 Tbs. chopped parsley
- 1 level tsp. salt
- ¼ level tsp. pepper

These are nicest if the meat is cut in the thinnest possible slices. Cut each slice to approx. 4 ins. by 3 ins. Spread a little forcemeat on each and roll up tightly. Fasten with wooden toothpicks or tie with fine string. Melt the butter or oil and fry the meat until brown all over. Add in the onion towards the end of frying. Place the meat in a casserole and add the flour to the frying pan and mix well. Add the stock and stir until it boils. Add parsley and seasoning and pour over the olives. Cover and cook very gently until tender. Remove the string or toothpicks and arrange on a dish with the sauce poured over.

One portion. Carbohydrate 5 g. Calories 240.

320. Veal Blanquette

Quantities for 4. *Cooking time* 1¾–2 hrs (1 hr pressure-cooking).

1½ lb. stewing veal
½ level Tbs. salt
1 onion, stuck with a clove
1 carrot, chopped
Pinch of mixed herbs
Piece of celery, chopped
¾ oz. (1½ level Tbs.) butter or margarine
½ oz. plain flour (1½ level Tbs.)
Pepper
2 oz. mushrooms, sliced
6 small pickling onions (optional)
1 egg yolk
Juice of ½ lemon
1½ Tbs. cream
2 Tbs. chopped parsley
Grilled bacon rolls
Wedges of lemon (optional)

Cut the veal in small pieces as for a stew. Put in a pan with 1 pt water and the salt, onion, carrot, herbs, and celery. Simmer for 1 hr, or pressure-cook (using ½ pt water) for ¼ hr. Strain. Make a sauce with the butter or margarine, flour, and ½ pt of the strained stock. Season to taste. Add mushrooms, peeled onions (if used) and boil gently for ¾ hr. Mix the egg yolk, lemon juice, and cream. Remove the sauce from the heat and add the egg mixture and the meat. Heat again without boiling. Serve sprinkled with chopped parsley. If liked, serve with the grilled bacon rolls and wedges of lemon.

One portion (without bacon). Carbohydrate 5 g. Calories 306.

321. Casserole of Veal (*low-fat*)

Quantities for 4. *Cooking time* 1–1½ hrs. *Temperature* 300 °F. No. 2.

1 lb. fillet of veal, cubed
1 onion, sliced
2 oz. (½ c.) mushrooms, chopped
Pepper
Salt
Bouquet garni
1 Tbs. lemon juice
1 pt (2 c.) fat-free stock or water
1–2 level Tbs. cornflour
Skimmed milk
Chopped parsley

Remove any fat from the meat. Put meat, vegetables, flavourings, and stock in a casserole and cover. Simmer until the meat is tender. Thicken the liquid with a little cornflour blended with skimmed milk. Sprinkle with chopped parsley.

One portion. Carbohydrate 5 g. Calories 150.

322. Creamed Veal or Chicken

Quantities for 4

12 oz. freshly cooked meat
½ pt (1c.) Béchamel sauce (No. 93)
Chopped parsley to garnish

Dice the meat and reheat in the sauce, being sure to simmer for a few minutes. Serve on toast, in a border of mashed potatoes, Duchess potatoes, or boiled macaroni. Garnish with chopped parsley.

One portion. Carbohydrate 10 g. Calories 350.

Variations. 1. Add 2 oz. sliced cooked mushrooms. 2. Make the sauce a little thinner than usual and add 2 egg yolks and the juice of ½ lemon just before serving. Do not allow to boil again. 3. Add a little cream or evaporated milk just before serving. 4. *Low-fat diet.* Make a fat-free sauce instead of the Béchamel. 5. *Modified-fat diet.* Use a sauce made with oil, and mashed potatoes No. 349 (7) with oil. 6. *Gluten-free diet.* Use gluten-free flour for the sauce.

323. Veal Cutlets with Cider

Quantities for 4. *Cooking time* 20–25 mins.

4 veal cutlets
2 oz. butter or oil (4 Tbs.)
2 medium onions, chopped
2 level Tbs. plain flour
¼ pt (½ c.) dry cider
¼ pt (½ c.) water
Salt and pepper
Chopped parsley

Heat fat and fry cutlets brown, about 10 mins. Remove and keep hot. Add onions and fry until pale brown. Add flour and mix well. Cook 1–2 mins. Add cider and water and stir until it thickens and boil for a few minutes, seasoning to taste. Return the cutlets for about 3 mins. to reheat. Serve sprinkled with chopped parsley.

One portion. Carbohydrate 8 g. Calories 346.

324. Veal Flan

Quantities for 4. *Cooking time* ¾ hr. *Temperature* 450 °F. No. 8 then 375 °F. No. 5.

- 6–8 oz. short pastry (4 oz. (¾ c.) flour, 2 oz. (4 level Tbs.) fat)
- 8 oz. freshly cooked veal
- 2 oz. fat bacon rashers (2 rashers)
- 1 small onion, chopped
- 2 level Tbs. plain flour
- ½ pt (1 c.) stock
- ¼ level tsp. salt
- Pinch of pepper
- Pinch thyme and rosemary
- 2 eggs
- 4 Tbs. double cream
- 2 oz. grated Parmesan cheese (½ c.)

Roll out the pastry to line a shallow 1½-pt oven-proof dish. Cut veal in ½-in. cubes. Fry bacon gently without added fat or grill until crisp. Drain on absorbent paper and crumble when cool. Fry the onion in the bacon fat, add flour, and cook a little; add the stock and stir until boiling. Add seasoning, bacon, and veal and pour in pastry case. Bake at 450 °F. for 20 mins. or until the pastry is cooked. Beat the eggs and mix with cream and cheese. Pour on top of the meat and return to the oven at 375 °F. for 15 mins. to set and brown the top. Serve hot or cold.

One portion. Carbohydrate 30 g. Calories 615.

325. Veal Mould (*low-fat*)

Quantities for 4. *Cooking time* 1½–2 hrs (½ hr pressure cooker)

- 1 breast veal (about 1¾ lb.)
- 1 carrot cut in chunks (4 oz.)
- ¼ bayleaf
- A strip of lemon rind
- ¾ pt (1½ c.) water (½ pt (1 c.) for pressure cooking)
- Salt and pepper
- Chopped parsley

Cut the meat in pieces to fit the stew pan comfortably. Simmer the meat, carrot, bayleaf, lemon rind, and water for 1½–2 hrs (½ hr pressure cooking). Remove the veal, take out the bones, and shred or cut the meat in small pieces. Place it in a mould.

Strain the stock, season well, add chopped parsley, pour over the meat and leave to set. Unmould when firm.

One portion. Carbohydrate a trace. Calories 132.

Variation. For other than low-fat diets, replace some of the veal with mild cured ham or bacon.

326. Veal Parmesan

Quantities for 4. *Cooking time* 10–15 mins.

- 1 lb. fillet veal
- A small piece of garlic
- 1–2 oz. (2–4 level Tbs.) butter
- 3 level Tbs. grated Parmesan cheese
- 3 level tsp. paprika pepper
- Salt and pepper
- A little hot stock

Have the veal cut in ½-in. slices and then beaten out flat. Chop the garlic finely. Heat the butter in a frying pan. Add the garlic, then the veal. Sprinkle the veal with cheese, paprika pepper, salt, and pepper, and fry gently until brown on one side. Turn and finish cooking, giving about 10–15 mins. in all. Serve with the pan drippings dissolved in a little hot stock.

One portion. Carbohydrate Nil. Calories 267.

327. Veal Ragoût with Green Peas

Quantities for 4. *Cooking time* 1¾ hrs

- Veal bones for stock
- 1 lb. stewing veal (no bones)
- ½ oz. (1 Tbs.) butter or olive oil
- ½ oz. (1 level Tbs.) lard
- 2 level Tbs. plain flour *or* 1 level Tbs. cornflour
- 8 small onions or shallots
- ¾ pt (1½ c.) veal stock
- Bouquet garni
- 1 level tsp. salt
- ¼ level tsp. pepper
- 1 pt (2 c.) shelled green peas

Make the veal stock with the bones and water to cover (½ hr in pressure cooker). Cut veal in suitable pieces for serving. Melt the fats and add the flour or cornflour. Stir and cook until it turns yellow, then add the veal and peeled onions and cook for 10 mins. stirring occasionally. Add the stock, bouquet garni, salt, and pepper and bring to the boil. Add the peas, cover, and cook gently 1½ hrs or until the meat is tender. Stir occasionally.

One portion. Carbohydrate 16 g. Calories 250.

328. Veal Stewed with Sherry

Quantities for 4. *Cooking time* 40–45 mins.

6 Tbs. olive oil
1½ lb. veal chops or 4 chops
1 stalk celery, chopped
1 carrot, chopped
1 onion, chopped
1 Tbs. tomato paste
¼ pt (½ c.) dry sherry
Salt and pepper
Chopped parsley

Heat the oil and fry the chops brown. Add vegetables and mix well. Cover the pan and cook 10 mins. or until the vegetables are tender. Mix tomato purée and sherry and add to the meat, together with the seasonings. Cover and cook until meat is tender (about 20 mins.), adding water during cooking if necessary to prevent burning. Sprinkle with chopped parsley.

One portion. Carbohydrate 7 g. Calories 433.

Variation (*low-sodium diet*). Omit the salt, use Cirio brand tomato paste. Add some salt-substitute at the end if allowed. Also you could add a little chopped rosemary with the vegetables for extra flavour.

VEGETABLES AND SALADS

329. Cooking Vegetables for Sick People

Methods are very important to make the vegetables look pleasant, be palatable, and have the maximum possible vitamin value. The only sources of vitamin C in a diet are vegetables and fruit and all sick people need plenty of this vitamin for its healing properties.

To preserve vitamin C all vegetables should be cooked in the shortest possible time, in very little water and until just tender. They should then be served as soon as cooked and not kept waiting or reheated.

All vegetables cook more quickly if cut in small pieces, e.g. slicing carrots, shredding cabbage, breaking cauliflower into sprigs. Use about 1 in. water in the pan, get it boiling first, add salt, and when the vegetables are in keep the lid on to retain the steam. Any cooking liquid should be kept for sauces and soups.

When vegetables have to be sieved for a patient, do this as quickly as possible, reheat, and serve at once.

330. Vegetables au Gratin

Quantities for 4. *Cooking time* ½ hr. *Temperature* 450° F. No. 8

1–1½ lb. vegetables
½ pt (1 c.) cheese sauce (No. 81)
Buttered crumbs (No. 521)

Boil the vegetables, saving any liquid for the sauce, put vegetables and sauce in layers in a pie-dish, finishing with a layer of sauce, and cover with buttered crumbs. Brown in a hot oven or under the grill.

Suitable vegetables. Cauliflower sprigs, Brussels sprouts, shredded cabbage, celery, onions, leeks.

Variations. 1. *High-protein diet.* Add 2–4 chopped or sliced hard-boiled eggs to the vegetables. 2. *Low-protein diet.* Instead of cheese sauce put the vegetables in layers with grated cheese (from the allowance) finishing the top with cheese and dabs of butter or margarine. Brown under the grill. 3. *Low-carbohydrate diet.* As for 2, but use as much cheese as liked.

331. Vegetable Ragoût

Quantities for 4. *Cooking time* ¾–1 hr

1 oz. (2 level Tbs.) fat
2–4 oz. bacon, chopped (2–4 rashers)
1 onion, sliced
1 level Tbs. plain flour
½–¾ pt (1–1½ c.) stock
2 lb. mixed vegetables, sliced or diced
Bouquet garni
3 Tbs. wine vinegar
Salt and pepper
Chopped parsley

Melt the fat and fry the onions and bacon until just beginning to brown. Add the flour and cook until it turns yellow. Add the stock, and stir until it boils. Add the vegetables and bouquet garni and cook gently, stirring occasionally, until the vegetables are tender. Add vinegar and taste for seasoning. Sprinkle with chopped parsley and serve hot.

332. Macédoine of Vegetables

Quantities for 4. *Cooking time* ½ hr

½ pt (1 c.) diced carrots (½ lb.)
¼ pt (½ c.) diced turnips (¼ lb.)
½ pt (1 c.) shelled or frozen peas (½ lb.)
¾ oz. (1½ Tbs.) butter or margarine
¾ oz. plain flour (2 level Tbs.)
½ pt (1 c.) vegetable stock
Salt and pepper
Pinch nutmeg or mace
1 egg yolk
Chopped parsley

Boil the vegetables in a little salted water. Drain and use the water for the sauce. Make this from the butter or margarine, flour, and vegetable stock. Cook 2–3 mins. and season to taste. Add the vegetables and reheat. Add the egg yolk just before serving. Sprinkle with chopped parsley.

Variation. Add one Tbs. double cream with the egg yolk. Alternatively use other vegetable mixtures.

One portion. Carbohydrate 14 g. Calories 150.

333. Mixed Strained Vegetables

Quantities for 2. *Cooking time* 5 mins.

½ level Tbs. cornflour
¼ oz. (½ level Tbs.) butter
1 can strained peas *and*
1 can strained green beans *or* 8–9 oz. (227–255 g.) of any other mixture
½ level tsp. yeast extract
Salt and pepper

Work the cornflour and butter together to make a smooth paste. Heat the strained vegetables, add the cornflour paste, stir, and cook 3–4 mins. Add seasoning and yeast extract and serve at once.

One portion. Carbohydrate 4 g. Calories 50.

334. Broad Beans and Bacon

Quantities for 4. *Cooking time* 20–30 mins.

- 3–4 lb. beans in the pod or 1 lb. frozen
- 2 oz. (4 level Tbs.) butter or margarine
- 1 oz. (3 level Tbs.) plain flour
- $\frac{3}{4}$ pt ($1\frac{1}{2}$ c.) vegetable water or stock
- 2–4 oz. chopped bacon (2–4 rashers)
- Salt and pepper
- 1 level tsp. sugar
- 2 Tbs. chopped parsley
- 2 Tbs. vinegar

Shell fresh beans. Melt the fat and mix in the flour, cooking one to two minutes. Add the water and stir until it boils. Add bacon and beans. Cover and cook gently until the beans are tender. Season to taste, and add sugar, vinegar, and parsley. Serve hot.

One portion. Carbohydrate 13 g. Calories 300.

335. Cauliflower Polonaise

Quantities for 4. *Cooking time* 20 mins.

- 1 medium cauliflower (1 lb. prepared)
- $\frac{1}{2}$ oz. fine breadcrumbs (2 level Tbs.)
- 1 hard-boiled egg, chopped
- $\frac{1}{2}$ oz. grated cheese (2 level Tbs.)
- 2 level Tbs. chopped parsley
- 1 oz. (2 level Tbs.) butter

Prepare the cauliflower and boil in a little salted water. Drain and put in a hot serving dish, preferably in sprigs. Mix the crumbs, egg, cheese, and parsley and sprinkle on top. Heat the butter until sizzling and pour over. Serve at once.

One portion. Carbohydrate 5 g. Calories 130.

336. Chicory Polonaise

Quantities for 4. *Cooking time* ½ hr

1 lb. chicory (8 small pieces)
½ oz. (1 level Tbs.) butter or margarine
2 Tbs. milk
4 Tbs. stock
Salt
1 hard-boiled egg, chopped

Wash and drain the chicory. Heat fat in a pan and put in the chicory in layers. Add the milk, stock, and salt and cover and cook gently for ½ hr or until tender. When the chicory is cooked, sprinkle the egg over and serve hot.

One portion. Carbohydrate 2 g. Calories 70.

337. Carrots Vichy

Quantities for 4. *Cooking time* 25 mins.

1 oz. (2 level Tbs.) butter or margarine
1 lb. young carrots, sliced (4 medium)
1 level tsp. sugar
½ level tsp. salt
1 Tbs. chopped parsley

Melt the fat and add all the other ingredients except for the parsley. Cover and cook until tender, shaking the pan occasionally. Serve with the parsley sprinkled over.

One portion. Carbohydrate 10 g. Calories 100.

338. American Fried Cabbage

Quantities for 6. *Cooking time* 15 mins.

1 oz. (2 level Tbs.) margarine or butter
1½ lb. cabbage shredded coarsely
1 oz. chopped onions (½ a small)
Pinch of nutmeg
1½ level tsp. salt
½ oz. sugar (1 level Tbs.)
Few grains cayenne pepper
3 Tbs. vinegar
2 Tbs. chopped parsley

Melt the fat in a stew pan over a low heat. Add cabbage, onion, nutmeg, and salt and cover and cook for 10 mins. over a low heat, stirring frequently and taking care the vegetables do not brown. Add sugar and cayenne to the vinegar and mix well.

Pour over the cabbage, mix well, and cook 5 mins. longer. Serve hot, sprinkled with chopped parsley.

One portion. Carbohydrate 6 g. Calories 80.

339. Chestnut Stew

Quantities for 4. *Cooking time* 1 hr

- 1½ lb. chestnuts
- 1½ oz. (3 level Tbs.) lard
- 1½ oz. plain flour (4½ level Tbs.)
- 1 pt (2 c.) stock
- 2 oz. carrot, chopped (1 small)
- 2 oz. onion, chopped (1 small)
- Pinch ground cloves and mace
- Salt and pepper

Slit the chestnuts and place under the grill until the skins begin to separate and they will peel easily. Make a brown roux with the lard and flour, add the stock, and stir until it boils. Add chestnuts, vegetables, and seasoning and stew gently until the chestnuts are tender.

One portion. Carbohydrate 63 g. Calories 388.

340. Chicory with Cheese and Bacon

Quantities for 4. *Cooking time* 1 hr. *Temperature* 400 °F. No. 6.

- 1 lb. chicory (8 small pieces)
- 1 Tbs. lemon juice
- ½ pt (1 c.) cheese sauce (No. 81)
- 4 oz. lean thin bacon rashers or ham (4 rashers)
- 4 Tbs. buttered crumbs

Boil the chicory in a little salted water with the lemon juice. When tender, drain and put in a baking dish in layers with the sauce and bacon or ham cut in pieces. Finish with a layer of sauce, cover the top with the crumbs and bake in a moderate oven for 20 mins. or until heated through and brown on top.

One portion. Carbohydrate 20 g. Calories 360.

341. Braised Celery

Quantities for 4. *Cooking time* ½–1 hr. *Temperature* 275–375 °F. Nos. 2–5.

1 head celery (1 lb.)
½ oz. (1 level Tbs.) fat
½ level tsp. salt
Pinch pepper
1–2 Tbs. water
Chopped parsley

Wash the celery and cut in convenient-sized picces. Put in a casserole with fat, seasoning, and water. Cover and cook slowly until tender. Serve sprinkled with chopped parsley.

One portion. Carbohydrate 2 g. Calories 45.

342. Red Cabbage

Quantities for 4. *Cooking time* ½–¾ hr

1 oz. (2 level Tbs.) fat
1 lb. (8 level cups) red cabbage, shredded
1 large onion, sliced
1 large apple, sliced
2 Tbs. stock *or* water
2 Tbs. vinegar
1 level tsp. salt
Pinch of pepper
1 level Tbs. brown sugar

Melt the fat in a saucepan and add the other ingredients. Cover closely and boil gently until tender. Stir occasionally and watch to see it does not boil dry. All the liquid should be used up by the time the cabbage is cooked.

One portion. Carbohydrate 10 g. Calories 106.

343. Stuffed Cabbage Leaves

Quantities for 4. *Cooking time* ½ hr

4 large cabbages leaves
1 oz. (2 level Tbs.) fat
1 small chopped onion
3 oz. rice (⅓ c.)
½ pt (1 c.) stock
1 oz. cooked chopped liver *or* other meat
Salt and pepper
Cornflour to thicken

Make the stuffing by frying the onion in the fat in a strong pan until it begins to brown. Add rice and cook 2 mins. longer.

Add the stock and cook until all is absorbed and the rice tender. Season to taste. Add meat. Cool a little. Pour boiling water on the cabbage leaves to soften them. Drain. Place some stuffing on each leaf and roll up tightly. Pack closely in pan and add a very little stock. Cover and cook gently for ½ hr. Lift out and thicken stock with cornflour. Season well and pour over the cabbage.

One portion. Carbohydrate 25 g. Calories 170.

Variation. Stuff with half minced meat (No. 254) or with partly cooked sausage meat. Alternative sauces are cheese and tomato.

344. Cauliflower with Bacon Sauce

Quantities for 4. *Cooking time* 30 mins.

- 1 large cauliflower
- 2 oz. (4 level Tbs.) fat
- 2 oz. chopped bacon (2 rashers)
- 1 Tbs. chopped onion
- 6 level Tbs. plain flour (2 oz.)
- 1 pt (2 c.) vegetable stock
- Salt and pepper
- 4 Tbs. chopped parsley

Wash the cauliflower and divide into sprigs. Boil in a little salted water. Use the trimmings to make the stock. Fry bacon and onion in the fat in the saucepan. Add the flour, mix, and cook a minute or two, and then add the stock. Stir until it boils and cook 5 mins., seasoning to taste. Add parsley and pour over the drained cauliflower. Serve hot.

One portion. Carbohydrate 14 g. Calories 240.

345. Leeks Skelton

Quantities for 4. *Cooking time* 45 mins. *Temperature* 375 °F. No. 5.

- 2 lb. leeks
- 4 oz. (1⅓ c.) grated cheese
- 6 Tbs. double cream
- Salt and pepper

Boil the leeks in salted water until almost tender. Sprinkle a layer of cheese in a shallow greased dish. Drain the leeks and arrange on this. Cover with more cheese, add the cream and the final layer of cheese. Bake until golden brown and hot. Serve as a separate course or as a vegetable with chicken or veal or fish.

One portion. Carbohydrate 5 g. Calories 240.

346. Cooking Mushrooms

Fried mushrooms soak up a lot of fat and tend to be rather indigestible. For sick people it is wiser to grill or bake them with a small nut of butter or margarine in the middle. For a low-fat or low-calorie diet they can be grilled without any fat. Another good way is to poach them in cream, milk, or skimmed milk and then thicken the milk with a little cornflour to make a sauce. Alternatively, stew in a little water.

347. Glazed Onions

Quantities for 4. *Cooking time* ¾ hr

1 lb. small onions or shallots
2 oz. (4 level Tbs.) butter or margarine (50 g.)
1 oz. sugar (2 level Tbs.)

Peel onions and boil in salted water until nearly tender. Drain well. Melt the fat and cook the onions in it until brown. Sprinkle on the sugar and cover the pan. Cook gently a few minutes longer until the onions are quite tender. Serve hot.

One portion. Carbohydrate 15 g. Calories 170.

Variation (*low-sodium diet*). Boil the onions without salt. This is one of the ways of preparing vegetables when the absence of salt does not seriously affect the flavour. Use unsalted butter or margarine.

348. Baked Stuffed Potatoes

Quantities for 1 potato. *Cooking time* 45 mins.–1 hr. *Temperature* 400–425 °F. Nos. 6–7.

1 large potato
1–2 Tbs. milk
½ tsp. butter or margarine
Pinch of pepper
¼ level tsp. salt
1 Tbs. chopped parsley *or* minced ham, corned beef, grated cheese, *or* ½ Tbs. chopped fried onion

Scrub the potatoes and brush the skin with oil or rub with greased paper. Place on a baking shelf and cook until it feels soft when squeezed with a cloth. Cut in half lengthwise and scoop out the inside carefully. Mash this with the milk, fat, seasonings and other chosen ingredients. Put back in the shell, brown in a hot oven for a few minutes.

Variations. 1. Plain baked potato. Cut a slit in the top after cooking and insert a piece of butter. 2. *Low-fat diet.* For the filling use cooked minced lean meat or flaked white fish. Moisten with a little of one of the fatless sauces and add some chopped parsley. 3. Mix the mashed potato with a little vegetable extract and moisten with skimmed milk. 4. Mix the mashed potato with skimmed milk, cottage cheese, and chopped green herbs.

349. Creamed or Mashed Potatoes

Quantities for 4. *Cooking time* 45 mins.

1 lb. potatoes (4 medium)
1 oz. (2 level Tbs.) butter or margarine
4 Tbs. hot milk
Salt and pepper
Chopped parsley or chives (optional)

Scrub the potatoes and boil in their jackets. Peel and mash. Beat in the butter or margarine melted in the hot milk. Beat thoroughly until light and creamy. Do this over a light heat or reheat potatoes before serving. Season to taste and add chopped parsley or chives for extra flavour.

CAUTION. Use freshly cooked potatoes and finish and serve the dish quickly or the flavour and vitamin content deteriorate.

One portion. Carbohydrate 24 g. Calories 166.

Variations. a. Low-fat diet. Beat in ½ oz. dried skimmed milk powder or ¼ oz. Casilan powder. Omit the butter or margarine and use more skimmed hot milk to make it of the desired texture. Add 4 oz. cooked tomatoes for additional flavour. *b. Complan.* Instead of the dried milk add 2 oz. Complan. Milk may be omitted. *c. Low-salt diet.* Omit salt in cooking. Use salt-free butter or margarine and add ¼ oz. chopped water-cress. (Edosol may be used in place of the milk.) *d. High-protein.* Omit the milk and add 2 oz. grated cheese (½ c.), 2 egg yolks, 1 oz. butter (2 level Tbs.) a pinch of paprika pepper. *e. Duchess potatoes.* Use only 2 Tbs. milk and add 2 egg yolks. *f. Protein-enriched potatoes.* Add 1 oz. dried skimmed milk powder (2½ level Tbs.) to the potato and beat in well before adding the milk. *g. Oil.* Use hot skimmed milk or Alfonal milk in the proportions of 4 Tbs. milk to 1 lb. potatoes and add 2 Tbs. of oil. *h. Purée of Potatoes.* Any of the above mixtures with the potatoes sieved or put through a potato ricer to make sure they are smooth.

350. Fried Potatoes with Cheese

Slice cold boiled potatoes and fry them brown in shallow fat. Sprinkle with grated cheese and allow the cheese to begin to melt before serving.

Low-protein diet. For one person use ½ lb. potatoes and ½–1 oz. cheese.

351. Grilled Potato and Cheese Balls

Quantities for 4. *Cooking time* 45 mins.

- 1 lb. potatoes (4 medium)
- 1 oz. (2 level Tbs.) butter or margarine
- 3–4 oz. (1⅓ level c.) grated cheese
- Salt and pepper
- Pinch ground mace
- Chopped parsley

Boil the potatoes in their jackets. Peel and mash with the butter or margarine and beat in the cheese and flavourings. Shape into balls and grill or bake until brown.

CAUTION. Use freshly cooked potatoes and finish and serve the dish quickly or the flavour and vitamin content will be poor.

One portion. Carbohydrate 25 g. Calories 275.

352. Pommes de Terre au Lard

Quantities for 4. *Cooking time* 45–50 mins.

1 lb. potatoes (4 medium)
2 oz. lean bacon (2 rashers)
1 oz. fat (2 level Tbs.)
1 oz. (2 level Tbs.) chopped onion
1 level Tbs. plain flour
¼ pt (½ c.) stock
3 Tbs. white wine
Pinch mixed herbs
Salt and pepper
Chopped parsley

Peel potatoes and cut in pieces about half the size of an egg. Dice the bacon and fry it in the fat until just beginning to brown. Remove from the fat and add the onion. When tender add the flour and cook a little. Then add the stock, wine, herbs, and seasoning. When blended add the potatoes and bacon and simmer gently until the potatoes are tender. Sprinkle with chopped parsley and serve hot.

One portion. Carbohydrate 30 g. Calories 252.

353. Potato and Bacon Cakes

Quantities for 8 cakes. *Cooking time* 45 mins. *Temperature* 375 °F. No. 5.

1 lb. potatoes (4 medium)
1½–3 oz. bacon, chopped (1½–3 rashers)
6 level Tbs. chopped onion
2 tsp. meat or vegetable extract
½–1 level tsp. salt
Pinch of pepper
Milk and breadcrumbs for coating

Boil the potatoes in their jackets. Skin and mash. Heat the bacon until the fat runs, add onion, and fry both until golden brown. Add to the potatoes together with the extract and seasoning. Form into 8 cakes. Brush with milk and dip in crumbs. Bake in a moderate oven until firm.

1 *cake.* Carbohydrate 12 g. Calories 96.

354. Potatoes and Carrots

Mix equal quantities of mashed or sieved freshly boiled potatoes and carrots. Season with salt and pepper. The mixture may also be creamed as in recipe No. 349, put in small heaps on a baking tray and browned in the oven, or a stiff mixture may be rolled in balls and browned under the grill.

CAUTION. Use freshly cooked potato and finish and serve the dish as quickly as possible or the flavour and vitamin content will be poor.

355. Potato Croquettes

Quantities for 8 or more croquettes. *Cooking time* Fried 2–3 mins. Grilled 10 mins. Baked 15–20 mins. *Temperature* 450 °F. Nos. 7–8.

1 lb. potatoes (4 medium)
2 Tbs. milk
1 level tsp. salt
¼ level tsp. pepper
2 level Tbs. chopped parsley
1 tsp. onion juice or use onion powder
¼ level tsp. ground mace

Coating
1 beaten egg
Dry breadcrumbs

Boil the potatoes, strain, and mash with the milk, seasoning, parsley and onion, and mace. Leave the mixture to stand in a cool place before shaping into rissoles or croquettes. Dip in egg and then in crumbs and either fry in deep fat or oil or grill or bake.

1 *croquette* (grilled or baked). Carbohydrate 12 g. Calories 65.

356. Roast Potatoes with Oil

Quantities for 4. *Cooking time* 1–1¼ hrs. *Temperature* 400 °F. No. 6.

Allow 6 Tbs. oil to 1½ lb. potatoes. They are best cooked separately from the meat. Peel and dry the potatoes. Heat the oil and add the potatoes, turning to coat well. Put in a part of the oven which browns well and turn the potatoes once at about half time. Sprinkle with salt and serve.

357. Gnocchi

Quantities for 4. *Cooking time* 45 mins.

1 lb. potatoes (4 medium)	½ pt. (1 c.) tomato sauce (No. 106 or 108)
5 oz. (1 level c.) plain flour	1½–2 oz. (½ c.) grated Parmesan cheese
½ level tsp. salt	

Peel and boil the potatoes. Mash thoroughly or sieve. Add salt and the flour gradually, kneading to a smooth dough. Divide into 4 pieces and roll each to a long sausage about ¾ in. thick. Cut in ¾-in. pieces, dip in flour, and drop into fast-boiling salted water (1 level Tbs. salt to 1 qt water). Boil hard for 10 mins., drain in colander, and serve on a hot dish with the tomato sauce poured over. The cheese is served separately.

One portion. Carbohydrate 48 g. Calories 283.

358. Cooking Tomatoes

To prevent fried tomatoes from becoming greasy and indigestible, be careful not to overcook them. Halved tomatoes should have the cut side dipped in seasoned flour, to form a sealing. Grilled or baked tomatoes are best for most diets. Cook small ones whole, halve the others. No fat is required. Grilling takes about 10–15 mins. and baking in a moderate oven about 20 mins.

To skin tomatoes. Plunge in boiling water for a minute or two and then in cold water when the skins should peel off quite easily. Very ripe tomatoes will skin without this treatment.

359. Tomatoes Concassé

Is a useful way of preparing fresh tomatoes for garnishing when skins and seeds must be omitted from the diet. Skin the tomatoes as above, cut in half, and remove the seeds with a small spoon. Chop the flesh with a sharp knife. Use as a garnish.

360. Tomato Purées and Paste

Tomato purées are made by sieving cooked or raw ripe tomatoes or by pulping in an electric blender. With the latter method it may be necessary to strain to remove the seeds. Concentrated purée or tomato paste has been boiled to reduce it to a thick pulp and then canned or put in tubes. Used undiluted, it gives a richer tomato taste to sauces, soups, etc., than ordinary purée.

361. Tomato Flan

Quantities for 4. *Cooking time* about ½ hr. *Temperature* 450 °F. No. 8.

Pastry
4 oz. (¾ c.) flour
2 oz. (4 level Tbs.) fat

Filling
1 oz. (2 level Tbs.) fat
4 oz. onion, peeled, and chopped finely (1 medium)
12 oz. tomatoes, skinned and sliced (6 medium)
5 oz. peeled and sliced cucumber (½ small one)
2 tsp. chopped fresh herbs *or* ½ tsp. dried herbs
Salt and pepper
1 oz. grated cheese (4 level Tbs.)
Chopped parsley

Make the pastry and roll to line a 7-in. flan ring or sandwich tin. Bake 'blind' for 15–20 mins. and keep hot. Meanwhile heat the fat and fry the onions until they are almost cooked, add tomatoes and cucumber and continue cooking to give a soft mixture. Add herbs, seasoning, and cheese and pour into the hot pastry case. Decorate with chopped parsley and serve hot.

One portion. Carbohydrate 26 g. Calories 350.

362. Tomato Jelly (*low-fat*)

Quantities for 4

2 level Tbs. gelatine
8 Tbs. boiling water
1 pt (2 c.) tomato juice
Celery salt to taste
Pinch sugar
Pinch pepper
Paprika pepper

Dissolve the gelatine in the boiling water and mix all the ingredients together. Seasoning to taste. Pour into a mould to set. Unmould and serve with cold meat or salad.

Variations (*low-sodium*). Omit the celery salt and use salt-free tomato juice. Add a little Dietade tomato sauce if liked for extra flavour.

One portion. Carbohydrate 9 g. Calories 36.

363. Tomatoes à la Provence

Quantities for 4. *Cooking time* 20 mins. *Temperature* 375 °F. No. 5.

1¼ lb. tomatoes (10 medium)
Salt, pepper
Sugar
1 oz. (4 level Tbs.) fresh breadcrumbs
1 oz. (4 level Tbs.) grated cheese
1 finely chopped onion
2 Tbs. chopped parsley

Cut the tomatoes in half and put in a single layer in a flat dish, sprinkle with salt and pepper and a pinch of sugar. Mix the breadcrumbs and cheese and sprinkle over. Add the onion. Bake in a moderate oven until tender and serve sprinkled with the chopped parsley.

One portion. Carbohydrate 10 g. Calories 25.

364. Stuffed Tomatoes

Quantities for 4. *Cooking time* 15–20 mins. *Temperature* 400 °F. No. 6.

8 medium-sized tomatoes (1 lb.)
8 oz. (1 c.) cooked minced meat
4 Tbs. gravy or brown sauce (No. 96) *or* stock
4 level Tbs. fresh breadcrumbs
Salt to taste
1 Tbs. chopped parsley

Wash and dry the tomatoes. Cut a slice off the end away from the stem and, using the handle of a teaspoon, scoop out the pulp into a small basin. Remove all fat and gristle from the meat and mince it. Mix all ingredients with the tomato pulp and use to stuff the tomato shells. Replace the slice as a lid, put in a baking dish and cook in a moderate oven until heated through and the tomatoes tender, but be careful not to overcook. Serve hot.

Variations. 1. *Gluten-free diet.* Use gluten-free breadcrumbs and 1 Tbs. of the stock to moisten. 2. Instead of the meat mixture use 1 oz. breadcrumbs, 2 oz. chopped mushrooms, 1 oz. finely chopped onion, chopped parsley, and salt and pepper to taste.

One portion. Carbohydrate 7 g. Calories 40.

365. Salad Suggestions

Cauliflower, raw or lightly cooked sprigs, with chopped walnuts.

Cauliflower with chopped mint or orange segments.

Chopped celery and raisins.

Potato and cucumber with chives.

Lightly cooked cauliflower sprigs with parsley and chives and French dressing.

Pineapple cubes and grated raw carrot.

Cooked peas and carrots with raw celery.

Raw diced apples, chopped celery, shredded cabbage heart, and a little mint.

Shredded red cabbage and red dessert apple.

Shredded pineapple, red cabbage, and parsley.

Endive, beetroot, and watercress.

Shredded cabbage, grated raw carrot, chopped celery, and sweet peppers.

Grapefruit, orange, and watercress.

Chopped apple, diced celery, and shredded carrot.

Shredded cabbage heart with pineapple and chopped walnuts.

Chicory and diced tomato.

366. American Tomato and Egg Salad

Quantities for 4

1 lb. tomatoes, sliced (8 medium)
4 hard-boiled eggs, sliced
French dressing
4 gherkins, chopped
1 oz. watercress ($\frac{1}{4}$ bunch)

Arrange the tomatoes and eggs in overlapping layers in a serving dish. Sprinkle over the dressing and the chopped gherkins. Garnish with watercress.

One portion. Carbohydrate 5 g. Calories 341.

367. Boiled Beef Salad

Quantities for 4

6 oz. sliced cold boiled beef
8 oz. cold boiled waxy or new potatoes, fresh or canned (4 medium)
2 hard-boiled eggs, sliced
Chopped chives or parsley
French dressing

Arrange slices of beef in a flat dish. Surround with slices of potato and egg. Sprinkle with chives or parsley and French dressing.

One portion. Carbohydrate 22 g. Calories 718.

368. Beef and Lettuce Salad with Mustard Sauce

Quantities for 4. *Cooking time* 10 mins.

½ oz. (1 level Tbs.) butter or margarine
1 Tbs. finely chopped onion
½ level Tbs. plain flour
1 level tsp. dry mustard
Pinch salt
Pinch pepper
⅛ pt (5 Tbs.) stock
1 tsp. Worcester sauce
1 Tbs. vinegar
4 oz. corned beef
1 small lettuce *or* other salad vegetables and a few cooked peas to garnish

Fry the onion in the butter or margarine. Add flour and mustard, mix, and cook for a few minutes. Add stock and stir until it boils. Boil for a few minutes. Add vinegar, chopped corned beef and seasonings, and leave to become cold. Line a bowl with the lettuce leaves or arrange on individual plates. Pile the filling in the centre. Garnish with the green peas.

One portion. Carbohydrate 3 g. Calories 200.

369. Savoury Banana Salad

Quantities for 4

1 lettuce
4 bananas
4 Tbs. salad dressing
4 tomatoes

Make a nest of lettuce in a salad bowl. Peel and slice the bananas and mix with the dressing at once. Pile in the centre of the lettuce and surround with sliced tomatoes.

One portion (without dressing). Carbohydrate 5 g. Calories 63.

370. Carrot and Apple Salad

Quantities for 4

1 lettuce
4 dessert apples
4 carrots
3 oz. (½ c.) raisins
Salad dressing to moisten

Grate the apples and carrots and mix with the stoned raisins. Mix with salad dressing and pile in a nest of lettuce leaves.

One portion (without dressing). Carbohydrate 27g. Calories 104.

371. Cauliflower and Anchovy

Boil cauliflower in small sprigs. Drain and cool. Dress with French dressing or mayonnaise and garnish with chopped parsley and anchovy fillets drained of oil.

372. Celery and Sprout Salad

Mix equal quantities of very finely sliced raw Brussels sprouts with finely chopped crisp celery. Moisten with any salad dressing and serve at once. Garnish with egg and/or slices of canned or cooked beetroot.

373. Chicken and Mushroom Salad

Quantities for 4

8 oz. (2 c.) cooked diced chicken
4 oz. cooked or canned mushrooms
8 oz. (1 c.) diced celery
Mayonnaise or salad dressing to moisten
Salt and pepper
1 lettuce

Cook the mushrooms in a little water till tender. Mix the ingredients together and serve in a nest of lettuce leaves.

One portion. Carbohydrate 1 g. Calories 127.

Variations. Instead of the chicken use shrimps, tunny fish, salmon, or turkey. (*Low-sodium diet.*) Use fresh mushrooms and omit the salt and use Dietade salad cream or home-made salt-free dressing, see Nos. 110 and 114.

374. Chicory Salad

Quantities for 4

- 8 oz. chicory (2 medium pieces)
- 3–4 oz. cooked beetroot (1 small)
- 1 oz. (3 level Tbs.) sultanas
- 1 box mustard and cress
- Salad dressing to moisten

Cut the chicory in ½-in. pieces and dice the beetroot. Mix the sultanas thoroughly with the dressing and then combine with the vegetables. Pile in the centre of a serving dish and then surround with the mustard and cress.

One portion. Carbohydrate 8 g. Calories 37.

375. Corned Beef Salad

Quantities for 4

- 12 oz. (3 c.) corned beef, diced
- 1 carrot, grated
- 4 oz. shredded cabbage heart or Brussels sprouts
- 2 oz. mixed sweet pickle *or* chutney
- ¼ pt (½ c.) French dressing
- 1 lettuce

Mix the beef, carrot, cabbage, and pickle with French dressing to moisten. Serve individual portions in a nest of lettuce leaves or on a bed of shredded lettuce.

One portion (without dressing). Carbohydrate 11 g. Calories 450.

376. Crab Salad

Quantities for 4

- 1 large crab
- 3 Tbs. vinegar
- 3 Tbs. oil
- ½ level tsp. salt
- 1 level tsp. mustard
- Few grains cayenne pepper
- 1 lettuce
- 4 tomatoes

Remove flesh, discard shell. Mix the seasonings with the oil and vinegar and mix with the crab. Wash and drain the lettuce. Wash the tomatoes. Make a nest of lettuce leaves on each plate, arrange the crab in this. Decorate with sliced tomatoes and serve at once.

One portion. Carbohydrate 2 g. Calories 182.

377. Cottage Cheese Salad (*low-fat*)

Arrange crisp lettuce leaves on a dish. Place a mound of skimmed milk cottage cheese in the centre and surround this with sections of grapefruit. Serve with lemon juice or one of the fatless dressings.

378. Tangerine or Orange and Cottage Cheese (*low-fat*)

Make as above but surround with sections of canned tangerines or fresh oranges and a few slices of tomato.

379. Stuffed Tomatoes with Skimmed Milk Cottage Cheese

Mix the cheese with a little vinegar or fatless dressing. Use this to stuff tomatoes. Serve on lettuce leaves. For other than low-fat diets, serve with mayonnaise or oil dressings.

380. Dutch Salad Bowl

Quantities for 4

- 1 cucumber, sliced
- 12 stuffed olives, sliced
- 8 oz. Dutch cheese, cubed
- French dressing
- 4 oz. watercress (1 bunch)

Combine the cucumber, olives, cheese, and dressing. Line a

salad bowl with the watercress and pile the mixture in the middle. If preferred, a mayonnaise or thick dressing may be substituted for the French dressing.

One portion (without dressing). Carbohydrate a trace. Calories 192.

381. Fish Salad (*low-fat*)

Quantities for 4

Mix 1 lb. cold, flaked fish with one of the fatless salad dressings, or with the fish cocktail sauce (No. 118). Serve on a bed of lettuce or with other salad vegetables. A small portion may be served as a first course in place of soup or fruit juice.

Variation. For other diets, use mayonnaise or French dressing to mix with the fish.

382. Grapefruit and Beetroot Salad

Quantities for 4

4 large grapefruit
4 medium beetroot
1 lettuce
French dressing

Peel and slice or segment the grapefruit. Skin and slice the beetroot. Line a serving dish with lettuce leaves. Arrange the grapefruit and beetroot alternately in it. Pour over the French dressing, which is nicer if made with some grapefruit juice instead of the vinegar.

One portion (without dressing). Carbohydrate 5 g. Calories 20.

383. Herring Salad

Quantities for 4

2 salt or 2 fresh herrings
8 Tbs. vinegar
4 Tbs. water
2 level tsp. sugar
Pepper
Salt if needed
1 lb. diced cooked potatoes (4 medium)
4 oz. chopped gherkins
8 oz. chopped apple (2 medium)
1 lb. (2 c.) chopped cooked beetroot
2 Tbs. chopped onion
1 hard-boiled egg
Chopped parsley

Clean the salt herrings, remove the heads, and soak the fish in cold water overnight. Drain, skin, fillet, and slice. Steam or grill the fresh herrings. Skin, fillet, and flake. Mix vinegar, water, sugar, pepper, and add all the other ingredients except the egg and parsley. Season to taste. Pack into a basin or mould. Unmould on to a serving dish and decorate with egg and parsley.

One portion. Carbohydrate 41 g. Calories 197.

384. Ham Roll Salad

Spread thin slices of cold cooked ham with seasoned cottage cheese or a mild cheese sandwich spread. Roll up loosely. Arrange on a nest of lettuce leaves or on a bed of other green salad. Garnish with a little thick mayonnaise or serve any salad dressing separately.

385. Leeks Vinaigrette

Quantities for 4. *Cooking time* 15–20 mins.

Salt and pepper
1½ lb. leeks, halved
¼ level tsp. made mustard
2 Tbs. oil
1 Tbs. vinegar
½ level tsp. each of finely chopped gherkins, shallots, and parsley

Wash the leeks and boil in a little salted water until tender. Drain and cool. Mix the remaining ingredients and pour over the leeks. Serve cold.

One portion. Carbohydrate 7 g. Calories 69.

386. Nut Salad with Peas

Quantities for 4

2 oz. lettuce (1 small)
2 oz. (⅓ c.) shelled almonds blanched
2 oz. shelled walnuts
2 oz. Brazil nuts
6 oz. (¾ c.) peas, cooked
4 oz. (¼ c.) celery, chopped
1 oz. watercress (¼ bunch)
French dressing made with lemon juice

Chop the nuts finely and toss in French dressing. Arrange the lettuce leaves around the dish and pile the nuts and peas in the centre. Decorate with celery and watercress.

One portion (without dressing). Carbohydrate 6 g. Calories 281.

Variation. Use nuts of one kind only.

387. Orange Salad (*To serve with cold lamb, duck, etc.*)

Quantities for 4

4 oranges	1 Tbs. vinegar
Chopped tarragon and chervil	2 tsp. lemon juice
2 Tbs. oil	Watercress or lettuce

Peel the oranges and remove the pith. Slice thinly, removing all pips. Sprinkle with the chopped herbs. Mix oil, vinegar, and lemon juice and pour over the oranges. Leave to stand for a while. Surround with watercress or lettuce.

One portion. Carbohydrate 8 g. Calories 100.

388. Parisian Salad

Quantities for 4

8 oz. cold cooked veal	4 tomatoes, sliced
2 hard-boiled eggs, sliced	French dressing
4 boiled potatoes, diced	1 small lettuce or a few leaves
2 small onions, parboiled and chopped	2 tsp. chopped parsley

Cut the meat in thin strips. Mix meat, potatoes, onions, eggs, and tomatoes. Combine with the dressing. Add the lettuce torn roughly or left whole if the leaves are small. Sprinkle with parsley and serve.

One portion (without dressing). Carbohydrate 26 g. Calories 288.

389. Pineapple and Lettuce Salad

Quantities for 4

4 large lettuce leaves	1 Tbs. salad dressing
4 rings pineapple	1 oz. watercress to garnish ($\frac{1}{4}$ bunch)
$\frac{1}{4}$ medium cucumber	

Wash, drain, and dry the lettuce leaves. Put one on each plate, put a pineapple ring on each and section it. Chop the cucumber and mix with salad dressing. Pile on the centre of the pineapple, and decorate with watercress.

One portion (without dressing). Carbohydrate 10 g. Calories 39.

390. Potato Salad

Quantities for 4

- 1½ lb. potatoes, new or a waxy kind (6 medium)
- 1 level Tbs. finely chopped onion
- ¼ pt (½ c.) French dressing
- 1 level Tbs. chopped mint, parsley, or other green herbs

Scrub potatoes and boil them in their jackets. While they are still warm, peel them, and cut in neat dice. Mix with the onion and dressing and leave to become cold. Add the chopped herbs. If new or waxy potatoes are not available it is advisable to leave the potatoes to become quite cold before peeling and dicing and take great care not to over-cook them in the first place.

One portion (without dressing). Carbohydrate 27 g. Calories 114.

391. Swiss Salad

Quantities for 4

- 8 oz. (2 c.) diced cooked chicken
- 8 oz. (1 c.) diced cucumber
- 4 oz. (1 c.) chopped walnuts
- 8 oz. (1 c.) cooked or canned green peas
- Salad dressing
- 1 lettuce

Mix the chicken, cucumber, walnuts, and green peas with enough salad dressing to moisten. Serve in a nest of lettuce leaves.

One portion (without dressing). Carbohydrate 7 g. Calories 309.

392. Tomato and Sweet Pepper Salad

Quantities for 4

8 oz. tomatoes (4 medium)
2 canned or cooked sweet red peppers
1 small onion, chopped
½ level tsp. salt
Pinch pepper
½ Tbs. wine vinegar
1 Tbs. olive oil
1 Tbs. chopped parsley

Slice the tomatoes. Remove peel and seeds from the peppers and slice them. Put in a dish with the tomatoes and the onions. Mix seasoning, vinegar, and oil and pour over; sprinkle with chopped parsley.

One portion. Carbohydrate 3 g. Calories 49.

393. Tomato Salad

Quantities for 4

1 lb. firm, ripe tomatoes (8 medium)
3 Tbs. French dressing
¼ level tsp. sugar
1 level Tbs. chopped parsley or tarragon

Wash, dry, and slice the tomatoes. Arrange in overlapping rows in a shallow dish. Sprinkle with sugar and then with the French dressing. Sprinkle the herbs on top and serve at once.

One portion (without dressing). Carbohydrate 3 g. Calories 16.

394. Waldorf Salad

Quantities for 4

4 red apples
16 lettuce leaves
4 sticks chopped celery
4 Tbs. chopped walnuts
8 Tbs. salad dressing

Core the apple but leave the skin on. Cut in small dice. Mix all ingredients together, keeping a little red apple for garnishing. Put the mixture in a nest of lettuce leaves and decorate with the pieces of apple.

One portion (without dressing). Carbohydrate 16 g. Calories 136.

FRUIT PUDDINGS

395. Fruit Cocktails

These are mixtures of fruit served in sundae glasses or large wineglasses as a first course.

They should not be too sweet, and may consist of fresh, canned, or frozen fruit. They may contain liqueur or other alcohol, but not necessarily, and they may also have some water ice for variation. The fruit should be cut small and mixed well with any flavourings used. A little lemon juice improves most of them.

Suggested Mixtures

Grapefruit and orange
Grapes, orange, and pineapple
Orange, melon, and grapes
Grapes, banana, and strawberry
Grapefruit, strawberries, and raspberries
Orange and crystallized ginger
Melon, lemon, or orange juice
Orange and cider

Garnishes

Small sprigs of mint
Glacé or Maraschino cherries

396. Fruit Fools

Quantities for 4. *Cooking time* ½ hr

½ pt (1 c.) thick fruit purée from raw or cooked fruit
Sugar to taste
Lemon or orange juice or spices or other flavouring to taste
¼ pt (½ c.) chilled evaporated milk (No. 137), or ½ pt (1 c.) whipping cream, *or* ¼ pt custard plus ¼ pt whipping cream

Sweeten the fruit purée and flavour to taste. Whip the evaporated milk or cream and fold in the purée. Pour into individual glasses and chill. Garnish to taste.

Variations (*low-sodium diet*). Use custard made with Edosol milk and double cream or use double cream only.

397. Fruit Juice Custard

Quantities for 4. *Cooking time* 10–15 mins.

1 level tsp. arrowroot
¾ pt (1½ c.) fruit juice (orange, grapefruit, pineapple)
3 egg yolks
Sugar if necessary, or sugar substitute for low carbohydrate diets

Mix arrowroot with a little cold juice. Add egg yolks and mix. Add the rest of the juice and put in a pan. Heat gently, stirring until it thickens slightly. Add sugar if needed. Remove from heat, cool a little, and pour into individual glass dishes. Cool and then chill. This is meant to be a fairly thin custard. More arrowroot may be used if liked thicker. Serve with biscuits, e.g. langue de chat, made with the egg whites.

One portion (orange juice). Carbohydrate 12 g. Calories 120.

398. Fruit Meringue (*low-fat diet*)

Quantities for 4. *Cooking time* 20 mins. *Temperature* 350 °F. No. 3.

½ pt (1 c.) thick fruit purée
Sugar to taste
2 egg whites

Sweeten the purée to taste. Beat the egg whites until stiff. Fold half of this into the purée and put in a baking dish. Add 1 oz. sugar to the rest of the egg white and pile on top of the fruit. Bake in a slow oven until the meringue is set. Serve cold.

399. Fruit Mousses (*with gelatine*)

These are made with either well-flavoured fruit juices or a fairly thin fruit purée, with the addition of evaporated milk or single cream.

Quantities for 4

¼ oz. gelatine (½ level Tbs.)
2 Tbs. hot water
½ pt (1 c.) sweetened purée or juice
¼ pt (½ c.) evaporated milk or single cream
1 egg white

Dissolve the gelatine in a little hot water and add sweetened fruit juice or purée. Chill until just beginning to set and then add the evaporated milk or cream and whisk until light. (An electric beater is a help here.) Beat the egg white until stiff and fold into the fruit mixture.

Many people think it is an improvement to reserve ½ oz. sugar to beat into the egg white as with a meringue. Chill before serving.

Best fruits to use are raspberries, apricots, loganberries, strawberries, bananas (with lemon juice) or orange juice.

400. Fruit Mousses (*without gelatine*)

These all consist basically of a very thick fruit purée, sweetened to taste, which may be further thickened by heating with egg yolks. It is finished by folding in beaten egg whites only (lowest calorie and fat content), or by folding in yogurt or whipped cream, and then the egg whites. It is fairly soft and best poured into individual serving glasses before chilling and serving. The amount of fruit needed to give ½ pt thick purée is approximately 1 lb. fresh or frozen, ½ lb. dried, and with canned fruits it depends on the ratio of fruit to juice, that is, on the brand. Surplus juice in each case should be drained off before making the purée.

401. Plain Fruit Mousse

Quantities for 4

½ pt (1 c.) very thick purée sweetened to taste (saccharin, Saxin, or Sweetex makes it low-calorie, low-carbohydrate)
2 eggs

Method as in No. 400.

402. Fruit Mousse with Cream

Quantities for 4

½ pt (1 c.) very thick purée, sweetened to taste (saccharin, Saxin, or Sweetex will make it low-carbohydrate but not low-calorie)
1 egg
¼ pt (½ c.) cream, whipped

Method as in No. 400.

403. Raspberry and Yogurt

Quantities for 3–4

Use ½ lb. raspberries and 2 oz. (4 level Tbs.) sugar to make the sweetened purée. Chill and fold in one jar yogurt, approximately ¼ pt (½ c.), and then one egg white, beaten. Use another ½ lb. raspberries for decoration.

One portion. Carbohydrate 23 g. Calories 108.

404. Apple Mousse (*sharp and refreshing flavour*)

Quantities for 4

1 lb. apples (4 medium) to make the purée, sweetened with 2 Tbs. redcurrant jelly melted in the hot fruit.

Fold in one beaten egg white. Sprinkle top with ground cinnamon or nutmeg and chill.

One portion. Carbohydrate 18 g. Calories 70.

405. Fruit Purée Dessert

Quantities for 4

1 lb. fruit
Sugar to taste
1 oz. flour or arrowroot or fine semolina or ground rice or custard powder (3 level Tbs.)
Pinch of salt
Flavouring, lemon, or spices
½ oz. (1 level Tbs.) butter or margarine
Single cream

Stew the fruit, if possible without adding any water. Sieve fruit and make up to 1 pt with water. Sweeten to taste. Blend the cornflour or alternative, with a little cold water. Heat the fruit purée and pour on to the blended mixture. Return to the pan and stir until it thickens. Cook for a few minutes. Flavour to taste and add the butter or margarine. Pour into individual serving dishes and sprinkle the top with caster sugar. Leave to become cold. Run a little single cream on top and serve.

406. Fruit Salad with Cider

Any fresh or frozen fruit.
Syrup proportions. Make enough to cover the fruit.

2 oz. honey (2 level Tbs.)
⅛ pt (5 Tbs.) water
⅛ pt (5 Tbs.) cider

Mix, pour over the fruit, and leave to stand some hours.

Full syrup recipe. Carbohydrate 46 g. Calories 194.

407. Fruit Soufflé

Quantities for 4. *Cooking time* 20 mins. *Temperature* 375 °F. No. 5.

2 egg whites
Pinch of salt
1 oz. sugar (2 level Tbs.)
½ pt (1 c.) thick fruit purée
½ level tsp. grated lemon rind or juice

Beat the egg whites and salt until stiff. Beat in the sugar. Fold in the fruit purée and lemon rind or juice. Pour into a baking dish and cook in a moderate oven until risen and lightly set. Serve at once with cream or a fruit sauce (No. 142), or with a piece of cake or biscuit.

408. Fruit Whip (*low-fat*)

Quantities for 4

1 oz. instant dried skimmed milk powder (2 heaped Tbs.)
⅛ pt (5 Tbs.) cold water
Juice of 1 lemon
½ pt (1 c.) thick fruit purée
Sugar to taste
Flavouring (see below)

Combine the dried skimmed milk powder and cold water and beat until smooth. Refrigerate or chill for 1 hr. Add lemon juice and beat until like whipped cream. Fold in the purée sweetened to taste and add flavourings, for example: cinnamon, nutmeg, or ginger with apple, almond essence with apricot, or cinnamon or grated orange rind with plums or prunes.

Variations. In low-carbohydrate diets use sugar substitute and fresh fruit purée.

409. Fruit Whip

Quantities for 4

- ¼ pt (½ c.) evaporated milk
- 2 Tbs. lemon juice
- ½ pt (1 c.) thick sweetened fruit purée or mashed ripe fruit

Chill the milk in the freezing tray of the refrigerator and chill the mixing bowl. Alternatively, prepare the milk for whipping as described in No. 137. Whip the milk, add strained lemon juice and the fruit. Chill until ready to serve.

Variations. 1. Vary the flavour by adding, a little grated orange or lemon zest, a pinch of mixed spice, nutmeg, or cinnamon, or a little rum or liqueur. 2. Use whipping cream instead of the evaporated milk. This will give a higher fat and calorie content, but less protein. 3. *Low-fat diet.* Instead of evaporated milk, use machine-sweetened condensed milk and do not sweeten the fruit pulp. Acid fruits will be found best for this, for example plums, damsons, apples, or loganberries.

410. Apple Crumble

Quantities for 4. *Cooking time* 1½ hrs. *Temperature* 350 °F. No. 3.

- 1 lb. cooking apples (4 med.)
- ¼ level tsp. ground cinnamon
- ⅛ pt (5 Tbs.) water
- 3 oz. (⅔ c.) flour
- 2 oz. (¼ c.) sugar
- 1 oz. (2 level Tbs.) butter

Peel and core apples and slice finely. Put in baking dish and sprinkle with cinnamon. Add the water. Mix flour and sugar and rub in the fat until it looks like fine crumbs. Sprinkle this on top of the fruit. Bake in a slow to moderate oven until golden brown and the apples are cooked.

One portion. Carbohydrate 42 g. Calories 230.

Variations. 1. Make with rhubarb, berries, or plums. More sugar will be needed for sour fruit. 2. For high-fibre diets use wholemeal flour or rolled oats or substitute some wheatgerm for some of the flour. 3. *Low-sodium diet.* Use salt-free butter.

411. Cinnamon Apples

Quantities for 4

Stew cooking apples to a pulp with very little water. Sieve if necessary. Sweeten to taste and add powdered cinnamon in the proportions of $\frac{1}{2}$ level tsp. to 1 lb. apples (4 medium) and 2–4 oz. ($\frac{1}{4}$–$\frac{1}{2}$ c.) sugar. Serve cold in individual dishes. If allowed in the diet, serve a biscuit, cake, or cream with it.

One portion. Carbohydrate 25–40 g. Calories 100–150.

Variation (low-carbohydrate diet). Sweeten with saccharin and serve with cream.

One portion. Carbohydrate 11 g. Calories 40.

412. Jellied Apples

Quantities for 4. *Cooking time* about $\frac{1}{2}$ hr

- 1 lb. cooking apples (4 medium)
- 1 Tbs. lemon juice
- 4 oz. ($\frac{1}{2}$ c.) sugar
- 4 oz. (4 level Tbs.) redcurrant jelly

Peel and core the apples. Put peel and core into a saucepan with the apples and water to half cover. Add lemon juice and sugar and put on a tightly fitting lid. Poach gently until just tender but still whole. Lift out the apple and strain the liquid. Return liquid to pan with the jelly and boil rapidly until thick and syrupy. Pour over the apples and leave until cold.

One portion. Carbohydrate 60 g. Calories 227.

413. Apple Snow

Quantities for 4. *Cooking time* 1 hr. *Temperature* 400 °F. No. 6.

- 1 lb. cooking apples (4 medium)
- 1 oz. sugar (2 level Tbs.) or to taste
- Juice of one lemon
- 2 egg whites
- Custard sauce (No. 139) using egg yolks

Wash the apples and bake until tender or slice and boil unpeeled, adding only enough water to prevent them burning. The resulting pulp must be very thick. Sieve and keep hot. Add the sugar and lemon juice. Beat the egg white. Put basin over a pan of boiling water, add the apple pulp, and whisk for 4–5 mins. to cook the egg. Cool and then chill. Serve with the hot egg custard sauce (No. 139), made with the egg yolks.

One portion (without the sauce). Carbohydrate 19 g. Calories 75.

Variation. For low-carbohydrate, low-calorie diets the sugar may be replaced by sugar substitute, when the carbohydrate values become 9 g., calories 37.

414. Baked Stuffed Apples

Cooking time 40–50 mins. *Temperature* 400 °F. No. 6.

For stuffings use any of the following: dates, honey and ground cloves, honey and ground cinnamon, brown sugar, raisins, chopped peel, jam mixed with chopped nuts. Core the apples and either peel or slit the skin in a ring round the top. Stuff and put in a baking dish. Add water and 1 level Tbs. sugar, treacle, syrup, or honey for each apple, and ¼ in. water or cider in the baking dish. Bake in a moderate oven until the fruit is tender, basting occasionally. Test with a fine skewer to see if done in the middle. Serve hot or cold.

415. Stuffed Stewed Apples

Quantities for 4

Peel and core 4 small apples and cook them in syrup (½ pt water and 4 oz. sugar) in a saucepan, turning them occasionally and taking care not to over-cook or break them. Place in a serving dish and fill the centres with red jam mixed with dried fruit. Boil the syrup to thicken it, and pour round the apples. Serve cold. If the diet allows, cream or custard may be added.

416. Swedish Apple Cake

Quantities for 4. *Cooking time* 35 mins. *Temperature* 375 °F. No. 5.

- 1½ lb. apples (6 medium)
- 4 oz. (½ c.) sugar
- 4 oz. (1⅓ c.) breadcrumbs
- ½ oz. (1 level Tbs.) margarine or butter
- 1½ oz. (3 level Tbs.) grated chocolate
- Custard sauce (No. 139) or single cream

Peel, core, and slice the apples and stew to a pulp with 2 oz. sugar and no water. Heat margarine or butter in frying pan, add breadcrumbs and rest of sugar, and fry until golden brown, stirring frequently. Grease a shallow 7-in. cake-tin or deep pie-plate. Put in a layer of crumbs, then apple, and repeat layers, finishing with crumbs. Bake ½ hr and leave to cool. Turn out on a large dish and sprinkle the chocolate on top. Cut in wedges to serve and hand the sauce or cream separately.

One portion (without sauce). Carbohydrate 63 g. Calories 285.

Variations (*low-sodium diet*). Use salt-free breadcrumbs and salt-free butter or margarine.

417. Baked Bananas

Quantities allow 1 per person. *Cooking time* 20 mins. *Temperature* 375 °F. No. 5.

Various methods. 1. They may be baked in their skins for a low-fat diet. First remove skin, squeeze lemon juice over the banana and then put back in skin carefully and bake in a moderate oven until tender. 2. Bake out of the skin with a little butter or margarine and lemon or add orange juice or other fruit juice and a little grated lemon or orange rind. 3. Bake as in 2. Add a little rum towards the end of cooking and set light to it just before serving (flambé).

One portion. Carbohydrate 16 g. Calories 66.

418. Baked Bananas and Prunes

Quantities for 4. *Cooking time* 20 mins. *Temperature* 375 °F. No. 5.

4 bananas
1 tsp. grated lemon rind
1 Tbs. lemon juice
10 oz. cooked or canned prunes (284 g.)

Peel bananas and cut in four lengthwise. Arrange in a shallow baking dish and sprinkle with the lemon rind and juice. Stone the other fruit and put on top of the bananas. Pour over enough prune juice barely to cover and bake in a moderate oven. Serve warm or chilled.

One portion. Carbohydrate 25 g. Calories 100.

419. Banana and Chocolate Cream

Quantities for 4

4 bananas
1 oz. caster sugar (2 level Tbs.)
¼ pt (½ c.) double cream
Vanilla
Juice of one lemon
2 oz. (4 level Tbs.) grated chocolate
Glacé cherries

Mash the bananas with a fork and add the sugar, cream, and vanilla to taste. Add lemon juice and mix well. Put in individual dishes and top with a layer of grated chocolate. Decorate with glacé cherries and serve cold, but do not put in the refrigerator.

One portion. Carbohydrate 32 g. Calories 336.

Variation (*gluten-free diet*). Use chocolate from list on page 70–1.

420. Banana Mould

Quantities for 4

1 level Tbs. gelatine
4 Tbs. hot water
4 ripe bananas (1 lb.)
1 Tbs. lemon juice
1 oz. sugar (2 level Tbs.)
½ pt (1 c.) single cream
⅛ pt (5 Tbs.) whipped cream to garnish

Dissolve gelatine in the hot water. Mash or sieve the peeled banana. Mix all ingredients thoroughly and pour into two wetted moulds. Leave to set. Meanwhile whip some cream and tint pale green. Use this to decorate the moulds when they have been turned out.

Alternative method. Dissolve gelatine as before. Put the whole, peeled banana and all the other ingredients into an electric blender and mix until smooth. Mould as before.

One portion. Carbohydrate 23 g. Calories 235.

421. Dried Fruit Compôte

8 oz. ($1\frac{1}{2}$ c.) dried apricots
1 pt (2 c.) water
4 oz. ($\frac{1}{2}$ c.) seedless raisins
Piece of lemon rind
1 apple

Wash apricots and soak with the water, overnight or for several hours. Add raisins and lemon and cook gently until tender. Peel and core the apple and cut into eighths. Lay the sections on top of the other fruit, cover the pan, and cook gently until the apple is tender. Dish carefully and serve hot or cold.

One portion. Carbohydrate 44 g. Calories 180.

Variation. Add some chopped canned pineapple to the cold compôte.

422. Parisian Sweet

4 oz. dried figs
4 oz. dates
4 oz. shelled walnuts or other nuts
Lemon juice
Icing sugar

Remove stalks from the figs and stones from the dates. Put all through a fine mincer and mix with lemon juice to taste. Knead on a board dredged with icing sugar. Roll and cut into small squares.

Total recipe. Carbohydrate 138 g. Calories 1148.

Variations. Any other mixtures of dried fruits may be used, including some peel and crystallized ginger.

423. Gooseberry and Banana Compôte

Quantities for 3

1 banana
1 orange
3 oz. canned or stewed gooseberries (85 g.)
3 oz. ($\frac{1}{2}$ c.) chopped dates
Lemon juice

Peel banana and slice into a serving dish. Divide the orange into sections, saving all the juice and removing pith and membrane. Mix banana and orange with the gooseberries and dates and moisten with orange and lemon juice and some syrup from the gooseberries if needed. Serve cold.

One portion. Carbohydrate 25 g. Calories 98.

424. Grapefruit and Prune Salad

Quantities for 4

- 2 grapefruit (12 oz.)
- 8 oz. cooked prunes (about 4 oz. raw) ($\frac{3}{4}$ c.)
- Juice of 2 oranges ($\frac{3}{4}$ c.)
- Sugar only if required

Peel the grapefruit, removing all skin and pith. Cut grapefruit in slices and put in serving dishes. Decorate slices with cooked, stoned prunes, and sprinkle with orange juice. Sugar may be sprinkled on the grapefruit or cooked with the prunes.

One portion (without sugar). Carbohydrate 36 g. Calories 149.

425. Grapefruit and Date Salad

Quantities for 4

- 2 large grapefruit
- 4 oz. ($\frac{2}{3}$ c.) dates, chopped
- 2 oz. ($\frac{1}{2}$ c.) chopped nuts

Peel the grapefruit and remove all pith and membrane. Cut it up small. Mix with the dates and sprinkle with the nuts. Serve cold with cream if allowed.

One portion (without cream). Carbohydrate 24 g. Calories 145.

426. Grilled Grapefruit

Quantities allow $\frac{1}{2}$ grapefruit per person. *Cooking time* 5–7 mins.

Prepare the fruit in the usual way for serving in its skin. Sprinkle with brown sugar (1 level Tbs. per portion). Place about $\frac{1}{4}$ oz. of butter over the hole in the centre. Grill gently until lightly browned. Serve hot.

One portion. Carbohydrate 18 g. Calories 125.

Variation (*low-calorie or low-carbohydrate diets*). Sprinkle with sherry or marsala instead of the brown sugar.

427. Grapes and Tangerines

Quantities for 4

The flesh of 1 lb. tangerines
8 oz. grapes
1 Tbs. lemon juice
¼ pt (½ c.) sweet or sour cream (optional)

Remove peel, pith, and membrane from the tangerines. Save all the juice. Cut grapes in half and remove the stones (and skins if necessary). Mix tangerine flesh and grapes in a serving dish. Mix tangerine juice with the lemon juice and pour over the fruit. Serve the cream separately.

One portion (without cream). Carbohydrate 15 g. Calories 62.

428. Honey, Apple, and Nut Salad

Quantities for 4

8 oz. dessert apples (diced) (4 medium)
4 oz. (⅔ c.) stoned dates, chopped
2 oz (½ c.) shelled walmuts, chopped
4 oz. (4 level Tbs.) honey
¼ pt (½ c.) water
2 Tbs. lemon juice

Mix the fruit and nuts. Dissolve honey in water, add lemon juice, and pour over the fruit. Serve cold.

One portion. Carbohydrate 47 g. Calories 256.

429. Mango Fool (*low-fat*)

Quantities for 4

1 lb. tin of mangoes
1 oz. instant dried skimmed milk powder (2 heaped Tbs.)
Grated nutmeg or ground cinnamon

Drain the fruit from the syrup and rub through a sieve. Beat in the dried skimmed milk using an electric blender or a rotary beater. Thin with the juice if desired. Pour into serving dishes and chill well. Sprinkle with the nutmeg or cinnamon.

430. Caramel Oranges

Quantities for 4. *Cooking time* 5 mins.

- 4 large oranges
- 1 oz. (2 level Tbs.) caster sugar
- Brandy or liqueur (optional)
- 6 Tbs. water
- 3 oz. granulated sugar (6 level Tbs.)
- Whipped cream and chopped nuts optional

Peel oranges, taking care to remove all the pith. Cut in slices. Arrange in layers in a fireproof serving dish. Sprinkle each layer with caster sugar and liqueur. Heat the 4 oz. granulated sugar with the water, stirring until dissolved, and then boil rapidly without stirring until it turns pale brown. Pour over the oranges and leave in a cold place several hours, when the caramel will gradually dissolve to form a syrup. Decorate with whipped cream and nuts if liked.

One portion (without cream and liqueur). Carbohydrate 41 g. Calories 160.

Variation. Make the caramel with only half the water, add the rest and dissolve to make a sauce to pour over the oranges. Serve as soon as cold.

431. Orange and Grapefruit Cup

Quantities for 4

- 1 grapefruit
- 3 oranges
- 1 lemon
- Caster sugar
- 3–4 cherries or grapes

Peel fruit and remove all pith. Slice thinly. Squeeze lemon juice and place fruit in alternate layers in serving glasses, sprinkling a little sugar between each layer. Pour the lemon juice over and garnish with a cherry or grape. Chill before serving.

Variation. For low-carbohydrate and low-calorie diets omit sugar or use sugar substitutes.

One portion (using sugar substitute, or no sugar). Carbohydrate 12 g. Calories 45.

432. Stuffed Oranges

Quantities for 4

4 large oranges
8 oz. white grapes

Choose oranges with a flat enough end to enable them to stand upright. Cut a slice off the other end and remove the pulp with a grapefruit knife or teaspoon for the last bits. Remove all pith and membrane and put the pulp, cut in small pieces, into a basin. Cut grapes in half and remove pips. Mix with the orange pulp and return to the prepared cases. Chill.

One portion. Carbohydrate 24 g. Calories 96.

433. Orange and Rhubarb Compôte

Quantities for 4. *Cooking time* 20–30 mins. *Temperature* 300–350 °F. Nos. 3–4.

1 lb. rhubarb
3 oz. sugar (6 level Tbs.)
2 oranges

Cut the rhubarb in inch-long pieces and put it in layers in a casserole with the sliced, peeled orange and the sugar. Cover and bake in a slow to moderate oven until the rhubarb is tender. Serve hot or cold with custard or cream, if desired.

One portion (without cream or custard). Carbohydrate 29 g. Calories 116.

434. Pears in Red Wine Sauce

Quantities for 4. *Cooking time* depends on the pears

4 pears (1 lb.)
$\frac{1}{4}$ pt ($\frac{1}{2}$ c.) water
2 oz. ($\frac{1}{4}$ c.) sugar
$\frac{1}{4}$ pt ($\frac{1}{2}$ c.) red wine
Strip of lemon rind
Pinch of ground cinnamon
1 level Tbs. arrowroot or potato starch ($\frac{1}{3}$ oz.)

Peel, halve, and core the pears. Boil the water, sugar, wine, lemon, and cinnamon together until it forms a thin syrup. Poach the pears in it until they are just tender but not broken. Remove pears and thicken the liquid with the arrowroot blended with a little cold water. Serve cold.

One portion. Carbohydrate 26 g. Calories 124.

435. Prunes in Cider

Quantities for 4. *Cooking time* ½ hr

8 oz. (1½ c.) prunes
½ pt (1 c.) water
2 oz. sugar (4 level Tbs.)
3 pieces preserved ginger, chopped
⅛ pt (5 Tbs.) cider
Cream

Soak the prunes overnight in the water. Drain and add sugar to the liquid. Boil until dissolved. Add prunes, ginger, and cider, and simmer ½ hr. Serve cold with cream.

One portion (without cream). Carbohydrate 40 g. Calories 153.

436. Pineapple and Orange Mould (*low-protein*)

Quantities for 6. *Cooking time* 10 mins.

1 large tin pineapple (1 lb.)
2 oranges
1½ oz. arrowroot (4½ level Tbs.)
1 oz. sugar, optional (2 level Tbs.)
Cream

Drain the pineapple, keeping the syrup. Grate the yellow rind of the oranges finely. Squeeze the juice into a measure and make up to one pt with pineapple syrup. Blend arrowroot with a little of this and boil remainder with the orange rind. Pour into the arrowroot, return to the pan, cook and stir until it thickens. Add sugar if needed to sweeten it and add chopped pineapple. Pour into wetted mould and leave to set. Unmould and serve with more chopped pineapple rounds and with cream handed separately.

One portion (without cream). Carbohydrate 42 g. Calories 161.

437. Summer Pudding

Quantities for 4

1 lb. fresh or frozen fruit
1–2 oz. sugar (2–4 level Tbs.)
¼ pt (½ c.) water
4–6 oz. stale bread or cake (4–6 slices of a large loaf)

The best fruit to use are raspberries, loganberries, black-currants, or red plums. The amount of sugar will vary with the fruit and whether bread or cake is used. Stew fruit with the sugar and water until tender. Remove crusts and cut the bread or cake into ¼-in. thick slices. Cut enough pieces in fingers or triangles to line a 1-pt basin, reserving enough whole slices to give a lid. Half fill the lined basin with fruit, then a layer of the bread or cake, then the rest of the fruit, and finally a lid of bread or cake. Pour over the juice and cover with a plate or saucepan lid small enough to fit inside the basin. Put a weight on top and leave in a cold place for several hours. Unmould and serve with custard or cream.

Variation (low-sodium diet). Use salt-free bread.

OTHER PUDDINGS

438. Chocolate Mousse No. 1

Quantities for 4. *Cooking time* 10 mins.

4 oz. plain chocolate (132 g.)
4 Tbs. water
4 eggs
Vanilla essence to taste
1 Tbs. rum or brandy

Melt the chocolate and 3 Tbs. water in a pan over hot water or directly over a very gentle heat. Add the egg yolks beaten with another Tbs. of water until very light. Remove from the heat and add the flavouring. Beat the egg whites stiff and fold in. Pour into small glasses. Chill if possible for 12 hrs in a refrigerator.

One portion. Carbohydrate 15 g. Calories 263.

439. Chocolate Mousse No. 2 (*enriched*)

Quantities for 4. *Cooking time* 15 mins.

½ oz. cocoa (1½ level Tbs.)
1–2 oz. sugar (2–4 level Tbs.)
¼ pt (½ c.) water
2 eggs
2 oz. Complan (6 level Tbs.)
¼ oz. gelatine (½ level Tbs.)
2 Tbs. hot water
Pinch of salt
Vanilla
Cream (optional)

Blend cocoa and sugar in a small pan and mix in the water. Bring to the boil and cook for a few mins. Remove from the heat. Separate the whites and yolks of the egg. Beat the yolks and add to the cocoa mixture. Cook until it thickens without boiling. Remove from the heat and beat in the Complan. Dissolve gelatine in the hot water and add to the mixture. Add salt. Beat egg whites and fold the cocoa mixture into them. Add vanilla to taste. Pour into individual dishes and leave to set. If liked, garnish with whipped cream.

One portion (1 oz. sugar, no cream). Carbohydrate 21 g. Calories 221.

Variation. Omit the Complan and add 2 oz. of dried skimmed milk powder (5 level Tbs.) to the sugar and cocoa. Stir and watch carefully to see it doesn't catch. Proceed as before.

440. Baked Custard

Quantities for 4. *Cooking time* 1½ hrs (4 mins. pressure-cooking). *Temperature* 350 °F. No. 3.

1 pt (2 c.) milk	Pinch salt
3 eggs	Flavouring to taste
½ oz. sugar (1 level Tbs.)	Grated nutmeg (optional)

Heat the milk. Beat the eggs, salt, and sugar just enough to break up the eggs. Pour hot (not boiling) milk on to the eggs. Stir well and flavour to taste. Pour into an ovenproof dish and sprinkle the nutmeg on top.

To bake. Stand the dish of custard in a shallow pan of hot water which should keep hot but not boiling. To test for setting, slip the blade of a knife into the custard half-way between the centre and the side, and it should come out clean if the custard is done. The centre of the custard will finish cooking with the residual heat in the dish.

To pressure-cook. Cover the heatproof dish with a piece of aluminium foil or greaseproof paper. Place in the pressure cooker with ½ pt water. Bring to pressure (15 lb.), and cook

4 mins. exactly. Allow pressure to drop slowly before removing custard.

One portion. Carbohydrate 10 g. Calories 180.

Variations. 1. *Caramel custard.* Boil 2 oz. (4 level Tbs.) sugar in a small pan with 2 Tbs. water until toffee coloured. Dissolve this in the hot milk, and make the custard as above but leave out the sugar. 2. *Orange baked custard.* Add the finely grated rind of 1 orange to the custard and bake as before. Sprinkle the top thickly with brown sugar and place under a moderate grill to melt the sugar. Leave to become cold. Arrange some overlapping slices of canned mandarin oranges or fresh sliced oranges on top. Serve plain or with cream. 3. *Low-carbohydrate.* Use the basic recipe, omitting the sugar and using saccharin or Saxin instead. 4. *Low-sodium.* Use Edosol milk and 4–5 egg yolks.

441. Crème au Caramel

Quantities for 4. *Cooking time* 1 hr (or 4 mins. pressure-cooking). *Temperature* 350 °F. No. 3.

Caramel

2 oz. sugar (4 level Tbs.)
2 Tbs. water

Custard

4 eggs
½ oz. sugar (1 level Tbs.)
1 pt (2 c.) milk
Vanilla essence

Grease one large or 4 small moulds. Boil the sugar and water, stirring until the sugar dissolves. Then boil hard without stirring until it turns light brown. Pour quickly into the moulds. Beat eggs slightly and add sugar. Heat the milk and when hot (not boiling) pour on to the egg. Add vanilla to taste. Pour into the moulds and cover. Bake in a slow oven or in a pan of hot water in a moderate oven or cook in a saucepan with water half-way up the mould. In both cases the water should be kept just below boiling. In the pressure cooker use ½ pt water and time very carefully and exactly.

Turn out and serve hot, or leave in the moulds to cool. They may be stored in the refrigerator in their moulds.

One portion. Carbohydrate 26 g. Calories 257.

Coffee custard mould. Omit the caramel and add soluble coffee to the hot milk. Serve cold, decorated with whipped cream and chopped nuts.

442. Floating Island

Quantities for 4. *Cooking time* 20 mins.

- ¾ pt (1½ c.) milk
- 2 eggs
- 3 oz. sugar (6 level Tbs.)
- Pinch of salt
- Vanilla or sherry to flavour

Scald the milk in a wide saucepan. Separate the whites and yolks of the eggs. Beat the whites until stiff and fold in half the sugar. Divide in 8 spoonsful and poach for 2–3 mins. on top of the hot milk. Remove and put in the serving dishes. Mix the yolks with the remaining sugar, pour on hot milk, return to the pan, and cook gently without boiling until it thickens slightly or begins to coat the wooden stirrer. Flavour to taste. Pour round the egg white. Serve cold with a crisp biscuit.

One portion (without the biscuit). Carbohydrate 25 g. Calories 200.

443. Orange Custard (*low-fat*)

Quantities for 4. *Cooking time* 10 mins.

- 1 oz. custard powder (3 level Tbs.)
- 2 oz. sugar (4 level Tbs.)
- 1 pt (2 c.) skimmed milk
- Pinch of salt
- 1 level tsp. grated orange rind
- 2 oranges
- 4 oz. (4 level Tbs.) redcurrant jelly
- 2 Tbs. water

Make a custard sauce with the first five ingredients. Pour into serving dishes and sprinkle the tops with sugar to prevent a skin from forming. Leave to cool. Peel oranges, remove pith and pips and divide in segments. Arrange oranges on top of the custard. Melt the jelly and water together over a low heat and pour it over the oranges. Leave to cool.

One portion. Carbohydrate 57 g. Calories 248.

444. Snow Custard (*low-fat*)

Quantities for 4. *Cooking time* ¾–1 hr. *Temperature* 350 °F. No. 4.

1 pt (2 c.) skimmed milk
2 oz. (4 heaped Tbs.) instant dried milk powder
½ oz. (1 level Tbs.) sugar
4 egg whites
Pinch of salt
Vanilla essence

If fresh skimmed milk is not available use water and double the amount of milk powder. Warm the milk. Beat the egg whites and salt together until the egg is broken up but not frothy. Add sugar, milk and flavouring and pour into 4 small, greased dishes. Stand the dishes in a pan of hot water. Bake until set. Serve plain or with stewed or canned fruit or fresh fruit salad.

One portion. Carbohydrate 18 g. Calories 124.

445. Ice Cream (*gluten-free*)

Quantities for 4

½ pt (1 c.) whipping cream or 7-oz. (198 g.) tin chilled evaporated milk (see No. 137)
Flavouring, see Nos. 446–9.

Set the refrigerator at cold. Whip the cream or milk, add the chosen flavouring, and pour into two freezing trays. Freeze without stirring.

446. Chocolate Ice Cream (*see No. 445*)

Soften 2 oz. plain chocolate in a bowl over hot water. Add 2 Tbs. of the unbeaten cream or evaporated milk and 1 oz. sugar (2 level Tbs.). Stir and warm until the sugar is dissolved. Add to the whipped cream or milk and beat to blend well. Freeze, without stirring.

One portion. Carbohydrate 16–21 g. Calories 183–433.

447. Coffee Ice Cream (*see No. 445*)

Mix 1 level Tbs. powdered coffee (soluble) with 1 oz. sugar (2 level Tbs.) and 2 Tbs. of the unbeaten cream or milk. Add to the whipped mixture and freeze as before. For variety add 1 Tbs. rum before freezing.

One portion (without rum). Carbohydrate 9–14 g. Calories 107–358.

448. Coffee-Chocolate Ice Cream (*see No. 445*)

Soften 2 oz. plain chocolate in a bowl over hot water. Add a level Tbs. soluble coffee, 2 Tbs. of the unbeaten cream or milk, and ½ oz. sugar (1 level Tbs.). Warm until the sugar is dissolved and then add to the whipped mixture, beating to blend well. Freeze as before.

One portion. Carbohydrate 14–17 g. Calories 171–422.

449. Fruit Ice (*see No. 445*)

Replace half the cream or evaporated milk with a fruit purée, e.g. banana, strawberry, raspberry, cooked dried apricots, or blackcurrants. Add 1 oz. icing sugar (¼ c.) and a little finely grated lemon or orange rind (optional). Freeze as before.

450. Banana and Blackcurrant Sundae

Peel and slice 1 banana per person and dress with lemon juice. Pour blackcurrant syrup over a portion of vanilla ice cream or a mixture of strawberry and vanilla ice. Surround with the sliced banana and sprinkle with chopped nuts.

451. Peach Melba

Use fresh peaches if possible. Peel and cook gently in vanilla-flavoured syrup. Chill. Put a portion of vanilla ice cream in the serving dish. Rest one peach half on top and coat with 1–2 Tbs. fresh or frozen raspberry purée or sauce Melba (No. 146).

452. Meringue Glacé

Join two meringues together with vanilla or chocolate ice. Serve with fresh fruit purée or chopped fresh fruit.

453. Chocolate Ice Cream Cake

Sandwich 2 slices of sponge cake with a portion of vanilla ice cream. Pour chocolate sauce over and sprinkle with chopped nuts.

454. Frozen Vanilla Mousse (*gluten-free*)

Quantities for 4

½ pt (1 c.) whipping cream	½ tsp vanilla
1 oz. (¼ c.) sifted icing sugar	1 egg white

Set the refrigerator control at cold. Whip cream and add the sugar and vanilla. Beat the egg white stiff and fold into the cream. Freeze without stirring. Serve plain or as a basis for sundaes.

One portion. Carbohydrate 11 g. Calories 263.

455. Frozen Fruit Mousse (*gluten-free*)

Quantities for 4

1 level tsp. gelatine	3–4 oz. (6–8 level Tbs.) sugar
1 Tbs. hot water	½ pt (1 c.) cream or ⅓ pt (⅔ c.) evaporated milk
½ pt (1 c.) fruit purée	

Set the refrigerator control at cold. Dissolve the gelatine in the hot water. Add to the fruit and sugar and leave until cold. Beat well. Whip the cream or evaporated milk and fold it into the fruit mixture. Freeze without stirring. Best fruits to use are: raspberries, loganberries, strawberries, blackcurrants, damsons, apricots, peaches, pineapple, and rhubarb.

One portion. Carbohydrate 75 g. Calories 437.

456. Pineapple Sherbet (*low-fat, gluten-free*)

Quantities for 4

4 oz. (½ c.) granulated sugar	1 Tbs. lemon juice
½ pt (1 c.) water	2 Tbs. orange juice
½ level tsp. gelatine	
¼ pt (½ c.) crushed or chopped pineapple	

Set the refrigerator control at cold. Boil the sugar and water gently for 5 mins. Soak the gelatine in 1 Tbs. cold water. Add the hot sugar syrup and stir to dissolve the gelatine. Cool and add the pineapple, lemon, and orange juice. Freeze. When half frozen, fold in the stiffly beaten egg whites. Re-freeze.

One portion. Carbohydrate 25 g. Calories 133.

457. Lemon Water Ice (*low-fat, gluten-free*)

Quantities for 4

- 3 very thin strips lemon rind
- ¼ pt (½ c.) water
- 3 oz. (6 level Tbs.) sugar
- 2 oz. (2 level Tbs.) syrup or honey
- 1 level tsp. gelatine
- ⅛ pt (5 Tbs.) lemon juice

Set the refrigerator control at cold. Bring the lemon rind and water to the boil and strain into the sugar. Return to the pan and boil for 5 mins. Soak the gelatine in another ¼ pt cold water and add it to the hot lemon mixture together with the syrup or honey and lemon juice. Cool and then freeze until it is beginning to set round the edges. Stir thoroughly with a small whisk or fork and then re-freeze. Then set the control back to normal.

One portion. Carbohydrate 35 g. Calories 180.

458. Lemon Sherbet

When the above mixture is beginning to freeze round the edges, turn out into a cold basin and mix well. Fold in one stiffly beaten egg white, return to the tray, and freeze as before.

459. Other Water Ices

1½ c. of any unsweetened fruit juice may be substituted for the lemon and water in the two previous recipes. Juices with a fairly strong flavour are the best to use because freezing reduces the flavour.

460. Fruit Purée Ice or Sherbet (*low-fat, gluten-free*)

Quantities for 6

1–2 oz. (2–4 level Tbs.) sugar
⅛ pt (5 Tbs.) water
½ pt (1 c.) thick fruit purée
1 egg white
1–2 Tbs. lemon juice (optional)

Set the refrigerator control at cold. Dissolve the sugar in the water and boil for 2–3 mins. Cool and add to the purée. Put in the ice tray and freeze until it is beginning to set round the edges. Scrape out into a bowl. Beat until smooth and fold in the stiffly beaten egg white. Continue freezing. Turn the control back to normal to keep the ice in a suitable condition for serving.

One portion. Carbohydrate 23 g. Calories 90.

461. Coffee Creams (*gluten-free*)

Quantities for 4. *Cooking time* 10–15 mins.

2 eggs
1 oz. (2 level Tbs.) sugar
½ pt (1 c.) milk
¼ oz. (½ level Tbs.) gelatine
2 Tbs. hot water
Soluble coffee to taste
¼ pt (½ c.) evaporated milk or whipping cream
Whipped cream to decorate

Make a custard with the eggs, sugar, and milk (see No. 139). Dissolve the gelatine in the hot water and add to the custard slowly, together with soluble coffee to taste. Whip the evaporated milk or cream and fold into the other mixture. Pour into a mould and chill. Unmould and decorate with whipped cream.

One portion. Carbohydrate 15–23 g. Calories 165–255.

462. Coffee Spanish cream

Quantities for 4. *Cooking time* 15–20 mins.

1 level Tbs. soluble coffee
½ pt (1 c.) hot water
¼ pt (½ c.) milk
2 oz. (4 level Tbs.) sugar
¼ oz. (½ level Tbs.) gelatine
2 Tbs. hot water
Pinch of salt
3 large eggs
½ tsp. vanilla
Cream

Dissolve the coffee in the ½ pt hot water and put in a saucepan with the milk and half the sugar. Heat to boiling, stirring frequently. Separate the egg whites and yolks and beat the yolks with the rest of the sugar. Pour on the boiling coffee, return to the pan, and stir. Cook until it thickens slightly, without boiling. Add the gelatine dissolved in the 2 Tbs. hot water. Add the vanilla and salt. Beat the egg whites until stiff and fold them into the mixture. Pour into a mould and leave to set and then chill. Unmould and serve with single cream or garnish with whipped cream.

One portion (without the cream). Carbohydrate 15 g. Calories 180.

Variation. If sugar substitute is used the carbohydrate value then becomes 2 g.

463. Egg Jelly

Quantities for 4

½ oz. (1 level Tbs.) gelatine
1 pt (2 c.) water
Yellow peel of 2 lemons
3 oz. (6 level Tbs.) sugar
4 eggs
Juice of 2 lemons
2 Tbs. sherry *or* 1 Tbs. rum

Mix the gelatine, water, lemon rind, and sugar in a pan, and bring to the boil, stirring well. Remove from the heat, cover and infuse for 10 mins. Beat the eggs and lemon juice together slightly. Add the hot liquid, stir, and strain back into the pan. Stir over gentle heat continuously until it begins to thicken a little. Flavour to taste and pour into moulds. Cool and chill. Turn out and serve with cream or fruit salad or just plain.

One portion (without cream or fruit salad). Carbohydrate 23 g. Calories 160.

Variation (*low-carbohydrate diets*). Replace the sugar with sugar substitute, when the carbohydrate value will be 1 g., calories 76.

464. Home-made Jelly

These take only a few minutes longer to make than the packet variety and are usually more delicate in flavour and colour. It costs a little more to make your own, but the nutritive value (especially for vitamin C) is usually higher and this is important for a sick person. The usual proportions are: ½ oz. gelatine (1 level Tbs.) to 1 pt liquid, but it is best to follow the dircctions supplied with the brand of gelatine you are using. The usual method is to dissolve the gelatine in a little hot water or to heat it gently in a small portion of the fruit juice. Add the sugar and dissolve it, and then add the remaining liquid before pouring into the moulds. Fresh or canned fruit may be set in these jellies in the usual way, and the fruit juice from canned fruit used as part of the liquid and sugar in the recipe. Where the jellies are suitable for low-carbohydrate diets if sugar substitutes are used, this has been indicated.

465. Blackcurrant Jelly

Quantities for 4

¼ pt (½ c.) blackcurrant syrup	No extra sugar needed. Add
¾ pt (1½ c.) water	a little lemon juice if liked

Method as in No. 464. Unmould and serve with green grapes and decorate with cream.

One portion (jelly only). Carbohydrate 22 g. Calories 81.

466. Grapefruit Jelly

Use the canned juice and add extra sugar only if needed. Very refreshing without any. Make as No. 464. Alternatively, make in the same way as fresh orange jelly (No. 467). For low-carbohydrate and low-calorie diets use sugar substitute.

467. Fresh Orange or Lemon Jelly

For 1 pt jelly use ⅞ pt water and ⅛ pt juice. Infuse the thinly peeled rinds in the water for 5–10 mins., strain, and dissolve the recommended amount of gelatine in it. Add sugar and the juice. For low-carbohydrate and low-calorie diets use a sugar substitute. Use this jelly for setting fruits and for puddings such as Charlotte Russe (No. 509).

468. Coffee Jelly

Use soluble coffee to make the liquid into a strong coffee brew before adding the gelatine. Flavour with vanilla and add sugar or sugar substitute to taste. Serve with cream.

469. Golden Jelly

Quantities for 4

- ½ oz. (1 level Tbs.) gelatine
- Rinds of two lemons (yellow part only)
- 1 pt (2 c.) water
- 6 oz. (6 level Tbs.) golden syrup
- 4 Tbs. lemon juice

Make as in No. 467.

One portion. Carbohydrate 75 g. Calories 140.

470. Crème de Menthe

Make lemon jelly (No. 467), flavour with a very little peppermint essence but not enough to cover up the lemon flavour. Colour pale green. Pour into shallow dishes. Serve single cream or custard separately.

471. Port Wine Jelly

Quantities for 4

- Grated yellow rind of ½ lemon
- ½ pt (1 c.) water
- 1 oz. (2 level Tbs.) sugar
- 1 tsp. redcurrant jelly
- ¼ oz. (½ Tbs.) gelatine
- ¼ pt (½ c.) port wine
- Juice of ½ lemon

The lemon rind is simmered 5 mins. with the water and sugar, and then the redcurrant jelly dissolved in it. The gelatine and port wine are soaked together and then the hot mixture strained in and stirred to dissolve the gelatine. The strained lemon juice is added last.

One portion. Carbohydrate 11 g. Calories 68.

472. Milk Jelly

Make fruit juice jelly using only $\frac{3}{4}$ pt ($1\frac{1}{2}$ c.) juice. Cool and add $\frac{1}{4}$ pt ($\frac{1}{2}$ c.) undiluted evaporated milk.

Variations. 1. When on the point of setting, beat the jelly to make it light and fluffy. 2. Add chopped fresh or canned fruit.

473. Low-fat Milk Jelly

Beat in 1–2 oz. dried skimmed milk powder (2–4 heaped Tbs.) when the jelly is still warm.

474. Apricot Cream (*low-fat*)

To 1 pt lemon jelly add apricot purée made from the drained fruits of a 10-oz. (284 g) can. Beat in 1–2 oz. (2–4 heaped Tbs.) dried skimmed milk powder.

475. Custard Jelly Cream

$\frac{1}{2}$ pt (1 c.) fruit juice jelly plus $\frac{1}{2}$ pt (1 c.) custard powder sauce. Add to it $\frac{1}{4}$ pt ($\frac{1}{2}$ c.) whipped cream and fold into the jelly.

476. Cider Jelly

Quantities for 4

$\frac{1}{2}$ pt (1 c.) water
4 oz. ($\frac{1}{2}$ c.) sugar
1 oz. (3 level Tbs.) gelatine
$\frac{1}{2}$ pt (1 c.) dry cider
2 Tbs. lemon juice

Simmer sugar and water 20 mins. Dissolve the gelatine in it and add cider and lemon juice. Pour into moulds to set.

One portion. Carbohydrate 32 g. Calories 162.

Variations. 1. Use the jelly as a basis for setting fruit. 2. Omit sugar, to give: carbohydrate 1 g., calories 43.

477. Various Fruit and Jelly Combinations

1. Canned tangerine segments set in orange jelly.

2. Sliced ripe bananas in a lemon jelly.

3. $\frac{1}{2}$ pkt jelly, $\frac{1}{2}$ evaporated milk, or thin custard or fortified milk, see No. 1. The packet jelly should be made with only half the usual amount of water.

478. Lemon Snow

Quantities for 4

- The rind and juice of 1½ lemons
- 1½ oz. (3 level Tbs.) sugar
- ½ pt (1 c.) water
- ½ oz. gelatine (1 level Tbs.)
- 1 egg white
- Whipped cream

Peel off the yellow part of the lemon. Put in a small pan with the sugar and water. Bring to the boil and strain into the gelatine. Stir until dissolved and allow to cool and then chill until just beginning to set. Add the lemon juice and egg white and whisk until frothy. Pile into a glass dish and garnish with whipped cream, slightly tinted if desired.

One portion (without cream). Carbohydrate 12 g. Calories 60.

Variation. Sugar is replaced by sugar substitute and the carbohydrate value then becomes negligible. Calories 20 without the cream.

479. Norwegian Trifle (*gluten-free*)

Quantities for 4

- ¼ oz. gelatine (½ level Tbs.)
- ¼ pt (½ c.) water
- 2 eggs
- 2 oz. sugar (4 level Tbs.)
- ½ tsp. grated lemon rind
- 2 Tbs. lemon juice
- 2 oz. raspberry jam (2 level Tbs.)
- ¼ pt (½ c.) whipping cream

Dissolve the gelatine in half the water. Beat egg yolks with 1 oz. sugar, add the lemon rind and remaining water. Put this in a small pan over gentle heat, or in the top of a double boiler and cook, stirring frequently, until the mixture thickens a little. Add the dissolved gelatine and mix well. Remove from the heat and add the lemon juice. Whisk the egg whites. Add remaining sugar and beat until thick. Fold the lemon mixture into the egg whites and pour into serving dishes. Leave to set. Cover with a layer of raspberry jam and decorate with whipped cream.

One portion. Carbohydrate 25 g. Calories 309.

480. Junket

Quantities for 4. *Time to set* 20–30 mins.

1 pt (2 c.) milk
Pinch salt
½ oz. sugar (1 level Tbs.)
Rennet, junket powder, or tablets, according to the makers' instructions
Flavouring to taste

Heat the milk until just lukewarm (90 °F.). Pour into serving dishes and stir in the salt, sugar, and flavourings. When the sugar is dissolved add the rennet and leave in a warm place undisturbed until set.

One portion. Carbohydrate 11 g. Calories 109.

Variations. Chocolate. Mix 2 level Tbs. cocoa and 2 Tbs. boiling water and add this to the milk, then proceed as before. *Coffee.* Add soluble coffee or coffee essence to taste. *Coloured.* For children add a few drops of colouring. *Jam.* Spread 2 oz. thick red jam (2 level Tbs.) in the bottom of the dish. Mix the junket in another dish and pour on gently. *Rum or brandy.* Add 1–2 Tbs. of the spirit. Serve with whipped cream on the top. *Low-carbohydrate.* Use sugar substitute, when the carbohydrate value becomes 7 g.

481. Lemon Cream

Quantities for 4. *Cooking time* 10 mins.

2 lemons
1½ oz. (4½ level Tbs.) cornflour
1 pt (2 c.) water
2 eggs
Sugar
Whipped cream
Angelica

Wash and dry the lemons. Peel off the yellow part of the rind only. Blend the cornflour with a little of the cold water and put the rest of the water in a pan with the lemon rind. Infuse by bringing slowly to the boil. Strain on to the cornflour, mixing well, and return to the pan, stirring until it boils; boil for 3 mins. Beat the eggs and lemon juice together, add, and cook gently until thickened. Sweeten to taste, cool, and pour into glasses. Chill. Decorate with cream and angelica.

One portion (2 oz. sugar). Carbohydrate 27 g. Calories 140.

482. Chocolate Pie Crust

Quantities for 4

- 3 oz. semi-sweet biscuits (9 biscuits)
- ¾ oz. (1½ level Tbs.) butter
- 1 oz. golden syrup (1 level Tbs.)
- 1 oz. plain chocolate
- Vanilla

Crush the biscuits into fine crumbs. Cream the butter and syrup and melt the chocolate over hot water. Add chocolate to the creamed mixture together with the vanilla and then mix in the crumbs. Press into a deep 7-in. pie-plate, or flan ring placed on a serving dish, and chill thoroughly. Remove flan ring. Fill with a cooled pie filling such as lemon (No. 491) and chill again.

One portion. Carbohydrate 22 g. Calories 200.

483. Currant Patties (*high-fibre*)

Line patty tins with thin short pastry. Fill with currants and sugar in alternate layers, put in a small nob of butter or margarine and a little chopped mint, amount according to taste. Cover with pastry and bake in a hot oven for 10–15 mins. 450 °F. No. 8.

484. Fruit Squares (*high-fibre*)

Quantities for 9 squares. *Cooking time* 30 mins. *Temperature* 450 °F. No. 8.

Pastry

- 8 oz. (1½ level c.) S.R. flour
- ¼ level tsp. salt
- 4 oz. (½ c.) fat
- Water to mix

Filling

- 4 oz. (½ c.) sultanas
- 4 oz. (½ c.) seedless raisins
- 1 oz. (2 level Tbs.) chopped mixed peel
- 1 medium apple, grated (4 oz.)
- 1½ oz. (½ c.) wholemeal bread-crumbs
- 1 level tsp. mixed spice
- 5 oz. (5 level Tbs.) black treacle, melted

Make the pastry. Divide in two and roll half thinly to line a shallow tin. Soak the sultanas and raisins for a few minutes in boiling water, drain, and rinse. Add the rest of the ingredients and mix well. Spread this on the pastry. Cover with the other piece of pastry, brush with milk, and sprinkle with sugar. Bake until the pastry is lightly browned. Cut in squares and serve hot as a pudding or cold as a cake.

Each square. Carbohydrate 50 g. Calories 300.

485. Lemon Cheese Meringue

Quantities for 4. *Cooking time* 40–45 mins. *Temperature* 450 °F. No. 8. 350 °F. No. 3.

Pastry
4 oz. (¾ c.) plain flour
2 oz. (4 level Tbs.) fat

Meringue
2 egg whites
2 oz. (6 level Tbs.) caster sugar

Filling
12 oz. (3 c.) cottage cheese
2 egg yolks
2 Tbs. lemon juice
Grated lemon rind
½ oz. (1 level Tbs.) sugar

Roll the pastry to line a 7-in.-diameter flan tin or pie-plate. Bake blind in a hot oven for about 10 mins. Sieve the cottage cheese or beat smooth and add the other filling ingredients. Pour into pastry case and bake until set, about ½ hr. Beat egg whites stiff, fold in the sugar, and put meringue on top of the filling. Bake at the lower temperature until the meringue is set and lightly coloured (about 15 mins.). Serve hot or cold.

One portion. Carbohydrate 60 g. Calories 525.

486. Oil Pastry

8 oz. (1½ c.) plain flour
½ level tsp. salt
3 fl. oz. (6 Tbs.) oil
2½ Tbs. cold water

Sift the flour and salt into the bowl and make a well in the centre. Blend the oil and water with a fork and pour into the flour. Mix with a fork until a dough is formed. Knead lightly and roll out.

Full recipe. Carbohydrate 176 g. Calories 1,592.

Variation (*cheese pastry*). Add 4 oz. finely grated cheese to the flour.

487. Gluten-Free Pastry

8 oz. ($1\frac{1}{2}$ level c.) wheat-starch or gluten-free flour
3–4 level tsp. special baking powder (see page 66)
Pinch of salt
2 oz. (4 level Tbs.) lard
2 oz. (4 level Tbs.) margarine
1 egg
Few drops lemon juice
Milk to mix

Sift the wheat-starch, salt and baking powder into a basin. Rub in the fat. Add the beaten egg, lemon juice and enough milk to make a pliable dough, softer than ordinary short pastry. Knead well and roll out on a board sprinkled with wheat-starch. Roll fairly thickly. Shape and bake in the usual way for short pastry.

488. Refrigerated Flan (1) (*gluten-free*)

Quantities for 4

$1\frac{1}{2}$ oz. ($1\frac{1}{2}$ c.) cornflakes *or* other cereal
2 oz. (4 level Tbs.) margarine *or* butter
$\frac{1}{4}$ oz. ($\frac{1}{2}$ level Tbs.) sugar
1 oz. (1 level Tbs.) golden syrup

Crush the cornflakes medium fine, using a rolling pin, or crush by hand. Cream the other ingredients, add flakes, and mix well. Put in a 7-in. flan ring on a serving dish or in an oven-glass pie-plate, pressing the mixture in with the back of a spoon to make it come up the side in the usual flan shape. Chill 24 hrs Fill and serve.

One portion. Carbohydrate 17 g. Calories 180.

489. Refrigerated Flan (2) (*gluten-free*)

Quantities for 4

2 oz. (4 level Tbs.) butter or margarine
2 oz. (4 level Tbs.) caster sugar
$1\frac{1}{2}$ oz. ($\frac{1}{2}$ c.) crushed cornflakes or other cereal

Cream the fat and sugar and work in the cereal. Press into a 7-in. flan ring on a serving dish or into a glass pie-plate. Chill for several hours or keep in the refrigerator until wanted. It will keep several days. Add cooked fillings. Serve.

One portion (of main recipe). Carbohydrate 45 g. Calories 315.

Variation to Recipe 2. Use semi-sweet biscuits instead of flakes, and less sugar.

490. Fillings for Refrigerated Flans

Peach flan. Arrange in the flan one large tin of sliced peaches, pour over ¼ pt nearly set lemon jelly.

491. Lemon Filling

½ pt (1 c.) water	1 oz. (3 level Tbs.) cornflour
Grated rind and juice of 1 lemon	1½ oz. (3 level Tbs.) margarine *or* butter
1 egg	3–4 oz. (6–8 level Tbs.) sugar

Mix the cornflour to a smooth paste with a little of the water. Heat the rest of the water with the grated lemon rind, and, when boiling, pour on to the cornflour, mix well, return to the pan, and boil 3 mins. Add the slightly beaten egg and cook for a minute or two but do not boil. Add the lemon juice, margarine, and sugar to taste. Mix well and put into the pastry case.

One portion. Carbohydrate 25 g. Calories 170.

Variation (*low-sodium diet*). Use 2 egg yolks instead of the whole egg. Use salt-free margarine or butter.

492. Caramel Rice Cream (*gluten-free*)

Quantities for 4. *Cooking time* ½–1 hr or longer in a double boiler

3 oz. (6 level Tbs.) rice	2½ oz. (5 level Tbs.) sugar
1 pt (2 c.) milk	2 Tbs. water
2 strips lemon rind	¼ pt (½ c.) cream or evaporated milk

Wash the rice and simmer with the milk and lemon rind, until all the milk is absorbed. When cooking over a naked flame, this is best done in a double boiler. Add 1 level Tbs. sugar, cool a little, and remove the rind. Make a caramel of the remaining sugar and the water, boiling together without stirring until toffee-coloured. Pour into the rice and stir until melted. When quite cold stir in the whipped cream or evaporated milk. Put in glass dishes and chill.

One portion. Carbohydrate 50 g. Calories 325.

493. Low-Fat Milk Pudding

These may be made with fresh or dried skimmed milk, or fortified skimmed milk, see No. 1 (f).

Variety can be achieved in the following ways:

1. Flavour the pudding with a very little finely grated orange or lemon rind.
2. Put a layer of jam on top after cooking (firm texture needed here) and then cover with meringue.
3. Dissolve carmelized sugar in the milk before making the pudding. (For caramel see No. 441 or serve with caramel sauce No. 131 or 132.)
4. Other suitable sauces for blancmanges and other fairly solid milk puddings are: fruit juice sauce (No. 142), jam sauce (No. 143), rose-hip syrup, or blackcurrant syrup or purée.
5. Dried fruits such as raisins may be added during cooking and mixed in afterwards.

494. Lemon Meringue Rice (*gluten-free*)

Quantities for 4. *Cooking time* 30–40 mins. *Temperature* 350 °F. No. 3.

1½ oz. (3 level Tbs.) rice
1 pt (2 c.) milk
1½ oz. (3 level Tbs.) sugar
2 egg yolks
Pinch salt
½ oz. (1 level Tbs.) butter or margarine
Grated rind of 1 lemon
1½ Tbs. lemon juice

Meringue
2 egg whites
1 oz. (2 level Tbs.) sugar

Wash the rice and cook in a double boiler with the milk until thick and the rice tender. Add the egg yolks and sugar beaten together. Add the remaining ingredients. Pour into a greased baking dish. Beat the egg white stiff and fold in 1 oz. sugar. Put on top of the rice and bake in a slow oven until the meringue is set. Serve hot or cold.

One portion. Carbohydrate 32 g. Calories 222.

Variation (*low-sodium diet*). Use Edosol milk and salt-free butter or margarine. Leave the meringue for the rest of the family and have a little jam instead.

495. Pear Condé (*gluten-free*)

Quantities for 4. *Cooking time* 45 mins.

1½ oz. (3 level Tbs.) rice
1 oz. (2 level Tbs.) sugar
Pinch of salt
1 pt (2 c.) milk
1 egg
½ oz. (1 level Tbs.) butter
4 pears, halved and poached in vanilla-flavoured syrup
Arrowroot or potato flour

Cook the rice, sugar, salt, and milk in a double boiler until the rice is done (about ½ hr). This is best carried out in the top of a double boiler. Beat and add the egg, cook until the mixture thickens, add butter, cool, and make into a flat mound on a serving dish. Arrange the cooked pears on the rice, thicken the syrup with a little (2 level tsp. to ¼ pt) arrowroot or potato flour and pour over as a glaze, coloured if desired.

Variations. 1. Sprinkle chopped stem ginger between the pears. 2. Peaches and other fruits may be served in the same way. 3. *Low-sodium diet.* Omit salt, use Edosol milk, and salt-free butter. Also use two egg yolks instead of one whole egg.

496. Rice Soufflé (*gluten-free*)

Quantities for 4. *Cooking time* 1–1½ hrs. *Temperature* 375 °F. No. 5.

1½ oz. (3 level Tbs.) rice
1 pt (2 c.) milk
1½ oz. (3 level Tbs.) sugar
Grated rind of 1 lemon
2 eggs

Wash the rice and cook gently with the milk and lemon rind in a double boiler until tender and thick. Add the egg yolks and sugar beaten together and then fold in the beaten whites.

Pour into four small dishes and then bake 15–20 mins. or until risen and light brown. Serve at once with jam or fruit sauce or with a little rose-hip syrup or blackcurrant syrup.

One portion (without the sauce). Carbohydrate 30 g. Calories 222.

497. Lemon Sago (*gluten-free, low-protein*)

Quantities for 4. *Cooking time* 15 mins.

2 oz. (4 level Tbs.) sago
1 pt (2 c.) water
Pinch salt
Grated rind and juice of 2 lemons
3 oz. (3 level Tbs.) golden syrup *or* honey

Wash the sago. Boil the water and sago and cook until clear (about 15 mins.). Add the lemon and sweetening. Pour into individual dishes and leave to thicken and become cold. Serve with fruit salad and/or cream.

One portion. Carbohydrate 30 g. Calories 114.

498. Canary Pudding

Quantities for 4 individual puddings. *Cooking time* 40 mins. steaming, 20–30 mins. baking. *Temperature* 375 °F. No. 5.

4 oz. (½ c.) butter or margarine
4 oz. (½ c.) caster sugar
2 eggs
Little grated lemon rind
4 oz. (¾ c.) plain flour
½ level tsp. baking powder
Pinch of salt
Milk if necessary

Grease individual pudding moulds. Cream the fat and sugar, beat in the eggs, and add lemon rind. Sift flour, baking powder, and salt. Stir in gently, adding milk if needed to make a soft consistency. Put into the moulds and bake, or steam (covered with foil lids). Unmould and serve with jam, lemon, orange, or custard sauce.

One portion. Carbohydrate 53 g. Calories 488.

499. Eve's Pudding

Quantities for 4

Use half the recipe (No. 498). Put 8 oz. sliced apples (2 medium) in a pie-dish with 1–2 oz. (2–4 level Tbs.) sugar. Put the sponge mixture on top and bake for 30–45 mins. Serve with custard sauce or cream.

500. Chocolate Sponge

Quantities for 4

Sift ½ oz. cocoa (1½ level Tbs.) with the flour in recipe No. 498. Use vanilla essence in place of the lemon rind. Steam or bake, and serve with chocolate sauce or custard sauce.

501. Carrot Plum Pudding

Quantities for 4. *Cooking time* 3–4 hrs

- 4 oz. (1 level c.) raw grated carrot
- 4 oz. (¾ c.) raw grated potato
- 2 oz. (¼ c.) sugar
- 6 oz. (1 level c.) mixed dried fruit
- 4 oz. (¾ c.) plain flour
- ½ level tsp. bicarbonate of soda
- ½ level tsp. salt
- ½ level tsp. ground nutmeg
- ½ level tsp. ground cinnamon
- 1½ oz. (3 Tbs.) melted fat

Grate the vegetables on the coarse part of an ordinary household grater. Sift the flour, salt, soda, and spices together. Mix all the ingredients together with the melted fat. Put in a greased basin and steam. Serve with lemon sauce (No. 144) or custard sauce (No. 139). It may be cooked in individual moulds but will still need about 2 hrs steaming at least to make it a good colour and to cook the vegetables. It makes an excellent and light substitute for Christmas pudding.

One portion. Carbohydrate 65 g. Calories 353.

Variation (*gluten-free diet*). Use gluten-free flour.

502. Christmas Pudding (*Oil*)

Quantities for 8 or more. *Cooking time* 6 hrs and 2–3 on day of using

8 oz. (1½ level c.) plain flour
4 oz. (½ c.) soft brown sugar
1 level tsp. bicarbonate of soda
½ level tsp. salt
½ level tsp. cinnamon
½ level tsp. nutmeg
½ level tsp. mixed spice
4 oz. (½ c.) raisins
4 oz. (½ c.) currants
4 oz. (½ c.) sultanas
4 oz. (½ c.) chopped mixed peel
⅛ pt (5 Tbs.) oil
3 fl. oz. (6 Tbs.) milk
3–4 Tbs. rum or brandy
1 egg

Grease a 2-pt pudding basin. Sift the dry ingredients together into a mixing bowl and add the prepared fruit. Whisk together the oil, milk, rum or brandy, and egg. Add to the dry ingredients and mix well. Put in the basin, cover closely with aluminium foil, and steam 6 hrs. Then keep 6 weeks or several months and steam 2–3 hrs on the day of use. Serve with sweet white sauce flavoured with rum or brandy.

One portion. Carbohydrate 90 g. Calories 475.

503. Ohio Pudding (*low-fat*)

Quantities for 4. *Cooking time* 3 hrs

3 oz. S.R. flour (¾ c.)
1 level tsp. salt
1 level tsp. bicarbonate of soda
3 oz. sugar (6 level Tbs.)
3 oz. raw potato, grated (½ c.)
4 oz. raw grated carrot (1 c.)
2 oz. fresh breadcrumbs (⅔ c.)
4 oz. dried fruit (⅔ c.)
Milk to mix

Sift the flour, salt, and soda and add all the other ingredients together with enough milk to make a soft mixture. Put in a lightly greased basin, cover with foil, and steam for 2 hrs. Serve with a custard made with custard powder and skimmed milk or with an orange or lemon sauce (No. 144 or 145).

One portion. Carbohydrate 77 g. Calories 306.

504. Sponge Pudding (*low-sodium*)

Quantities for 4. *Cooking time* ¾–1 hr steaming, 20–30 mins. baking. *Temperature* 375 °F. No. 5.

3 oz. (6 level Tbs.) salt-free margarine or butter
2½ oz. (5 level Tbs.) caster sugar
2 small eggs or 1 large
Flavouring: spice or a little grated lemon or orange rind or vanilla
4 oz. (¾ c.) plain flour
1 level tsp. special baking powder see p. 139
Water if needed

Cream fat and sugar and beat in eggs gradually. Add flavouring and the sifted flour and baking powder with water if needed to give a soft consistency. Put in greased moulds or a basin, cover with foil, and steam ¾–1 hr. Unmould and serve with jam or marmalade sauce (No. 143).

One portion (without the sauce). Carbohydrate 38 g. Calories 370.

Variations. 1. Put in large dariole moulds or an ovenproof dish or tin and bake 20–30 mins. Serve with sauce or stewed fruit. 2. *Eve's Pudding.* Use half the above mixture. Put 8 oz. sliced apples in a pie-dish with 1–2 oz. sugar. Put the sponge on top and bake for 30–45 mins. Serve with salt-free custard powder sauce or lemon sauce (No. 144).

505. Steamed Sponge Pudding (*gluten-free*)

Quantities for 3 individual puddings. *Cooking time* 45 mins.

Recipe 1

2 oz. (4 level Tbs.) margarine or butter
1½ oz. (3 level Tbs.) caster sugar
1 egg
4 oz. (¾ c.) wheat-starch
2 level tsp. special baking powder, see page 66
Pinch of salt
2 fl. oz. (4 Tbs.) milk
Flavouring, see below

One portion. Carbohydrate 51 g. Calories 380.

Recipe 2

2 oz. (4 level Tbs.) margarine or butter
2 oz. (4 level Tbs.) caster sugar
1 egg
3 oz. ($\frac{1}{2}$ c.) wheat-starch
1 level tsp. special baking powder, see page 66
Pinch of salt
2 Tbs. milk
Flavouring, see below

One portion. Carbohydrate 46 g. Calories 360.

Both are mixed by the usual creaming method. Recipe 1 makes a lighter and drier sponge, Recipe 2 is sweeter and richer. Put in greased individual moulds, cover with aluminium foil or greaseproof paper and steam. Serve with jam sauce or any sauce allowed on the gluten-free diet.

Flavourings. 1. Grated lemon or orange rind added to the creamed mixture or put red jam or raisins in the bottom of the mould before adding the pudding mixture. 2. *Chocolate pudding.* 2 level Tbs. cocoa added with the flour and some vanilla essence to the creamed fat. Serve with chocolate sauce.

506. Apple Trifle

Quantities for 4. *Cooking time* 20–30 mins.

1 egg
$\frac{1}{2}$ pt (1 c.) milk
$\frac{1}{2}$ oz. (1 level Tbs.) sugar
$\frac{1}{2}$ oz. (1 level Tbs.) gelatine
3 Tbs. hot water
2 oz. (2 level Tbs.) golden syrup
$\frac{1}{4}$ pt ($\frac{1}{2}$ c.) hot juice from the stewed apple
1 tsp. lemon juice
$\frac{1}{4}$ pt apple purée
4 sponge cakes or 1 small sponge sandwich (2 oz.)
Whipped cream to decorate
Glacé cherries

Make a custard with the egg, milk, and sugar (see No. 139). Cool. Dissolve gelatine in hot water and add the syrup, apple-juice, lemon juice, and apple purée. Leave to cool until it begins to thicken. Split the sponge and put half in a serving bowl. Spread on half the custard, put the other half of the sponge on top, and then the rest of the custard. Leave to soak. Cover with the apple mixture. Chill. Decorate with whipped cream and glacé cherries. If preferred it may be made in a mould, turned out, and the top 'iced' with the whipped cream.

One portion (without the cream and cherries). Carbohydrate 20 g. Calories 110.

Variation (*gluten-free diet*). Use sponge cake recipe (No. 572).

507. Baked Trifle

Quantities for 4. *Cooking time* approx. 1 hr. *Temperature* 350 °F. No. 3.

¾ lb. stewed or canned sweetened purple plums drained of syrup
3 oz. sponge cake
2 eggs
½ pt (1 c.) hot milk
2–4 oz. (¼–½ c.) sugar

Sieve or pulp the plums and put them at the bottom of a 1½-pt baking dish. Cut the sponge in slices and put on top of the plums. Beat the egg yolks slightly with ½ oz. sugar, add the milk, and pour over the sponge. Bake in a slow oven until set (about ¾ hr). Make a meringue with the egg whites and 2 or more oz. sugar. Pile on top of the custard and cook in a very slow oven until the meringue is set and lightly coloured (about 15 mins.). Serve hot.

One portion (using 4 oz. sugar). Carbohydrate 50 g. Calories 445.

Variations. Use ¾ lb. of any other fruit. *Gluten-free diet*. Use sponge recipe (No. 572).

508. Trifle

2 egg yolks
¼ oz. (½ level Tbs.) sugar
½ pt (1 c.) milk
Almond essence
2½ oz. sponge cake
1 oz. (1 level Tbs.) sieved red jam or jelly
¼ pt (½ c.) fruit juice
2 Tbs. sherry
½ pt (1 c.) whipping cream
Garnish as allowed in the diet

Mix egg yolks and sugar and add the milk. Stir over a gentle heat until the mixture just begins to thicken and coat the back of the wooden stirring spoon. Add almond essence to taste. Cool. Split the sponge cakes and spread with jam or jelly. Place in serving dishes (or one large dish). Pour in the fruit juice and sherry and leave to soak. Pour on the cold custard and leave in a cold place. Decorate with whipped cream and garnish as allowed in the diet, e.g. cherries and angelica for some, or a little sieved red jam or jelly for those not allowed whole fruit.

Variation (*low-fat diet*). If the patient is allowed whole eggs, trifles may be made with ordinary sponge, and skimmed milk custard. Otherwise use home-made angel cake (see No. 548 or 549) and custard powder custard made with skimmed milk. The cake may be spread with sieved jam or fruit and the trifle decorated with syrup cream (No. 149). As both the angel cake and the cream are very sweet it is advisable to omit sugar from the custard and use a rather sharp fruit purée or jam, or alternatively sprinkle the cake with a little lemon juice.

509. Charlotte Russe

Quantities for 4

1 small pkt sponge fingers
½–¾ pt (1–1½ c.) lemon jelly (No. 467)
Glacé cherries
Angelica
¼ oz. (½ level Tbs.) gelatine
2 Tbs. hot water
¼ pt (½ c.) double cream
⅛ pt (5 Tbs.) milk
1 oz. (2 level Tbs.) caster sugar
Vanilla or other flavouring

Prepare the jelly and put to cool. Trim the ends of the sponge fingers to make them fit neatly round the edge of a 1-pt soufflé dish or straight-sided tin or mould. Remove, and rinse the mould. Pour ¼-in. layer of jelly into the bottom of the mould and chill to set the jelly. Decorate with cherries and angelica and pour in more jelly to make ½-in. depth. Chill to set the jelly. Brush each sponge finger with jelly and arrange them round the edge of the mould. Chill again. Dissolve gelatine in hot water. Whip the cream and gradually add the milk and sugar, beating all the time. Fold in the gelatine and flavouring, and pour into the mould. Leave to set. Turn out and decorate with chopped jelly.

One portion. Carbohydrate 65 g. Calories 500.

Other flavourings. Liqueurs, grated yellow rind of orange or lemon, chopped preserved ginger, using some of the syrup and some vanilla, or chopped crystallized fruits added to the cream mixture with sherry or liqueur.

510. Cabinet Pudding

Quantities for 4–6. *Cooking time* 1–1¼ hrs

Glacé cherries, angelica, raisins, or peel for decoration
8 oz. savoy biscuits or sponge cake
3 eggs
1 oz. (2 level Tbs.) sugar
1 pt (2 c.) milk
Almond essence or other flavouring

Grease a 2-pt pudding basin or plain mould and decorate the bottom with one or more of the fruits. Split the biscuits or cut finger slices of the sponge cake and use them to line the sides of the basin. Cut the cake trimmings into dice and use them to fill the centre loosely. Beat eggs and sugar just enough to mix them, add milk and flavouring to taste. Pour over the cake and cover with a lid of foil. Leave to stand for 20 mins. Steam until the pudding is firm enough to turn out of the mould. Unmould and serve with Egg Custard Sauce (No. 139), flavoured with sherry or brandy.

One portion (without sauce). Carbohydrate 30–46 g. Calories 246–370.

Variations (*low-fat diet*). Make the custard with skimmed milk. (*Gluten-free diet*). Make the sponge with recipe No. 566 or 572.

511. Bread Pudding (*low-fat*)

Quantities for 4. *Cooking time* 20–30 mins. *Temperature* 375 °F. No. 5, then 350 °F. No. 3.

½ pt (1 c.) skimmed milk
4 oz. (1 level c.) stale breadcrumbs
1 oz. (2 level Tbs.) sugar
2 oz. (⅓ c.) sultanas
Vanilla or grated lemon rind
Sieved jam or fruit purée
Meringue
2 egg whites
2–4 oz. (4–8 level Tbs.) sugar

Heat the milk and pour on to the crumbs, sugar, and sultanas, mixed. Soak for ½ hr. Add the flavouring and bake in a moderate oven until set. Spread the jam or purée on top. Make the meringue, by beating egg whites stiff and folding in the sugar, and decorate the top of the pudding with it. Bake the meringue at the lower temperature until set, about 15 mins. Serve hot with a fruit juice sauce (see No. 142).

One portion. Carbohydrate 42 g. Calories 280.

BREAD AND SCONES

512. Gluten-free Yeast Bread

Quantities for a 1 lb. loaf. *Cooking time* 30 mins. *Temperature* 350 °F. No. 4.

¼ pt (½ c.) warm water
½ oz. fresh yeast or ¼ oz. dried
¼ oz. (½ level Tbs.) sugar
6 oz. (1¼ level c.) wheat-starch or gluten-free flour
½ level tsp. salt
2 oz. (4 heaped Tbs.) instant dried skimmed milk
¼ oz. (½ Tbs.) melted fat

Line the tin with non-stick paper or grease it heavily. Crumble or sprinkle the yeast into the warm water, add the sugar and stand it in a warm place for 15 minutes. Mix the starch, salt and milk powder in a basin. Add the yeast mixture and the melted fat. Mix to a smooth, thick batter, adding more warm water if necessary. It should be the consistency of thick cream. Turn into the tin. Stand the tin in a warm place until the mixture rises almost to the top of the tin. Bake fairly near the top of the oven until the centre feels firm and springy. Turn out on a rack and remove the paper. When the loaf is cold, store it in a polythene bag.

The mixture can also be baked in heavily greased patty tins or tins lined with foil, to make bread rolls. Bake at 375 °F No. 5 for 15–20 mins. Leave in the foil to cool.

513. Ways of Using Gluten-free Bread

This high-protein, gluten-free bread keeps moist longer than others.

It makes excellent toast. Deep-frozen loaves can be sliced and toasted frozen. ½-in. slices can be baked in a slow oven to make rusks. To make sweet rusks, dip in a sugar or honey and water mixture before baking.

514. Quick Gluten-free Loaf

Quantities for a 1 lb. loaf. *Cooking time* 30 mins. *Temperature* 425 °F. No. 7.

8 oz. gluten-free flour (1½ level c.)
4 level tsp. special baking powder (see p. 66)
½ level tsp. salt
2 oz (4 level Tbs.) margarine
½ pt (1 c.) milk or ¼ pt (½ c.) milk plus 1 egg

Line the tin with non-stick paper or grease it heavily. Sift the dry ingredients into a bowl. Rub in the margarine. Add the milk, or milk and egg beaten together, and mix to a soft dough. Turn into the tin and make the top even. Bake quickly until firm. Cool and slice and use like bread.

Variation. For a sweet loaf add 1–2 oz. sugar (2–4 level Tbs.).

515. High-Protein, Low-Sodium Bread

Quantities for 2 1-lb. loaves. *Cooking time* 35 mins. *Temperature* 425 °F. No. 7.

8 oz. (1½ level c.) plain flour
1½ oz. (4 level Tbs.) Casilan
½ oz. yeast
½ oz. (1 level Tbs.) sugar
½ pt (1 c.) lukewarm water
½ oz. (1 Tbs.) melted butter *or* margarine

Sift flour and Casilan into a basin and rub in yeast. Add water, sugar and fat. Beat well and add more flour (about 12 oz.) to make a fairly stiff dough. Knead well. Put basin in polythene bag and put to rise until double its bulk. Knead well and shape into two loaves. Put in the greased tins. Brush tops with melted unsalted margarine and put in polythene bag to rise to double the bulk. Remove bag. Bake in a hot oven until brown.

516. Plain Low-Sodium Bread (*By Courtesy of the Flour Advisory Bureau*)

Quantities for 2 1-lb. loaves. *Cooking time* 45 mins. *Temperature* 450 °F. No. 7.

1 lb. (3 level c.) plain flour (wholemeal, or a mixture of white and wholemeal, or all white)
2 level tsp. sugar
½ oz. fresh, or 2 tsp. dried yeast
1 Tbs. salad oil
½ pt (1 c.) water

Method 1 (using fresh yeast). Mix flour and sugar in a bowl. Rub fresh yeast into the flour mixture. Add oil and water and mix with the hand or wooden spoon until the dough leaves the side of the bowl clean. Turn out on a very lightly floured board and knead for about 1 min. Shape into a roll about 1 ft long. Cut and place each half in a well greased tin. Place each tin in a greased polythene bag and tuck the end under, so that the dough is in a draught-free place. Leave to rise in a warm place until the dough doubles in size. It is ready when the dough rises back after pressing with a floured finger. Time required approx. 45 mins. Bake in a hot oven. When cooked, the loaf should have shrunk from the sides of the tin and the bottom of the loaf will sound hollow when tapped. Cool loaves on a wire rack.

Method 2 (using dried yeast). Dissolve the sugar in water, sprinkle in yeast mixture with 1 tsp. flour on top. Leave in warm place until frothy (about 15 mins.). Put yeast liquid into flour, add oil, and mix with the hand or wooden spoon until the sides of the basin are clean. Finish the bread as for method 1.

Cold rising gives good results. If it is more convenient the dough can be mixed overnight with cold water and placed in a greased polythene bag in a cold larder or refrigerator. In the larder it will take from 12 to 24 hrs to rise; dough left in a refrigerator will need to recover in a warm place for up to 2 hrs before baking. If the dough becomes over-risen because no one is available to deal with it at the right moment, there is no need to throw it away. It can be knocked back or re-kneaded and risen again as before.

517. Soft Dinner Rolls (*Oil*)

Quantities for 8 rolls. *Cooking time* 12 mins. *Temperature* 400 °F. No. 6.

- 2 fl. oz. (4 Tbs.) milk
- ¾ level tsp. salt
- ¾ oz. (1½ level Tbs.) sugar
- ¼ oz. yeast
- 1 Tbs. oil (see page 150)
- 5 oz. (1 level c.) plain flour
- 2 fl. oz. (4 Tbs.) warm water

Scald milk. Add salt and sugar and cool to lukewarm. Crumble yeast and sprinkle over warm water in mixing bowl. Stir until dissolved. Add milk mixture, and oil. Add half the flour and beat smooth. Add rest of flour to make a soft dough. Turn out on floured board and knead until smooth. Place in oiled bowl and brush top lightly with oil. Cover and rise to double its bulk. Time required 1–1½ hrs. Divide dough in half and roll each into a circle about ¼-in. thick. Cut in 2½-in. rounds. Crease through centre, brush with oil, and fold over. Put 1 in. apart on greased sheets, but for soft-sided rolls put them close together. Cover and rise to double their bulk (about ¾ hr). Bake in a hot oven until brown and firm.

518. Quick Baking-Powder Bread

Quantities for 1-lb. loaf tin. *Cooking time* 1 hr. *Temperature* 375 °F. No. 5.

- 8 oz. (1½ level c.) plain flour
- ½ level tsp. salt
- 4 level tsp. baking powder
- 2 oz. (4 level Tbs.) sugar
- 1 egg
- 1 oz. (2 Tbs.) melted butter *or* margarine
- 6–8 fl. oz. (¾ c.) milk

Sift the flour, salt, and baking powder into a bowl. Add the sugar. Beat the egg and add it together with the melted (not hot) fat and enough milk to make a dropping consistency. Put in a greased tin and bake until brown and firm. Cool, slice, and spread like bread.

Variations. 1. *Nut bread.* 2 oz. chopped nuts. 2. *Low-sodium bread.* Omit salt and use 6 level tsp. special baking powder (page 128), unsalted butter and margarine, and Edosol milk (the milk powder can be sifted with the flour, in which case use water for mixing).

519. Brown Baking-Powder Bread (*high-fibre*)

Quantities for 1-lb. loaf tin. *Cooking time* ¾–1 hr. *Temperature* 375° F. No. 5

- 8 oz. (1½ level c.) 100 per cent wholewheat flour
- 4 oz. (¾ c.) plain white flour
- ½ level tsp. salt
- 2 level tsp. cream of tartar
- 2 oz. (2 level Tbs.) black treacle
- 1 level tsp. bicarbonate of soda
- ½ pt milk

Grease the loaf tin. Put wholemeal flour in a bowl and sift in the white flour, salt, and cream of tartar. Melt treacle but do not make very hot. Dissolve soda in milk. Use treacle and milk to mix the dry ingredients. Put in a tin and bake. Leave 24 hrs before cutting and spreading.

520. Poor Knight's Fritters

Quantities for 4. *Cooking time* 5–10 mins.

- 4 slices stale bread ¼ in. thick from a 1-lb. loaf
- 2 eggs
- ¼ level tsp. salt
- Butter or margarine for frying

Cut bread in eight pieces. Beat egg and salt and dip bread in this until it is evenly coated. Heat fat and fry the bread golden brown on both sides. Drain and serve with bacon for breakfast or as a sweet course with jam or syrup.

521. Buttered Crumbs (*for topping gratin and similar dishes*)

Quantities for the top of a 2-pt pie-dish

1 oz. (2 level Tbs.) butter or margarine
3 oz. (1 level c.) fresh breadcrumbs

Melt fat in a small pan, add crumbs, stir until well coated. Use to top sweet and savoury dishes and gratin dishes. It gives a better finish than dry crumbs dotted with fat.

Full recipe. Carbohydrate 44 g. Calories 420.

522. Fairy or Melba Toast

Cut very thin slices of stale bread. Put them on baking trays and dry in a very slow oven until they are crisp. Cool and store in an air-tight tin.

523. Bread Rusks

Cut stale bread into slices ½ in. thick and then cut up into fingers. Bake in a cool oven until they are pale brown and crisp. For variety, before baking dip the rusks into one of the following mixtures: 1. Marmite mixed with a little water. 2. Jam or honey dissolved in a little milk (skimmed milk for low-fat) and a little water mixed together.

524. Brown Honey Scones (*high-fibre*)

Quantities for 12 scones. *Cooking time* about 15 mins. *Temperature* 425 °F. No. 7.

8 oz. (1¼ level c.) 100 per cent whole wheat flour
3 level tsp. baking powder
½ level tsp. salt
2 oz. (4 level Tbs.) butter or margarine
2 oz. (2 level Tbs.) honey
A little milk, if necessary
1 egg

Mix flour, baking powder, and salt in a basin and rub in the fat. Melt the honey but do not make it hot. Beat the egg. Use the egg and honey and a little milk, if necessary, to make a very soft dough. Roll out on a well-floured board to about ½ in. thick. Cut in shapes. Bake in a hot oven until brown. These do not rise as much as scones made with white flour but are very crisp and nutty to eat.

Variation. Add some chopped dates or sticky raisins (1–2 oz.).

525. Treacle Loaf (*low-fat*)

Quantities for 1-lb. loaf tin. *Cooking time* 1 hr. *Temperature* 350 °F. No. 4.

- 8 oz. (1½ level c.) S.R. flour
- Pinch salt
- 1 oz. (2 heaped Tbs.) dried skimmed milk powder
- 1 level tsp. bicarbonate soda
- ¼ pt warm water
- 8 oz. (½ c.) black treacle

Sift the flour, salt, and dried skimmed milk into a bowl. Dissolve the soda in the water. Warm the treacle and mix all the ingredients together. Pour into the lightly greased tin and bake until risen and set. Keep four days before using to allow it to soften and become moist. Serve plain, as cake, for the patient. The family can have it spread with butter or margarine. Thin slices of this with cottage-cheese filling make a delicious sandwich for tea.

526. Doughnuts (*gluten-free*)

Quantities for 1 doz. *Cooking time* 10 mins.

- 8 oz. (1½ level c.) wheat-starch
- Pinch salt
- 1 oz. (2 level Tbs.) butter or margarine
- ½ oz. yeast
- 1 level tsp. sugar
- Approximately 7 fl. oz. (¾ c.) of lukewarm milk
- Jam
- Oil for frying
- Caster sugar

Sift wheat-starch and salt into a basin and rub in the fat. Cream yeast and sugar and add some milk. Use this, together with the rest of the milk, to make a dough which is stiff enough to handle but not stodgy. Roll in balls, make a depression in each, insert a little jam, and close up smoothly. Put to rise in a warm place for about 20 mins. Fry in oil, drain, and roll in caster sugar.

SANDWICH FILLINGS

527. Closed Sandwiches

Cooked Ham

Minced ham and liver with chopped capers and gherkins and a binding sauce.

Minced ham and chutney.

Minced ham and chicken with chopped olives and lemon juice and a binding sauce.

Minced ham with mashed baked beans and lettuce leaves chopped.

Minced pickled pork with shredded Brussels sprouts and mayonnaise.

Minced ham with chopped hard-boiled egg and binding sauce.

Cooked lamb, beef, or veal

Minced with chopped beetroot and sauce to bind.

Minced with grated carrot and sauce to bind.

Minced and mixed with skinned chopped tomato and sauce to bind.

Fish

Cooked flaked fish mixed with salad dressing.

Flaked canned salmon with chopped gherkin or cucumber and salad dressing.

Cheese

Cottage cheese mixed with chopped chives or pickles.

Cottage cheese and skinned chopped tomato.

Grated cheese and chopped celery with salad dressing to bind.

Cottage cheese and raw grated carrot.

Grated cheese mixed to a paste with onion juice and hot water.

Eggs

Chopped hard-boiled egg with gherkins and salad dressing.

Scrambled eggs with fine chopped bacon.

Scrambled eggs with curry powder.

Liver

See liver pâté (No. 303 or 304) and liver terrapin (No. 308).

Banana

Mashed ripe banana with lemon juice.

528. Open Sandwiches

Cooked Ham

Ham and fried egg.
Ham and Russian salad.
Ham and scrambled egg with watercress.
Ham and cooked mushrooms in white sauce.
Ham with orange slices and lettuce.
Ham with baked beans and watercress.
Ham with slice of cheese and pickle.
Ham with sliced poached apple and maraschino cherry.
Ham with pineapple rings.

Cheese

Thin slice of cheese garnished with pickles or a slice of meat or tomatoes.

Egg

Scrambled egg in lettuce nest with pickles to garnish.
Scrambled egg with a slice of cold ham.
Scrambled egg with tomato.
Hard-boiled egg and shrimps, prawns, or pickle.

Fish

Sardines with egg and watercress.
Flaked cooked fish in sauce with parsley as garnish.
Thin slices of smoked salmon or eel with sliced lemon.

529. Asparagus Rolls

Use sliced new brown bread with crusts removed. Spread with butter and put a piece of fresh-cooked or canned asparagus on each one with a little mayonnaise. Roll up like a small Swiss roll and press to keep in place.

530. Neapolitan Sandwiches

Quantity for 4

8 oz. bread (16 thin, small slices)
2 oz. (4 level Tbs.) butter
4 oz. ham
4 hard-boiled eggs
8 oz. tomato (4 medium)

Spread the bread with butter and sandwich in four layers with tomato at bottom, then bread, then egg, then bread again, and finally tomato topped with bread. Press well together and trim if necessary. It is a help to leave it for a while with a small weight on top. Cut in portions to serve.

Variation. Mince the ham, chop the egg, and bind with sauce or salad cream.

One portion. Carbohydrate 31 g. Calories 41.

531. Herring Roe Spread

8 oz. canned soft roes (227 g.)
½ oz. (4 Tbs.) chopped parsley
Salt and pepper

Mash the roes with the chopped parsley and season to taste. Use on toast or as a sandwich filling.

532. Cottage Cheese and Celery Spread (*low-fat*)

4 oz. (1 c.) cottage cheese
1 oz. finely chopped celery (2 level Tbs.)
Chopped gherkins and capers to taste
Salt and pepper to taste

Mix all together.

533. Herring Spread

6 oz. herring flesh (2 fish)
½ oz. (1 level Tbs.) margarine
½ oz. chopped onion (½ level Tbs.)
½ level tsp. salt
Pinch pepper
1 level Tbs. chopped parsley
2 tsp. vinegar

Steam or grill the herrings, remove all bones, and flake the fish. Fry onion in margarine and mix in all the other ingredients to form a smooth paste. Use for sandwich fillings or on toast.

BISCUITS

534. Almond Biscuits

Quantities for 48 biscuits. *Cooking time* 20–25 mins. *Temperature* 350 °F. No. 4.

8 oz. (1 c.) margarine or butter	12 oz. (2½ c.) plain flour
8 oz. (1 c.) caster sugar	¼ level tsp. salt
1 egg	2 level tsp. baking powder
A little almond essence	24 blanched almonds

Cream fat and sugar and beat in egg. Add essence and sifted dry ingredients. Flour hands, roll mixture in balls or force using a plain tube. Press half an almond on each and bake slowly until pale brown and crisp. Cool and store in an air-tight tin. They keep very well.

Variations (*low-sodium diet*). Omit the salt, and use unsalted margarine or butter and 1½ level tsp. of special baking powder (see page 139).

One biscuit. Carbohydrate 11 g. Calories 100.

535. Almond Biscuits (*gluten-free*)

Quantities for 10 biscuits 2½ in. across. *Cooking time* 15–20 mins. *Temperature* 350–375 °F. No. 4–5.

2 oz. (4 level Tbs.) margarine or butter	½–1 oz. (2–3 level Tbs.) ground almonds
1 oz. (1 level Tbs.) honey	4 oz. (¾ c.) gluten-free flour

Cream fat and honey. Add almonds and wheat-starch and work until thoroughly mixed. Roll out and cut into shapes. Place on well-greased trays and bake in a moderate oven until just beginning to colour.

One biscuit. Carbohydrate 13 g. Calories 110.

536. Almond Fingers (*gluten-free*)

Quantities for 24 biscuits. *Cooking time* 30–40 mins. *Temperature* 350 °F. No. 3–4.

4 oz. (¾ c.) cornflour
2 oz. (4 level Tbs.) caster sugar
2 oz. (4 level Tbs.) butter
1 Tbs. sherry
1 tsp. egg yolk

Topping
1 egg white
1 oz. (2 level Tbs.) caster sugar
1 oz (¼ c.) chopped blanched almonds

Mix cornflour and caster sugar in a basin and work in the butter by rubbing and kneading. Combine sherry and egg yolk and use to bind the mixture to a stiff consistency. Roll ⅛ in. thick and cut into fingers or shapes. Beat egg white until stiff, then beat in the sugar. Spread this on the biscuits like an icing and sprinkle chopped almonds on top. Bake slowly until the biscuit is crisp and the topping firm and just coloured.

CAUTION. The biscuits must be rolled thinly or they will not cook in the same time as the topping. When the biscuits are rolled to ⅛ in., the topping will give the right amount for covering the biscuits.

One biscuit. Carbohydrate 8 g. Calories 52.

537. Arrowroot Cookies

Quantities for 2 dozen. *Cooking time* 10–15 mins. *Temperature* 375 °F. No. 5.

2 oz. (4 level Tbs.) butter or margarine
2 oz. (4 level Tbs.) caster sugar
1 egg
Vanilla essence
2 oz. (½ c.) plain flour
1½ oz. (4½ level Tbs.) arrowroot
Jam

Cream fat and sugar and beat in the egg. Add vanilla. Stir in the sifted flour and the arrowroot. Drop on a tray in small spoonsful, or pipe with a plain tube, leaving a little room for spreading. Bake until very pale brown. Cool and serve plain or join in pairs with jam.

1 *cookie*. Carbohydrate 6 g. Calories 49.

538. Bran Biscuits (*high-fibre*)

Quantities for 24 biscuits. *Cooking time* 20 mins. *Temperature* 375 °F. No. 5.

2 oz. (4 level Tbs.) butter or margarine
1 oz. (2 level Tbs.) granulated sugar
1 egg
4 oz. plain flour (¾ c.)
2 level tsp. baking powder
Pinch salt
2 oz. washed bran (1¼ c.)

Cream fat and sugar and beat in the egg. Mix in the sifted flour, baking powder, and salt, and bran. Knead and then roll out about ¼ in. thick and cut into rounds (about 2–2½ in.) or squares. Bake in a slow oven until crisp, but do not allow to brown or they become bitter. Cool and store in an airtight tin. When serving spread with butter.

539. Chocolate Crisps (*gluten-free*)

Quantities 12–18 biscuits

4 oz. milk or bitter chocolate
Rice Krispies

Break chocolate in pieces and melt in a basin over hot (not boiling) water. Stir in Rice Krispies until they are generously chocolate coated. Place in small heaps on a greased tray and allow to set. Stored in an airtight tin they will keep for some time.

540. Jumbles

Quantities for 24 cakes. *Cooking time* 20–30 mins. *Temperature* 350 °F. No. 4.

4 oz. (½ c.) butter or margarine
6 oz. (¾ c.) caster sugar
1 egg
Vanilla essence
8 oz. (1½ c.) plain flour
Pinch of salt

Cream fat and sugar. Beat in egg. Add vanilla essence and then sifted flour and salt. Mix thoroughly. Roll in balls or ovals. Dip in sugar. Bake slowly until very pale brown. Cool and store in an airtight tin. They keep very well.

One cake. Carbohydrate 15 g. Calories 100.

Variation (low-sodium diet). Omit salt and use unsalted butter or margarine.

541. Lemon Finger Biscuits (*for a biscuit forcer*)

Quantities for 48 biscuits. *Cooking time* 15–20 mins. *Temperature* 350 °F. No. 4.

4 oz. (½ c.) butter or margarine
4 oz. (½ c.) caster sugar
1 egg
Finely grated rind of 1 lemon
8 oz. (1½ c.) plain flour
1 level tsp. baking powder
¼ level tsp. salt

Cream fat and sugar and beat in the egg. Add lemon rind and finely sifted dry ingredients. Force into long strips, mark in finger-lengths, and bake. Cook slowly until crisp but hardly coloured at all. Leave a few minutes before removing from the trays. Cool and store in an airtight tin. They keep well.

Variation (low-sodium diet). Omit salt and use unsalted butter and margarine and 1½ level tsp. special baking powder, see page 139.

One biscuit. Carbohydrate 6 g. Calories 47.

542. Langues de Chat

Quantities for 48 biscuits. *Cooking time* 20–30 mins. *Temperature* 350 °F. No. 4.

4 oz. (½ c.) butter
4 oz. (½ c.) caster sugar
Vanilla essence
3 egg whites
Pinch of salt
4 oz. (¾ c.) plain flour
1 oz. (3 level Tbs.) cornflour

Cream the butter and sugar until very thick and light. Add the essence and beat in the egg whites one at a time. Beat until very light and fluffy. Sift the flour, salt, and cornflour together and stir into the creamed mixture. Pipe on to well-greased trays in small finger shapes, using a ½-in. plain forcing tube. Leave room for spreading a little. Bake in a slow oven, watching them well, as they burn easily. They should only colour slightly. Leave a moment or two on the tray to set and then remove to a wire rack.

One biscuit. Carbohydrate 10 g. Calories 78.

543. Macaroons (*gluten-free*)

Quantities for 36 small ones. *Cooking time* 30–40 mins. *Temperature* 350 °F. No. 3–4.

- 2 egg whites
- Pinch of salt
- 6 oz. (1¼ level c.) ground almonds
- 8 oz. (1 level c.) caster sugar
- ½ oz. (1 level Tbs.) ground rice
- 36 blanched almonds

Beat the egg whites until stiff. Fold in the salt, ground almonds, sugar, and ground rice. Put in rounds on either rice paper, silicone paper, or aluminium foil, placed on baking trays. Put an almond on each. The easiest way to shape them is to roll the mixture in small balls in the hands or, better still, to put through a piping bag with a plain nozzle. Bake in a slow oven until lightly coloured and firm.

One macaroon. Carbohydrate 14 g. Calories 110.

544. Nutties (*high-fibre*)

Quantities for 18 pieces. Tin about 6 in. by 9 in. *Cooking time* 30–45 mins. *Temperature* 350 °F. No. 3–4.

- 4 oz. (½ c.) butter or margarine
- 1 oz. (1 level Tbs.) syrup
- 4 oz. (½ c.) brown sugar
- 7 oz. (2 level c.) rolled oats
- ½ level tsp. salt
- ½ tsp. vanilla
- 2 oz. (½ c.) chopped walnuts *or* roast peanuts

Melt the fat and syrup together but do not allow to become too hot. Mix the other ingredients together, pour in the melted mixture, and combine well to make a crumbly mixture. Spread in a flat greased baking tin, smoothing the top with a knife. Cook very slowly until lightly browned. Mark in fingers and leave in the tin until almost cold.

One piece. Carbohydrate 16 g. Calories 141.

545. Oat Biscuits (*Oil*)

Quantities for 36 small biscuits. *Cooking time* 15–20 mins. *Temperature* 350 °F. No. 3–4.

- 2 oz. (2 level Tbs.) golden syrup
- 1 Tbs. water
- 2 Tbs. oil (see page 150)
- 3 oz. (6 level Tbs.) brown sugar
- 3 oz. (¾ c.) rolled oats
- ½ level tsp. bicarbonate of soda
- 2 oz. (⅓ c.) plain flour
- Pinch of salt

Warm syrup and water together, add oil. Add to dry ingredients and mix well. It should be a dropping consistency. Form into small balls, flatten, and place 2 ins. apart on an oiled baking tray. Bake until delicately brown. Cool and store in an airtight tin.

One biscuit. Carbohydrate 7 g. Calories 36.

546. Raisin Cookies (*low-fat*)

Quantities for 12 cookies. *Cooking time* 10–15 mins. *Temperature* 375 °F. No. 5.

- 1 egg white
- 2 oz. (4 level Tbs.) caster sugar
- Pinch of cream of tartar
- 2 oz. (6 level Tbs.) S.R. flour
- Pinch of salt
- Pinch of nutmeg, cinnamon, cloves, all-spice, mace
- 1 oz. (2 level Tbs.) raisins
- Few drops vanilla

Beat the egg white, cream of tartar, and sugar together until thick and white. Stir in the sifted dry ingredients. Add raisins and vanilla. Drop tsp. of the mixture on to rice paper or silicone paper placed on baking trays, allowing room for spreading a little. Bake in a moderate oven. They look rather like little white rock cakes and are very pleasant to eat. They will keep quite satisfactorily for several days.

One cookie. Carbohydrate 10 g. Calories 42.

547. Shortbread

Quantities for 2 6-in. rounds. *Cooking time* 30–45 mins. *Temperature* 350 °F. No. 3–4.

4 oz. (½ c.) butter
2 oz. (4 level Tbs.) granulated or caster sugar
6 oz. (1¼ level c.) plain flour
Pinch of salt

Have all ingredients warm. Cream butter and sugar and work in the flour and salt gradually. Knead very thoroughly. Press into two 6-in. rounds or roll out ¼–½ in. thick and cut into 16 biscuits. Prick well and bake until just beginning to colour. Cut rounds in pieces while still warm or mark and separate slightly before baking. Cool and store in an air-tight tin.

Variation (*low-sodium diet*). Omit salt and use unsalted butter.

Cut into 16 pieces (per piece). Carbohydrate 15 g. Calories 121.

CAKES

548. Angel Cake (*low-fat*)

Quantities for a 7-8-in. border mould. *Cooking time* 45 mins. *Temperature* 350–375 °F. No. 4–5.

1½ oz. (4½ level Tbs.) arrowroot
1½ oz. (4½ level Tbs.) plain flour
1 level tsp. baking powder
½ level tsp. cream of tartar
Pinch of salt
4 egg whites
4 oz. (½ c.) caster sugar
Vanilla or almond essence

Sift the arrowroot, flour, salt, and raising agent two or three times to blend thoroughly. Beat egg whites stiff, fold in the sugar and flavouring. Fold in the dry ingredients very gently and pour into an ungreased border mould or savarin mould, having it only half full to allow plenty of room for rising. Bake in a moderate oven until it feels springy to the touch. Turn upside down on a wire rack and leave to cool before removing from the tin.

Whole cake. Carbohydrate 192 g. Calories 800.

549. Angel Cake (*gluten-free and low-fat*)

Quantities for a 7-in. tin. *Cooking time* 40 mins. *Temperature* 350–375 °F. No. 4–5.

4 egg whites
Pinch of salt
2 oz. (6 level Tbs.) wheat-starch
3 oz. (6 level Tbs.) caster sugar
1 level tsp. special baking powder (see p. 66)
½ level tsp. cream of tartar
Almond or vanilla essence

Grease the tin lightly and coat with ½ level Tbs. wheat-starch and ½ level Tbs. caster sugar mixed. Beat egg whites stiff. Sift in the dry ingredients and fold in gently with the flavouring. Pour into the prepared tin and bake in a moderate oven for about 40 mins. or until it feels firm in the centre.

Whole cake. Carbohydrate 143 g. Calories 582.

550. Fairy Cakes (*gluten-free*)

Quantities for 1 doz. cakes. *Cooking time* 15–20 mins. *Temperature* 400 °F. No. 6.

2 oz. (4 level Tbs.) butter or margarine
2 oz. (4 level Tbs.) caster sugar
1 large egg
3 oz. (½ c.) gluten-free flour
¼ level tsp. special baking powder (see p. 66)
Milk to mix
Water icing (optional)
Glacé cherries and angelica

Grease tins and dust with wheat-starch. Cream fat and sugar thoroughly and beat in the egg. Sift and mix in the starch and baking powder. Mix to a soft consistency with milk. Put in the tins and bake until lightly browned and firm. Cool on a rack; ice if desired.

One cake. Carbohydrate 12 g. Calories 85.

551. Christmas Cake (*gluten-free*)

Quantities for a 7-in. tin. *Cooking time* 2 hrs. *Temperature* 325 °F. No. 2–3.

- 8 oz. (1¼ level c.) currants
- 8 oz. (1¼ level c.) sultanas
- 1 oz. (2 Tbs.) glacé cherries
- 1 oz. (2 level Tbs.) mixed peel, finely chopped
- 4 oz. (½ c.) butter or margarine
- 4 oz. (½ c.) brown sugar
- ½ tsp. glycerine
- 3 oz. (¾ c.) ground almonds
- 1 oz. (1 level Tbs.) black treacle
- Essence to taste, e.g. almond or vanilla
- 3 eggs
- 5 oz. (1 level c.) gluten-free flour
- Pinch special baking powder (see p. 66)
- Pinch of mixed spice
- Caramel to colour

Prepare fruit. Line the tin with silicone paper. Cream together the butter, sugar, glycerine, almonds, and treacle. Add essence. Add eggs one at a time, beating in thoroughly and adding some of the sifted wheat-starch, baking powder, and spices to prevent curdling. Add colouring, the rest of the starch, and the fruit. Put in a tin and smooth the top. Bake until a skewer inserted comes out clean.

Whole cake. Carbohydrate 498 g. Calories 3,448.

552. Fruit Cake (*gluten-free*)

Quantities for a 6-in. tin. *Cooking time* 50 mins. *Temperature* 350 °F. No. 4.

- 4 oz. (½ c.) butter or margarine
- 4 oz. (½ c.) caster sugar
- 2 large or 3 small eggs
- Flavouring, e.g. lemon juice or essence or vanilla
- 6 oz. (1¼ level c.) gluten-free flour
- Pinch of special baking powder (see p. 66)
- 6 oz. (1 level c.) sultanas or other fruit

Line a tin with silicone paper. Cream fat and sugar. Beat the eggs and flavouring and add gradually to the creamed mixture, beating well after each addition. Sieve the starch and baking powder and add together with the sultanas. Put in the tin and bake until a skewer inserted comes out clean.

Whole cake. Carbohydrate 466 g. Calories 2,470.

553. Plain Fruit Cake (*oil*)

Quantities for a 2-lb. tin. *Cooking time* 1½ hrs. *Temperature* 350 °F. No. 4.

3 oz. (½ c.) sultanas
3 oz. (½ c.) currants
2 oz. (⅓ c.) chopped mixed peel
10 oz. (2 level c.) plain flour
2 eggs
6 oz. (¾ c.) caster sugar
4 fl. oz. (8 Tbs.) oil (see page 150)
3 Tbs. milk
Pinch of salt
2 level tsp. baking powder
Grated rind of ½ lemon

Brush the tin with oil and line with paper. Prepare the fruit and dredge with a little flour. Beat eggs, sugar, and oil together. Mix in the remainder of the flour, sifted with the salt and baking powder. Add milk and finally the fruit and grated lemon rind. Put in the prepared tin, smooth the top, and bake until a skewer inserted comes out clean. After baking turn out on a rack to cool. Store in an airtight tin and leave 24 hrs before using.

554. Rich Fruit Cake (*oil*)

Quantities for a 7-in. tin. *Cooking time* 2¼–2¾ hrs. *Temperature* 325 °F. No. 3, then reduce to 300 °F. No. 2.

8 oz. (1½ level c.) plain flour
2 level tsp. baking powder
¼ level tsp. salt
5 oz. (⅔ c.) caster sugar
¼ pt oil (see p. 150)
2 eggs
2 Tbs. milk
10 oz. (1½ level c.) mixed dried fruit (including some sliced almonds)
4 oz. (⅔ c.) glacé cherries, chopped
2 oz. (¼ c.) mixed chopped candied peel

Grease a tin and line with paper. Sift flour, baking powder, salt, and sugar into a basin. Make a well in the centre. Pour in the oil and break in the unbeaten egg. Add the milk. Using a wooden spoon stir thoroughly for not less than 2 mins. Add and mix in the dried fruit. Turn into the tin, smooth the top, and bake at the higher temperature for 1 hr and then reduce for a further 1¼–1¾ hrs until a skewer inserted comes out clean. Turn out on a rack and cool. Store in an airtight tin and keep at least one day before cutting.

Variations. For additional flavour add some essence or grated orange or lemon rind, or a little mixed spice with the flour.

555. Wholewheat Fruit Cake (*high-fibre*)

Quantities for an 8-in. tin. *Cooking time* 1½–2 hrs. *Temperature* 350 °F. No. 4.

- 8 oz. (1 level c.) butter or margarine
- 8 oz. (1 level c.) fine brown sugar
- 3 eggs
- 8 oz. (1½ level c.) plain white flour
- 4 level tsp. baking powder
- 2 level tsp. mixed spice
- 8 oz. (1½ level c.) 100 per cent whole-wheat flour
- ½–1 lb. (1½–3 level c.) raisins or mixed fruit
- Approx. ¼ pt milk
- Split almonds, optional

Line the tin with paper. Cream fat and sugar and beat in the eggs one at a time. Sift the white flour, baking powder, and spice and add to the creamed mixture, together with the wholewheat flour and fruit. Add milk to make a soft consistency. Put in the tin, sprinkle almonds on top and bake until it comes out clean when tested with a skewer. Leave in the tin to cool.

556. Wholewheat Gingerbread (*high-fibre*)

Quantities for a 6-in.-by-9-in. tin. *Cooking time* 45 mins. *Temperature* 350 °F. No. 4.

- 4 oz. (¾ c.) plain white flour
- 1 level tsp. spice
- Pinch of salt
- 3 level tsp. ground ginger
- 4 oz. (¾ c.) 100 per cent wholewheat flour
- 1½ oz. (3 level Tbs.) brown sugar
- 2 oz. (⅓ c.) sultanas
- 1 oz. (2 level Tbs.) chopped peel or preserved ginger
- 4 oz. (½ c.) butter or margarine
- 8 oz. (½ c.) golden syrup or treacle
- 1 level tsp. bicarbonate of soda
- ¼ pt (½ c.) warm milk
- 1 egg, beaten
- Some split almonds

Line the tin. Sift white flour, salt, and ginger into a bowl and add wholewheat flour and brown sugar, and add the dried fruit. Melt the fat and syrup but do not make hot. Dissolve soda in milk and use both liquids and egg to mix the dry ingredients. Pour into the tin and arrange split almonds on top. Bake until it comes out clean when tested with a skewer. Cool and cut in squares.

557. Fatless Gingerbread

Quantities for a 6-in.-by-9-in. tin. *Cooking time* ¾–1 hr. *Temperature* 350 °F. No. 4.

8 oz. (1½ level c.) S.R. flour
Pinch of salt
1 tsp. ground ginger
6 oz. (½ c.) syrup or honey
1 level tsp. bicarbonate of soda
¼ pt (½ c.) tepid water

Line the tin. Sift the flour, salt, and ginger into a bowl and make a well in the centre. Add the syrup or honey. Mix the soda and water. Mix all ingredients together. Pour into the tin and bake in a moderate oven until it feels firm in the centre. Turn out and cool. Do not cut for at least two days. Store in an airtight tin.

558. Treacle Gingerbread

Quantities for an 8-in.-sq. tin. *Cooking time* 1 hr. *Temperature* 350 °F. No. 4.

8 oz. (1½ level c.) plain flour
3 level tsp. ground ginger
1 level tsp. mixed spice
Pinch salt
4 oz. (½ c.) butter or margarine
3 oz. (6 level Tbs.) brown sugar
4 oz. (4 level Tbs.) black treacle
¼ pt (½ c.) boiling water
1 level tsp. bicarbonate of soda

Line the tin. Sift flour, ginger, spices, and salt into a basin. Heat fat, sugar, and treacle together, and add to the dry ingredients. Stir in the boiling water and add the soda dissolved in a little warm water. Mix well. Turn into the tin and bake in a moderate oven. Turn out and cool on a rack and store in an airtight tin. Keep a week before cutting.

559. Kolac (*high-fibre*)

Quantities for a 12-in.-by-9-in. tin. *Cooking time* 35–40 mins. *Temperature* 375 °F. No. 5.

8 oz. (1½ level c.) wholemeal flour
1 level tsp. baking powder
¼ level tsp. salt
4 oz. (½ c.) butter
3 oz. (½ c.) brown sugar
1 egg, beaten

Filling
2 apples and 2 bananas *or* 1 lb. red plums
2 oz. (½ c.) cottage cheese or more
2 oz. (4 level Tbs.) brown sugar
½ oz. (1 level Tbs.) butter

Mix flour, baking powder, and salt and rub in the butter. Add brown sugar and mix to a stiff dough with the egg. Roll out to fit the greased tin (e.g. Swiss-roll tin). Peel and chop the apple and banana or stone and chop the plums. Cover pastry with the fruit and sprinkle the cottage cheese over the top. Cover this with a generous layer of soft brown sugar, and dot with ½ oz. butter. Bake in a moderate oven. Cool and cut in squares.

560. Madeira Cake

Quantities for a 7-in. tin. *Cooking time* 1 hr 50 mins. *Temperature* 350 °F. No. 3–4.

8 oz. (1 level c.) butter or margarine
8 oz. (1 level c.) caster sugar
4 eggs
8 oz. (1½ level c.) plain flour
1 level tsp. baking powder
Pinch of salt
Grated rind of 1 small lemon, or other flavouring

Line the tin. Cream fat and sugar very thoroughly. Beat in eggs one at a time. Or beat eggs separately until very thick and light and then mix them in. Stir in the sifted flour, baking powder, salt, and flavourings. Put in a tin and bake until, when tested with a skewer, the skewer comes out clean. Turn out on a rack to cool.

Variation (*low-sodium diet*). Use unsalted butter or margarine, and special baking powder (see page 139).

561. Madeleines

Quantities for 24 small cakes. *Cooking time* 15–20 mins. *Temperature* 375 °F. No. 5.

5 oz. (10 level Tbs.) butter
6 oz. (¾ c.) caster sugar
2 large eggs
Grated rind of 1 lemon or
pinch of mace or vanilla or
1 Tbs. brandy
5 oz. (1 level c.) plain flour
1 oz. (3 level Tbs.) cornflour

Grease and flour small fluted tins or bun tins. Cream butter and sugar and beat in the eggs. Add flavouring and fold in the sifted flour and cornflour. Two-thirds fill the tins and bake until golden brown.

One madeleine. Carbohydrate 13 g. Calories 112.

562. Cornflour Meringues (*gluten-free*)

Quantities for 18 meringues. *Cooking time* 20 mins. or more. *Temperature* 350 °F. No. 3–4.

2 egg whites
4 oz. caster sugar (½ c.)
1½ oz. cornflour (4½ level Tbs.)
Flavouring
Whipped cream or butter cream

The flavouring can be vanilla or other essence or a little finely grated orange or lemon rind, or use a flavoured cornflour. Beat egg whites until stiff. Gradually beat in half the sugar and continue beating until stiff. Mix the remaining sugar and cornflour and fold in. Grease a baking tray or cover with aluminium foil or rice paper. Either shape the meringues with two spoons or force with star tube. Bake in a slow oven until firm and dry. Use plain or sandwiched with whipped cream or butter cream.

One plain meringue. Carbohydrate 9 g. Calories 35.

563. Meringues (*gluten-free, low-fat*)

Quantity for 18 meringues. *Cooking time* 1 hr or more. *Temperature* 275 °F. No. 1.

2 egg whites
4 oz. (½ c.) granulated sugar
Vanilla essence

Beat egg whites until stiff but not dry. Add half the sugar and beat again until the mixture is very thick. Fold in the rest of the sugar and the flavouring. Force from a tube or put spoonsful on a greased tray or cover the tray with aluminium foil, silicone paper, or rice paper. Bake in a slow oven until quite dry, and just coloured. When cold store in an air-tight tin.

One plain meringue. Carbohydrate 7 g. Calories 26.

Variations. (*Lemon meringues.*) Add the finely grated rind of 1 lemon. (*Cornflake meringues.*) Add 2 oz. cornflakes (2 level c.). (*Coffee meringues.*) Add ½–1 level tsp. soluble coffee powder.

564. Pavlova Cake (*gluten-free, low-fat*)

Quantities for an 8–9-in. tin. *Cooking time* 1 hr. *Temperature* 300 °F. No. 2.

- 3 egg whites
- Pinch of salt
- 6 oz. caster sugar (¾ c.)
- 1 level tsp. cornflour
- 1 tsp. vinegar
- ½ tsp. vanilla essence
- Fresh or canned fruit

Line the tin with greased paper. Use a shallow cake tin or a very deep sandwich tin. Beat the egg whites and salt until stiff. Beat in half the sugar. Mix the cornflour with the rest of the sugar and fold in gently. Add the essence and vinegar and mix. Spread in the tin and bake slowly until firm on the outside but still soft inside. Turn upside down on a large dish and leave to cool, when it will shrink a little. Arrange the fruit on top. Serve as a cake or pudding. It is better to use a fairly tart fruit as the cake is very sweet. Alternatively, the fruit may be dressed with lemon juice. For those who are allowed it, serve a jug of single cream.

Whole cake. Carbohydrate 191 g. Calories 755.

565. Queen Cakes (*oil*)

Quantity for 18 cakes. *Cooking time* 15–20 mins. *Temperature* 375 °F. No. 5.

2 eggs
4 Tbs. oil (see p. 150)
4 oz. (½ c.) caster sugar
4 oz. (¾ c.) S.R. flour
2 oz. (⅓ c.) currants
Flavouring essence or grated lemon rind

Oil patty tins and dredge with flour or prepare paper cases. Beat eggs, oil, and sugar together thoroughly. Mix in the sifted flour and the fruit and flavouring. Half-fill the tins and bake in a moderate oven until lightly browned and set. Cool on a rack.

One cake. Carbohydrate 12 g. Calories 60.

Variation. Omit the fruit and use the mixture for fairy cakes.

566. Butter Sponge (*gluten-free*)

Quantities for 12-in.-by-8-in. tin *or* two 7-in. sandwich tins. *Cooking time* 20–25 mins. *Temperature* 375 °F. No. 5.

3 eggs
4 oz. (½ c.) caster sugar
3 oz. (½ c.) wheat-starch
½ oz. (1½ level Tbs.) cornflour
1 oz. (2 Tbs.) melted butter

Grease the tins and dust with cornflour. Warm eggs and sugar and beat until very thick and light. Sift wheat-starch and cornflour and fold into the eggs gently. Lastly, fold in the melted (not hot) butter and pour into the prepared tins. Bake until springy to the touch but do not overcook or it will be very dry. Turn out and cool. Fill with jam or any other filling allowed. Or use as a basis for gluten-free trifle and other puddings. It keeps well in a deep-freeze; in fact it improves, as it becomes more moist.

Whole cake. Carbohydrate 200 g. Calories 1,300.

567. Chocolate Swiss Roll (*gluten-free*)

Quantities for 1 Swiss roll tin. *Cooking time* 7–10 mins. *Temperature* 400 °F. No. 6.

3 eggs	Pinch of salt
2 oz. (¼ c.) fine brown sugar	¼ tsp. vanilla
1 oz. (3 level Tbs.) cornflour	Whipped cream
1 oz. (3 level Tbs.) cocoa	

Grease the tin and dust with cornflour. Beat the eggs until light and then add the sugar and beat until very light and thick, so that when the beaters are removed the impression remains for a few seconds. Sift cornflour, cocoa, and salt, and fold in gently. Pour into the tin and spread evenly. Bake until springy. Turn out on a piece of greaseproof paper, dusted with caster sugar. Trim off the edges and roll up with the paper inside. When cold, unroll, and fill with whipped cream.

Whole cake. Carbohydrate 96 g. Calories 728.

568. Genoese Sponge

Quantities for a 10-in.-by-8-in. tin *or* two 8-in. sandwich tins. *Cooking time* 25–30 mins. *Temperature* 375 °F. No. 5.

3 eggs	1 level Tbs. cornflour
4 oz. (½ c.) caster sugar	3 oz. (6 Tbs.) melted butter
3 oz. (⅔ c.) plain flour	or 3 Tbs. oil (see p. 150)

Warm the mixing bowl. Sift flour and cornflour. Grease and flour the tin. Beat the eggs until light. Add the sugar and beat again until very thick and light so that when the beater is lifted out the mixture takes a little while to fall back into place. Fold in the flour gently and finally the melted butter, which must not be hot. Pour into the prepared tin and bake until it feels springy when pressed lightly on top. Leave a few minutes in the tin before turning out on a rack. When cold, sandwich with cream, jam, jelly, lemon curd, or in any way the patient is allowed. Pieces of the plain sponge are pleasant to serve with fruit salad or other puddings. It keeps well in a tin.

CAUTION. It is difficult to make a good sponge unless you have an efficient egg beater. A large whisk made of a wire spiral is very good, or a large rotary whisk or an electric beater.

Whole cake. Carbohydrate 186 g. Calories 1,702.

Variation (*gluten-free diet*). Use wheat starch in place of flour.

569. Hot Water Sponge (*low-fat*)

Quantities for two 8-in. sandwich tins. *Cooking time* 20 mins. *Temperature* 375 °F. No. 5.

- 3 eggs
- 6 oz. caster sugar (¾ c.)
- 4 oz. plain flour (¾ c.) *or*
- 3 oz. flour plus 1 oz. cornflour
- 1 level tsp. cream of tartar
- ½ level tsp. bicarbonate of soda
- 3 Tbs. boiling water

Grease and flour the tins. Warm the eggs and sugar and whisk until very thick and light. When the beaters are removed the impression should remain for a few seconds. Sift in the flour and cream of tartar and fold in gently. Dissolve the soda in boiling water and fold in. Divide evenly into the greased and floured tins and bake until springy to the touch. Leave a few minutes before turning out. When cold fill with jam or cream or any filling allowed in the diet (see fatless lemon filling (No. 576) and banana honey (No. 577)). Dust top with sifted icing sugar.

Whole cake. Carbohydrate 296 g. Calories 1,348.

Variations. 1. For *chocolate sponge*, sift 3 level Tbs. cocoa with the flour. 2. Add ¼ tsp. grated orange or lemon rind after the flour.

570. Sponge Sandwich (*oil*)

Quantities for two 7-in. sandwich tins. *Cooking time* 20 mins. *Temperature* 375 °F. No. 5.

- 2 eggs
- 4 oz. (½ c.) caster sugar
- ½ tsp. vanilla essence or other flavouring
- ½ level tsp. salt
- 3 Tbs. milk
- 3 Tbs. water
- 4 oz. (¾ c.) plain flour
- 2 level tsp. baking powder
- 3 Tbs. oil, see page 150

Oil the tins and line with oiled or silicone paper. Warm the bowl and whisk the eggs and sugar very thoroughly until thick and light, so that when the beaters are removed the impression remains for a few seconds. Add flavouring. Heat the milk, water, and oil together. Fold in the sifted flour, baking powder, and salt. Add the hot, not boiling, liquid and stir gently until well blended. Pour into the tins and bake until springy to the touch. Turn out on a cake rack. When cold, sandwich with jam or other filling.

Whole cake. Carbohydrate 210 g. Calories 1,454.

571. Sponge Drop Kisses (*gluten-free*)

Quantities for 12 completed kisses. *Cooking time* 5–7 mins. *Temperature* 425 °F. No. 7.

- 2 eggs
- 2 oz. (4 level Tbs.) caster sugar
- 2 oz. (6 level Tbs.) gluten-free flour

Beat eggs and sugar together until thick and light so that when beaters are removed the impression remains for a few seconds. Sift the wheat-starch and fold into the eggs lightly. Drop the mixture in teaspoonsful on greased trays, leaving room for spreading a little. Bake in a hot oven until they feel springy. When cold, sandwich together with jam or butter icing.

One kiss (no filling). Carbohydrate 10 g. Calories 50.

572. Swiss Roll (*gluten-free*)

Quantities for 1 Swiss roll tin. *Cooking time* 20–30 mins. *Temperature* 375 °F. No. 5.

- 4 eggs
- 4 oz. caster sugar (½ c.)
- 2 oz. gluten-free flour (6 level Tbs.)
- 2 oz. ground rice (6 level Tbs.)
- Jam

Line the tin with silicone paper. Warm the eggs and sugar and beat until very thick and light, so that when the beaters are removed the impression remains for a few seconds. Mix the wheat-starch and rice and fold in gently. Pour into the prepared tin and bake until springy to the touch but take care not to over-cook it or it will be dry and will crack when rolled.

Turn out on to a piece of greaseproof paper sprinkled with caster sugar. Trim off the edges, spread with jam, and roll up quickly. It keeps well in the deep-freeze.

Whole cake. Carbohydrate 221 g. Calories 1,220.

573. Swiss Roll

Quantities for 1 Swiss roll tin. *Cooking time* 7–10 mins. *Temperature* 400 °F. No. 6.

2 eggs
3 oz. granulated sugar (6 level Tbs.)
3 oz. plain flour ($\frac{2}{3}$ c.)
1 level tsp. baking powder
Pinch of salt
Jam

Grease and flour the tin. Warm the eggs and sugar and beat until very thick and light. When the beater is withdrawn the impression should remain for a few seconds. Sift the flour, baking powder, and salt and fold in gently. Pour into the tin and bake until springy to the touch. Take care not to overcook or it will be dry and will crack when rolled. Turn out on a piece of greaseproof paper sprinkled with caster sugar. Trim off the edges, spread with warm jam, and roll up quickly.

Whole cake. Carbohydrate 155 g. Calories 820.

Variation. Use 2 oz. caster sugar and 2 oz. flour and omit the baking powder.

574. Treacle Parkin (*high-fibre*)

Quantities for an 8-in.-by-10-in. tin. *Cooking time* 1$\frac{1}{4}$ hrs. *Temperature* 350 °F. No. 4.

6 oz. (1$\frac{1}{4}$ level c.) plain white flour
2 level tsp. baking powder
2 level tsp. ground ginger
4 oz. ($\frac{1}{2}$ c.) margarine
12 oz. (1$\frac{1}{2}$ level c.) medium oatmeal
2 oz. (4 level Tbs.) brown sugar
1 lb. (1 level c. plus 2 level Tbs.) syrup or black treacle melted
1 egg, beaten

Grease the tin. Sift flour, baking powder, and ginger into a bowl. Rub in the margarine. Add oatmeal and sugar. Melt syrup but do not make hot. Use this and the beaten egg to mix the dry ingredients. Spread in the tin and bake until firm to the touch. Cool in the tin. Cut in squares and store in an airtight tin. Keep for two weeks or longer before eating.

575. Victoria Sandwich

Quantities for two 7-in. tins. *Cooking time* 15–20 mins. *Temperature* 375 °F. No. 5.

- 4 oz. (½ c.) butter or margarine
- 4 oz. (½ c.) caster sugar
- 2 standard eggs
- 4 oz. (¾ c.) plain flour
- 1 level tsp. baking powder
- Pinch of salt
- Flavouring, e.g. vanilla or a little grated lemon or orange rind

Grease and flour the tin. Cream the fat and sugar and beat in the eggs gradually. Add flavouring and sifted dry ingredients and mix in gently and lightly. Spread evenly in the tins and bake until it shrinks from the sides. Turn out on a rack and cool. Join with jam and dust the top with icing or caster sugar.

Whole cake. Carbohydrate 207 g. Calories 1,940.

Variation (*low-sodium diet*). Omit the salt and use unsalted butter or margarine and 1½ level tsp. of special baking powder. See p. 139.

576. Lemon Jelly Filling (*gluten-free*)

- 2½ level Tbs. arrowroot or potato starch
- ½ pt (1 c.) water
- Grated rind and juice of 1 lemon
- 4 oz. (½ c.) sugar

Mix arrowroot smooth with a little of the cold water. Boil the rest with the lemon rind and pour on to the arrowroot. Return to the pan and stir until it boils. Add sugar and lemon juice and use when cold.

577. Banana Honey (*low-fat, gluten-free*)

3 bananas
1 orange
Rind and juice of 1 lemon
⅛ pt (5 Tbs.) water
An equal weight of sugar

Peel and mash bananas, squeeze the juice from the orange, and weigh all the ingredients. Add an equal weight of sugar. Boil 20–30 mins. or until thick, stirring frequently. Pour into hot jars and tie down when cold. Use alone or as a sponge filling for fatless diets or, with cream, for others.

Manufacturers' Names and Addresses

Alfonal Ltd, Alfonal House, Oyster Lane, Byfleet, Weybridge, Surrey.
Andomia Products Ltd, Grant St, Bradford 3, Yorkshire.
Bayer Products, Winthrop House, Surbiton-upon-Thames, Surrey.
Boots Pure Drug Co. Ltd, Station Road, Nottingham.
Burroughs Wellcome and Co., The Wellcome Building, 183 Euston Road, London NW1.
Carlo-Erba, 28–30 Great Peter St, London SW1.
J. & J. Colman Ltd, Carrow Works, Norwich.
'Coronet' fat-free yogurt: Unigate Creameries Ltd, Trowbridge, Wiltshire.
Dietade Foods, Eustace Miles Food Co. Ltd, Colnbrook, Bucks.
Edenvale Ltd, Victoria Road, South Ruislip, Middlesex.
Energen Foods Bureau (The), Ashford, Kent.
Farley's Infant Food Ltd, Torr Lane, Plymouth.
Glaxo Laboratories Ltd, Greenford, Middlesex.
Hermes Sweeteners, Zurich, Switzerland.
Howards of Ilford Ltd, Ilford, Essex.
Kerfoot (Thomas) & Co. Ltd, Bardsley Vale, Ashton-under-Lyne, Lancashire.
Liga Food Products (UK) Ltd, Liga House, 23 Saxby St, Leicester. LE2 ONL.
Marmite Ltd, Enfield, Middlesex.
Procea Ltd, Alexandra Road, Dublin 1, Eire.
Ryvita Co. Ltd, Old Wareham Road, Poole, Dorset.
Trufood Ltd, London Road, Guildford, Surrey.
Welfare Foods (Stockport) Ltd, 63/65 Higher Hillgate, Stockport, Cheshire.

Index of Diets

These references are to page numbers

Index of Recipes

These references are to recipe numbers

Breads, Scones, and Sandwiches

Cakes

Cheese

Eggs

Fish

Meat and Poultry

Soups

Stocks

Vegetables

MORE ABOUT PENGUINS AND PELICANS

Modern Vegetarian Cookery

Walter and Jenny Fliess

As founders and owners of the famous vegetarian 'Vega' restaurants in Cologne and London, Walter and Jenny Fliess built up an international reputation for themselves many years ago.

In this cookbook they compressed a good slice of their life's work into some 500 recipes for vegetarian dishes of all kinds, soups, sauces, sweets, and uncooked meals. They are not directly concerned here with the broader theory of vegetarianism or food reform, and their book will simply and engagingly recommend itself to most readers as a very practical one.

These fresh and imaginative recipes open up new culinary worlds and remove the sting from the injunction to 'eat plenty of fruit and vegetables'.

'Recipes to tempt even meat-eaters' – *Financial Times*

'500 recipes explain how to make everyday vegetables delicious and exciting' – *Vogue*

'The clearly set out recipes are easy to follow ... One could well live on vegetable fare' – *Tatler*

'A solid work of professional competence which many of our chefs might find intriguing' – *Culinarian* (U.S.A.)

'The idea that vegetarian cooking is necessarily dull is routed by the contents of this attractive book' – *House and Home* (South Africa)

The Penguin Cookery Book

Bee Nilson

'My choice for a young housewife's first cook book – particularly if she is tied to a strict budget – is *The Penguin Cookery Book* by Bee Nilson' – Ambrose Heath in *Ideal Home*

'A book which is likely to find a grateful and useful place in many homes ... Here are over 850 basic recipes, given in both weights and measures, indexed and cross-referenced ... Should the beginner require more than that, he or she will also find advice on kitchen equipment, food values, how much food to buy for how many, cooking time, temperatures, and a glossary of French terms. Finally there are diagrams, to assist in identifying the different cuts of meat and in preparing fish' – *Listener*

The third edition includes over 990 recipes.